Some Other Frequency

Penn Studies in Contemporary American Fiction
A Series Edited by Emory Elliott,
University of California at Riverside

A complete list of books in the series is available from the publisher.

Some Other Frequency

Interviews with Innovative
American Authors

Larry McCaffery

PENN

University of Pennsylvania Press

Philadelphia

Published by
University of Pennsylvania Press
Philadelphia   19104-6097

Library of Congress Cataloging-in-Publication Data
    McCaffery, Larry, 1946–
    Some other frequency : interviews with innovative American authors / Larry
McCaffery
        p.   cm. — (Penn studies in contemporary American fiction)
    Includes bibliographical references.
    ISBN 0-8122-3201-1 (cloth: alk. paper). — ISBN 0-8122-1442-0 (paper: alk. paper)
    1. Experimental fiction, American—History and criticism—Theory, etc.   2. Avant-
garde (Aesthetics)—United States—History—20th century.   3. American fiction—20th
century—History and criticism—Theory, etc.   4. Authors, American—20th century—
Interviews.   5. Postmodernism (Literature)—United States.   6. Experimental fiction—
Technique.   I. Title.   II. Series.
PS374.E95M33   1996
813′.54091—dc20   96-19112
                                                                            CIP

For CHARLES BERNSTEIN, ROBERT COOVER, RAYMOND
FEDERMAN, and RONALD SUKENICK—for their contributions
to the contemporary literary scene above and beyond their
creative writing.

And for SINDA GREGORY.

The form of the "book" is now going through a period of general upheaval, and while that form appears less natural, and its history less transparent, than ever . . . the book form alone can no longer settle . . . the case of those writing processes which, in practically questioning that form, must also dismantle it.

—Jacques Derrida, *Dissemination*

There are strings in the tragic distance. They are against the blue.

—Lyn Hejinian, *My Life*

Contents

Acknowledgments

My thanks first of all to the authors for welcoming me and my collaborators into their lives, books, and homes. They not only patiently sat through a barrage of questions but also worked with me throughout the editing process until we had a version we were all satisfied with. Likewise, my collaborators — Sinda Gregory, Jerzy Kutnik, Brian McHale, Marjorie Perloff, Tom Marshall, and Harry Polkinhorn — provided direct and immediate help in conducting and editing a number of these interviews, as well as in writing the introductions.

Special thanks to Emory Elliott, Editor of the University of Pennsylvania Press's Studies in Contemporary American Fiction series, for his patience, encouragement, and trust in this project. Without the sort of long-range commitment provided by Professor Elliott throughout the process of assembling this volume, long-term and nontraditional scholarly works such as *Some Other Frequency* would rarely see the light of day. Thanks, too, to Carlton Smith, who worked with me during the final stages of editing and proofreading. Carlton provided valuable suggestions, helped track down bibliographical information, and otherwise assisted me in preparing the final version of the manuscript.

I also owe a sincere debt of thanks to the University of Pennsylvania Press's Mindy Brown and Ridley Hammer for their editorial assistance during the later stages of preparing the final manuscript, and to my diligent copy-editor, Jennifer Shenk, for her attention to details generally — and for supplying me with the accurate citation for a quotation by Lily Tomlin's Ernestine in particular.

I'd also like to express thanks to Frederick Barthelme, editor of the *Mississippi Review*, for supporting and publishing my interview work over the years. Rick: I was in China back in '89 and so was unable to offer my condolences when your bro' Don Juan departed for places unknown; please note that I am here issuing a public word of thanks to Donald Barthelme for the tall tales and tequila-and-tonics he offered me in a bar one night during Bob Coover's 1988 Unspeakable Practices Festival. Yo, Don: I'll get the next round.

Cara Thompson, Ken Jones, Mike Kinney, Sean Anderson, Mike Norton, Sandro Sondaro, and Jim McMenamin all provided transcription assistance, with Jim also supplying editorial suggestions. The San Diego State University Foundation and the College of Arts and Letters provided grants that helped defray some of the expense for transcriptions and travel to conduct the interviews.

Grateful acknowledgment is also made here to the magazines and literary journals in which excerpts from the following interviews first appeared: *African American Review, Atticus Review, Chicago Review, Central Park, Mondo 2000, Mississippi Review, Positive Magazine* (Tokyo), and *The Review of Contemporary Fiction.*

Thanks, too, to numerous individuals who provided professional assistance of various sorts during the completion of this manuscript. I was assisted on a daily basis by the staff of San Diego State University's English Department and its intrepid Media Technology Center; Jim Edwards and Rachel Litonjua-Witt (of the Media Center) were exceptionally generous with their time and professional expertise.

I once again owe a great deal to Jim McMenamin, who has been an active collaborator with me during all my interview projects of the past decade. My son, Mark Urton, ever philosophical and levelheaded, has been an inspiration to me ever since I first engaged him in a serious conversation about life and literature back in 1970 (he was three, I was twenty-three). A steady stream of letters, phone calls, faxes and words of encouragement from Brooks Landon, Chip Delany, Robert Coover, Raymond Federman, Brian McHale, Takayuki Tatsumi, Bruce McPherson, and David Blair helped remind me that another world still existed outside of *Some Other Frequency*. Thanks—I needed that.

There's also my chief collaborator on this and all my other projects, Sinda Gregory. Without her ongoing input, suggestions, admonitions, and encouragement, *Some Other Frequency* would have faded away like the radio-sound of the Indiana-Kentucky NCAA basketball game back in '75 while we were driving through the Smoky Mountains.

Postmodern Realism(s) on Some Other Frequency—Introduction

Larry McCaffery

At this point in . . . history, the relevant question is, "What exactly does a composer do?"

—John Zorn, "John Zorn on His Music"

Turning On

The title of this collection of interviews is taken from the famous scene that occurs near the opening of Thomas Pynchon's *The Crying of Lot 49*, in which Oedipa Maas gazes out over the vast "sprawl" of San Narciso's suburban housing projects and freeway interchange systems and experiences the same peculiar sensation that she once had when she opened up a transistor radio and saw her first printed circuit. Since the passage has a variety of specific resonances for the following interviews, it is worth quoting at some length:

Though she knew even less about radios than about Southern Californians, there were to both outward patterns a hieroglyphic sense of concealed meaning, of an intent to communicate. There'd seemed no limit to what the printed circuit could have told her (if she had tried to find out); so in her first minute of San Narciso, a revelation also trembled just past the threshold of her understanding. . . . As if, on some other frequency, or out of the eye of some whirlwind rotating too slow for her heated skin even to feel the centrifugal coolness of, words were being spoken. She suspected that much. (22)

It turns out, of course, that Oedipa's intuition regarding this "intent to communicate" is right on the money: she has just stumbled upon (or been subtly guided toward) her first important revelation concerning the existence of the Tristero, a hidden community of individuals who are writing and speaking to each other outside the "official channels" of the American communications network. One of my intentions in presenting the fourteen interviews that comprise *Some Other Frequency* is to verify the existence of an analogous Tristero-like community of writers who are publishing formally daring and thematically rich works of fiction, mostly outside the "official channels" of our commercial presses.[1]

I am aware, of course, that in the 1990s any claim for the existence of this sort of vital literary communication flies in the face of what one hears so often these days regarding the "death of the novel," the "death of the author," the disappearance of originality, and so forth. Writing and reading, we are told, especially in print-bound media like books, have grown increasingly irrelevant, their roles usurped by word processors and new forms of electronic communication, the global flow of data, and the development of multimedia hypertext systems.[2] I would argue, however, that many of the people circulating these dire pronouncements have been, like Oedipa, paying too much attention to the literary equivalent of AM radio shows; and even the commercial publishing equivalent to FM "alternative" stations—Farrar/Straus, Harmony/Crown, Random House, Grove Press, New Directions, and so on—have *highly* limited play lists to choose from. For all such people—

1. Most of this work has been published through the network of quality small presses and literary journals that have arisen in the wake of the well-documented multinational takeovers of the New York publishing industry in the 1970s and its subsequent diminishing interest in serious fiction. Readers can obtain a fairly comprehensive (though by no means exhaustive) listing of the small presses, university presses, and literary journals that are keeping serious fiction alive in America by consulting the individual bibliographies I've provided for each of the authors included in *Some Other Frequency*.

2. "Hypertext" is a term coined by Theodor H. Nelson in the 1960s and refers to a radically new information technology, a mode of publication, and a form of electronic text. By "hypertext," Nelson explains, "I mean nonsequential writing—text that branches and allows choices to the reader, best read at an interactive screen" (Landow, 4). As it is usually conceived, then, hypertext denotes texts composed of blocks of text (what Roland Barthes calls a *lexica*)—and the electronic links that join them. Hypermedia—certain to be the next crucial step in the transformation of our concepts of writing and reading—simply extends the notion of the text in hypertext by including visual information (moving pictures can now be scanned into hypertext documents), sounds, animation, maps, diagrams, images, and virtually anything else whose information can be stored through digital microstorage. Although I feel certain that hypertext represents the next crucial stage in which innovations in fiction are likely to be played out, I deliberately have chosen not to include interviews with any of its leading practitioners (someone like Michael Joyce would have been an obvious inclusion here, for example) due to my conviction that hypertext represents a fundamentally different medium for storytelling and fiction-making than print-bound media such as books, magazines, and so forth.

both academic specialists and ordinary readers alike—I suggest tuning into *Some Other Frequency*. Those who do will discover that recent rumors concerning various and sundry deaths (of the author, of the novel, of originality, of realism, of serious fiction) have been greatly exaggerated.

Tuning In

> I came from the fictional womb as I am, the postmodern battles had already been fought and won, so I was never interested in those battles. It simply never occurred to me to write traditional, mimetic, plotted narratives.
>
> —Mark Leyner

So who are these writers communicating in *Some Other Frequency*? My collaborators and I began interviewing these fourteen "radically innovative" American authors in 1987 and have continued our interrogations even as this manuscript is going to press. For most of this period my working title for this volume was "Interviews with Fiction Writers of the Postmodern Avant-Garde," and although I subsequently decided that this title was misleading on several accounts,[3] it nonetheless provides a generally accurate sense of what sorts of authors I wanted to include in this volume—namely, those working outside the usual conventions of traditional realism (usually far outside) who had produced works I judged to be of superior quality. In particular, I was interested in having these authors discuss a crucial series of concepts and tropes—including "textuality," "defamiliarize," "narrative," the "I" narrator, "realism," "history," "reality," "originality," "collaboration," "invention," "appropriation," "authority," "representation," and others that struck me as being central to our current understanding of what the term "fiction" *means* at this point, what its boundary lines are, how and where these lines have expanded or contracted, and for what reasons.

One thing that is safe to say about these authors is that they are an

---

3. Misleading in the sense that (1) it is becoming increasingly obvious that "postmodernism," like Melville's white whale, is forever destined to elude all human efforts to categorize and define it; (2) very few of the authors interviewed here feel any sense of kinship to the concept of "postmodernism" however that term is defined (the only notable exceptions to this disavowal of postmodernism are Kathy Acker and Harold Jaffe); and (3) although the term "avant-garde" is easier to define and establish historical and aesthetic precedents for, its relevance as an artistic movement may have permanently ended during the 1960s, when artists like Andy Warhol helped dismantle the distinction between an aesthetically radical, adversarial "underground" and the "mainstream." For a discussion of this dismantlement and an assessment of how the avant-garde and mainstream culture are currently interacting with one another, see my essays "Everything Is Permitted: The North American Novel at the Quincentennial Moment" and "Avant-Pop: Still Life after Yesterday's Crash."

eclectic group. They range from writers like Lydia Davis, whose work at first glance appears to rely on relatively traditional storytelling methods (those of "minimalism," for example), to Richard Kostelanetz, whose own approach to "minimalism" has resulted in a series of books consisting entirely of numbers, straight lines, and of one/two/three/four words, to "maximalist" word-drunk figures like William T. Vollmann, who has already published a half dozen huge, encyclopedic "prose assemblages" that include reportage, personal narrative, collaborative "rewrites" of prior materials, maps, illustrations, glossaries, and numerous other forms. They range in age from relative youngsters like Mark Leyner and Vollmann—perhaps the hippest of the current cult figures in the pop-underground—to writers a generation older who began publishing in the 1970s during the aftermath of the first phase of postmodern experimentalism (Davis, Kathy Acker, Harold Jaffe, Gerald Vizenor, Lyn Hejinian, Ken Gangemi), to members of the 1960s breakthrough period (Kostelanetz, Robert Kelly, Clarence Major, David Antin), to octogenarian Marianne Hauser, who published her first book some sixty years ago.

One of the reasons the works of these writers seem so varied in texture, theme, and formal concerns undoubtedly has to do with the diversity of personalities, aesthetic inclinations, and backgrounds that helped shape their individual sensibilities. For instance, although I didn't plan things with this goal in mind, *Some Other Frequency* turned out to be most definitely *not* a book of interviews with ivory-towered "academic writers." True, several of the authors here now hold full-time positions at universities (Vizenor in the Native American Department at the University of California at Berkeley, Kelly in the English Department at Bard, Jaffe in San Diego State's English Department, and Antin in the Art Department at the University of California at San Diego), but only Mark Leyner emerged from a creative writing program. On the other hand, a listing of some of the jobs these writers have held at various times during their careers gives some rough sense of the variety of creative sensibilities and "content" found in their works. A partial survey of these jobs include: bartending (Ken Gangemi),[4] translating (Lydia Davis,

4. Gangemi, who was an engineering major at college, was also a jet pilot in the Air Force and has written a "travel guide" to Mexico, *The Volcanoes from Puebla. Puebla,* which consists of an alphabetically arranged sequence of entries on topics unlikely to be found in most guidebooks (e.g., "Mangoes," "Americans," "Motorcycle Helmets"), was published originally as nonfiction; but after Charles Caramello (in *Silverless Mirrors*) extensively analyzed the book as being a species of "experimental novels," Gangemi himself became convinced that it was indeed fiction, which is how recent editions of the book have been categorized. *Puebla* thus offers a striking example of the ways traditional literary cate-

David Antin, Lyn Hejinian),[5] working in steel mills (Clarence Major) and live sex shows (Kathy Acker), journalism (Gerald Vizenor, William Vollmann), computer programming (William Vollmann), playing semipro basketball (Harold Jaffe), providing ad copy for a pharmaceutical company (Mark Leyner), and publishing pornographic material for *Playboy* and *Screw* (Derek Pell). Robert Kelly, Lyn Hejinian, and David Antin are all well known as poets, but Kelly's fiction has to date received little attention and the works of Hejinian and Antin have never, to my knowledge, previously been considered "fiction" at all. Likewise, most of Derek Pell's work—which includes text-and-collage works, mail art, book objects, and gallery exhibitions—appears to have as much to do with conceptual and performance art as with fiction.

As might be expected from a book focusing on radical forms of innovative writing, many of these writers have achieved little popular recognition, or even critical attention, outside "serious" literary circles. In fact, most of the writers here have been working so much in isolation and so far removed from the norms of conventional realism that critical consensus hasn't solidified sufficiently to generate labels or categories for their work. There are a few exceptions to this: Robert Kelly, for instance, was a leading theorist and practitioner of the "deep image school" of poetry back in the 1960s; Lyn Hejinian is a leading figure in (and spokesperson for) the "language school" of poetry; David Antin is probably best known for his "talk" pieces; Mark Leyner has been

---

gories—particularly distinctions between autobiography, reportage, and "fiction"—have been all but obliterated by many of the authors in *Some Other Frequency*.

5. The topic of translation and "mistranslation" as a specific influence on writing practices is raised in several of the interviews here (most notably in the conversations with Lydia Davis and Lyn Hejinian). But translation's association with numerous other experimental collaborative methods of writing—appropriation, plagiarism, pastiche, cut-up, sampling, and other forms of authorial interaction with (or "translations" of) prior material—make it a recurrent trope in these conversations, one that indicates the willingness of innovative fiction writers to create works that do not rely on authorial "invention" to supply "material." Such methods point to the ways that nearly all the authors in *Some Other Frequency* have abandoned the romantic concept of authorial "originality" and "creativity" in favor of what I refer to later in this introduction as the "Textual 'I.'" Examples of this tendency can be seen in Kathy Acker's "rewrites" of famous traditional novels (*Great Expectations, Don Quixote*), Gerald Vizenor's "trickster" interventions into historical narratives (*The Heirs of Columbus*), Harold Jaffe's use of media names as an arbitrary springboard for his improvisation (*Madonna and Other Spectacles*), Robert Kelly's monumental reworking of the Percival legend, William Vollmann's similarly grand treatment of Norse legends, the Iceland sagas, and other historical materials (in his sequence of "dream" novels), Lyn Hejinian's transformations of Russian and other literary material in her highly subjective autobiographical works, *My Life, Oxota*, and the series of "textual transformations" that Derek Pell subjects the Warren Commission Report to in *Assassination Rhapsody*.

frequently (and misleadingly) associated with science fiction's "cyber-punk" movement;[6] Kathy Acker has been variously labeled a feminist and "postfeminist"; and the term "avant-pop" has been recently used to describe Leyner, Vollmann, Jaffe, and Pell.[7] But with the exception of Kelly and Hejinian, there is no real justification for connecting any of the writers in *Some Other Frequency* with the sorts of manifestos, shared goals, or exchange of ideas one expects from literary movements. Quite the contrary, what has struck me throughout the process of conducting and editing the interviews in *Some Other Frequency* is that these are writers who have been working through their own private sets of personal ob-sessions and aesthetic concerns with a diligence and dedication that is defiantly individualistic.

In short, like the people who are part of Pynchon's mysterious Tris-tero, the writers interviewed here are less a cohesive "movement" sharing specific backgrounds, literary assumptions, and aesthetic goals than a kind of spiritual community of individuals bound together primarily by a shared interest in employing aesthetic innovation in their writing as a means of enlarging their readers' perceptions and injecting meaning-ful choices, diversity, and unprogrammable possibilities into lives and imaginations that seem to be increasingly drained not only of originality but of "the real" itself.

This is not to say that a certain amount of overlap can't be detected among their work in terms of theme and formal orientation. As Lydia Davis points out in our interview, it is hardly surprising to find such commonalities, even among a group of writers whose backgrounds and interests are so widely divergent: "Writers can try and maintain this sense of creative isolation as much as they like, but at a certain point identifiable similarities in even the most barricaded sensibilities are eventually going to start emerging. These things . . . are simply 'in the air' somehow." I will return to the issues of "overlap" and of things that are "in the air" in a moment, but at this point let me briefly address what sorts of factors helped launch this project in the first place.

My rationale behind my choice of "radically innovative writers" for

6. I myself have been directly involved in this misrepresentation. For instance, I selected Leyner's "i was an infinitely hot and dense dot" as the lead story for the special issue of the *Mississippi Review* devoted to cyberpunk that appeared in 1988; I also later included this story in the cyberpunk anthology I edited, *Storming the Reality Studio: A Case-book of Cyberpunk and Postmodern Fiction*.

7. See my discussion of Leyner, Vollmann, Jaffe, and Pell's work as being part of the "Avant-Pop Phenomenon" in "Everything Is Permitted: The North American Novel at the Quincentennial Moment," in "Tsunami" (my introduction to *Avant-Pop: Fiction for a Day-dream Nation*), and in "Avant-Pop: Still Life after Yesterday's Crash" (my introduction to *After Yesterday's Crash: The Avant-Pop Anthology*).

the focus of this volume is essentially the same as the one offered by William T. Vollmann to explain his fascination with extremity in his work. "I'm . . . attracted to the extreme," he says, "because frequently the extreme case illustrates the general case—and sometimes it can do so more forcefully and memorably than the ordinary is able to." When I began working on *Some Other Frequency*, I had already published *Anything Can Happen* (1983) and *Alive and Writing* (1986), two earlier interview volumes that had collectively presented a fairly comprehensive survey of what might be termed "mainstream" postmodern American fiction, and I was nearing completion on a third volume, *Across the Wounded Galaxies* (1990).[8] *Galaxies* seemed to mark a departure from my earlier interview work in that it focused exclusively on a particular area of innovation— contemporary science fiction and its various hybrid forms. But as I explained in my introduction, this focus was actually a natural extension of my ongoing interest in postmodernism generally:

My premise is that SF's formal and thematic concerns are intimately related to characteristics of other postmodern art forms, that SF has been influencing and influenced by these forms. Science fiction can, in fact, be seen as representing an exemplar of postmodernism because it is the art form that most directly reflects back to us the cultural logic that has produced postmodernism. (2–3)

As my reference here to science fiction as "an exemplar of postmodernism" clearly indicates, *Galaxies* could also be seen as being an early application of Vollmann's "extremity principle." At any rate, with *Some Other Frequency* I set about using a different set of the "extreme" examples—writers whose approach to formal issues was "radical," highly unusual, *extreme*—confident that talking to such writers would result in a greater understanding of what had been occurring recently in the "general case" of postmodern American fiction.

As had been true for the earlier interview collections, I found it best to begin *Some Other Frequency* with only a general working premise in

---

8. These earlier interview collections are: *Anything Can Happen: Interviews with Contemporary American Authors* (with Tom LeClair), which included interviews with John Barth, Donald Barthelme, Robert Coover, Don DeLillo, E. L. Doctorow, Stanley Elkin, Raymond Federman, William H. Gass, John Hawkes, John Irving, Diane Johnson, Steve Katz, Joe McElroy, Toni Morrison, Tim O'Brien, and Ronald Sukenick; *Alive and Writing: Interviews with American Authors of the 1980s* (with Sinda Gregory), interviews with Walter Abish, Max Apple, Ann Beattie, Raymond Carver, Samuel R. Delany, Barry Hannah, Russell Hoban, William Kennedy, Ursula Le Guin, Thomas McGuane, Tom Robbins, Ron Silliman, Edmund White; and *Across the Wounded Galaxies: Interviews with Contemporary American Science Fiction Authors*, with Gregory Benford, William S. Burroughs, Octavia Butler, Samuel R. Delany, Thomas M. Disch, William Gibson, Ursula Le Guin, Joanna Russ, Bruce Sterling, and Gene Wolfe.

mind (here, formal extremity), thus allowing the selection process and the topics to evolve without regard to preset slots or rigidly defined prescriptions. Indeed, it seemed important for me *not* to assign a specific definition to these terms or to fix in advance precisely what I meant by "traditional," "innovative," "radically innovative," or, even the most essential term of all, *fiction*. Rather, I decided to enter into this round of interviewing with an open mind about these areas—to rely on my intuition and personal judgment about them. Beyond that, the only thing I knew in advance was that I wanted to talk with authors whose works struck me as being genuinely "extreme" in their approaches to form/content issues, whose radicalism seemed aesthetically interesting and significant, and who had produced works that I judged to be of superior quality rather than selecting authors because of their critical reputation, influence, representativeness, or even diversity.[9]

At the same time, there were a series of more specific topics that grew naturally out of my focus on radically experimental fiction writers. One of the most important of these involves the assessment of what areas of formal innovation remain viable and interesting to contemporary writers today. I was anxious to get a sense of what narrative strategies have—and haven't—been exhausted during the experimental fervor characterizing fiction in the sixties and seventies, and to gain insights about what sorts of *new* areas of experimentation have emerged. A related issue had to do with the ways that the rapid expansion of the "media culture" has affected contemporary authors' approach to writing. How had the formal principles associated with television, music, the cinema, and (of increasing importance) word processors and hypertext systems affected the ways that authors today organize and think about their writing? Further, how had developments in contemporary critical theory (in structuralism, poststructuralism, Marxist perspectives, and so on) influenced fiction writing?

Connected to these topics were several other issues that wound up being raised in most of the interviews here: For instance, how have authors been responding to the dilemmas of producing "original" art in the age of the death of the author, with the consequent destabilization of authorial "meaning" and textual priorities? How are authors responding to our current age's suspicions about such concepts as authorial originality and the ability of texts of any sort to provide reliable "outside" perspectives regarding causality and psychological motivation? How has this role been transformed by the blurring of traditional boundaries

9. Another factor concerning my selection process that should be mentioned is my decision not to interview authors who were included in my earlier interview books.

between fiction and history, reportage, autobiography, and other discourses previously seen as lying outside the usual parameters of the novel and short-story form?

I had anticipated that many of the most radical fictional innovators would have been influenced by sources outside fiction per se, but it soon became clear that nearly all these writers were not only familiar with and influenced by such sources but had been actively and creatively involved in them at some point in their careers. To cite a few specific examples, Kostelanetz, Pell, Gangemi, Vizenor, Kelly, Antin, Hejinian, and Major had all written books of poetry; Kelly, Hejinian, Gangemi, Vizenor, Vollmann, Jaffe, Antin, and Kostelanetz had all written books of literary theory or nonfiction; Leyner, Kostelanetz, and Hejinian worked in musical forms; Davis, Antin, Acker, Vizenor, and Kelly had published translations of foreign authors; Kostelanetz, Pell, Vizenor, Major, Acker, and Vollmann had worked in visual media (painting, video, text-and-collage forms, and so on).

Conclusion(s): The Death of the Death of the Author

> Maybe I think that all my fiction is realistic and that so far it has simply been misunderstood as otherwise.
> —Robert Coover interview in *Anything Can Happen*

There are dozens of fascinating conclusions to be drawn from these interviews concerning the current status of formal innovation in postmodern fiction, including several points that openly challenge a number of key views expressed by many of the most influential postmodern critics and theorists. The most significant of these areas has to do with fundamental changes that have been occurring in the way contemporary authors conceive of the composition process and how this process relates to concepts such as "originality," "truth," and "reality." Jazz musician and theorist John Zorn's observation that "Whether we like it or not, the era of the writer as composer as autonomous musical mind has just about come to an end" strikes me as being equally valid for the creation of fiction, and indeed, for all aesthetic constructs today. In varying degrees and in very different sorts of contexts, the works of most of the writers in *Some Other Frequency* relentlessly interrogate the notion of "autonomy"—of the self, of reality, of words and sentences, of the creative imagination—*in all its guises.* Central to this interrogation is an almost casual acceptance of the view that both reality and the self are in fact *discontinuous* entities. This acceptance finds expression in a series of works by these authors that reconfigure assumptions concerning relationships between author and story, inner and outer, self and other, history and imagination, truth and reality that have been central to the whole realist tradition of fiction since its rise in the eighteenth century. One perhaps surprising result of this reconfiguration is a refutation of the view that postmodernist literary experimentalism has been non- or antirealistic in nature—that it represents above all a collective retreat from reality into the endlessly (self-) reflecting "mirror stage" of Barth's funhouse.[10] To the contrary, what emerges from these interviews is the sense that even the most radically innovative American authors retain an allegiance to realism's dictum to "tell it like it is." It is the *nature of the telling*, as well as of the "it," that have been transformed as writers increasingly recognize that fiction's inability to produce *truth-functions* concerning our shared postmodern condition in no way precludes its ability to render "the real" in a realistic manner. There is also a growing awareness on the part of our best writers that the "real"—of the self and of the world we live in—is not some discrete, isolable entity that can be represented objectively but is in actuality a *network of relationships* that can be rendered "realistically" only via formal methods that emphasize rather than deny the fundamentally fluid, interactive nature of this network. Thus, for example, Mark Leyner's insistence that he considers his work to be realistic despite its seeming strangeness and exoticism because it "presents the world the way people like you and I actually live in it, the way we receive and perceive it" sounds a note that recurs throughout *Some Other Frequency*.

One direct corollary of the view that reality and our experience of reality are fundamentally discontinuous and interactive has been the replacement of the romantic conception of artistic creation and the Artistic Self—that is, the work of fiction as a discrete entity produced in isolation by an autonomous author, who is solely responsible for the creation of meanings, which emerge out of his or her own unique set of experiences, attitudes, and perceptions—by what might be termed the "textual assemblage" and the "textual 'I.'" This is a model of textuality as a dynamic, open-ended, and fundamentally unstable system of codes,

---

10. The numerous critical studies that have proposed the reflexive, metafictional, fabulous, and antimimetic nature of postmodern aesthetics include my own early study, *The Metafictional Muse: The Works of Robert Coover, Donald Barthelme, and William H. Gass*; Jerome Klinkowitz, *Literary Disruptions: The Making of a Post-Contemporary American Fiction* and *The Self-Apparent Word*; William H. Gass, *Fiction and the Figures of Life, Habitations of the Word*, and *The World Within the Word*; Raymond Federman, *Surfiction: Fiction Now and Tomorrow*; Robert Scholes, *Fabulation and Metafiction*; Brian McHale, *Postmodernist Fiction*; Ronald Sukenick, *In Form: Twelve Digressions Towards a Theory of Fiction*; John Gardner, *On Moral Fiction*; Linda Hutcheon, *Narcissistic Narrative: The Metafictional Paradox*; Gerald Graff, *Literature Against Itself*; Tony Tanner, *City of Words*; and Fredric Jameson's *Postmodernism, or the Cultural Logic of Late Capitalism*.

information, citations from and references to other books, other texts, other sentences. Such a model has far-reaching implications indeed, for it encourages authors to see the composition process as fundamentally collaborative, one that produces not a single meaning placed there by the author and retrievable by a careful reader, but a multiplicity of meanings and perspectives that are disseminated as its component features intersect and interact with other texts and contexts. And although not all the writers in *Some Other Frequency* acknowledge having either read or been directly influenced by the recent explosion of interest in critical theory, it should be obvious that this "textual model" is very close to ones proposed by such leading critical theorists as Derrida, Barthes, and Foucault, as well as those proposed by hypertext advocates like George Landow and Brooks Landon.[11]

Postscript: A Few Words About Methodology and Organization

These interviews are all based on actual "live" conversations with the authors. The conversations were taped and transcribed, at which point they underwent a considerable amount of editing, which included eliminating trite or repetitious materials, recasting (or "translating") unclear or unmemorable replies (or suggesting rephrasing to the authors), and rearranging sections of the interview to create a greater sense of continuity or dramatic impact.[12] The revised transcripts were then sent to the authors for their changes, deletions, and corrections; once I received these revisions, I continued editing and reediting the materials. The

11. For the ways that multimedia text and data processing systems such as hypertext have begun to literalize some of the models for reading and writing suggested by recent critical theorists, see George Landow, *Hypertext: The Convergence of Critical Theory and Technology.* Among the interviews in *Some Other Frequency* in which authors discuss their interest in recent critical theory are those with Kathy Acker, David Antin, Lydia Davis, Lyn Hejinian, Harold Jaffe, Derek Pell, and Gerald Vizenor. I did not become familiar with hypertext until I was nearly finished conducting the interviews here, so I did not have the opportunity to query any of the authors in *Some Other Frequency* concerning their interest in working with it; to my knowledge none of them have yet begun working in hypertext, although for writers like Acker, Jaffe, Kostelanetz, and (particularly) William T. Vollmann, this next step seems inevitable. Certainly a great deal of investigation needs to be made into the manner in which critical theory has begun to reconfigure our notions about what constitutes the reading and writing of fiction; and, as the examples of Kathy Acker and Harold Jaffe in this volume clearly demonstrate, sometimes the influence of critical theory on a writer's work has been direct and profound indeed.

12. For a more detailed description of the methodology involved in my interview work, along with a summary of my views concerning the aesthetics of the interview as a literary form and the ways this form relates to the postmodern notion of discourse generally, see the interview with me conducted by Lewis Shiner in the *Mississippi Review—Interview Issue.*

bottom line: the versions that appear in *Some Other Frequency* are meant to be seen as collaborative texts based on an actual conversation rather than as a direct rendering of that conversation. Thus, the question-and-answer format has been employed here throughout for its economy of means and dramatic potential rather than to suggest any sort of adherence on my part to the traditions of mimesis.

The interviews are arranged alphabetically by author and each is preceded by a brief critical introduction with a selective bibliography of primary and secondary materials that I hope will encourage readers to leave behind the literary "maps" included in *Some Other Frequency* and strike out on their own for the actual territories themselves. My choice of an alphabetical arrangement for the volume, rather than ordering the interviews according to chronology, category, or some other method of organization is deliberate. Relying on this sort of "random" organizing principle allowed me to avoid creating the false impression that there is a "proper" or "most revealing" sequence in which to read the interviews. Such an arrangement also encourages readers to create their own connections and draw their own conclusions—often ones that neither I nor my collaborators could possibly have anticipated.

Works Cited

Caramello, Charles. "*The Volcanoes from Puebla* and Other Reflections." In *Silverless Mirrors*, 348–77. Tallahassee: University Presses of Florida, 1982.

Federman, Raymond. *Surfiction: Fiction Now and Tomorrow.* Chicago: Swallow Press, 1975.

Gardner, John. *On Moral Fiction.* New York: Basic Books, 1978.

Gass, William H. *Fiction and the Figures of Life.* New York: Knopf, 1970.

———. *Habitations of the Word.* New York: Knopf, 1982.

———. *The World within the Word.* New York: Knopf, 1978.

Graff, Gerald. *Literature against Itself.* Chicago: University of Chicago Press, 1979.

Hutcheon, Linda. *Narcissistic Narrative: The Metafictional Paradox.* New York: Methuen, 1980.

Jameson, Fredric. *Postmodernism, or the Cultural Logic of Late Capitalism.* Durham, NC: Duke University Press, 1991.

Klinkowitz, Jerome. *Literary Disruptions: The Making of a Post-Contemporary American Fiction.* Urbana: University of Illinois Press, 1975.

———. *The Self-Apparent Word: Fiction as Language/Language as Fiction.* Carbondale: Southern Illinois University Press, 1984.

Landow, George P. *Hypertext: The Convergence of Contemporary Critical Theory and Technology.* Baltimore, MD: Johns Hopkins University Press, 1992.

LeClair, Tom, and Larry McCaffery. *Anything Can Happen: Interviews with Contemporary American Authors.* Urbana: University of Illinois Press, 1983.

McCaffery, Larry. *Across the Wounded Galaxies: Interviews with Contemporary American Science Fiction Authors.* Urbana: University of Illinois Press, 1990.

———. *Alive and Writing: Interviews with American Authors of the 1980s* (with Sinda Gregory). Urbana: University of Illinois Press, 1986.

————. "Avant-Pop: Still Life after Yesterday's Crash." Editor's critical introduction. In *After Yesterday's Crash: The Avant-Pop Anthology*. New York: Penguin, 1995.

————. *The Cyberpunk Controversy: Mississippi Review* (special double issue devoted to Cyberpunk) 47, 48 (1988).

————. "Everything Is Permitted: The North American Novel at the Quincentennial Moment." In *The Novel of the Americas*, ed. Raymond Williams, 96–110. Boulder, CO: University of Colorado Press, 1992.

————. "The Fictions of the Present." In *The Columbia Literary History of the United States*, ed., Emory Elliott, 1161–1172. New York: Columbia University Press, 1988.

————. *The Metafictional Muse: The Works of Robert Coover, Donald Barthelme, and William H. Gass*. Pittsburgh: University of Pittsburgh Press, 1983.

————. *Storming the Reality Studio: A Casebook of Cyberpunk and Postmodern Fiction*. Durham, NC: Duke University Press, 1991.

————. "Tsunami." Editor's critical introduction. In *Avant Pop: Fiction for a Daydream Nation*, 15–31. Normal, IL: Black Ice Books, 1993.

McHale, Brian. *Postmodernist Fiction*. New York: Methuen, 1987.

O'Donnell, Patrick. "From the Editor." *Modern Fiction Studies* 38, 4 (winter 1992): 817–19.

Pynchon, Thomas. *The Crying of Lot 49*. 1967. New York: Bantam, 1993.

Scholes, Robert. *Fabulation and Metafiction*. Urbana: University of Illinois Press, 1979.

Shiner, Lewis. "An Interview with Larry McCaffery." *Mississippi Review — Interview Issue* 20, 1 and 2 (1991): 155–67.

Ronald Sukenick. *Down and In: Life in the Underground*. New York: Beech Tree Books, 1987.

————. *In Form: Twelve Digressions Towards a Theory of Fiction*. Carbondale, IL: Southern Illinois University Press, 1985.

Tanner, Tony. *City of Words: American Fiction, 1950–1970*. New York: Harper and Row, 1971.

The Path of Abjection
An Interview with Kathy Acker

Larry McCaffery

A narrative is an emotional moving.
— *Great Expectations*

Like the dissolving, schizophrenic "I's" that speak to us from Kathy Acker's novels, the "real" Kathy Acker is likely to strike people as a bundle of contradictory parts that combine to create the jagged unity of a Rauschenberg collage: part streetwise gutter snipe, radical feminist critic, and punk artist, and part vulnerable woman on the verge of being torn apart by rapacious phallic society; part cynic, and part visionary idealist. Kathy Acker has also produced a major body of experimental, shocking, and highly disturbing "prose assemblages" (to refer to them as "novels" misses the point) that have produced perhaps the most devastating and (a point missed by too many readers) *wickedly funny* critiques of life-under-late-capitalism since William Burroughs's great mid-1960s works.

During the somnolent, repressive 1980s decade of Reagan/Bush/Helms/Bennett, Kathy Acker established herself as one of postmodernism's boldest and most original fiction innovators—and one of its most controversial, as well. Her major works during this period included her "rewrites" of classic Western novels (*Great Expectations* [1982] and *Don Quixote* [1986]), as well as several other novels that pastiched a broader variety of prior literary works: *Blood and Guts in High School* (1984), a book that combined Acker's own drawings and "dream maps" with plagiarized sections of Jean Genet, Gilles Deleuze, and Félix Guattari, obscure pornography, and radical feminist criticism to produce a grotesque "coming of age" novel quite unlike any other; *Empire of the Senseless* (1988), a book which clearly displayed Acker's movement away from "deconstructive" methods, toward a more positive "constructive" literary approach, and which included striking interventions into William Gibson's "cyberpunk" classic, *Neuromancer*; and perhaps her most personal and passionate novel to date, *In Memoriam to Identity* (1990), which appropriated materials ranging from ancient Japanese fiction to Rimbaud and Faulkner as a means of reexploring the myth of romance.

The following interview was conducted at Acker's Greenwich Village apartment. Acker had returned to settle in the United States in the late eighties after spending nearly a decade living in London, where she had gained recognition on the basis of having published a series of radically experimental texts with small presses during the 1970s. These early works included *The Childlike Life of the Black Tarantula by the Black Tarantula* (1973); *I Dreamt I Was a Nymphomaniac!: Imagining* (1974); *The Adult Life of Toulouse Lautrec by Henri Toulouse Lautrec* (1975); and *Kathy Goes to Haiti* (1978).

But it was in England that Acker wrote *Great Expectations* (1982), the first of her major works that was directly influenced by her growing awareness of poststructuralist critical theory and feminism. As perhaps the most visible "weird American artist" in London, Acker soon was having her novels published (with spectacular Robert Mapplethorpe photographs on their covers) by major commercial houses (Picador in England, Grove in the United States). Controversy inevitably followed, as Acker was attacked not only by the predictable sources of conservative opinion but by feminists, many of whom felt uncomfortable with Acker's unabashed depictions of emotional and sexual masochism, her obscenity, and her ongoing, devastating portrayal not only of political and cultural repression but of many of the utopian ideals usually associated with 1960s liberalism and hippiedom.

Acker's fiction resembles other authors' in *Some Other Frequency* (for example, that of Vollmann, Leyner, Jaffe, Hejinian, and Antin) in its tendency to appropriate, sample, defamiliarize, and otherwise collaborate with prior texts drawn from the realms of both "high" and "pop" culture. It also illustrates the ways that authors in the eighties and nineties increasingly tend to blur the distinction between author and character— a device that emphasizes the individual's imaginative role in constructing *any* version of "reality" and the interaction of "fiction" and "fact" in our media-soaked environment. In works like *In Memoriam to Identity* and *My Mother: Demonology*, Acker, in typically bold maneuvers with point of view, adopts gender-bent perspectives of both figures involved in two of the most intensely passionate—and painful—love stories in Western fiction: Rimbaud *and* Verlaine and Heathcliff *and* Cathy in Emily Brontë's nineteenth-century masterpiece, *Wuthering Heights.*

But of course "retelling" a familiar story within a contemporary context permits readers to rethink the assumptions and "meanings" they bring to such materials. "Reanimated" by Acker's surrealist imagination and fiercely political vision, the familiar elements of the historical circumstances of the Rimbaud-Verlaine affair and of Brontë's novel are transformed into a nightmarish vision of the sexual longings, gender confusions, and injustices to be found in contemporary society.

Acker's recent work has increasingly focused on *the body* as a literal and symbolic site of struggle between individuals seeking self-empowerment and the forces of patriarchal control that seek to regulate people's lives. As we sat talking in her apartment, it was obvious that this focus on *the body* is grounded in more than abstract political concerns. As a real woman and not just a narrative person, Acker is her own text, her own gallery. Embedded in one of her front teeth is a jagged chunk of bronze. She's a bodybuilder in more than the usual way: her muscles animate spectacular tattoos, a combination that she feels allows her to seize control over the sign systems through which people "read" her. Meanwhile, the overall effect of her work resembles that found in earlier radical artists like Sade, Artaud, Burroughs, and Rimbaud—artists who felt the need to invent an entirely new way of using language and narrative structures that do not so much deconstruct dogmatic and life-negating narratives as model a *deconditioning process* readers can apply when they close their books.

We primed ourselves for the interview with sushi and sake at a quiet Japanese restaurant, where the conversation ranged from mutual West Coast acquaintances (during the 1970s Acker lived for periods in San Diego and San Francisco) to Acker's *Village Voice* article about Peter Greenaway's film, *The Cook, the Thief, His Wife, and Her Lover,* to our mutual fascination with tattooing, blood-and-splatter films, punk, and the work of artists such as Sade, Baudelaire, Rimbaud, Bataille, Genet, and Burroughs—disparate forms of extremist cultural production from which Acker clearly draws inspiration. Acker is an articulate and energetic talker who moves easily and authoritatively among widely divergent realms of discourse; she is also a disarmingly open woman whose laughter and self-irony often punctuate her anecdotes, discussions of aesthetics and intimate personal history, and heavily theoretical forays into French feminist theory, the history of the novel, and the evolution of postmodern art and culture.

*   *   *

Kathy Acker: Selected Bibliography

Books of Fiction

Politics. Papyrus Press, 1972.
The Childlike Life of the Black Tarantula: Some Lives of Murderesses (under the
    pseudonym of The Black Tarantula). San Diego: Community Congress Press,
    1973. Expanded edition published as *The Childlike Life of the Black Tarantula by
    the Black Tarantula.* New York: Vanishing Rotating Triangle Press, 1975.
I Dreamt I Was a Nymphomaniac!: Imagining. San Francisco: Empty Elevator Shaft
    Press, 1974.
Florida. Providence, RI: Diana's Bimonthly Press, 1978.
The Adult Life of Toulouse Lautrec by Henri Toulouse Lautrec. New York: TVRT, 1975;
    rpt. New York: TVRT and Printed Matter, 1978.
Kathy Goes to Haiti. Toronto: Rumor, 1978.
Blood and Guts in High School. New York: Grove Press, 1984. Published in En-
    gland as *Blood and Guts in High School Plus Two* (includes *Great Expectations* and
    My Death, My Life). London: Picador, 1984.
Great Expectations. San Francisco: RE/Search Productions, 1982, Reprinted New
    York: Grove Press, 1983.
Don Quixote. New York: Grove Press, 1986.
Empire of the Senseless. New York: Grove Press, 1988.
In Memoriam to Identity. New York: Grove Weidenfeld, 1990.
My Mother: Demonology. New York: Pantheon Books, 1993.
Pussy Cat Fever. San Francisco: AK Press, 1995.
Pussy, King of the Pirates. New York: Grove Press, 1996.

Collected Fiction, Novellas, and Stories Published Individually

I Don't Expect You'll Do the Same/Clay Fear. San Francisco: Musicmusic Corp., 1974.
The Persian Poems by Janey Smith. New York: Borzeau of London Press, 1980.
Hello, I'm Erica Jong. Chapbook. New York: Contact II, 1982.
Implosion. New York: Wedge, 1983.
Algeria: A Series of Invocations Because Nothing Else Works. New York: Printed Mat-
    ter, 1984; London: Aloes Books, 1984.
New York City in 1979. Novella. Buffalo, NY: Top Stories, No. 9, 1981; rpt., New
    York: Top Stories, 1986.
Literal Madness: Three Novels (includes *Kathy Goes to Haiti, My Death, My Life by Pier
    Paolo Pasolini,* and *Florida*). New York: Grove Press, 1988.
The Seven Cardinal Virtues. London: Serpent's Tail, 1990.
Hannibal Lecter, My Father. Miscellaneous collection. New York: Semiotext(e),
    1991.
Portrait of an Eye: Three Novels (includes *The Childlike Life of the Black Tarantula, I
    Dreamt I Was a Nymphomaniac!: Imagining,* and *The Adult Life of Toulouse Lautrec
    by Henri Toulouse Lautrec*). New York: Pantheon, 1992.

Other

Variety. Screenplay. Horizon Films, 1985.
The Birth of the Poet. Text for opera. Music by Peter Gordon. Performed at the

Brooklyn Academy of Music, 1985. Included in *Wordplays: An Anthology of Five American Dramas*. New York: PAJ Publications, 1986.

Pussy, King of the Pirates. Album. Lyrics and narration by Mekons and Kathy Acker. Chicago: Quarterstick Records, 1996.

As Editor

Throat. San Francisco Art Institute, December 1992.

Black Ice Magazine ("Kathy Acker Ice Picks: New Writing" Special Section). Boulder, CO, 1991.

Reviews and Commentaries about Acker's Work

[Note: The 1989 special Acker issue of the *Review of Contemporary Fiction*, edited by Ellen Friedman and Miriam Fuchs, is probably the best single source of critical discussions of her work. See below for individual listings.]

Dix, Douglas Shields. "Kathy Acker's *Don Quixote*: Nomad Writing." *Review of Contemporary Fiction* 9, 3 (1989): 56–62.

Friedman, Ellen. " 'Now Eat Your Mind': An Introduction to the Works of Kathy Acker." *Review of Contemporary Fiction* 9, 3 (1989): 37–49.

Friedman, Ellen, and Miriam Fuchs. "Introduction to Kathy Acker Issue." *Review of Contemporary Fiction* 9, 3 (1989): 7–11.

Jacobs, Naomi. "Kathy Acker and the Plagiarized Self." *Review of Contemporary Fiction* 9, 3 (1989): 50–55.

LeClair, Tom. "The Lorde of La Mancha and Her Abortion." Review of *Don Quixote*. *New York Times Book Review*, 30 November 1986, p. 10.

McCaffery, Larry. "The Artists of Hell: Kathy Acker and 'Punk' Aesthetics." In *Breaking the Sequence: Women's Experimental Fiction*, ed. Ellen Friedman and Miriam Fuchs, 215–30. Princeton, NJ: Princeton University Press.

Sciolino, Martina. "Confessions of a Kleptoparasite." *Review of Contemporary Fiction* 9, 3 (1989): 62–63.

———. "Kathy Acker and the Postmodern Subject of Feminism." *College English* 52, 4 (April 1990): 437–48.

Siegle, Robert. "Kathy Acker." In *Suburban Ambush: Downtown Writing and the Fiction of Insurgency*, 47–123. Baltimore: Johns Hopkins University Press, 1989.

Tillman, Lynne. "Selective Memory." *Review of Contemporary Fiction* 9, 3 (1989): 68–70.

Walsh, Richard. "The Quest for Love and the Writing of Female Desire in Kathy Acker's *Don Quixote*." *Critique: Studies in Contemporary Fiction* 32, 3 (spring 1991): 149–69.

Willis, Holly. "Wild Dogs Howl beneath the Gangrened Limbs of the Old: Kathy Acker's Fucking Literature." *Frighten the Horses* 11 (Winter 1993): 36–41.

Interviews

Friedman, Ellen. "An Interview with Kathy Acker." *Review of Contemporary Fiction* 9, 3 (1989): 11–23.

McCaffery, Larry. "An Interview with Kathy Acker." *Mississippi Review* 20, 1 and
2 (1991): 83–97.
————. "An Interview with Kathy Acker." *Shift* 6, 1 (1992): 30–34.
————. "Reading the Body: An Interview with Kathy Acker." *Mondo 2000* 4 (Fall
1991): 72–77.

*   *   *

LARRY MCCAFFERY: Do you write with the conscious aim of shocking
your readers? Or, let me ask this by creating what may well be a false
opposition: do you think you write shocking works because the world is
shocking, or is shock more of an aesthetic effect you adopt because you
think it is valuable in and of itself?

KATHY ACKER: Except really minorly, I don't think I've ever written
with the idea of shocking anyone. It took me a long time to even have an
audience in mind. At the very beginning I didn't even care if there was
an audience. I'd still say I write mainly for myself and maybe my friends.
I like the idea that people read my books, but during the act of writing it
has always been just myself I'm aware of. Obviously Baudelaire's dictum
Il faut épater le bourgeois, "surprise the bourgeois," is relevant here, and
an element of shock always reverberates here. The idea that shock can
help you to break through these perceptual blinders of habit is a theme
that comes through in my books again and again. But I'm not sure shock
is the best way to break through habit. You can do that better by the
breaking of taboos, or through transgressions—which both in form and
in content run through my work endlessly. That's not the same thing as
shock, although shock might accompany this. After all, the people in
our culture positively *live* off shock: in our media, we feed on it, but this
doesn't seem to have any positive effect in the sense of helping people
to break perceptual habits. This whole area of shock, what produces it
and why, is actually a very hot subject, because if you really went into it
you'd see all the hypocrisies and the real political bases of the society.

LM: Let me trace a certain lineage: Sade, Baudelaire, Rimbaud, Lautréamont, Jarry, the surrealists and dadaists, Bataille, Artaud, Genet, Burroughs, Johnny Rotten, Patti Smith, Charles Bukowski. Is that pretty
much the lineage you see yourself working out of? And if so, to what
extent do you see yourself as working out of a fairly clear tradition of
the extremist avant-garde who shared certain aesthetic and thematic impulses?

KA: I wouldn't call those people you listed really "avant-garde." I always
trace the lineage of the "avant-garde" in America through a completely
different tradition: John Cage, for instance. But there's also no doubt
that I place myself in that lineage you cited. Definitely. And I very much

hope I do enough significant work that I can someday be seen as belonging to that lineage. If someone tries to place me in another lineage, they're mistaken.

As to how my work relates to what they were doing, I'd say one thing we all share is a deeply sexual perspective which insists upon the connections between power and sexuality. It's basically a world-view. There's also the use of non–social realist language and imagery that is very involved with areas of the mind which are not rational. It's almost like we all have the same favorite color—black. Of course, there are differences. For instance, Apollinaire was not that "black" of a writer, in fact he was always trying hard as hell not to be. But then I'm not sure if Apollinaire is quite in that lineage.

LM: I'd say one of the things shared by all these writers is the sheer *excess* of their imaginations, the ways their works strain to defy perceptual limitations; that defiance has to do with the idea that daily reality is partly a lie covering up emotions and sexuality—and the body generally.

KA: I very much agree that their art was finally always about transcending limits. What that lineage of people are all expressing in their work is finally always about *seeing*. And they certainly share a view of excess as being not exactly what reality *is* but what you want to see reality *as*. Seeing almost becomes reality itself. You could say that for Baudelaire the act of perception was everything, and that his particular way of seeing has to do with excess. Most of these guys believed that you can't see properly unless you have gone over the limit. Certainly Bataille was very much about the opposition between the daily, workaday world and the transgressive or the ecstatic world—and the balance between these worlds. But this balance goes beyond transgression. In a sense, Bataille was trying to set up a stable form of transgression, where you can go back and forth. They were all concerned with that idea in one way or another. Which makes for political stances.

LM: Right. It's no accident that Sade is writing *The 120 Days of Sodom* while he's a prisoner in the Bastille just before the French Revolution. What he's writing really is a specific response to the beginning of the rise of industrialism and rationalism.

KA: Absolutely. In a very deep and profound sense, Sade was attacking rationalism. His work is profound partly because its excesses create all those emotional responses that make it impossible to argue about his work successfully. Sade wasn't really interested in sadism per se but in how the political realities of rationalism deny the body. I love Sade's work because you can argue endlessly and no fucking person agrees. You can go through Klossowski, de Beauvoir's, all the essays on him, and *nobody*—Bataille, Sarduy, anybody—can reach any agreement whatsoever. It's magnificent! Being an upper-class boy, Sade created a wonderfully

diabolical machine for attacking rationalism, especially political rationalism (which is what postindustrialization is) and capitalism. And this
machine works so bloody well that nobody can touch it. He never allows
you to rest in any meaning. It's not like language poetry, where you're
apart from meaning—you're just not allowed to be comfortable, intellectually, with the meaning he gives you. And, of course, Sade is truly,
profoundly, *shocking*.

LM: Your books constantly return to the site of the body in all kinds of
ways: as a source of power, as a center of struggle for power, as refuge
from brutality and banality, as the place we finally exist in (as opposed
to our thoughts). Why generally are you so interested in the body, as
opposed to whatever else you might be exploring in your work?

KA: Because when reality (or the meanings associated with reality) is up
for grabs—which is certainly Wittgenstein's main thing and one of the
central problems in philosophy and art ever since the end of the nineteenth century in the Western world—then the body itself becomes the
only thing you can return to. You can talk about sexuality as a social
phenomenon, so that it's up for grabs. You can talk about any intellectual thought and *it* is up for grabs because anything can mean anything,
any thought can lead into another thought and thus be completely per-
verted. You get to Baudrillard's black hole. But when you get to the
actual physical *act* of sexuality, or of bodily disease, there's an undeniable materiality which *isn't* up for grabs. So it's the body which finally
can't be touched by all our skepticism and ambiguous systems of belief.
The body is the only place where any basis for real values exist anymore.
Something like Mishima's *Sun and Steel* is fascinating because he returns
again and again to the body.

LM: But doesn't it seem that in our postmodern context whatever refuge
we have ever had from the "outer"—the state, the media, the church, or
whatever—is being systematically invaded? Even our sense of beauty or
our identity is no longer our own. Even our basic sense of desire. That's
why I'm wondering if even the body is finally untouchable . . .

KA: These erosions of the self and our imagination are obviously happening, and they may even be entering into the realm of body in some
way. But I still think there's something undeniably different in kind
about the body. I don't mean there is a "reality" there (we are too much
into postmodernism for that), but that with the body there is something that's essentially untouchable. And therefore transgressive. I guess
what I mean by untouchable—because I certainly don't mean "real"—
is what is taboo. I've been deeply into this whole area of taboo because
that's where you get into the stuff you just have to leave alone. And this
stuff is still very powerful. Otherwise why would pornography be such a
charged political issue?

LM: Do you think that today your work, or the works of any artists, can have significant effects on the world around you? Have we lost the avant-garde's early optimism about art's ability to produce significant change? **KA:** That all depends on what you mean by whom you want to affect. Audience is a big question for any novelist. The pressure is always on you to go for a commercial audience, to reach as many people as possible. Then the question becomes: Could one shock those people? Well, who are you going to shock? Would audiences who support all the censorship cases that have been brought against museum directors and book publishers be shocked if they read my work? Probably not—they'd be more likely to just blank out. They probably just wouldn't get it. I am guessing. I imagine if someone explained what I was doing to them they'd be shocked. And I know from what people have told me and from people's reactions that some people are certainly shocked when they read my work. But I see this as being like talking to people: you really only talk to someone who understands your language somewhat. I wouldn't really be shocking an audience of readers who don't at least somewhat get where I'm at because they have no idea of what I'm doing. Or the reasons they're shocked would be superficial. The people I'm really shocking in my work are mostly my brothers and my sisters.
LM: The early Russian experimentalists had a different take on this. Their idea wasn't so much to "shock" their audience in the sense we're talking about (i.e., through transgression and taboos) but to "shock" or assault their consciousness by exposing them to radically experimental works that would change their way of looking at things.
KA: Right, which is pretty much my own sense. I'm really not interested in shocking people in the usual sense but the idea of shock as a form of teaching. I want to "shock my audience," yes, meaning I want to show them that their perceptual habits are distorted, too rigidified. I also think most writers who want to shock their readers are a lot more conscious about content issues when they're writing than I am. They make an artistic machine that's structured to accomplish the task that they have in mind beforehand. Well, I don't have a clue what I am going to do when I start writing. It's what I said earlier about using my writing to find out about things, not to relay messages or ideas I have before I start. In that sense, I'm much more like a cockeyed journalist than a fiction writer. It takes me a while to realize my subject matter, and it's usually only about two-thirds of the way into a book that I have the range of a subject matter, thematically, so that I have an idea of the territory I am exploring. That's why you could say that pirates and explorers are the image or metaphor of how I work.
LM: You began writing your books back in the seventies, before the term "postmodernism" was even popular yet. But obviously even your

very earliest works seem to contain features that later on would be called postmodernism. How do you now situate yourself in this area?

KA: I certainly had no idea what the term meant when I started out writing, and I'm still not sure I understand it today. When I started out, I didn't know about the work of Foucault or—what would be more important to me—Deleuze and Guattari. I knew I wanted to plagiarize, but I didn't have a clear theoretical justification for what I was doing—or why. So I just started finding these different texts and putting them together. The first book I wrote seriously (at least, the first one I'd even want to talk about) would be *Tarantula*. At that point I was fascinated by schizophrenia and the model of the centralized "I" (and I don't think I would've even used the word "centralized" in those days). I was reading R. D. Laing and David Cooper. In *Tarantula* I was trying to see if, rather than trying to integrate the "I," if you could *dis*-integrate it and find a more comfortable way of being. The question on my mind was, "What was this 'I'?"

LM: Was this a question about *you*—that "I" that is Kathy Acker? Or was it more of an investigation into the nature of the textual "I"—the kind of thing Rimbaud is talking about when he says "'I' am another"?

KA: It was the "I" in the text, not "I" of *me*. I wasn't interested in autobiography or in diary writing, but in what that textual "I" looked like. So I set a real autobiography next to fake autobiography—that is, I took some biography and made it into an autobiography. I took what I figured out "I" wasn't, which was a murderess. Figuring that out wasn't as simple as it sounds (it's hard to tell what you aren't or haven't got if you just list qualities), but I knew I wasn't a murderess because I hadn't murdered anybody. So at the beginning of the whole process I placed the fake autobiography of murderesses next to a lot of quotation marks— the real autobiography—to see what would happen. After working some of these ideas through in several books, I found I wasn't so interested in that area of textual identity anymore. It was a false problem.

LM: How do you mean that it was a "false problem"—that textual identity is always "scripted" rather than "real" somehow?

KA: Just that when you're writing you aren't using language (with all its problematics) to "express identity" at all. What I realized was that language doesn't *express* anything, it *creates*, it makes, it creates something that didn't exist before. This goes back to Joyce. And if you're making rather than expressing, then identity isn't a problem. What was much more interesting was the actual text itself. It was right about that point when I started *Great Expectations*.

LM: That kind of textual juxtaposition and manipulation resembles what Burroughs was doing. Was he one of the sources for the kind of experimentation you were doing?

KA: Burroughs has probably been the main influence on my work. I started out coming from the poetry world, the Black Mountain School. People like Charles Olson, Jerry Rothenberg, and David Antin were my teachers. Burroughs was important to me early on because I wanted to write fiction and not poetry, and Burroughs was about the only prose model around at that point interested in what I was—which was in writing essentially nonnarrative prose. I took *The Third Mind* and went through it carefully, imitating it basically—you know, doing all the experiments and writing as I thought Burroughs wrote. I wrote so many pages a day, and I did all the experiments with diary materials and taking two tapes and messing around. I more or less taught myself how to write by imitating Burroughs. Then I forgot about him as I became interested in other things. The last few years I'm finding I'm really interested in him again.

LM: So would you compare what you were doing early on with the Burroughs cut-up or fold-in methods?

KA: I wasn't really doing the same thing as the cut-up because it wasn't conceived with the idea of attacking the image-system. The main impulses in my work early on were actually coming from outside literature altogether. I was very influenced, for example, by Bob Ashley's music; the way I would have spoken about what I was trying to do at that time was to talk about making a text that was an "environment" rather than a centralized, meaningful narrative. What I wanted was a "de-narrative," if there is such a word. You see, there was no way I had of really talking about it until the punk movement came along and I met Sylvère Lotringer. That was about 1976. Sylvère introduced me to the work of Félix Guattari, Gilles Deleuze, and Foucault. Derrida was never as important. And I never took to Baudrillard's work. But it was only then that I began to find a language for what I was doing. Especially the ideas of decentralization and different notions of sexuality, and of the relation of sexuality to language and politics. All that. Reading Kristeva's *Powers of Horror* was another step, but it had nothing to do with Sylvère.

LM: Your comments about recognizing that writing doesn't *express* identity but that it *creates* it seems related to your work's ongoing interrogation of creativity and originality—which, again, is another of postmodernism's signatures . . .

KA: Certainly I was attacking the traditional notion of originality from the very beginning, but I'm not sure how all these concerns really add up to something that holds together as a movement called "postmodernism." I mean, suppose I put some of Sarduy's essays (which I've just read) next to those of someone like Baudrillard. They're both in the postmodern canon, but I am moved very deeply by Sarduy whereas Baudrillard just leaves me cold. That writers representing such very different kinds of ideas and viewpoints can both fit comfortably under a single term makes "postmodernism" seem mainly just a loosely conceived catchall phrase.

LM: Aside from the attractive political features of these writers that Sylvère Lotringer introduced you to—Deleuze and Guattari, Foucault, and so forth—were there any ways that they had a specific impact on your own work, your sense of form-content issues? I would imagine that something like *Anti-Oedipus* or the whole Foucault program would have appealed to someone who was experimenting the way that you were in switching your characters' sexual genders (and doing just about every other kind of semiotic slippage imaginable!). Even in those early books, like *Tarantula* and *I Dreamt I Was a Nymphomaniac*, you seem to use this slippage and textual transformations to literalize the notion that identity is unfixed, and to question the whole concept of stable feminine and masculine identities.

KA: Mainly those people helped me begin to see more clearly some of the deeper sources for certain kinds of impulses that had been operating in my work without my really understanding. For instance, I really had no idea *why* I was switching sexual genders in my novels and jumping from one narration to another. I knew what I *didn't* want to do, mind you—I didn't want to write a John Cheever short story or a John Updike novel. But at the time I was writing those early books, those issues you mentioned weren't consciously involved in what I was doing. One of the things that made my discovery of Deleuze and Guattari and the others so useful was precisely that it helped me gain an understanding of how they *might* apply to what I had been doing, and how I could explore them differently in other ways. But back then (and I'm very aware that in talking about what was *now*, I'm applying a theory to a past act) I honestly did not understand why I was doing what I was doing. I knew I was very angry. I knew I didn't want any centralized meaning, I can say that. Even though I have great respect for Robert Creeley and that range of work, I also hated it because it was so male, and I just didn't want to be that male.

LM: Obviously finding an appropriate means to escape that "male centralized meaning" in writing fiction requires some pretty radical adjustments on the part of the novelist, if only because the novel evolved with such a rationalist-empiricist bias that foregrounded centralized meanings. What it requires, obviously, is the fictional equivalent of a "deconstructive aesthetic"—which is one way I'd describe the underlying aesthetic of your work.

KA: My own escape mechanism from that (which was initially purely intuitive, you understand) was to keep my interest in writing as purely conceptual as I could. So I wasn't interested in "saying" anything in my work. If anything, the only thing I could use my works to say is "I don't want to say things!" I couldn't say anything beyond that, certainly nothing about all the slippage that was going on or why I just didn't give a damn if one character was another or not—I couldn't even remember who my characters *were*! Of course, I also couldn't understand why anyone would read me. I honestly thought I was writing the most unreadable stuff around. And then suddenly when I read this stuff that Sylvère turned me on to, I had a theory for what I was doing. Even more importantly, it was a theory that made sense to me because it wasn't just abstract theoretical garbage but something grounded very much in the political and social world I saw around me. It explained my own anger, which was very much an anger against the "centralization of the phallus," to put it in academic terms. And it kind of went together with feminism, and then postmodernism, so that I could finally actually say, "*That's* what I'm doing" or "This is what I'm aiming to do." Now that I understood that, I could start using some of this stuff more consciously, with a greater degree of control and precision about what I was doing. By the time of *Empire of the Senseless* I could even *plan* things! Whereas before I never even wanted to touch anything that was rational, because I felt that would intrude on whatever was going on. I had known all along that *something* was going on, but it was just too much for me to handle on my own. Reading this theory gave me a handle, and the first book I wrote after reading this stuff was *Pasolini*.

LM: This was after *Blood and Guts*—the novel that first received a lot of attention for your work?

KA: *Way* after. *Blood and Guts* was actually a very early book, even though it wasn't published until 1984. It can actually be considered part of *Great Expectations* in that it helped me see something about what I wanted to do, which led me to *Great Expectations*. *Blood and Guts* was written when I was still working through that business about the meaning of textual identity. When I was finished with it I simply didn't take it that seriously. In my demented mind at that time, I thought that I was writing a rather commercial novel.

LM: "Commercial" in what sense?

KA: Its narrative component. Other than *Kathy Goes to Haiti* (which was written for strange reasons and really off to the side of what I had been doing), *Blood and Guts* was the first book where I used plot (an episodic plot) as a device to structure my materials. That came about only in the final draft, where I put something like a plot on top of everything. So I tried to make Janey seem like one person, and take her from the time she was fourteen and trying to get rid of Daddy up until her death. That was the first time I had done that. Of course, I abandoned plot in some of my later books, so that in something like *Great Expectations* I couldn't have cared less about it.

What was most interesting and enjoyable to me about *Blood and Guts*, though, wasn't the plotted aspect but what I was doing with this Genet material. I remember saying to myself that using these other texts is what I want to start doing more with. Which is how I arrived at *Great Expectations*, where I really felt I was doing something I loved.

LM: You mentioned earlier that *Pasolini* was the first book you wrote after you had been exposed to some of the theory you had been absorbing . . .

KA: Yes. There I was putting things together not by narrative but based on puns, and generally trying to put together a book out of various noncausal ways of ordering. That approach grew partly out of Deleuze and Guattari's *Anti-Oedipus*—and with me consciously and obsessively fighting against Oedipal structuring. I probably wound up being *too* obsessive in this regard and I don't ever want to go that far again. Partly as a result I think the book is almost unreadable.

LM: Your use of appropriation seems to change just about the time of *Great Expectations*.

KA: Appropriation is not a literary strategy I've chosen. I have always used appropriation in my works because I simply can't write any other way. I mean that very literally. When I was in my teens I grew up with some of the Black Mountain poets who were always giving lectures to writers to the effect that, "when you find your own voice, then you are a poet." The problem was, I couldn't find my own voice. I didn't *have* a voice, as far as I could tell. And yet I wanted very badly to write. So I began to do what I *had to* if I wanted to write: appropriate, imitate, and find whatever other ways I could to work with and improvise off of other texts. In high school I was always imitating Shakespeare, redoing poems from *Romeo and Juliet*, and so on. It's been that way ever since. What this comes down to, I think, is that I've never liked the idea of originality, and so my whole life I've always written by taking other texts, inhabiting them in some way so that I can do something with them.

LM: Why inhabit other texts rather than starting out with something of your own?

KA: The honest answer has to do with my personality, even with my sexuality. Kristeva's *Powers of Horror* opened up this area for me so that I could understand certain aspects about myself and my creative process. She starts out with some boring Freudian stuff, but then develops a brilliant analysis of Céline where she talks about "abjection." She takes the Husserl model of the mind turning in upon itself in order to understand itself; it eventually reaches a kind of nothingness, and then some under-

standing takes place. She also talks about this sexual personality structure which wants to follow the "black path" or *poète maudit* tradition—the
path of "abjection," which is the way writers like Genet and Céline work.
Her analysis appealed to me because I never accepted the way most
critics tend to put writers down who have followed that path by saying,
"Oh, they're fucked up, they just love evil"—as if loving "evil" meant
they loved petty crime or something rather than giving them access to a
certain kind of knowledge about themselves and the world. Critics who
say that don't understand what Baudelaire meant by the word "evil."

   What I also recognize now is that I am passive. Deeply, deeply passive.
So the quality of making or creation that comes out in me—whatever it
is in me that has to do with making—is based on a reactive rather than
an active principle. I don't see a blank page when I'm writing. Ever. Or
when I do, nothing happens. I can't even write letters to people or apply
for a grant. Literally, I just can't do it. For me, the blank page is like an
invitation to paralysis, not to creative activity.

LM: Do you identify what you've been doing with the term "deconstruction"?

KA: Sure. But that's true mainly from the period of *Great Expectations*
until *Empire of the Senseless*, when I was taking texts and trying to see what
they were really saying in a social, political, and sexual context—which
is essentially the program of deconstruction. I was trying to show that
mostly texts are not presented in context. News stories are presented
to us as objective reports, but without really knowing the politics of the
newspaper readers are actually being presented with basically a con. My
books like *Great Expectations* and *Don Quixote* were attempts to write my
way through the cons.

LM: Give me an example.

KA: I'd often take texts that were either sexual or political—usually
fairly *hot* texts, like the beginning of *Great Expectations*, where there's that
incredible Pierre Guyotat text—and I put these next to the stuff about
my mother's suicide. Now one speaks about one's mother's suicide in a
certain way, especially autobiographical material. And one speaks about
sex during wartime—which is what Pierre Guyotat is writing about—in
another way. I put them both together as if they were the same text.
Doing that uncovered a lot of stuff.

LM: And part of the point of this is . . .

KA: There really wasn't a "point," at least not in an abstract sense that I
was doing this deconstructive activity trying to bring out specific content
or ideas. See, that is when I was working basically intuitively, introducing different materials that just felt right. If I was doing that *now* I could
have a theory about what I was doing—I could talk about women's roles,
what my mother's suicide was, why I had to stick that next to a war text,

why I wouldn't deal with it sentimentally. And what the function was of including that kind of sex which a lot of feminists would call very sexist (to say the least). Placing those Telweit texts on Nazi fantasies next to the Guyotat text is very interesting from a theoretical standpoint, right? Because according to a certain brand of feminism they're the same text.

LM: So when you're doing these kinds of deconstructive operations on texts *now*, you're doing so with a greater self-consciousness about what's going to result from these interactions.

KA: To a certain extent, yes. But it's finally all reactive, right? When I started out doing this I was interested in finding out how this society worked. My main reason for writing *Great Expectations* and *Don Quixote* was to see how texts that had already established themselves within our societal matrix worked—or I wanted to destroy them, or do something else with them. So I would take a text that confused or puzzled me, or that I even thought was great, and let these things interact with other texts. But this "it" was always a given, and what I was doing was producing a reaction to it. I wasn't constructing anything except my own reaction to it, so it was directly a process of deconstructing. I was tearing things apart, like a kid does sometimes, and using every strategy I could think of for tearing things apart. Then at the end of *Quixote* I no longer wanted to do that sort of thing anymore.

LM: What reasons did you have for choosing the framing texts for *Great Expectations* and *Don Quixote*? For example, did you start out with *Don Quixote* thinking you wanted to shatter this great myth of the romantic male hero whose blindness is gradually revealed, or—

KA: No. *Don Quixote* was chosen by random, although once I got started with the book I kept with it for certain specific reasons. *Quixote* happened to be the book I had taken with me to the hospital when I was about to have an abortion. In fact, the first scene in *Don Quixote* is exactly what I wrote prior to the abortion. I couldn't think while I was waiting, so I just started copying *Don Quixote*. It was my version of a Sherrie Levine painting, where you copy something with no theoretical justification behind what you're doing. I keep being asked if I chose *Don Quixote* out of any kind of feminist perspective, but that wasn't really it. There were some places in the book where I wound up dealing with feminist issues—like there's one part where I was trying to deal with Andrea Dworkin's view that men are totally evil and responsible for all the shit that's ever existed in the world. And after I got into the middle of it, I began to see that the book was, in a way, about appropriating male texts and about trying to find your voice as a woman (I deal with that a lot in the second part of the book). But I started out mainly being fascinated with this Levine notion of seeing what happens when you copy something for no reason. I kept with the book because once I started reading

Don Quixote (I had never read it before) I was fascinated about seeing how it worked. So deconstructing *Quixote* was an act of reading for me. In fact, all my writings are very deeply acts of reading.

LM: Was the same basic thing true with *Great Expectations?*

KA: Not exactly, because I *had* read the book before and what I wanted to do was take a grid and destroy this book that I had always absolutely loved. So I was working on the book for essentially the same reason (being fascinated by this original text), but my fascination with *Quixote* happened simultaneously with my reading of the book, whereas I knew *Great Expectations* very, very well, because as a kid the first adult books I'd ever read and loved were Hawthorne and Dickens. Talking about these books is almost like talking about my childhood. When I was a kid I always thought of books as more real than anything else. I had a bad childhood and books really *were* my reality. Dickens was a big part of that.

LM: Did you have anything particular in mind when you set out to "destroy" this book that you loved so much? I would assume one of the things you were taking on was this whole notion of "great expectations"—the way people are acculturated to have these, and so on.

KA: I certainly used that title totally ironically. But again, I don't mean to imply that I had a conscious program of specific points I wanted to make when I chose *Great Expectations.* I chose the book for emotional reasons, and when you do things for emotional reasons, you are often doing them for different reasons you don't know about. Whereas when you work totally rationally, you don't get that range. To my mind now, the book is about my mother's suicide. But I didn't know that when I started writing it, or if I did, that knowledge was buried somewhere deeply inside my emotions. Today it makes perfect sense that after my mother's suicide I would choose to write a book with the ironic title *Great Expectations.*

LM: In one of your earlier interviews, you say that you started *In Memoriam to Identity* with Rimbaud because Rimbaud "saw myth as a way out of this mess." Throughout *Empire,* you seemed to be searching for a society that can escape from the central myth of the phallus and can replace it with another one. Since that search seems to fail there, I wondered if you were drawn to retelling Rimbaud's story because he represents a myth that might succeed—maybe the artist who turns his back on the world, the myth of refusal.

KA: Not really. I was looking for a myth that we could say was ours, or that I could say was mine, but the myth I had in mind was the myth of romantic love. I set the book up by presenting these different models or stories (they're not really stories so much as myths). It's a book of several mirrors all reflecting this basic myth of romantic love. The first one of these mirrors is the Rimbaud-Verlaine material. Maybe I was consciously searching for a myth, but honestly this book just seemed to pour out of me; the searching was incidental to the compelled quality of what I was doing. Once I had that myth, then the other relationships followed from it and reflected it: Airplane and the rapist (which is from *Sanctuary*), then Capital and her father and brothers, Jason and Quentin, and so on.

LM: *In Memoriam* feels different to me than anything else you've written—there's less irony . . .

KA: It felt very strange for me, too. The fact that these different mirrors keep showing you the same thing made the range feel very constricted to me. It's also less theoretical than any of my last few books, and it's got a narrower range than I usually work with. It's more personal as well. If anything, I'd say the book is *too* narrow and personal. But it's done, and I like the way it's constructed. I also feel like it has a narrative power I've never had in any of my books.

LM: What drew you to start off the book with the Rimbaud material in the first place?

KA: I had originally set out to write the life of Rimbaud. But when I got to the end of the affair with Verlaine I thought, "This guy became a fucking capitalist! He's like a yuppie, I can't do this, I'm bored out of my mind!" The more research I did about Rimbaud (and I did quite a lot), the more I realized I didn't want to write this anymore [laughs]. That's why he eventually becomes Jason, and you get all these other reflections of different aspects of the patriarchy you find in the Rimbaud-Verlaine relationship—the stuff from *The Wild Palms* that I used at the end, Airplane's relationship with the German guy, Capital's with the husband. Are all those really one myth? Maybe so . . .

LM: In what sense is *In Memoriam* "less theoretical" than your other recent novels?

KA: Because up until *In Memoriam* (this is probably true of *Empire of the Senseless*, as well) the form of each book was pretty much determined by some sort of theory—or, in the case of the really early stuff, on some form of experiment. But the form of my recent books seems to be coming more organically in the sense that it's based on theme, which I think is more clearly laid out in *In Memoriam* than elsewhere. It's not as if I'm basing my work on any kind of centralization but that I'm not working out of deconstruction any longer.

LM: You said that when you began writing *Empire* you decided pretty consciously to try and look for something "constructive"—what was that?

KA: A myth that people could live by. What was involved in the writing itself was a dialectic between trying to get to another society and realizing you can't. So in the first part of the book I basically took the world of patriarchy and then killed the father on every level I could imagine. Part of this involved my attempt to find a way to talk about taboo—those basic transgressions patriarchy is responsible for but tries to cover over and deny. In the second part of the book I tried to imagine a society where you didn't have any of these taboos because it wasn't defined by Oedipal considerations. But even though I wanted to get to that world, I couldn't get there (or in terms of the metaphor I used in the book, the "CIA" intervened). And so in the last section, there's only that sense of, "Well, what the fuck do we do now?" That section is the synthesis of what you have in the first two parts of the dialectical movement: the wanting to get to that society of taboo and freedom from the central phallus, but realizing this is impossible. Finally *Empire* isn't just about getting to another society (which is a literal impossibility) but about searching for some kind of myth to replace the phallic myth.

LM: Does Abhor find that myth at the end, with the motorcycle gang, the James Dean scene?

KA: Partially. She's still stuck in all that isolation and loneliness, but she's trying to deal with that somehow. Her relationship with Mark and the other guys shows that Abhor at the end is not dependent on the phallic myth at all. Mark, by the way, was based very directly after a real person who said to me after he read the book, "What this is really about is your, my, and Don's relationship, and it shows that it wasn't at all phallically defined." The most "constructive" part of the book is the sense that this is the myth about friendship, and about what relationships can be in our world. Even under the conditions of a society which hasn't changed.

LM: Given your obvious distaste for the patriarchal society that we live in—and given the extremely negative portrayals you've had of most of your male characters generally (and the father, always)—why haven't you been drawn more to the radical lesbian feminist program? Is it simply because separatism won't work, that it's unrealistic?

KA: Because it's the hippie line, the sixties line, and all you have to do is look around at the world today to see that they didn't work. And basically I see lesbian separatism as being part of the sixties. Anything separatist is going to have the same problems the hippies had. You can't separate yourself from the society at large—the milkman still has to deliver the milk [laughs]. It just doesn't work. Either the whole thing changes or nothing changes. This doesn't mean you don't change things slowly, or on a person-to-person basis (that's what I was suggesting at the end of *Empire of the Senseless*), but a model based on separatism just doesn't work. I also don't feel comfortable with the simplistic descriptions you get from a lot of radical lesbians about what a human being is—say, the ideal of someone free from jealousy, free from all the bad stuff. And I certainly don't find the general dislike of power, which you find among some feminists, as being at all satisfying.

LM: Your comment about myth in regard to *In Memoriam* also made me think of the myth of childhood. There's a way in which your work often seems "childish" in the positive way Rimbaud envisioned. It's like you're speaking through some voice that hasn't been socialized, controlled, or restrained by the repressive adult world. Was Rimbaud's impulse to recover childhood something that was relevant to your treatment of him in *In Memoriam*?

KA: In a sense, when I started the Rimbaud I was trying to recover my own childhood. Rimbaud had been important to me when I started out writing in the late sixties, and at a certain point I wanted to remember why because I'd forgotten. About the time that *Empire* came out, watching several programs about the European hippie scene that was happening in England and France in '68 made me start thinking again about those times. One of the programs showed how there was this huge outcry in the English press about how much they *hated* that kind of stuff, how they really loved Thatcherism (this is when Thatcherism was doing very well, and it was very trendy to be a yuppie, and all the punks were now wearing suits, and whatever). Then when *Empire* came out, everyone in England hated it because they thought it was preaching hippie politics. That's when I started wanting to remember why Rimbaud had meant a lot to us. I felt I needed to go over all this material again, so I could remember where I came from. Because when I saw all this '68 stuff I was feeling like history was disappearing. And maybe intelligence, along with it, because if we don't have history, our intelligence is going to disintegrate. We're not going to have models or ranges of possibility.

So that's why I started to want to remember my own history (the myth of my own childhood) and got interested in Rimbaud again. But then, maybe because I was in England and missing America, these concerns became connected with the myth of America. That's where the Faulkner material started coming in. I've always felt Faulkner was *the* American writer, and gradually the book started taking off.

LM: Rimbaud's program with poetic language—his interest in the relationship between language and the body, and language in memory, and language in childhood—would seem to be something you'd be sympathetic with. What was your main impression of these things when you went back and began to look at his works at this stage in your life?

KA: All those things were on my mind when I started translating his poems (or my "version" of them—when I'm working with these texts now, I get into them and just let myself go; like a jazz riff); but what most struck me was how bloody *honest* they were. I'd never really read them in terms of his relationship with Verlaine, but this time it struck me, "My god, there's nothing mysterious about what he's saying—he's writing direct autobiography!" Childhood for him *was* like being with Verlaine, a period of pure happiness, because his *real* childhood had been just bloody misery. What's ironic is that he *hated* his real childhood and his horrible mother and where he came from. And yet in the poems he keeps referring to his childhood as being a season of paradise. So I think that childhood was less literally about being four years old again than about getting into the happy world with Verlaine again.

LM: On the other hand, I don't think the underlying aesthetics of his work can be explained purely in those terms. He was working through some of this business about childhood representing this moment of pure "connection" with the world even before he met Verlaine, wasn't he?

KA: It was that, too. The problem is that we need the freedom to regain it. That's where drugs came in for him. Rimbaud wanted to live completely out on the edge where he could investigate perception and how the body worked. He didn't want to stop. He wanted to go all the way. But all Verlaine did was keep him waiting.

LM: Gertrude Stein's influence seems pretty obvious in your writing. What was it about Stein that interested you?

KA: Her attempt to make language *present*, and her equation of language and breath, in which language is absolutely primary, was important. I wanted to do a novel in which language was primary, so that it would have that power of breath. When I was starting out it seemed like what traditional novelists like Roth and Bellow were doing was mirroring reality, so that the function of language was secondary to their desire to express what they saw as reality, or society, or whatever. That seemed like an inverted set of values because I always felt that language was more real than what it was supposed to be mirroring. To me, that was what Stein was all about.

LM: Stein's break from the Balzacian form of the novel also strikes me as being very interesting from a feminist perspective.

KA: And in fact, if you look at the major women writers of the twentieth century—Virginia Woolf, Stein, Djuna Barnes, even Christa Wolf—you rarely see a centralized narrative.

LM: What does this have to do with? Power? Or meaning . . . ?

KA: Yeah! It's an attack on the control system, a refusal to uphold the centralized meaning. Whether or not this was theorized, these women don't want the centralized phallus. It's that simple. They don't want to be told what to do. There's a way in which the formal break from the Balzacian narrative tradition is very much a political move. I don't mean the sort of total disjunction you find in really avant-garde works, but the more mainstream experiments of Woolf. Roland Barthes does a nice job of analyzing what that Balzacian narrative is, politically. He says it's about property—and "ownership," of course, meant the ownership of the female by the male. So it's not surprising that you don't find women upholding this form.

LM: You say somewhere that "My father is not my *real father*"—the implication being that the basic problem women have isn't necessarily with men, per se. That the "real father" isn't necessarily the awful, power-wielding tyrant who keeps fucking over (and fucking) your women characters. It's an antiessentialist view—one that probably irritates certain feminists . . .

KA: I don't think the problem *is* with men. Take Cixous's argument against Kristeva, with Cixous saying that our problems all have their source in genital difference—so that the fact that men have cocks is what makes them evil. This being so, the only thing to do is escape from men. She's a separatist. And Dworkin's position is the same basic thing. Kristeva's argument that the real problem has to do with role models makes a lot more sense to me. This may not be a politically correct thing to say but *I like men*. I don't have any problem with guys. I just have a lot of problems with society.

Photograph by Byron Pepper

Matches in a Dark Space
An Interview with David Antin

Larry McCaffery, Marjorie Perloff, and Jerzy Kutnik

i was getting extremely tired of what i considered an unnatural language act going into a closet . . . because anything is possible in a closet in front of a typewriter and nothing is necessary

— talking at the boundaries

Poet, performer, art critic, linguist, literary theorist, filmmaker, social commentator, professor, and a founding chair of the Visual Arts Department at the University of California at San Diego, David Antin occupies a unique position in the poetry/art discourse of our late twentieth-century American moment. He is probably best known for his "talk poems," those transcriptions of taped oral improvisations made for particular occasions and confined only by the length of time allotted for a given "talk" (usually an hour). Neither verse nor prose (the texts avoid justified margins, conventional punctuation, and regularized spelling), the talk pieces create a new space for "natural" language—but a natural language always already transformed by *writing*. They fuse narrative, philosophical speculation, comic intervention, and learned digression into a genuinely new mode of discourse, consonant with the modes of perception and communication of our information age, in which knowledge has become increasingly problematized and "personal emotion" increasingly a product invented by the television networks for easy consumption.

Born in Brooklyn, New York, in 1932 into a family of East European Jewish immigrants with anarchist and radical leanings, Antin has always been a rebel, but an extraordinarily genial rebel who doesn't expect—or even necessarily want—others to agree with him. At City College in the early fifties, he struck up a friendship with poet Jerome Rothenberg; to this day, their relationship has a yin/yang quality, Rothenberg's visionary ethnopoetics offset by Antin's ironic, down-to-earth, disenchanted, cosmopolitan stance toward his world. Listening to a sparring match between Rothenberg and Antin is rather like reading Diderot's *Neveu de Rameau*, which happens to be one of Antin's favorite books.

Indeed, Antin's refusal to participate in this or that "movement" or to follow the going trend has made him, from the beginning, a controversial figure in the poetry and art world. His first two books (1967) were called *autobiography* and *definitions*: the former supplies no real autobiographical data and the second performs an elegant deconstruction of the process of definition itself. His "poetry" is closer to Wittgensteinian language game than to the lyric of the Beats or New York poets who were his contemporaries and often his friends. Ironically, Antin was thus a "language poet" *avant la lettre* even though—again ironically—the language poets have sometimes been critical of what they took to be his faith in a natural language. A further irony: his offbeat essay-writing mode (no statement of purpose, no proper footnotes, no topic sentences) is now being increasingly used as a model by academics who want to write in a more "playful," less conventional style than PMLA, or even *Social Text*, allows.

Antin's relation to the theory canon is equally complicated. His early essays on Marcel Duchamp, Robert Morris, video art, and so on have been widely reprinted and have become classics of their kind. But he has never allied himself with the dominant theoretical discourse, whether that of semiotics in the seventies, poststructuralism in the eighties, or cultural studies today. A skeptic about hard-line positions, whether Marxist, feminist, or psychoanalytic, Antin has over the years evolved his own theoretical base. In their deceptive but casual way, his three volumes of talk pieces, *talking at the boundaries* (1976), *tuning* (1984), and *what it means to be avant-garde* (1993), elaborate a complex theory of narrative and language use, of the visual and the verbal, of temporality and space. Accordingly, while so many of our "leading theorists" have already become hopelessly dated, Antin remains defiantly (and good-humoredly, for he is always good-humored) an original.

The following conversation took place in San Diego on a warm and hazy afternoon at the home of Larry McCaffery and Sinda Gregory, some twenty miles from Antin's own home in the Del Mar ranch country, where he has lived since 1976. Marjorie Perloff and the Polish critic Jerzy Kutnik, then a Fulbright fellow at Stanford, participated in the interview, and the poet Rae Armantrout was there for part of the time as an observer and kibitzer. Antin is such a great talker (and such an experienced one) that, not surprisingly, he is a slippery interviewee. Ask him a question that doesn't particularly interest him and he'll quickly turn the discourse in another direction. Ask him about the writers who "influenced" him, and he'll invariably give you a droll answer, launching into a spoof of Balzac or a demolition of Robert Lowell. A question about fiction will elicit a comment about the film scripts Antin has written—and intends to produce someday—with his wife, the well-known performance/installation artist and filmmaker, Eleanor Antin. A conversation with Antin is thus a heady experience. So much material comes up—ranging from Plato and Kant to Kathy Acker and cyberpunk, from Freud's *Interpretation of Dreams* to jazz improvisation—that the interview could last all day. But it doesn't for, despite the freewheeling and seemingly wholly digressive conversation, Antin's mind is very much in control. After three or four hours of taping (interrupted by snacks and drinks at various intervals), Antin remembered an appointment for dinner and took off, leaving the rest of us to dine at a local brasserie and try to process what we had been listening to.

Such processing is complicated by the fact that Antin is a rigorous editor of his own materials: he worked over the script of this interview with his usual fierce intensity and skepticism. "Did I really say that?" "What I really meant was . . ." The finished text thus gives us a state-of-the-art image of David Antin once again "talking at the boundaries," an artist quite literally at the cutting edge.

*   *   *

David Antin: Selected Bibliography

Books of Talk (Prose) Poems

Talking. New York: Kulchur Foundation, 1972.
talking at the boundaries. New York: New Directions, 1976.
Who's Listening Out There? College Park, MD: Sun and Moon Press, 1979.
The Principle of Fit, Part 2. Cassette tape. Washington, DC: Watershed Foundation, 1980.
tuning. New York: New Directions, 1984.
The Archaeology of Home. Two-hour cassette for tape recording. Los Angeles: Astro Artz, 1987.
what it means to be avant-garde. New York: New Directions, 1993.

Books of Poetry

Autobiography. New York: Something Else Press, 1967.
Definitions. New York: Caterpillar Press, 1967.

Code of Flag Behavior. Los Angeles: Black Sparrow Press, 1968.
Meditations. Los Angeles: Black Sparrow Press, 1971.
After the War: A Long Novel with Few Words. Los Angeles: Black Sparrow Press, 1973.
Poèmes Parles. Selection of poems from 1961 to 1981 published in French. Paris: Les Cahiers des Briscants, 1984.
Selected Poems: 1963–1973. Los Angeles: Sun and Moon Press, 1991.

Translations

Modern Theory of Molecular Structure, by Bernard Pullman. Rev. ed. New York: Dover Publications, 1962.
One Hundred Great Problems of Elementary Mathematics: Their History and Solution, by Heinrich Dörrie. New York: Dover Publications, 1965.
Physics of Modern Electronics, by Werner A. Gunther. Rev. ed. New York: Dover Publications, 1966.

As Editor

Some/Thing Literary journal co-edited with Jerome Rothenberg, 1965–70.

Commissioned Work

"Skypoem 1." Sky-written poem over Santa Monica, CA, May 1987.
"Skypoem 2." Sky-written poem over La Jolla, CA. La Jolla Museum and the National Endowment for the Arts. September 1988.
Word talks for Linear Park artist consultant for Land Group Linear Park Project. San Diego, 1989.

Selected Periodical Publications

"Biography." *Representations* (Fall 1986).
"The Stranger at the Door." *Genre* (Fall/Winter 1987).
"The Price." *Representations* (Fall 1989).
"Writing and Exile." *Tikkun* 5 (September/October 1990).
"Thinking about Novels." *Review of Contemporary Literature* 11, 2 (Summer 1991).
"determination suspension diversion digression destruction." *Conjunctions* 19 (Fall 1992).
"Fine Furs." *Critical Inquiry* (Fall 1992).
"Have Mind Will Travel." Catalog essay for 1994 Robert Morris exhibition, Guggenheim Museum, New York.
"the theory and practice of postmodernism—a manifesto." *Conjunctions* 21 (1993).

Reviews and Articles about Antin's Work

[*Note:* A special issue of *Review of Contemporary Fiction* devoted to Antin's work, edited by John Hanhardt, will be appearing sometime in late 1996 or early 1997.]

Altieri, Charles. "The Postmodernism of David Antin's *tuning.*" *College English* 48, 1 (January 1986).

Bromige, David. "Talking Antin as Writing." *Vort: Twentieth Century Pre-View* (David Antin and Jerome Rothenberg) 7 (1975): 2–3.

Damon, Maria. "Talking Yiddish at the Boundaries." *Cultural Studies* 5, 1 (1991): 14–28.

Davidson, Michael. "An Exchange." *Vort: Twentieth Century Pre-View* (David Antin and Jerome Rothenberg) 7 (1975): 72–76.

Garber, Fred. *Repositionings: Readings of Contemporary Poetry, Photography, and Performance Art.* University Park, PA: Pennsylvania State University Press, 1995.

Hartman, Charles O. *The Jazz Text: Voice and Improvisation in Poetry, Jazz, and Song.* Princeton, NJ: Princeton University Press, 1991.

Kenner, Hugh. "Antin, Cats, &c." *Vort: Twentieth Century Pre-View* (David Antin and Jerome Rothenberg) 7 (1975): 84–91.

Kroetsch, Robert. "Exchange of Correspondence." *boundary* 2 (Spring 1975): 594–650.

Lazer, Hank. "Thinking about It: David Antin's *Selected Poems: 1963–1973.*" *Virginia Quarterly Review* (1992).

———. "Thinking Made in the Mouth: The Cultural Poetics of David Antin and Jerome Rothenberg." In *Picturing Cultural Values in Postmodern America,* ed. William G. Doty. Tuscaloosa: University of Alabama Press, 1995.

Martone, John. "Augustine's Fate: Self Scriptural Conceptual Art and Horizons of Autobiography in America." *Southern Review* 23, 3 (Summer 1987).

Olson, Toby. "Antin: Some Notes on Context." *Vort: Twentieth Century Pre-View* (David Antin and Jerome Rothenberg) 7 (1975): 81–84.

Paul, Sherman. *In Search of the Primitive: Reading David Antin, Jerome Rothenberg, and Gary Snyder.* Baton Rouge: Louisiana State Press, 1986.

Perloff, Marjorie. "in the middle of the staircase i forgot to go down." Review of Antin's *Selected Poems: 1963–1973* and Rae Armantrout's *Necromance. American Book Review* (Winter 1992).

———. "John Cage and David Antin: The Poetry of Performance." In *The Poetics of Indeterminacy.* Princeton, NJ: Princeton University Press, 1981.

Phelps, Donald. "David Antin and Depressed Art." *Vort: Twentieth Century Pre-View* (David Antin and Jerome Rothenberg) 7 (1975): 55–56.

Rothenberg, Jerome. "[RE DEFINITIONS, autobiography, CODE OF FLAG BEHAVIOR, & MEDITATIONS]." *Vort: Twentieth Century Pre-View* (David Antin and Jerome Rothenberg) 7 (1975): 57–61.

Sayre, Henry. *The Object of Performance.* Chicago: University of Chicago Press, 1989.

Sorrentino, Gilbert. "Re Antin." *Vort: Twentieth Century Pre-View* (David Antin and Jerome Rothenberg) 7 (1975): 55.

Warren, Kenneth. "The Semantics of Political Labels." *Contact II* (Fall/Winter 1986–87).

Interviews

Abbott, Keith. "Talking with David Antin." *Vort: Twentieth Century Pre-View* (David Antin and Jerome Rothenberg) 7 (1975): 62–64.

Alpert, Barry. "An Interview with David Antin." *Vort: Twentieth Century Pre-View* (David Antin and Jerome Rothenberg) 7 (1975): 3–33.

Smith, Hazel, and Roger Dean. "Interview of David Antin." *Postmodern Culture* (Spring 1993).

*   *   *

MARJORIE PERLOFF: Given your conviction that writing and thinking should not be treated as different categories, why is it that you seem to have an aversion to having your work be seen as anything other than poetry?

DAVID ANTIN: I'm not interested in any forms where distinctions between "fictionality" and "factuality" can be clearly formulated. There's a Diderot story that's called *Ceci n'est pas un conte*, which translates literally into "this is not a story" but really means "this is not a fiction." Most of its characters seem to have had a historical existence, though there's no way of telling whether the romantic actions attributed to them or the motivations assigned to them were merely reported by Diderot or invented by him. Since it was circulated in Grimm's newsletter to the courts of distant countries, its readers were probably not in a much better position than we are to judge the facticity that the title lays a kind of claim to. So what the title does for Diderot is to tip the work into a space between gossip and fiction. And I think that the reason he wanted to do this was that he had something of the same problem with the idea of fiction that I have. "Fiction" is a label that positions all the works grouped under it too straightforwardly in the domain of the imaginary and the untrue, or at least contrafactual, and takes away its stakes as human experience. I don't want anybody to be sure whether what I say is a lie or a truth, whether I remembered it, heard it, imagined it, dreamt it, or invented it. I'd like the boundary between fact and fiction to be as unstable in my work as it is in my experience. Yet at the same time I have a strong desire to get at something I would call reality, however indeterminate that may be.

LARRY MCCAFFERY: In one of his letters to you, Robert Kroetsch referred to your "reckless recovery of narrative into poetry." Could you talk about why you've chosen poetry rather than novelistic or fictive forms to pursue this recovery?

DA: I've always had an interest in the force of narrative—its action as a kind of metaphor, parable, image, that lights up a space that couldn't be illuminated in any other way. I actually did work on a novel back in the late fifties, but that was the outcome of working for some time at a number of stories which preceded it. At that point I had a persistent interest in what I would then have called story and what I now call narrative. Narrative action may be similar to the way metaphor functions in some kinds of poetry—the difference being that storytelling is grounded in an even more widespread, common social practice. In the culture I come from people told stories to make points. Or at least pointed them toward something they had some intuition of. In Jewish culture if a storyteller goes on too long or the aim of the story seems somewhat obscure, people will impatiently demand, "Nu, vos is die sof" or "Well, so what's the point?" This question may arise from an overly didactic notion of story or an irritation with an obliquely angled or poetic discourse, but it has the value of recalling that significant narrative is born out of discourse and finds its justification in it. And in the Jewish folk tradition, with which I can only claim a casual acquaintance, it seems stories and jokes are nearly always discursively aimed, whether they're the Zen-like stories of the Hasidic masters or the ones your uncle tells you because he thinks you've chosen the wrong way to live.

Considered from this point of view, the novel is just a runaway example. But for me the idea of doing a novel was something of an accident. From around the age of sixteen I thought of myself as a poet. Poetry was the language art, and I wanted to be a language artist. Stories were central to language and one of the things a poet could do. Novels were more specialized and something of an applied form. If poetry was like mathematics, novels were like accounting—not something a mathematician would immediately set out to do.

LM: Don't those distinctions immediately break down once you consider writers like Stein, Burroughs (even Melville) or philosophers like Wittgenstein? Wittgenstein's metaphors in *Philosophical Investigations*, for instance, seem at once didactic, speech-driven, and yet still connected to story—and poetry . . .

DA: I never distinguished between poets and thinkers (I'm using the word "thinker" in a nonprofessional sense). For me Gertrude Stein, Wittgenstein, Kierkegaard, Heidegger all inhabited one world. I wrote an undergraduate thesis on Heidegger and Hölderlin at City College, where German literature was one of my nominal majors.

MP: Other than Stein (who seems like a very special case), are there any novelists you would regard as thinkers?

DA: Kafka, Dostoyevsky, Gogol, Diderot, Sterne, Stendhal, Tolstoy. All of *Anna Karenina* is driven by the opening one liner that all happy marriages are happy in the same way, while all unhappy marriages are unhappy in different ways. From there on the novel develops as a cautionary tale of the terrible marital consequences of a woman's desire for romantic love. I don't think much of Tolstoy's thinking; but no matter how stupid the argument, the argumentative force of *Anna Karenina* is very great. And what I miss in most novels is the discursive force out of which they may have originated, which seems to evaporate as the genre becomes more secure and acts as its own justification.

LM: But that discursive force isn't *inherently* lacking in the novelistic form. Did you begin to discover any inherent limitations in the form back when you first began working with it?

DA: First of all, I didn't like the orderly procedure of novels. They offer endless assurances to readers that the world they think they know is being presented in exactly the way they believe they know it. And then there's the idea of furniture. You throw in all sorts of recognizable bric-a-brac to make the story seem to occur in a recognizable world. Then there's the idea of character—which depends upon some set of plausible notions of human psychology, in which I was not very interested. And there were some assumptions about continuity that I found of limited value. The idea that the novel was a kind of textual continuum—that you didn't jump-cut language registers or fragment characters, and that if you intercut several stories they might be interrupted but still had to remain whole. And while there were individual examples of writers like Stein or Joyce or Dos Passos who violated some or even most of these assumptions, there weren't many of them and they didn't feel contemporary in 1957.

MP: Given your awareness of these limitations, what got you interested in doing a novel at all?

DA: It was a way for a writer to survive. One of my first publications was a story published in the *Kenyon Review* about 1959. I'd written it around '57 and hardly anybody wanted to consider it, but after it appeared I got a letter from a publisher suggesting that they would be interested in publishing my novel. My first response was "*what novel?*" Then I figured maybe I should write one. There was a market for novels back then, even so-called "serious novels," and I thought I could produce a work that looked something like a novel but was still the kind of work I was interested in. The first thing I decided was that it would have five separate sections, each of which would construct one essential image. The apparently central character of each of these sections might or might not be the same person. So either the book would consist of five separate elliptical stories or one significantly fragmented one.

LM: So right away you were instinctively pulling away from the traditional novel's empiricist bias, its illusion of being able to supply causal explanations. Its "authority."

DA: Sure, this ambiguity was absolutely central to my conception of the book. The central figure was a young woman. Or there were five female figures of different ages, the first of which spends a hot day at the beach shortly after the atomic bomb was dropped on Hiroshima, and the last one ends a philosophically romantic relation with a Kierkegaardian priest by either getting the stigmata or maybe not. There was no obvious connection between the five stories except they were all situated between August of 1945 and sometime in the late fifties, though they were based on a kind of cumulative intensity that culminates in the last section in which the young woman stabs herself to reveal the stigmata that she has expected to receive.

JERZY KUTNIK: What prevented you from finishing it?

DA: Formal problems I just wasn't able to resolve. I spent quite a bit of time trying to work things out, but I simply wasn't experienced enough as a writer at that point to figure out alternatives. I didn't have enough practice in writing against the grain in *any* form to simply forget about a lot of things. It was too much for me at the time. So I moved on.

JK: What kinds of formal problems were these?

DA: The most fundamental problem had to do with a kind of Flaubertian image I had of prose. This conception of "burnished prose" wound up draining the life from my novel, just as it was doing to most of the prose environment of that period. It encouraged writers to think of writing a story by writing and rewriting the first sentence endlessly, then rewriting sentence one and writing sentence two, then rewriting both one and two and starting sentence three, till the whole paragraph is beaten into shape like some kind of forged tool, and finally the whole story is a highly finished piece of hammered metal. Trying to write this awful, highly polished, utterly *lifeless* prose sapped the energies of the piece I was writing.

LM: Weren't people like Jack Kerouac and William Burroughs already developing alternatives to that Flaubertian conception for how prose might function in the novel?

DA: There's no question that Kerouac's example could have been helpful. But at the time I was working on my novel (this was the late fifties), I wasn't tuned to Kerouac. If I had started out writing fiction in the sixties, his work would have been more immediately available, and it might have been easier for me in all sorts of ways. When I finally ran across Kerouac's prose I was charmed by his light touch. But by that time I was already working in such a different way with found and collaged materials to construct a kind of poetry of definitions, lists, questionnaires, manuals . . . that I wasn't ready to go back to the idea of a novel.

MP: I can't think of a single example from your *Selected Poems* where the poem is presented from someone else's perspective. Why aren't you interested in assuming other people's voices—the dramatic monologue, and so forth?

DA: I don't like dramatic monologues. They're too stable. They place too clear a distance between a writer's voice and a constructed one. Which seems somewhat absurd, since the writer's own voice is also constructed, as much as any subject is constructed, and as far as I'm concerned multivocal enough. And at least you're putting your cards on the table. "Call me Ishmael" always sounded ridiculous to me as a beginning. I'd have preferred Melville to tell the whole story as a tall tale out of his own real, imaginary, or falsified experience. Fortunately Ishmael has the good grace to fade away whenever Melville wants to get rid of him, though he comes back for a kind of curtain call at the end. At the same time I dislike the practice of clearly cited quotations that claim a literal grasp on the words of another. Suppose I'm telling a story about what somebody did somewhere—how far will I go to render her speech? I might fragmentarily imitate the speech register, try to evoke an accent in my own speech, mimic a vocal tone, or cite a characteristic turn of phrase. There may be at least a dozen ways of evoking other voices and languages, and at least as many degrees and kinds of closeness or distance a writer can take up in relation to the voices he's invoking. At any given moment I might be making only a few minimal gestures in the direction of some other voice, enough to let you fill in the rest, while I still want to hold my distance from it. Part of my irritation with novels has to do with my sense that they commit themselves to quotation marks too early and too fully. European novels are somewhat less inclined to do this than American novels, which tend to fetishize quotation, even when the quotes are manifestly false or impossible to believe. Classical German or French novels make much less use of the full-fledged quote and make much more use of a kind of indirectly represented speech in which the narrator's voice appears to move fluidly back and forth between closer and more distant representations, or to slide freely and with infinite gradation between the two extremes of citation and summary.

JK: Are there aesthetic advantages in starting there, rather than projecting other voices?

DA: My own voice is a convenient carrier for a wide range of moves in relation to other voices. This is the traditional virtue of storytelling and the storyteller's voice. It allows an indeterminateness and flexibility of representation. It lets you evoke the voices and speech patterns of other people as you feel the need for them, not because you've got a novelist's contract with the reader to represent them. So I can evoke people's speech in ways that are more nuanced than quotation allows. Sometimes saying what they say in my own language, or one of my languages, at other times in language between my language and their language. I like the freedom of having an infinite number of gradations at my disposal between a remote diegetic account of what went on and a shamanistic rendering of the other's voice.

MP: You can see this in, say, the sections in *talking at the boundaries* which are rendered in what look like Yiddish intonations.

DA: In fact, not very many evoke Yiddish (which was not a language we spoke at home). When I do evoke it, I tend to evoke it fragmentarily.

You're probably thinking of the particular piece, "talking at the boundaries," which deals with the philosophical problem of translation. A key passage involves a story told me by a cabdriver, at the center of which was something he had said to a group of orthodox Jews who were attacking his wife for taking photographs at the Wailing Wall. What he had said was in Yiddish and he delivered it to me in Yiddish in the cab. It was a shocking comment, and he was completely unaware that it was shocking. And for me to give my full sense of it, I first quoted it in my free English translation, which I then examined and found insufficiently precise. So that I then quoted the Yiddish in my German-accented Yiddish (I understand the language reasonably well but don't really speak it), and tried to explain the fundamental difficulties involved in my translation. So there are at least three imperfect takes at representing what my cabdriver said, each one at a different distance from the source, in which the cabdriver was himself quoting something he had said in Jerusalem perhaps three or four years before. What comes across, I think, along with the representations, is their fundamental imperfections. So I very emphatically refuse to guarantee to deliver the voices of others, though I evoke them in a variety of partial representations, with a kind of range-finding movement, where I slide from focus to focus.

JK: Is that why other peoples' voices are so rarely set off by quotation marks in your works?

DA: Right. The sharp single focus implied by quotes suggests the full and continuous presence of this object of representation, whereas I don't believe these voices are continuously "there." So when I try to bring something into focus, it may not get there for more than a moment, sharply defined. My main intention, in other words, is not to use language to "produce" the object of my attention as much as to produce a sense of how that object comes into attention and is received by actual human beings.

LM: This intention almost seems like a postmodernist version of realism's "Tell it like it is" dictum—your aim being to suggest how reality continually slides in and out of focus. I'd say one of the key aims of postmodern fiction writers (and this is probably true of poets too) is to devise narrative strategies which present "character" more honestly, less illusionistically, by foregrounding the relationship between their own voice and character and the story or scene they are describing. You can see this back in the sixties, with writers like Barth, Coover, Federman, and Sukenick using metafictional, reflexive strategies that foreground the "self" of the author confronting the blank page with their creative imaginations, but without bothering to maintain the usual novelistic illusion of representing something outside the "self." The next generation of writers (William Vollmann, Kathy Acker, Susan Daitch, Mark Leyner) take this essential quality of the self-in-writing for granted—and push this premise on into new territories.

DA: But I'm not interested in the presentation of my "self," except insofar as I feel like putting my cards on the table. Out of convenience, my tendency is to work out of what I see as the trope of my experience— whatever that is. When I go to a place, I may want to talk about the theory of narrative. Or I've been rereading Freud, and I've been invited by a group of sociologists to Northwestern, where I want to talk about the sociology of dreams. Still, I'm trying to come at it from a ground in the circumstances I find myself in. I don't want to create the illusion of the kind of objective discourse that criticism and scholarship almost always fall back on. Everybody has some kind of place they're coming from whenever they say something. The subject that one "is" may, when closely inspected, be an unstable one, but you can never *not* start from somewhere, some ground. There literally is no "nowhere" in that sense, and you really can't get anywhere worth getting to without backpedaling to find it.

LM: Where is it that you want to arrive at with this backpedaling motion?

DA: I want to find my ground and get a purchase on it, in order to be able to go on to find out what it is I really want to think about. Not so much because I'm interested in my own subjectivity, but because I don't really know any other way to go on.

JK: This sounds like a less ego-driven version of the reflexive approach we associate with the sixties postmodernists (most of whom were *very* interested in their own subjectivity).

DA: It's probably not what most people think of as straightforward discourse, but it's not self-referential or reflexive in the usual way. Basically, it's that the only way I know to get beyond what I already know or think I know is to try to take stock and find out what that is.

LM: The way you often proceed in your talks seems to share a lot with the later Wittgenstein in that it relies less on discursive analysis and more on presenting examples that will illustrate and illuminate the thinking processes you want to examine.

DA: Wittgenstein is instructive for anyone interested in thinking. What's most instructive about Wittgenstein is the way he works by way of examples that proceed from his talking about thinking and thinking about talking. They're colloquial examples that light up the conversation with a flickering light and then they go out. There's something casual about them. They feel almost disposable. They're not patentable and they're not sculptural. At most they hang in the air like the grin of the Cheshire cat. Which might disappear immediately, though you almost always know where Wittgenstein is—because you can see him there right in front of you trying *obsessively* to go on. Because that's what he's doing—

not making sculpture, but trying to find his way forward. What I'm trying to do in my talks is somewhat similar. I'm not so much making things
up as picking them up and placing them in front of you, as proposals. So
my inventions are casual and not different from my borrowings, which
is why I use my friends' experiences, my uncles' experiences, Eleanor's
[Eleanor Antin] experiences alongside of my own experiences. Eleanor
says I've borrowed all of her relatives' experiences as well. And I don't
distinguish among them, or between them and anything I happen to invent.

LM: Doesn't inventing the specific details of these anecdotes in order to
illustrate your points tend to disguise your own subjectivity?

DA: What's involved is a different kind of "invention" from what you
find in a novelist like Updike or Bellow. Or a different function for the
invention. I suppose there are certain situations I make up. But they're
like experiments that are useful to test an idea I'm trying to consider.
And because they represent plausible or at least possible if extreme conditions, I'm not sure at all times whether they're literally true or not. But
I don't try to pretend otherwise. My sense is that since these unstable
aspects of memory and perception are fundamental to consciousness,
why shouldn't they be central to my linguistic representation? I find this
instability to be more meaningful in exploring the nature of my experience in the world—and most other people's experience in the world—
than the kind of stability created in most novels or fictions.

MP: This is just a rhetorical question, but why can't we write novels
today that begin: "Happy families are all alike. Each unhappy family is
unhappy in its own way. Everything was in confusion in the Oblonsky
household." Then it goes from there and seems totally natural. I just
reread *Anna Karenina* recently, my favorite novel. What makes such writing impossible today?

LM: Nabokov started *Ada* almost exactly that way . . .

DA: But Nabokov did so fully aware that you can't hold such an absurd
set of beliefs with anything like Tolstoy's amazing certainty. I probably
have as many absurd beliefs as Tolstoy, but they start to get hard to hold
onto as soon as I start writing (or talking). In fact it may be the great
virtue of contemporary writing that it plays a completely opposite role
to classical nineteenth-century writing, which seems aimed to stabilize
cultural beliefs, while our writing appears fated to bear witness to intelligent thinking and is compelled to undermine and destabilize cultural
commonplaces in the interests of truth. I have plenty of nostalgia, but
I'm not sure what it's worth. Kathy Acker has endless convictions. And
lots of nostalgia. And she undermines them from paragraph to paragraph. She throws one sentimentality after another. Till they kind of
annihilate each other. This is what creates the charm and ferocity of

Kathy's work, the staccato machine-gun-like quality of her prose. It's as though she's machine-gunning her sentimentality, her used up beliefs. So my sense is that the reason we can't write a classic novel is that the idea of writing, or in my case the idea of talking and thinking, will not allow the possibility of the intellectual stability on which that older novel was based—not even as fantasy. Which is why *Don Quixote* and *Tristram Shandy* and *Jacques the Fatalist* and *Rameau's Nephew* mean more to me than *Pamela* or *Tom Jones* or Balzac's whole *Human Comedy*.

LM: The avant-garde has been reacting against naturalism in various guises from the nineteenth century onward. Are the sources of this negative reaction today the same as they were a hundred years ago? For instance, there was a lot said back in the sixties and seventies about postmodernist writing being influenced by things like the theory of relativity, quantum mechanics, Heisenberg, and so forth. Was this a naive reaction for critics to take?

DA: Essentially, yes. Probably the sheer accumulation of naturalistic detail produced by naturalistic works is in any era finally going to reveal the poverty and banality of the point of view out of which they're generated. These works then stop working because they make a tiresome and pointless claim on the reader's attention and convictions.

LM: And on the attention and convictions of other writers.

DA: *Everybody's* attention. Writers are readers, after all. They read their own work. Talkers are listeners, and if you don't hear what you're saying you can't talk anyway. If you don't read what you write you can't write either. So in a very serious sense, you read a novel by somebody like Updike and the work is so firmly grounded in a kind of social naturalism, that while the words may be amusing, they have no force. They don't lay any justified claim to our attention, because whatever insights they provide are within a world that's taken for granted as a kind of given. They don't gain us any insight into the unachieved or unknown. For novelists of this type the world is very well known. They don't offer a new way to see. In fact, they actively prevent us from seeing. In effect they blind us. The accumulation of their predictable detail blinds us and deafens us, the way television does or newspapers do, with their always ready and banal explanations of just about everything. So they don't make any claim on my mind. Meanwhile the world keeps changing and our sense of it is changing, though maybe not fast enough to keep up with it, and these writers write books that are like a match that won't light. You go into a dark room and try to strike a match, and the match doesn't light and you're out of luck. The naturalist novel has become a match that won't light. Or a broken flashlight.

MP: Do such writers actually believe they're offering new ways of seeing? Or has this just become a kind of tic?

DA: I think they're looking for something different. I know I'm looking for someone to go in and strike a match in a dark space. I want some light and they want a literary pleasure. It's like the problem of the lyric in poetry: it provides a professional literary pleasure. Or maybe it's more than a professional pleasure. They get a reliable pleasure from a literary way of phrasing or of metaphorizing that produces from the words a seemingly solid and burnished thing. Novelists have more of an idea of reference, but it takes the form of a kind of incarnation—of using language to bring into being a kind of corporeal model. But that's also a kind of sculptural achievement that they have in mind.

LM: There remains a number of respected writers in America like Doctorow and even John Irving who continue to claim that their goal is a kind of historical accuracy or truth. But certainly your own work seems mainly interested in those areas of language that Marjorie examined in her study *The Poetics of Indeterminacy.* Does that inclination mean that you feel it's impossible for the writer to get at any kind of "truth" today?

DA: I don't think that my sense of instability has any direct relation to the Heisenberg principle. What do you want to know about subatomic particles, beyond where they are and how fast they're moving? And if it turns out that the more precisely you can specify how fast they're moving the less you know about where they are, all that tells you is that there's a paradox at the center of this discourse of measurement in a microworld where your measuring instrument has about the same wavelength as the particles you're interested in describing. Somehow, by the end of the twentieth century, this doesn't seem terribly surprising. It might have demoralized sociologists in the earlier part of the century because they were still suffering from physics envy, and maybe any writers who happened to believe that their job was based on the imaginary certainties of such a sociology. But the questions surrounding the discourse of human experience raise completely different issues—issues of the capabilities of language itself, the meaningfulness of notions of agency, intentionality, desire, or need, of their relation to the meaning of causality, the semiotic force of metaphor or narrative and their relation to some notion of truth. The early Wittgenstein of the *Tractatus* was nearly driven mad by the instabilities of verbal representation and would have liked to stabilize it by setting severe logical constraints on language, only to find that the notion of the truth that he could achieve in this manner was nearly totally trivial. Truth of this type—the propositional truth of the truth table—is framed by a very narrow context that isn't much use to you in most human situations. When you come to Wittgenstein's later work, the *Notebooks, Zettel,* the *Philosophical Investigations,* no matter how much he maintains a taste for the earlier fixation on nailing things down, he's at the same time become enchanted with the subversive tendencies of language and its multiple discourses. And so what happens is that narrative elements and metaphors, which made rare and mysterious appearances in the *Tractatus*, take over the whole work. And metaphors and narratives are not validatable or falsifiable in the same way. So it becomes the more difficult question of how much light they throw and whether it's the right light. Which raises the question of "the right light for what?" Or maybe it's not so much a matter of striking a match as of opening a door. Then the question will become, what doors do you close when you open this one?

JK: You're one of the few contemporary writers I'm aware of who is actually grounded in this material. Most writers would probably think of what we are calling indeterminacy as being just purely bad writing.

DA: What most of us are interested in, no matter how well or badly we approach it, is the slipperiness of experiential knowledge, and its adequacy or inadequacy. And we try to approach it through language. But experience is a complex fabric of sensations, perceptions, images, and motor habits and desires. And it's filled with slippage. Then we try to approach it through language, which doesn't seem to be able to keep up with it, because experience keeps changing; and language, even though it's grounded in history, seems too stable for it. And experience is only partially linguistic anyway—because it's filled with practices, which are not language, as anyone knows who has ever ground a tool bit or hit a baseball or danced or played a musical instrument. The paradoxes of subatomic physics—indeterminacy, complementarity—seem simple compared to this.

LM: As far as the question of finding some way to talk about experiential truth is concerned, there is a fairly clear distinction between the kind of work which you seem to be interested in and the more apocalyptic side of the avant-garde tradition. Crazed geniuses like Rimbaud and Artaud valorized the visionary quest and broke through rational discourse via hallucination, drugs, and even insanity, while your work comes more out of the tradition of Wittgenstein and other twentieth-century thinkers who used the gifts of rational thought, such as "clear thinking" or "language games," to clarify the nature of thinking itself.

DA: I've never been very interested in Artaud and Rimbaud. I never thought their visions or their idea of vision very interesting.

JK: Surrealism has never really been a direction in your work, either. Even early on.

DA: I was attracted to some aspects of Breton's work, to some of his poems, and a few prose pieces like *Nadja*. But I wasn't interested in the idea of intoxication and the derangement of senses, which I thought were trivial ideas. It seemed to me that everyday experience was considerably more bizarre and more interesting, once you began to question the assumptions underlying the points of view from which it was almost always considered. I thought drug experiences and madness were usually trivial and almost always boring—merely the other side of a banal naturalism.

LM: I have always felt that the Rimbaud/Artaud/Bataille/Acker line constitutes a less systematic, but nonetheless legitimate, attack on the language game called "rational discourse" (or "scientific discourse"). It was a way of recognizing that that discourse was the main game that people played, at least in the West. Your skepticism about this seems related to your interest, or rather lack of interest, in "deep" aspects of psychology, in the mysterious side of human consciousness. In a way your work is more phenomenological, staying on the surface . . .

DA: I've recently gotten very interested in Freud's *Interpretation of Dreams*, but as a book about narrative, not the unconscious.

MP: You and I both went to school at a time when poetry, not fiction, was considered *the* art form. Do you think that if you had gone to school later, when theory had become the big thing, you would have regarded your work less as poetry and more as essentially theoretical texts?

DA: I don't think poetry's preeminent position had much to do with my conception of my work. If poetry was *the* art when I went to college, it wasn't a poetry I was much interested in. Between 1950 and 1955 what was fashionable in the colleges seemed to be a poetry of manners, a kind of suburban pastoral. And most American novelists of the time weren't very experimental either. Either they were into some kind of naturalism or a novel of manners again. It wasn't till a couple of years later that I encountered Black Mountain or the Beat poets and novelists like Kerouac or Trocchi or Burroughs. And then, alongside of their looser structure, there was a kind of predictable naturalism in much of their work that I found uninteresting. I was a bit more interested in the French novelists—Robbe-Grillet, Sarraute, and Duras—but I didn't discover them till the end of the fifties. I wasn't fashionable then either. I think I did more reading in philosophy, and in the sciences, which interested me much more. Then I went on to graduate study in theoretical linguistics, and that probably spoiled me forever for most of the French structuralist tradition, which appeared to be involved with fairly primitive linguistic ideas.

JK: When did you realize that your "talks" were essentially poetic rather than discursive forms?

DA: My wife Eleanor was the one who first identified my talk pieces as poems, although I suppose I was moving in that direction. I had done a kind of free form talk at Cooper Union around 1970 or so, and then I was invited to speak at Pomona College. Ellie drove up with me, and on the way back she asked me to play back the talk on the tape recorder.

She listened for a while and said, that's really a poem. I thought about it, and realized she was right. She had put what I was doing in that frame, and I hadn't thought about what I was doing in any clear-cut way. But I realized she was right, and the realization helped articulate the way I went on.

JK: What sorts of things do you find yourself reading these days?

DA: Lately my reading has been sporadic and random. I'm not a very disciplined reader. I read pieces of things, whatever strikes my fancy at any given moment, but I don't read an awful lot of things that are called novels as novels. I'm not a dedicated, devoted reader of individual things. Aspects of writers like García Márquez appeal to me because he always seems to be making it up at the moment he's talking. Whatever comes out of his mouth he sticks with, and I like his way of going from moment to moment. I have enjoyed Toby Olson's work, which I was rereading recently, mainly because of the bizarre displacement of the relationship between the prose style and the metaphorical material. Mostly, though, I read pieces of this, pieces of that, pieces of critical work, pieces of writing on theory. I keep looking for something to turn me on. I keep trying to find things I can love. The greatest reading pleasure of recent days has been Gombrowicz's diaries; I love his impossible invention of himself. And I like his diaries much better than his novels, because he's a much more interesting invention than any of his other characters.

LM: What about Beckett?

DA: I've always liked Beckett's novels. The later, more minimal, material I find tiresome. It's like Kafka's rodent racing from the cat into the corner of the room with the space between the walls getting narrower and narrower. Beckett proves that no matter how narrow the space there is always a way to work in it, which is true, if somewhat obvious; as we know from Euclidean geometry or number theory, between any two given points you can always insert an infinity of points in a given line. I don't doubt this for a moment but I think the whole line is uninteresting: it's too fixed, too determined.

JK: What's your opinion of the few writers who are associated with the art world and the poetry world? Gilbert Sorrentino and Kathy Acker come immediately to mind, and maybe even some of the language poets who have written prose works.

DA: I enjoy Kathy's aggressive improvisational style, and I admire her radicality with respect to fixing on a subject, her willingness to assimilate virtually anything by a kind of incorporative act of will. What I find increasingly hard to deal with (which may no longer be the case in some of her more recent things not yet in print) is the staccato language, which seems monotonous to the point of becoming slightly tiring. There's a certain kind of staccato intensity that's like a frontal attack—Marines landing on a beachhead, wave after wave against a well-defended position, so they go down in these rows one after another. I'd like to see her try a flanking movement . . .

MP: Do you like Georges Perec? And what about Baudrillard?

DA: Baudrillard is a philosophical clown, but I'm tired of the performance. I like Perec, particularly some of his early work, and Walter Abish, who in some ways he's a lot like. I have more trouble with long works that pretend to be orthodox novels and covertly are not.

LM: How has your writing been shaped by your background outside of literature?

DA: There are a lot of people outside of literature whose work meant a great deal to me. Norbert Wiener's *Cybernetics* book. His negative feedback model played a large role in my thinking and in the argument I tried to develop in *tuning* to replace the notion of understanding. And behind Wiener was the work of the physiologist Walter Cannon, whose great book *The Wisdom of the Body* is a marvelous analysis of the ecology of the body. Both of these were books I've thought about since my college days, and have had an enormous impact on me. In fact one of the pieces in my *Selected Poems* is drawn partly from an account given by Cannon of the sense of thirst experienced by a guy who thought he was going to be executed by a group of Manchurian bandits. Then there was Chomsky. His work was a revelation in linguistics. For once there were proposals for thinking about language that were clear enough to be refuted. Thomas Kuhn and his *Structure of Scientific Revolutions,* and certainly the work of Wittgenstein also played a major role in a lot of the work I've done.

MP: What about the influence of visual artists?

DA: In the sixties I saw Minimalism and Pop as ways to break new ground, along with Fluxus, Happenings, Judson's dance, Godard's films. Though by the seventies I began to see much of the Pop and Minimal work as a kind of late modernist cul-de-sac, from which certain forms of conceptual art and performance work seemed the only reasonable ways out.

LM: Tell us a bit about the nature of the collaborations you've done with your wife, Eleanor.

DA: Eleanor is one of the few artists whose work I always find exciting. We have a kind of interactive relationship among equals. We talk to each other a lot, and in that way she has an impact on my work and I have an impact on hers. I've worked with her but not in a directly collaborative way. In a way Ellie's influence on me was to help radicalize my work, to help me become more outrageous. She's a totally off-the-wall sensibility.

Ellie is completely and insufferably herself at whatever she does, and you either love it or hate it. And she's willing to go all the way with it.

LM: What things have been involved in your choice of the particular form that you've focused the majority of your creative energies on and become best known for now—the "talk," and its subsequent representations in printed language? What made you feel the talk, rather than a "regular poem," was a more suitable way to address the issues you wanted to deal with?

DA: I don't know if it's suitable for it at all. When I started it, I was basically very much afflicted by the problem of being somewhere and not being there. I would go into a place to do a reading and I'd be reading words that I'd written before, and hearing those words began to annoy me. I would start reading and feeling like an actor reading somebody else's words, which didn't make much sense coming out of my mouth at that moment. So I started changing those words.

MP: But doesn't the actual process of being up in front of an audience— not that they're going to interject anything, but they're there and you know they're there—help you somehow go through the discovery process you need?

DA: I need that process to liberate me.

LM: That doesn't happen when you're in the closet by yourself with the typewriter?

DA: It would happen, but it seemed harder for it to happen, because at my typewriter I was too conscious of what I was doing and there were too many choices I could make. If you're going to talk in public, you have very little time to change your mind. And if you do change your mind, then the change becomes part of the work. So in a way the problem I had in the closet was having too many possibilities and too little urgency.

JK: What exactly is there about being in front of an audience, talking, that you find liberating?

DA: There's a letter of Schiller's, quoted by Freud in the *Interpretation of Dreams.* It was in response to some fledgling academic poet who was asking for advice about poetic composition, and Schiller suggests that the most important thing for a creative artist is to find some way to suspend your critical faculties long enough to allow any creation to take place. For me this was a real problem. I would start something and I would think about it too much before going on, would criticize it too fast. And then I think very quickly—too quickly for the mechanical process of writing—so that even though I'm a very fast typist I can't keep up with my mind. So that by the time I get it down I might have gone past that point in my mind . . . I used to jam up typewriters, trying to keep up with my thought. And though I didn't make many errors, after a while they'd accumulate, creating a kind of logjam on the paper. So I needed a kind of relationship of language to mind that was fast enough to let me keep moving. An audience usually helps me—by simplifying my choices, or at least they confront me with a particular concrete problem of address. Because reasonable social manners require that in some way I try to address them. So I have a kind of responsibility to them. At the same time I have a responsibility to the material I want to be working with—something I have on my mind and want to think about, which may be difficult or not immediately related to the audience's interests or capabilities. I have to find a way through whatever language I have available to resolve these responsibilities or interests. And I have to do it in a hurry.

JK: What preparation do you do before giving one of your talks? Do you go into these situations with a specific sequence of topics or incidents you want to cover, or is it more free-floating?

DA: It differs from talk to talk. I don't go in cold. I go in realizing I'm going to try to talk in relation to certain thematic issues. And I have whatever's been going on in my mind at the time.

LM: Having accumulated information for a talk, do you come to a point where you consciously start to develop stories or anecdotes to illustrate or clarify what you're talking about?

DA: Not usually. I usually have something on my mind that I want to think about—something that may seem a bit abstract, like the nature of desire or the structure of dreams or the meaning of explanations of human actions. And I've been thinking about these things and am still trying to get a grasp on them. And as I start talking and try to do this, I find myself trying out various ideas and models for the ideas in different situations, and, in trying to analyze them, sometimes they become more concrete and sometimes they seem to be slipping away. Often when they seem to be slipping away or disintegrating under a line of inquiry, a story may come to mind as a realization of the ideas, or maybe as an escape from a cul-de-sac or simply as a disappearing act. Maybe it's not a story at all, just a situation that might lead to a story or a joke—or just hang in the air as an unresolved image.

MP: Since you're bound by the frame of the thirty-minute or sixty-minute tape and since you're drawing not upon something you think up but upon a fund of information, what happens if the talk doesn't come to an appropriate juncture by the time the tape is up?

DA: I put in another reel of tape.

MP: But suppose they've only allotted you a specific time frame, say thirty minutes?

DA: I try to make it work, but it doesn't always. I have a reasonably good internal sense of tempo, and I have a rough sense of how much time I'll need to take a certain tack—how much time it would take me to develop a new line of inquiry, try another model for an idea or develop a narrative. But I'm not always right.

JK: How much of your talk, then, is truly "spontaneous"?

DA: I don't have a clear formal framework in mind. I can have no story at all, for instance. I've done at least half a dozen that have no fully developed story. Or I can have one story, or three stories. I can have an example that doesn't feel like a story but feels like an example, or something that feels like a joke at the center.

LM: Your model sounds like a jazz improvisation where you have, in a sense, the freedom to go with a riff as long as you want, with no preset ending.

DA: It's a bit like a Coltrane session of the sixties, though there is a difference in that he had other people to work with. I'm doing a solo. But, like a jazz musician, I start from a certain ground, I've got a sort of basic sequence that I've set up and I try to find a way to go with it, to work it over. Now, Coltrane had an interest in certain scales, in certain modes, in certain runs that he'd used before, and I also have habits. I have characteristic ways of getting from one place to another. Then sometimes I see another avenue, a way to go someplace I haven't been before, and sometimes I go someplace I was before and try to do it better. Sometimes I'll tell a story I've told before except that I see it better now. Or the context is a different context. So in a sense I'm trying to get to a better place than I was before. I really don't have a rule.

LM: Since one of the things you seem to be doing is trying to get at some kind of experiential truth, doesn't the introduction of the tape recorder (and the knowledge that its presence will be recorded later on in a written text) intrude into that experiential situation?

DA: I don't know if it does for most people, but I think it's a good thing for it to have a slightly alienating effect. It helps you put your cards on the table also. It says, "Look, I'm coming here to talk and I am talking to you, but I'm not *only* talking to you."

MP: But the talks are not the same as the texts that you publish?

DA: They're not the same, but they're like them, sometimes very like them except the texts are usually somewhat longer and more articulated. The relation is something like the one between a live session and a recording session. But there are lots of kinds of recording sessions.

MP: I recall your saying that sometimes you're not sure if something you've done is an essay or a talk piece.

DA: I don't really know how to make the distinction in formal terms, but I know it when I see it.

LM: One difference would seem to be that you write your essays more in the closet.

DA: Sometimes. The piece that I wrote for Marjorie's *Postmodern Genres* book, "The Stranger at the Door," was written in the closet. So was "Thinking about Novels," the piece on Toby Olson. Remember that the text of the talk pieces gets written in a closet too, but I have a kind of draft I can start working off. And the talk pieces have so loosened me up that I actually feel that I can write almost in the way that I talk—because of the computer and because I've gotten into the habit of moving much more quickly.

MP: Could you consider this interview we're conducting to be a collaborative talk?

DA: No. I'm more dutiful.

Deliberately, Terribly Neutral
An Interview with Lydia Davis

Larry McCaffery

Art is not some far off place.
   —"Extracts from a Life"

Lydia Davis is probably as well-known for her translations of the works of several leading French avant-gardists (notably Maurice Blanchot and Michel Leiris) as for her own fiction.[1] These experiences as a professional translator help account for the recurrence in Davis's work of a set of concerns that all fundamentally have to do with the slipperiness of language. These concerns include both abstract issues—metaphysical uncertainty, the ambiguity of all verbal expression and (hence) the inability of such semiologically based systems as logic and reason to arrive at the truth, the maddening disjuncture between words and feeling—as well as the more personal sense of frustration and insecurity that results from recognizing the implications of what Lyn Hejinian has referred to (in *My Life*) as the "tragic distance" between words and meaning.

Translation also occasionally appears in Davis's work more directly—as with her use of the form of an introductory French lesson to present clues about a mysterious murder (in "French Lesson I"), or her reworking of previously translated materials in several other stories (for

1. Davis has translated a number of the works of Blanchot, as well as Jean-Paul Sartre, Michel Foucault, and Georges Simenon; these include a number of cotranslations done with Paul Auster.

example, "Lord Royston's Tour" and "Extracts from a Life").[2] Davis's employment of themes and strategies derived from translation operates, however, rather differently from that found in other writers like Kathy Acker, William Vollmann, and Lyn Hejinian, who also deal variously with translated materials. Whereas Acker and Vollmann often recycle or appropriate materials translated from other sources as essentially "found materials" to be used as springboards for their own improvisations, Davis is usually drawn to such materials for more subtle reasons—their peculiarly rhetorical features (that is, their awkward, hypercorrect, stilted qualities) and the poignancy of their status as *failed systems,* which are unable to convey a sense of the *original* or the *other.* The influence of Davis's translation work often appears in less obvious ways as well—for instance, in the use of settings and voices that seem vaguely European and certainly distinctly non-American (this was especially true with her first collection, *The Thirteenth Woman* [1976]) and of narrative voices that often seem oddly distanced, in the awkward manner of English translations of foreign works.

The significance of Davis's ongoing work as a translator is underscored by the fact that she has only been able to devote her attention to her own fiction in spurts. This practical necessity, as opposed to a conscious aesthetic decision, has until recently compelled her (as it did Raymond Carver) to work almost exclusively in short fictional forms.

Davis's literary output includes one novel, *The End of the Story* (1995), three collections, *The Thirteenth Woman, Story and Other Stories* (1983), and *Break It Down* (1986), and a number of as yet uncollected pieces that have appeared during the past half-dozen years in such leading literary journals as *Conjunctions TriQuarterly, Antaeus, Fiction International,* and *The Partisan Review.* At first glance what is likely to strike most readers about her writing is not its innovative features but the ordinariness of its characters and situations (mainly women undergoing experiences that hardly seem extraordinary or even dramatic by most standards) and its matter-of-fact delivery. For instance, in the opening stories found in *Break It Down,* a woman reacts to a phone call from her boyfriend who says he's busy and won't be able to come over ("Story"); an old lady grows increasingly fretful about the dangers outside her home ("The Fears of Mrs. Orlando"); a woman dreams of a son who no longer lives with her ("Liminal: The Little Man"); a man sits in front of a typewriter trying to understand a broken relationship by calculating exactly how much money he spent during a recent (apparently disastrous) vacation trip with his ex-lover ("Break It Down"); a woman reads a story about a

---

2. "French Lesson I" and "Extracts from a Life" appear in Davis's story collection *Break It Down.* "Lord Royston's Tour" appeared in *Conjunctions* 15 (1990).

mouse while she's in the bathtub, and then later sees a mouse come out of a burner in her kitchen ("The Mouse"); a woman presents a series of brief observations concerning cockroaches ("Cockroaches in Autumn").

Summarized in this way, these stories probably sound much like those by Ann Beattie, Mary Robison, Frederick Barthelme, and other authors associated with the minimalist movement that gained prominence in the early 1980s. But such associations are imprecise for several reasons. For one thing, several of Davis's minimalist pieces appeared several years earlier than works by writers later associated with minimalism; these include Davis's early "micro-novel," *Sketches for a Life of Wassilly* (1981), as well as such stories as "Mothers" (included in her first story collection, *The Thirteenth Woman*), "Safe Love," and "How W. H. Auden Spends the Night in a Friend's House" (in *Story and Other Stories*), and "In a House Beseiged" (in *Break It Down*). As Richard Kostelanetz points out in his interview in *Some Other Frequency*, the critical use of the term "minimalism" to designate the work of Carver and others is basically misleading, since it implies a lineage with artists and musicians (for example, Jasper Johns, Steve Reich, Philip Glass) whose works were originally categorized as minimalist in the sixties, whose efforts to create art out of stripped-down elements obviously went much further than anything found in any of the eighties versions of minimalism—or in Lydia Davis for that matter. Kostelanetz goes on to claim that the only writer doing work analogous in its radical applications to the original minimalist impulse is himself—in, for example, his various books of fictions composed of one, two, or three words, or of numbers, or (the most extreme example) of lines.

Unlike the formal methods used by Carver, Beattie, and Frederick Barthelme, Davis's minimalist style was not developed as a reaction against the excesses of her postmodern contemporaries. Indeed, quite the contrary, both as a writer and a person Davis has evolved pretty much outside the context of contemporary American literary or cultural movements. Her chief formative influences, for instance, were nearly exclusively European—and male, at that. She cites Beckett, Nabokov, Joyce, Kafka, and the contemporary writer of short-short stories Russell Edson as having had the most important impact on her work, and she admits to feeling close to only a few women authors, among them, Jane Bowles and Grace Paley.

Davis is separated from most of the authors associated with minimalism by her personal background and basic aesthetic inclinations as well. Her intellectual background, her extended stays abroad, and her general immersion in art drawn from European and American "high culture" rather than rock music, the cinema, and other pop cultural forms all tend to make the textures of her work considerably different from the highly particularized here-and-now of Beattie's New England com-muter life, or the bleaker, scarier world inhabited by Carver's out of luck and out of work characters from the Pacific Northwest.

In fact, the closer one looks at Davis's work, the less it seems distinctly American at all. Her works are nearly devoid of the particularizing de-tails routinely used by most writers as a kind of shorthand method for introducing specific resonances that encourage the reader's empa-thy and understanding. In Davis's fiction surface details are emptied of such ready-made associations and instead are used as indicators of pri-mal fears, undercurrents of dread and existential nausea, a pervasive sense of betrayal, worthlessness, and loss evoked in Kafka or Beckett rather than the highly particularized anomie or bored-but-hyper atti-tudes found in most examples of American minimalism.

Davis's one-paragraph microfiction "The Fish" vividly illustrates this tendency. Beyond the vague references to the "mistakes" a woman has made on a "troubling day," Davis supplies no details that might clar-ify the specific set of circumstances that have led up to this ominous moment. We are given no exposition at all—no details about setting, personal background, not even the woman's name (Davis rarely uses anything but an indefinite pronoun to designate her protagonists). Nor does Davis provide any "analysis" of this hideous moment, nor any hint of self-awareness or understanding by the woman that might resolve her plight and lead to change.

What we are given instead is only a single, mysterious, powerfully resonant *image* that somehow seems to imply or contain—but does not refer to or depict (in the sense of exposition)—an entire lifetime of fail-ure, loneliness, and mistakes. These have led up to the moment in which her sense of utter alienation and victimization is finally revealed to her, "served up" in an image of a fish that, like her, has been stripped of its supporting structure, is now alone and powerless to undo the "irrevo-cable mistakes" that have been made, and is violated in this "final man-ner." In short, what we have here is something akin to a prose poem. Similarly eerie moments of paralyzing despair recur frequently in Davis's fiction, with the full measure of their pathos and despair often captured in the voice of highly unstable narrators who make doomed efforts to seize control of their situation by the only means at their disposal (lan-guage, logic, rational analysis, metaphor-making), whose unreliability is so obvious that even the narrators seem aware there's no way to pull out of their skid. Thus in stories from *Break It Down*, including "Story," "Break It Down," "Therapy," and "Five Signs of Disturbance," Davis's minimalist versions of Kinbote and Humbert Humbert are shown try-ing to find shelter from the mysteries of love and their own admitted insecurities in houses-of-words whose fragility and insubstantiality are, alas, all too apparent even to them.

The following interview is based on a conversation held on a bright May afternoon at Lydia Davis's home in Port Ewen, New York. The question-and-answer version that follows doesn't fully convey the general mood and tone of the actual interview, which was as warm as the weather outside. This conviviality was partly due to the reunion of sorts taking place between Davis and the other participants in the conversation, including Sinda Gregory and Edie Jarolim, two longtime friends who had met Davis in San Diego during the early eighties while she was teaching at the University of California at San Diego. After lunch, the exchange of gossip and the latest news, and commencement of nap-time for Lydia's two-year-old son, I found myself surprised once the interview proper began. Why? Quite simply because the woman with the soft voice and extraordinarily piercing eyes who began providing such articulate and measured replies to my questions bore no resemblance at all to the woman I (who should know better by now) assumed I would be talking to—namely, one of those neurotic, fragile figures depicted by Davis with such painful and darkly humorous accuracy.

Trust the tale not the teller? Not this time . . .

*   *   *

Lydia Davis: Selected Bibliography

Books of Fiction

The Thirteenth Woman and Other Stories. New York: Living Hand Editions, 1976.
Sketches for a Life of Wassilly. Barrytown, NY: Station Hill Press, 1981.
Story and Other Stories. Great Barrington, MA: The Figures, 1983.
Break It Down. New York: Farrar, Straus, and Giroux, 1986.
The End of the Story. New York: Farrar, Straus, and Giroux, 1995.

Uncollected Fiction

"E's Mistake." *Infolio 43* (England), 17 October 1986.
"Sixty Cents." *Northern Lit Quarterly* 88, 2 (Fall 1986).
"In the Proximity of Great Men." *Sulfur* 15 (Winter 1986).
"To Reiterate." *Pequod* 19–21 (Winter 1986).
"Jack in the Country." *Ottotle* 2 (Winter 1987).
"Wife One in Country" and "Foucault and Pencil." *City Lights Review* 1 (1987).
"The Race of the Patient Motorcyclists," "Killed by Monotony," "Almost No Memory," "Confusions," and "Television." *Conjunctions* 11 (1988).

"Disagreement," "Agreement," and "From Below, as a Neighbor." *Indiana Review* 12, 1 (Winter 1988).
"The Center of the Story." *Grand Street* 9, 1 (Autumn 1989).
"Soon after Falling Asleep," "Go Away," and "How He Is Often Right." *Conjunctions* 13 (1989).
"What Was Interesting." *Parnassus* 15, 2 (1989).
"Lord Royston's Tour." *Conjunctions* 15 (1990).
"The House Behind." *Antaeus* 67 (Autumn 1991).
"Pastor Arlene's Newsletter." *Pequod* 32 (1991).
"What I Feel," "The Actors," "Trying to Learn," and "Therapists." *Conjunctions* 17 (1991).
"The Professor." *Harper's* (February 1992).
"Affinity." *The Quarterly* 22 (Summer 1992).
"The Great-Grandmothers," "Our Kindness," "In the Garment District," "A Second Chance," and "The Lamplighter." *New American Writing* 10 (Fall 1992).
"Five Dark Tales." *Conjunctions* 18 (1992).
"Meat and My Husband." *TriQuarterly* 87 (Winter 1993).
"Old Mother and the Grouch." *Partisan Review* (Winter 1993).
"The Other." *Annandale* 133, 1 (1993).
"My Son," "My Sister and the Queen of England," and "Going South." *The World* (1994).
"The Mice," "The Outing," "Odd Behavior," "Fear," and "Lost Things." *Conjunctions* 24 (Spring 1995).

Translations

With Paul Auster, *Life/Situations*, by Jean-Paul Sartre. New York: Pantheon, 1977.
Death Sentence, by Maurice Blanchot. Barrytown, NY: Station Hill, 1978.
Fantastic Photographs, by Attilio Columbo. New York: Pantheon, 1979.
French Photography from Its Origins to the Present, by Claude Nori. New York: Pantheon, 1979.
With Paul Auster, *Aboard the Acquitaine in African Trio*, by Georges Simenon. New York: Harcourt Brace Jovanovich, 1979.
The Madness of the Day, by Maurice Blanchot. Barrytown, NY: Station Hill Press, 1981.
The Gaze of Orpheus and Other Literary Essays, by Maurice Blanchot. Barrytown, NY: Station Hill Press, 1982.
A Weed for Burning, by Conrad Detrez. New York: Harcourt, 1984.
When the Time Comes, by Maurice Blanchot. Barrytown, NY: Station Hill Press, 1985.
The Spirit of Mediterranean Places, by Michel Butor. Marlboro: Marlboro Press, 1986.
The Last Man, by Maurice Blanchot. Barrytown, NY: Station Hill Press, 1987.
Brisees: Broken Branches, by Michel Leiris. San Francisco: North Point Press, 1989.
Scratches: Rules of the Game, by Michel Leiris. New York: Paragon House, 1991.
The One Who Was Standing Apart from Me, by Maurice Blanchot. Barrytown, NY: Station Hill Press, 1993.
Scraps: Rules of the Game, II, by Michel Leiris. Baltimore: Johns Hopkins University Press, 1996.

Criticism

On Max Jacob and Malcolm de Chazal. *The Downtown Review* (Spring 1980).
On Jean Giono. *New York Times Book Review*, 4 July 1982.
On Clark Coolidge. *Poetics Journal* 4 (1983).
On Michel Rio. *New York Times Book Review*, 30 June 1985.
On Rae Armantrout. *Poetics Journal* 6 (Spring 1986).
Afterword. In *Sudden Fiction: American Short-Short Stories*, ed. Robert Shapard and
    James Thomas. Salt Lake City: Gibbs M. Smith, 1986.
On the fragment. *HOW(ever)* 4, 2 (October 1987).

Reviews and Commentaries about Davis's Work

Davis, Tracy. "Breaking It All Down: The Short Fiction of Lydia Davis." Thesis,
    Naropa Institute, Boulder, CO, 1993.
Haviland, Beverly. "Missed Connections." *Partisan Review* 56, 1 (1989).
Howe, Fanny. "Her Husband Isn't." *New York Times Book Review* 28 Septem-
    ber 1986.
Jarolim, Edie. "Ideas of Order." *Poetics Journal* 5 (May 1985): 143–45.
Kakutani, Michiko. Review of *Break It Down*. *New York Times*, 13 August 1986,
    p. 10.
Payne, Johnny. Chapter 5 of *Conquest of the New Word: Experimental Fiction and
    Translation in the Americas*, 142–94. Austin: University of Texas Press, 1993.
Perloff, Marjorie. "Fiction as Language Game: The Hermeneutic Parables of
    Lydia Davis and Maxine Chernoff." In *Breaking the Sequence: Women's Experi-
    mental Writing*, ed. Ellen Friedman and Miriam Fuchs, 198–214. Princeton,
    NJ: Princeton University Press, 1989.
Ziolkowski, Thad. "Lydia Davis." In *Contemporary American Short Story Writers: Post-
    1945*, ed. Patrick Meanor. Columbia, SC: Bruccoli Clark Layman, 1993.

*   *   *

LARRY McCAFFERY: Do you see your departures from traditional
storytelling methods having affinities with "postmodernism" generally?
Or with any other group of writers?
LYDIA DAVIS: I don't see myself as part of any group or associated with
any group.
LM: Maybe "group" is the wrong word. Do you see yourself doing things
in writing that are "in the air" that other writers may also be picking
up on?
LD: I do now, but for many years I felt that I wrote pretty much in
isolation. I simply did not read my contemporaries, either the more
traditional storytellers, or the more avant-garde writers. I read Kafka,
Beckett, and so on—the literary fathers, and uncles, and mothers, and
grandmothers of the postmodernists. These were my most important
early influences (in my early twenties I was really *studying* them unbeliev-

ably closely, as I discovered when I looked back at my notebooks from those years). But I kept very much apart from most contemporary writing.

LM: Why?

LD: I can't say, exactly. I do believe that writers can try and maintain this sense of creative isolation as much as they like, but at a certain point identifiable similarities in even the most barricaded sensibilities are eventually going to start emerging. These things, as you said, are simply "in the air" somehow. There are many features of different prose styles—even something like writing simple sentences or in the present tense—that you see in common, and the only way to account for them is just their being a product of the times. Everyone is depressed by the political situation to some extent, everyone feels a kind of helplessness—everyone this and everyone that. Everyone who grew up in the fifties grew up in the fifties. You can't escape it.

LM: Postmodernism seemed to emerge from the larger, cultural pattern of sixties disruption which (at least in my view) created an atmosphere of healthy skepticism regarding all sacred cows. Was that sixties zeitgeist something you identified with?

LD: Not really. I already came from a family that tended to challenge sacred cows, so I had that example. But then that made me skeptical even of the rebels of my generation. Yet a lot of other kids were excited by Beckett and Kafka when they got into college (or maybe I should say a handful). The list of writers who excited me, at least, isn't very surprising—they were all well known. Beckett amazes me stylistically. But I must say I came upon Beckett when I was only thirteen—*Malone Dies.* The amazing things he could do within legitimately structured sentences. He does so much with ellipsis and inversion—"Of it rid they too would be." He stands on his head but still keeps a nameable grammatical form. The acrobatics of that are simply remarkable. On the other hand, I didn't find him a sympathetic writer emotionally—in fact, I found his sensibility personally disturbing; but stylistically he was amazing. In the case of Kafka, whom I found much more sympathetic, it was the power and clarity of his vision, his logic—especially in his parables and paradoxes—although, again, it was very bleak and he can be chilly, distant.

LM: What made Kafka seem more sympathetic?

LD: His self-doubt, which shows through in every sentence. And he is more affectionate than Beckett. This preference perhaps says more about me than it does about either Kafka or Beckett. That sense you find in Kafka of his constantly striving to do better also seems appealing. Beckett would not have admitted to any of this quite so plainly. I left out another very important source of appeal in both these writers—their humor.

LM: I'm surprised that you didn't mention the French New Novelists.

LD: I was quite interested in some of them in college. Not Robbe-Grillet much at all, but one or two of Michel Butor's books intrigued me just for the absolute completeness of what he was doing. There was something fascinating and admirable about his *La Modification*, which is told from every possible point of view over and over and over again in exhaustive detail. The same worn pencil appearing again and again from different points of view. I'm very fond of the concrete object in literature, even though it doesn't appear a great deal in my own works. Butor left a lasting impression of moist French classrooms, smelling of pencil dust. It was very sensuous writing at the same time. Of course, Butor was also writing out of this program, which I don't have much sympathy with.

Nabokov also meant a great deal to me back then. I read many of his books one after another in high school—mostly the minor things, not *Lolita*—the way you do when you find a writer and then absolutely devour everything up to a certain point, and then become satiated. I admired very much his loving descriptions of the concrete, his exactness, and the lushness of his prose generally.

LM: You have mentioned Russell Edson as having an important effect on your writing. How so?

LD: Edson was the one who jolted me out of my stuckness in long conventional stories and into one-paragraph freedom. Not only freedom of length and form but freedom of subject matter: some of his stories were so uninhibited, or so absurd, that I saw that anything was appropriate and anything was possible. That revelation happened very specifically in the fall of 1973 when I was twenty-six (amazing how long it can take for someone to "find" a literary text that unlocks something so important!).

LM: It's interesting that there are no women on this list . . .

LD: I read them, but I did not get excited. I wasn't terribly taken even with the women writers you might have thought I would have enjoyed. Djuna Barnes I read in college and mildly liked but never read after. Stein and Woolf still only mildly interest me. I can't feel close to them in style or sensibility. I'm not interested in their characters either, yet I have been asked more than once if Stein was an important influence. I read Stein's *Paris, France* recently, but I'm afraid of reading much of her works, probably because I'm worried it will be too close to something I am already doing.

LM: Isn't doing a number of translations of a specific writer—as you have done with, say, Blanchot—even more dangerous?

LD: I don't have enough perspective to answer that very completely. Whatever affinity I have for an author I'm translating is already there in advance. I'm not going to be influenced by translating Blanchot so much as I *already* felt a kinship with him. Otherwise I would not be interested in translating him.

LM: What was there about Blanchot that made you feel this affinity?

LD: What happens in his novels is often very mysterious. You'll have something like, "N. left the room." (He often uses initials for names, though not always.) You're never quite sure who came, who went, what day it was, whether or not "this woman" is the same as "that woman." Yet it is all very urgent. Really, though, I shouldn't try to summarize him. Blanchot is utterly unique, truly different from any other writer I can point to. He manages to go very deeply into very small moments—someone going from one room to another. I find the way Blanchot will describe a concrete situation by jumping into an abstraction very interesting. He'll say something like, "It was as if the thought itself had moved into the room and done this and done that." And then the *thought* which we think of as abstract, becomes a concrete part of the interaction of the story, a character in the story. He may even move to a further level of abstraction and then yet another. That is part of the reason his writing becomes so very confusing, but also so very engrossing. And there is no question of how committed he is to it. Blanchot presents himself as very much another questioning, troubled person, like Kafka, someone who is always trying to understand the situation—which is something I find very appealing. His narrators are often very humble, very modest people, like Kafka's.

LM: You mentioned earlier that you didn't identify much with the sixties zeitgeist, and one of the ways your fiction differs from that of most of your contemporaries is the absence of reference to pop culture.

LD: My embrace of "high culture" instead of "popular culture" starts with my family's choices. My parents were fiction writers and teachers, my older sister was an excellent clarinetist, my brother played the cello. Meanwhile I was having piano lessons early on an old Steinway upright that my father learned on as a child; trips to Europe when my father was on sabbatical from Smith College and Columbia, a year spent in Europe during which I went to an Austrian Catholic school for my first grade, more or less learning to read German before English, and so on. This probably led to some sense of isolation from any "group" of kids in school and isolation in general. My passion as a teenager, or from eleven or twelve on, was classical music—listening to records, playing the piano, trying out my brother's cello, buying scores, et cetera. Later learning violin, guitar, in college playing violin in a string quartet. Writing was clearly in the picture, but not my passion.

LM: Do you think the sense of refinement or correctness that one hears in your narrator's voices grew out of that background?

LD: I'm sure it did. This "refinement" you see—though, believe me, there are times when I'm anything but refined!—would be influenced by the behavior of a father whose strongest expression of anger was "Drat!" and who was in general rather inhibited by nature. My mother less so but still relatively so. My father and mother were both hyperconscious of language in a way that went far beyond just correcting a mistake. Language was discussed constantly and naturally whenever and wherever it came up. Correctness: not only correct grammar but language correctly expressive, correctly pleasant to the ear also (my father would actually apologize if he repeated a word in a sentence!). Nobody used slang in the family, but not because it was frowned upon: it's hard to remember, but if I imagine my brother or me using a slang expression, I see a kind of spotlight of attention being turned on it for the curiosity it was, I see it being at the very least pointed out, at the most discussed, its origin pondered (my father would go several times a day to the dictionary, which was positioned on a bookstand open under a good strong light, and look up a word to announce, triumphantly, its curious origin). Both parents also had, and therefore passed on, a vivid curiosity about things—ideas, people, the natural world—and along with it went a concern for accuracy about the way things worked. This concern for accuracy stopped short of being pedantic because of the lively curiosity and the sense of humor, sensitivity to the absurd, that were always present.

LM: Even if this "spotlight" wasn't produced from pedantic motives, it must have contributed to your sense of isolation from your peer group, most of whom must have been using slang (maybe even drugs) and deeply involved in pop culture—the Beatles, and so on—in all sorts of ways . . .

LD: Yes. Despite all that, I did love the Beatles for a long time. Just as I loved Sidney Bechet and Charlie Parker for a while. The music was really a motley collection—Mozart, Bach, Brahms, Dvořák, yes, but also Gershwin, some movie score called "The Tiger Tamer"; it depended on what came into the house.

As for drugs, I experimented a little in college, but only a little. The whole idea just didn't interest me much. There was a pull in another direction: I couldn't do the things I liked to do best—reading, writing, playing the piano, et cetera—if I couldn't think straight!

LM: Is there any consistency to what gets you started on a particular work?

LD: The stories are often sparked by an odd piece of language or a paradoxical situation. Like everyone else I live with a number of ongoing problems that don't get solved and that don't even get addressed regularly or directly, consciously. Then a text or a question or someone else's story comes along to act as a catalyst to make this problem spring to life as something to be addressed then and there. But my stories don't ever start with an abstract idea about wanting to write about this sort of person, this sort of town, this sort of year. I usually begin from something very concrete—something that's happened to me or someone I know, or something I've read.

I usually write during, or immediately after, so soon after whatever it is that has happened that I'm particularly sensitive to for some reason. Then at some point I'll look back over what I have and usually one thing will pull everything else together. For instance, in "Five Signs" it was this absurd, utterly paralyzing incident that appears at the end of the story—trying to pay the toll, having these three quarters, and not knowing which two to give to the toll collector. This last image interested me philosophically—necessity and arbitrariness, plus the emotional incapacity to make a decision, what that incapacity implied, and everything that resonated around that idea. Fairly often that seems to be the way the longer narrative stories are written—something is just so compelling to me as an incident that I'll see how it could be supported and illuminated by a few other elements. It's as if the climax or epiphany is already there and I have to discover what produced that moment. The situations that intrigue me often combine a strongly humorous aspect and a very frustrating one—not tragic, but emotionally difficult. Somehow there is an odd emotional collision that lights a spark.

LM: How does a piece evolve once you have this initial spark?

LD: Each case is different. One factor that really has nothing to do with aesthetics is that I'm always working under a time constraint. I have probably (wrongly) set my life up in such a way that my writing doesn't have a large enough place. In other words, I try to earn money at a profession that doesn't pay very well (like translating) or I choose to have another child, knowing that this will cut away at my free time. The result is that I often write only five to eight hours a week, often less. There are certainly weeks (in extreme cases, *months*) when I don't do any writing at all. The time I give writing is snatched, I have the sense that I should be doing something else. This is good in that I don't follow through on things that aren't compelling. If something interests me, I'll write it down in my notebook. If I'm compelled enough, I'll start from that sentence and go on to write the whole piece, then and there, often without having planned to. Often I'm thinking I'm just doing a quick summary so I don't lose the ideas; then the summary gets more detailed and I try to grab the time, and go right through to the end in some form or other. It seems very important to get all the way through a piece in one go.

LM: Aside from the personal circumstances, are you drawn to the story format because the things you're specifically interested in doing with language and story aren't appropriate to the novel format?

LD: I think each idea demands its own form and length. "The Fish" required only a single image, a single paragraph. "Liminal," being a piece about insomnia, sleep, the night, needed a lot of space around brief dreamlike sections. "Break It Down" needed to have no space at all—one headlong flood of language. "Mrs. Orlando" and "Therapy" needed the regular, comfortable pacing of a more conventional short story form. But time constraints are a main factor for my having written mainly in short forms. With so little time a novel obviously isn't going to go very fast. I do think about novel-length projects quite often. And the draft of a novel I recently finished is just sitting there waiting for me to settle in to work.

But it is almost impossible for me to abandon the story form because I am always starting new stories before I finish the ones I'm working on. It's like a serial magazine that has three serials going at once: even if one serial ends, the other two are still continuing, so you always have to buy the next issue of the magazine. Having probably ten or fifteen stories at some stage of writing at a time (I mean stories actively in progress, not abandoned) is a slightly chaotic way to work. But I seem to need to be surrounded by these works-in-progress, working on each until I've done all I can to it for now, then turning to another. I'll find myself going back through my notebooks, picking out things to see what I've got and what might be done with them. It's as if each unfinished story is a living entity, not quite formed but very much alive.

LM: You've occasionally used first-person narrators in your stories—in "Break It Down," for example—but this seems fairly infrequent. Why is this?

LD: Especially if a story is based on incidences from my own life, writing it from a perspective other than the "I"—using "she," for example—allows me the distance I need to be able to see what I'm writing as a *made thing* rather than just a piece of autobiography. I do use "I" when I am occasionally stepping into the role of another character. That brings me closer to something that's already farther away. I use "she" for something that may be close.

But this is never a conscious choice, only something I understand later on. For instance, in the case of "Pastor Arlene's Newsletter," I didn't at any point consciously decide this piece ought to be written in first person plural instead of singular. It just came that way. It's only afterwards that I have to figure out why, because at a certain point I am aware that I'm using the first person plural for a singular—as in royalty. I probably wanted to adopt the generalizing tone of the sermon, the tone people use when they say, "We are often upset at so-and-so." The "we" is also a way of hiding in at least two respects: by taking refuge in the legitimate idea that this happens to all of us, and by simply refusing to come out and say "I"—that is, by pretending that there is more than one person. I could probably think of other reasons, too, but initially it's always an intuitive choice as to which person I use.

LM: A lot of your stories are narrated by impersonal pronouns—"he," "she," "we"—or the stories aren't given proper names. Is that absence of proper names a conscious decision in most cases?

LD: Usually not, although I am consciously bothered by the fiction pasting a name onto a character. Even back when I was twelve years old and writing stories for school assignments, I did not like to use a common name for a character. There is something about it that seems disturbingly arbitrary. A couple of times when I have put names to characters, they have come to me spontaneously but then I have seen the reason for them: the name of Mrs. Orlando, who is so afraid of everything, has associations with retirement communities in Florida. "Wassily" is spelled with two *s*s so that it can be separated into "was silly"—which he was. (Because of that spelling many people have asked if he is Wassily Kandinsky, and in a bio for a reading series the organizer went a step farther and actually listed that little book as "Sketches for a Life of Wassily Kandinsky.") But using "he" and "she" and no proper names causes a lot of technical problems, obviously, because it gets very awkward when you try to refer to more than one "he" or "she" in the same place. I guess my interest is more in creating or talking about the abstract situation of a "he" or "she" who could be anyone but happens to be particular (or pretends to be particular in this case). As soon as you say "Joe" and "Pete" you shift the emphasis—you pretend to be creating these two actual characters, Joe and Pete, in a specific, locatable situation. That's not really my intention.

The truth is that I resist locating *anything* too particularly. Often, when I think of naming something that would locate a story too specifically, I pull back and generalize it. After the fact I realize why: I know that I'll say, "She came from a large city in the East" instead of, "She came from New York" because as soon as I refer to "New York" readers will instantly bring in their own associations with New York—all that baggage about the "Big Apple" and so on. I don't want all those associations flocking in there.

LM: How much conscious choice is involved in the voices that you adopt?

LD: Conscious choice becomes involved mostly when I write something one way but know immediately that it isn't working; sometimes months or even years later, I'll decide to try a completely different approach. For instance, "The Center of the Story" was a piece that didn't work as a straight narrative because it did not have center. This part wasn't dra-

matic enough to be the center, and that part wasn't important enough—
so I managed to retrieve it by putting a frame around it involving a
woman setting out to write a story. It begins with this woman realizing,
"It was not a very good story," and so she showed it to a friend and the
friend said that it was not an interesting story. This frame worked because now the focus of the story was how it did not have a center. That
seemed to add a sense of conviction and structure that had been missing. It also added some distance, and perhaps also another perspective,
a depth . . .

LM: Your interest in the abstract instance of a person who could be anyone seems paradoxical for someone whose stories usually originate very
concretely from real people and real names.

LD: It has to do with keeping the focus on the question or problem
and resisting allowing the illusion that this thing might have happened.
When a specific person had something to do with inspiring the story,
then I sometimes use the actual name when I'm writing the first draft.
But I'm inhibited from keeping the name in the final draft because it's
too personal. Although there are exceptions. I have kept the real name
"Mitch" in a couple of stories for reasons a little obscure to me—maybe
because of associations with the use of that name going back years and
because it's an emphatic name with interesting rhymes: *itch, pitch, stitch,*
and *bitch.*

LM: This relates to Blanchot's leap from the particular to the abstract . . .

LD: Some of my stories are more or less unaltered recountings of an
episode, but even then what I consider the "fiction" in what I've written
is the *selection* of events. You can never really get it all, so you're always
selecting, and your selection is always biased, it's never really objective
or complete. I've certainly had people read the stories and then say,
"Wait a minute—this isn't what happened!" And of course it's not what
happened—for them; and it wouldn't be what happened for a third person. In other words, there is no one truth. I'm selecting from my experience, skewing it and slanting it, taking things out, adding others. Maybe
I'm painting a black picture instead of a rosy picture. There's a fiction, a
basic falsification, in any process of selection. But then another kind of
taking-from-life is taking not the incident but the pattern.

LM: Why rely on something "real" to get you started rather than just
making something up?

LD: I seem to have lost interest in making things up! I started out
making things up in college and just after, that's what I thought a story
should be and what I should be doing, and so I slaved away at constructing a proper story. But this did not feel very joyful. Some things in my
writing are still wholly invented, at least partially made up, because of

some internal necessity of the story, but I'm not interested in writing a traditional piece of fiction, although reading one by someone else is still perfectly enjoyable.

LM: This lack of interest in making things up is shared by several of the other writers in this interview book—Lyn Hejinian, for example, Ken Gangemi, Kathy Acker, Bill Vollmann. In fact, collaborative approaches to writing seems to be one of those things we mentioned earlier that is somehow "in the air." You hear about it (in a negative sense) in the discussions of the "death of the author" and "lack of originality" and "imagination as plagiarism" by poststructuralist critics. What is there about someone else's writing that might compel you to appropriate materials and begin to build your own story around them? Maybe you could talk about "Extracts from a Life" or "Lord Royston's Tour" as examples since they both take off from appropriation or collaboration.

LD: Those two are exceptional—my only "appropriations," so far anyway. But they both started with my reading something with pure delight and pleasure. The Suzuki book was something my son's piano teacher asked me to read—required me to read—in order to understand Suzuki's method and philosophy. The language delighted me so much that I started copying out sentences. At that point I wanted to make it my own, or bring out in it what was there potentially. I could either leave it alone, a book to be read by parents of Suzuki pupils, with all its oddities of language and thought, or I could extract from it what was really delightful and create a different work from it.

With the Lord Royston letters, I also felt that what I was doing was almost pure extraction. I rearranged and rewrote a little, but my idea was to leave the original material as untouched as possible beyond selecting. If I had to fiddle with it much, it wouldn't have appealed to me as a text in the first place; this other text seemed to be there *in potential*— there was something a great deal more interesting in it than what I was reading, the same language with a different shape and intention.

LM: That process seems to share a lot with translation.

LD: Yes, although it's obviously more of a transformation. But it must be related. Deciphering and isolating "meaning" becomes a very active mental exercise when I'm doing a translation, and I'm sure some of it winds up getting projected onto some of my characters when they're struggling with how to "read" or translate different things in their lives. For instance, Blanchot's essays (rather than fiction) are extremely dense and somewhat hard to follow. Before I translated those essays, I had never been confronted with such a horrendously frustrating task—trying again and again to make words yield their meaning and finding that they simply wouldn't. I mean actually reading a sentence over and over again, trying to hear it on this level and on that level and on that level, and still not being able to figure out what it meant. In that context "meaning" becomes very physical—I could feel my brain physically trying to grab hold of something. It was no longer an abstract thing but, especially with the Blanchot translations, a very frustrating, very difficult physical exercise.

My translation work also probably affects my fiction simply because it has forced me to examine syntax and structure so closely and because it has exposed me to different ways of writing—including the strange and oddly attractive language in poorly written things, the sort of thing that generated "Pastor Arlene." Something can be written very badly in French, and translating it into bad English or even worse English can be very interesting. I found a lot of enjoyment doing an extremely literal translation of one book that had very little literary merit and was written in a nauseatingly sentimental style—not in the final version, but in my notebook, where I would write down an absurdly accurate translation of a sentence that was already sentimental and stupid. Taking the language to the edge of cogent and meaningful writing interests me a great deal.

LM: Your stories are often about characters trying to "decodify" things from one set of terms to another (as in "Break It Down"), or to "translate" them into something that they feel more familiar with. Is translation perhaps one of the inspirations for this sort of investigation?

LD: I enjoy translating because I enjoy assuming a disguise, I'm borrowing from and piecing together other texts that *aren't* written the way I would write something. Writing like other people allows me to be able to do certain things—a long, lush description of a summer evening—that I have no place for in my own work. Stories of mine that don't have their origins in other pieces of writing (which are the vast majority) typically have very little local color in them at all—whereas you could say "Lord Royston" is nothing *but* local color. I shy away from including local color or exotic details. I often make stories deliberately rather sparse. If I bring in any concrete objects, there will only be those few that are absolutely necessary and that will sometimes become sort of talismans or objects of emotional speculation. It comes back to leaving in only what is *necessary*.

All this makes translation sometimes quite satisfying. Right now, for example, I'm translating Michel Leiris, who is a long-winded, syntactically complex writer, and I'm finding it a great pleasure to be able to write like him for a while. There's no doubt that I'm still creating something of my own, and yet I'm putting myself in someone else's shoes to do it. That is in addition to the very large pleasure of having this material transformed into English, my "home" language.

LM: What did you mean when you said that working with these prior materials, you want to make them your own?

LD: Saying you want to make something "your own" implies a notion of possessiveness that I'm really not comfortable with. I want to reshape the material of these works into something else. With the Suzuki and Royston materials, it wasn't so much a matter of making these things "my own," as taking from them a text that I sought, that was already there in potential somehow. What I'm after is not to leave my stamp on them with my voice or personal signature. I'm actually staying out of them except for selecting and arranging. I don't like "collaboration" as a term to describe what I've done because it implies a mutually agreed upon interaction between artists.

LM: This general area has interesting implications about aesthetic notions such as "originality"—that assumption so dear to Western notions of aesthetics that the goal of all serious art involves creation out of some unique expression of "the real" by the individual artist.

LD: I'm interested in a different kind of premise about what so-called "fiction writers" can be doing—a formal change that moves right out of the fiction genre and enters other genres at the same time, so that a text can be partly autobiography, partly fiction, partly essay, and partly technical treatise . . .

LM: And in your case, partly *poem* as well.

LD: Sure, partly poem—*and* partly story. Confusing the distinctions seems like a very healthy thing. Writing without those boundaries is what increasingly interests me most.

LM: Have you ever tried your hand at poetry?

LD: I wrote some in college, sitting in the back of my French literature class (and because I was sitting in the back of the room writing poems, I got a C in French literature!). But I was more interested in stories. My mother and father were both story writers, and both had some real success. Their involvement in publishing stories gave me the feeling when I was very young that writing stories was a perfectly legitimate thing to do with one's life. The rare times I have set out to write a poem, I've started it just the way you *can't* do it—which is to say, conceptually, from the outside, with the "subject" rather than from the inside, with the language I wanted to use and letting the poem grow in its own direction. It's still surprising to me how, after all these years of writing fiction, I haven't learned anything about writing poetry. Leaving aside whether or not some of my stories may be poetry, the problem of how to write an actual poem with line breaks still seems very interesting and mysterious. The truth is, I don't know how to do it.

LM: Do you see yourself working out of a specifically feminist perspective?

LD: I specifically *resisted* feminism when I was first writing. I have never had a program in my writing. I never said to myself that I was going to write about women's issues and speak for women. I suppose I have *acted* like a feminist in certain ways, and I have believed in most or all of the things that feminists believe in, so it wasn't that I was opposed to their goals theoretically or emotionally. But I've never been an activist.

I had the example of a very strong mother—very intelligent, very outspoken—who was a writer and felt frustrated because she was also trying to raise children and be a faculty wife. In retrospect now, it's obvious that she struggled with deep conflicts about her life. She wanted to be a good faculty wife, but she also resented the whole thing. She wanted to make a nice dinner and set a nice table, but she also resented making dinner. I've inherited a lot of those conflicts—and so have the characters I write about. After a while, though, I drew much closer to women writers. I read a lot of women writers now—contemporary women writers, women of a hundred years ago, everyone. I'm identifying with other women, their lives and struggles and so on, even though I still don't label myself a feminist as such. This is a complicated area because so much of what any writer does is blind. You can think you're a terrifically independent woman, but then you discover that what you're doing and thinking is what everyone else is doing and thinking or is in some way predetermined.

LM: These fears, this sense of powerlessness that you deal with so often, could also be felt by men; but somehow there's an emotional honesty in stories like "Mrs. Orlando"—a certain willingness to expose one's vulnerability—that rarely seems to surface in most male writing. I realize this gets us into gender stereotyping, but even though I could believe and even identify with the male narrator in "Break It Down," I still felt his perspective was "feminine" somehow.

LD: I know what you're suggesting. The character in "Wassilly" would be another example of a male who could be seen as being very feminine. He's a gentle, a timid man. But I'm not presenting "Wassilly" and "Break It Down" as typical of or identified with female writing as opposed to male writing.

LM: Most of your stories are not constructed to build up into a dramatic crisis that can be resolved. That lack of emphasis seems very "realistic" and appropriate for men and women—but maybe *especially* appropriate for women. Do women writers presently feel freer to write about these areas without feeling they have to present them dramatically or with a resolution?

LD: Probably, although this doesn't have so much to do with gender as with changing expectations about what is appropriate subject matter for fiction generally. You can find similar types of obsessive but "ordinary" sensibilities in books by men. It's not only women who are doing this.

LM: You were writing minimalist stories—for instance, "The Fish," "Safe

Love," and "The Problem"—years before this became common. What intrigues you about the form of these pieces? They seem to have less to do with narrative than with exploring a poetic image . . .

LD: What interested me in "The Fish" was the mental photograph I had of the fish on a slab of marble being looked at by this woman who feels she hasn't done much right today anyway—and now look what she's done! A description of a moment. That image didn't seem to require any more development than a paragraph. I could have figured out how to work this up into a whole story about this woman's life, what led up to this moment where she is looking at the fish, but that would have seemed artificial and laborious to me. Unnecessary exposition.

LM: "Cockroaches in Autumn" is almost like a haiku . . .

LD: That story was inspired and then written in much the same way as "Five Signs of Disturbance." The cockroach problem I was encountering where I lived at the time was so overwhelming that I began writing down each manifestation that was at all interesting. Finally they began to accumulate to the point where I had enough to make some kind of impact. What I liked was taking a literary, poetic tradition that generally serves more "poetic" subjects—sunsets, dawns, plum blossoms—and adopting it for cockroaches. "Cockroaches In Autumn"—because I was alternately looking at these cockroaches and looking out at a garden or a sunset, with the ugliness of the cockroaches being offset by the lyricism of the form, the horror offset by comedy or compassion.

With "Problem," which adopts the form of a logic problem, the minimalist treatment seemed right because going on much longer with that form wouldn't be interesting. Reducing those complex results of multiplied divorce and resettlement to this pattern of abstractions was interesting, but if I had gone much beyond what I included, it would have quickly become tiresome and predictable. The same thing was true with "Safe Love," where I began with a realistic woman talking about a realistic situation—having a crush on her child's doctor. But then it gets faster and faster, and more and more ridiculous, and further and further reduced until there isn't anywhere left to go with it. It's reached its logical end.

LM: In her review of *Break It Down* in the *New York Times*, Michiko Kakutani cited "Safe Love" as minimalist, and then attacked it for not providing these sorts of expository details by saying something like, "This piece has narrative possibilities, but it's not a story." What's your response to this?

LD: That's criticizing one form for not being another; it's like saying a cat has possibilities of being a tiger. It never occurred to me to write it as a traditionally developed story! The situation—a woman getting a crush on someone simply because there isn't anyone else in town—is so absurd to begin with, and yet obviously so common. There's no meaning to the crush, no meaning to the relationship. Reducing it was a way of playing off of a traditional set of associations and structures, instead of laboriously recreating them all again. It wasn't the situation that interested me but the language I could use to play with it.

LM: Several of your characters try to solve their particular dilemmas by writing things down to organize their responses so they can understand what is happening, how they should act, what to do, and so on. Do you use your own notebook writing like this?

LD: I write down anything that strikes me for whatever reason. If I am compelled enough by the material, it will demand to be continued into a story. Some people have very well developed instincts about how to live, how to do the right thing and interact with people. Others don't, and these people may use their brains rather than their feelings and instincts to try and figure out how to do something—dress, cook, talk to people. My stories often seem to reflect this divorce—the brain trying to teach the feelings how to behave.

LM: But you wouldn't say that your own writing is a method of understanding yourself?

LD: Not really. There are better ways to try to understand yourself. Each thing I have written has been done not because it might have some practical use for me but for the pleasure of making something out of something else. I doubt that writing helps *anyone* to live! On the contrary, it's rather troubling for me to find I've made a story I like out of a difficult situation while the difficult situation remains. As though I've exploited it.

LM: Isn't it a paradox for you to be suggesting that writing and language are finally of no real help in organizing the chaos of people's lives and emotional responses to things?

LD: That paradox is analogous to the cliché about translation being impossible: it's true theoretically, yet translations are done all the time. A writer has nothing but words to convey this ongoing struggle that everybody has—to make something of the interpretation of language, to be able to make language mean, to make language more trustworthy. Allowing this dilemma to enter openly into the work seems more useful and honest and interesting than doing otherwise.

About Mangoes, Two or Three Pages
An Interview with Kenneth Gangemi

Larry McCaffery
Sinda Gregory

In the darkness they could not see that I was an American and I could observe them undetected.

— *The Volcanoes from Puebla*

Until he began occasionally teaching creative writing and literature courses in the New York area in the early 1990s, Ken Gangemi was for many years a part-time bartender and full-time writer of highly unusual fiction, poetry, nonfiction, and various unclassifiable texts. Tending bar and writing literature are not nearly as disparate as they might seem. Indeed, one night, while spending a few hours watching Gangemi tend bar at J.G. Melon (the tavern on Manhattan's Upper West Side where he used to work each Saturday night), I discovered there were plenty of clues into the unique sensibility that has produced during the past twenty-odd years five distinctive and utterly original books, as well as numerous uncollected pieces.

Aspects of Gangemi's literary aesthetics can be discerned, for instance, in the way he greets most customers by name, and in the fastidious care with which he arranges every object on or behind the bar so that no wasted effort will be expended while he's working. As the bar begins to fill up with noisy, hungry, and thirsty Saturday night customers, Gangemi's mannerisms behind the bar resemble nothing so much as one of Hemingway's matador-code heroes: the epitome of grace under pressure. Even at 11 P.M., with the bar now in its most raucous weekend phase, his gestures—emptying an untidy ashtray while a customer is between smokes, placing the napkins, silverware, and necessary condiments in front of a hungry customer, cutting an orange slice and placing it delicately on the rim of the glass containing a bizarre concoction of carefully measured ingredients—remain unhurried and precise, blending the matador's sense of flair and economy of means. All the while Gangemi is maintaining a friendly patter with his patrons (though he does so politely, and only when encouraged to do so); in the space of a few minutes these brief exchanges are likely to cover everything from a discussion of the best passages in Joyce's *Ulysses*, to advice about where the best literary parties are going to be held in Manhattan this week (along with their exact addresses and the best subway routes to get there), to a discussion of the best strategies to use in bar fights.

Meanwhile, every few minutes Gangemi will reach unobtrusively around to his back pocket, pull out a pad of three-by-five-inch notebook paper, and jot down something he's overheard or seen. These jottings—the quirky name of a tourist's hometown in California ("Azusa"), the rumor that a man had been arrested earlier in the day during High Mass at St. Patrick's Cathedral for urinating on the altar, a patron's novelty photographs of an Eskimo riding a motorcycle and a Pygmy waterskiing—will accumulate over a several-year period, during which they will gradually be sorted into neatly labeled envelopes that are filed alphabetically in containers on top of the table at which Gangemi writes for twelve hours each day, every day, back at his spartan, rent-controlled studio apartment in the Lower East Side. After Gangemi's painstaking efforts to eliminate their excesses and purify their essences, some of these eventually find their way into the textures of his unadorned and yet instantly recognizable prose, where the exotic and the mundane are allowed to intermingle, *but always on their own individual terms*. These terms are rendered by Gangemi with an engineer's concern for accuracy and orderliness, with the innocent gentleness and ardor of a lover's first kiss—and with a bartender's generous appreciation for the rich variety, sensuousness, and beauty concealed in the ordinary.

Ken Gangemi's books are *Olt* (1969), a "miniaturized novel" that, somewhat in the manner of the French New Novel, uses a neutral-seeming presentation of the thoughts and actions of its protagonist to create a compressed but emotionally charged depiction of urban alienation and longings; *Lydia* (1970), a collection of poems, many of them in the form of unadorned lists of nouns or place names, which are almost haiku-like in evoking complex emotional responses from rigidly denotative forms; *Corroboree* (1977), a "book of nonsense" in the manner of Raymond Queneau and Lewis Carroll, in which Gangemi's remarkable tautness and control are used to wrest startling new meanings and resonances from improbable collisions of words and images; *The Volcanoes from Puebla* (1979), an apparent "travel guide to Mexico" whose mechanical structure (brief, alphabetically arranged sections about various people, places, and topics encountered by Gangemi on his motorcycle travels through Mexico) is balanced by a blatant subjectivity (under *B* one finds: Bach, Back in the USA, Bakery, Beggars, Bicycle, Bishop, Blanket, Bohemia, Books) to produce a new form—part travelogue, part fiction, and part autobiography—that critic Charles Caramello has dubbed a "postmodern *Bildungsroman*"; and *The Interceptor Pilot* (1980), a novel-disguised-as-a-screenplay that once again uses a seemingly distanced, objective manner of presentation to create a fiercely penetrating examination of the moral and psychological dilemmas of America's involvement in Vietnam.

*   *   *

Kenneth Gangemi: Selected Bibliography

Books of Fiction and Poetry

Olt. Novel. London: Calder and Boyars, 1969; New York: Orion Press, 1969. Reprint, Frankfurt: Marz Verlag, 1971; Paris: L'Herne, 1972; London and Boston: Marion Boyars, 1985; Copenhagen: Husets Forlag, 1991.
Lydia. Poetry. Los Angeles: Black Sparrow Press, 1970.
Corroboree: A Book of Nonsense. Humor and satire. Brooklyn, NY: Assembling Press, 1977.
The Volcanoes from Puebla. Fiction based on Gangemi's life and travels in Mexico. London and Boston: Marion Boyars, 1979.
Lydia/Corroborée. Includes English version of *Corroborée* and bilingual edition of *Lydia.* Paris: Christian Bourgois, 1980.
The Interceptor Pilot. Cinematic novel. London and Boston: Marion Boyars, 1980. Published originally in French translation as *Pilote de chasse.* Paris: Flammarion, 1975.

Short Stories and Fiction Excerpts

"The Snow-Lobsters." *Art and Literature* (Paris) 8 (Spring 1966): 184–91. Reprinted in *The Young American Writers,* ed. Richard Kostelanetz, 128–36. New York: Funk & Wagnalls, 1967.
"The Appointment." *Transatlantic Review* 27 (Winter 1967–68): 108–15.
"Second Miscellany," "The Politician," and "Sixth Miscellany." *El Uroqallo* (Madrid), 27–28 (May–August 1974): 94–97.
"The Restaurant," "Ninth Miscellany," and "The University." *Sun & Moon* 3 (Summer 1976): 41–44.
"The Party," "Questions and Answers," "The German-American's Tale," and "The Politician." *Foothill Quarterly* 2, 2 (1977): 12–17.

"Alarma!" and "Preferences." Special issue, *The Poets' Encyclopedia Of Unmuzzled Ox*, 4, 4/5 (1979): 6, 213–14.
"Back in the USA." *art press* (Paris) 38 (June 1980): 23.
"Miscellaneous." *Tel* (Paris) 7 (November 1982): 5.
"Greenbaum, O'Reilly & Stephens." *Conjunctions* 5 (1983): 208–23. Reprinted in *The Pushcart Prize, X: Best of the Small Presses*. Wainscott, NY: Pushcart Press, 1985, pp. 295–312.
"Hotels." *Europe* (Paris) 733 (May 1990): 121–29.

Uncollected Poetry

"Large Bottles." *Chouteau Review* 1, 3 (Fall/Winter 1976): 82.
"Seaport" and "Future." *Stardust* (Brussels) (1977): 10–11.
"USA." *Spirali* (Milan) 3, 10 (November 1980): 47.
"Reception," "Career Girl in a Supermarket," "Jones Beach," "American Museum of Natural History," "Donut Shop near Boston Common," and "Canada." *Blast* 3 (1984): 302–8.
"Names." *Ploughshares* 12, 4 (1986): 161–62.
"Random Reading in a Small Library." *Confrontation* 33/34 (Fall/Winter 1986–87): 36.
"A Streetcar Named St. Charles." *Confrontation* 35/36 (Spring and Fall 1987): 148.
"First Marriage." *Poetry East* 25 (Spring 1988): 53–56. Reprinted in *Men of Our Time: A Poetry Anthology*, ed. Fred Moramarco and Al Zolinas. Athens: University of Georgia Press, 1992.
"Ten Places," "A Few Preferences," "Running Heads in the Yellow Pages," and "Twenty Titles." *Fiction International* 18:1 (Spring 1988): 45–48.
"Confessions of an Ailurophile" and "Politics after Forty." *Abraxas* 37 (1988): 36–38.
"Tanks in Greenwich Village." *Rampike* 6, 3 (1988): 54.
"Waiting for the Biopsy." *Chelsea* 47 (1988): 88.
"Six Quatrains," "What They Said," "Skiing over Christmas Vacation," and "On the Road." *Transfer* 2, 1 (Fall/Winter 1988–89): 6–11.
"Susie Falls Asleep" and "Excerpts from Her Letters." *Central Park* 15 (Spring 1989): 169–71.
"The Art of Correspondence." *Lips* 16 (1990): 16–17.
"Calle Bolivar." *Gargoyle* 37/38 (1990): 85.
"Cover Lines from Magazines." *Poetry Project Newsletter* 139 (December/January 1990–91): 2.
"Notes of a Moonwatcher." *Amicus Journal* 13, 1 (Winter 1991): 53.
"Marked Lines," "Titles of Chinese Poems," and "The Chinese Poets." *Fiction International* 19:2 (Spring 1991): 47–50.
"The Time Machine." *Pequod* 33 (Febuary 1992).

Nonfiction

"Extraits de notes" and "Clippings." *L'Ennemi* (Paris) 1 (1980): 40–47.
"Notes on *Pilote de chasse*." *art press* (Paris) 38 (June 1980): 23.

Interviews with and Articles about Gangemi

Baumbach, Jonathan. Review of *The Interceptor Pilot*. *New York Times Book Review*, 18 January 1981.
Caramello, Charles. "On the Guideless Guidebooks of Postmodernism: Reading *The Volcanoes from Puebla* in Context." *Sun and Moon* 9/10 (Summer 1980): 59–99. Reprinted in *The Avant-Garde Tradition in Literature*, ed. Richard Kostelanetz, 348–77. Buffalo, NY: Prometheus Books, 1982.
———. "*The Volcanoes from Puebla* and Other Reflections." In *Silverless Mirrors*, 11, 28, 51, 143–44, 147–52, 157–73, 238–39n36, 239n37. Tallahassee: University Presses of Florida, 1983.
Chénetier, Marc. *Beyond Suspicion: New American Fiction Since 1960*. Philadelphia: University of Pennsylvania Press, 1995.
Klinkowitz, Jerome. "Directions in Contemporary Fiction." *American Book Review* 3, 3 (March–April 1981): 12–13.
———. "Experimental Realism." In *Postmodern Fiction: A Bio-Bibliographical Guide*, ed. Larry McCaffery, 67, 73–76. Westport, CT: Greenwood Press, 1986.
———. *The Self-Apparent Word*, 124–26, 132–33, 134. Carbondale: Southern Illinois University Press, 1984.
Kostelanetz, Richard. *The End of Intelligent Writing*, 172, 298, 301, 331, 347, 361, 365, 366, 376, 384, 388. New York: Sheed and Ward, 1974. Reprinted as *Literary Politics in America*. Kansas City, MO: Sheed Andrews and McMeel, 1977.
———. "Innovative Literature in America Today." In *Younger Critics of North America: Essays on Literature and the Arts*, ed. Richard Kostelanetz, 153–55. Fairwater, WI: Tom Montag/Margins, 1976.
———. "New Fiction in America." In *Surfiction*, ed. Raymond Federman, 88, 92. Chicago: Swallow Press, 1975.
———. In *The Old Fictions and the New*, 4, 159, 162–63. Jefferson, NC, and London: McFarland, 1987.
———. In *The Old Poetries and the New*, 126, 131–32, 143, 148. Ann Arbor: University of Michigan Press, 1981.
Lakoma, Agnieszka. "Kenneth Gangemi and the Question of Minimalism in Postmodern American Fiction." M.A. thesis, Maria Curie-Sklodowska University, Lublin, Poland, 1988.
Lemaire, Gérard-Georges. "Kenneth Gangemi." *Tel* (Paris) 7 (November 1982): 4–5.
———. Preface. "Rature ta vague littérature" (Mallarmé). *Pilote de chasse*, by Kenneth Gangemi. Paris: Flammarion, 1975.
———. Preface. "Solitudes d'un lexicographe." *Lydia/Corroborée*, by Kenneth Gangemi. Paris: Christian Bourgois, 1980.
Lewis, Peter. "The Book of the Script of the Film of . . ." Review of *The Interceptor Pilot*. *Times Literary Supplement*, 28 November 1980, p. 6.
McCaffery, Larry, and Sinda Gregory. "Sophisticated Innocence: An Interview with Kenneth Gangemi." *Mississippi Review* 20, 1 and 2 (December 1991): 63–75.
Myers, George, Jr. "Without the Trappings of Digression." In *Alphabets Sublime*, 132–39. Washington: Paycock Press, 1986.
———. "Kenneth Gangemi on Nonsense, Assemblages and the Mask of Fiction." *Gargoyle* 17/18 (Winter 1982): 47–49.
Saltzman, Arthur M. *Designs of Darkness in Contemporary American Fiction*, 7, 19–22, 60. Philadelphia: University of Pennsylvania Press, 1990.

*   *   *

LARRY MCCAFFERY: Let me try out a possible tabloid headline for your inspection: "Kenneth Gangemi—I led two lives. By day, avant-garde author (revered by the French); by night, Manhattan bartender (twenty-two years now)." What is the interaction between those two aspects of your life?

KENNETH GANGEMI: Bartending is like living in New York or California—a fifty-fifty trade-off of pluses and minuses. But the pluses are considerable. Writing is an isolated activity, with written matter in front of me all day. I get a few phone calls, but it is basically a very withdrawn existence. Writers tend to be reclusive in order to get their work done, but too much reclusiveness is unhealthy. When I change clothes and go out, however, when I am going to tend bar for the night, it is totally different, my life becomes more balanced. I'm not reading anything, I'm not straining my eyes. I'm on my feet, moving around, talking to people. It's the spoken language, not the written language. I'm not selecting the people I talk with, they're randomly selected. They are people from the general world, not the academic or creative world. "Powerful uneducated people," Walt Whitman would call some of them.

One of the best things about the job is the contact with my coworkers. I feel that I have much in common with them. Everyone I work with here in New York does something else. In addition to being in the theater, they are students, artists, writers, dancers, musicians, photographers. There is a great deal in people's heads that cannot be found in books and periodicals. And it is a wide selection of customers that I talk with, tourists from out of town, Europeans with thick accents, some with no education, some people who are very educated, people from thousands of different backgrounds and occupations. You learn to become a good listener. Even the least of them has something to tell me.

SINDA GREGORY: What you're describing maybe helps partially explain the eclecticism of materials that is so apparent in your work.

KG: My work naturally reflects the life I lead. And I don't mean only my experiences as a bartender. I've always preferred nonintellectual jobs. You sell your time and labor, but not your mind. I had some interesting jobs before I became a bartender. I've worked on a construction project in Connecticut, in a gold mine in Ontario, and on an offshore oil rig in Louisiana. I've traveled about forty thousand miles through Mexico, Florida, California, and the Southwest on three different kinds of motorcycles.

But there is certainly a lot of input from a night of tending bar. So much so that the only people I can really talk to about tending bar are other bartenders. It's like a brotherhood, an instant communication.

They are the only ones who really understand. Bartending is a powerful antidepressant. The next morning, after a night of work, I'm usually in a tremendously good mood. It's an incredible high, like being on drugs or something. What created this high is a combination of factors. Partly it is because I've been on my feet for seven or eight hours. Walking back and forth rapidly is almost aerobic, the pulse is up and the blood is circulating. Tending bar is also physical exercise, as you are constantly bending, leaning, and stretching. Also there is a certain amount of stress involved. Sometimes you find yourself in a confrontation, potential trouble, having to throw somebody out, and therefore a jolt of adrenaline. But always a lot of stimulation from the different people and various situations. Where else can I talk with a tattooed junkie? Or put a man out who's much bigger than I am? Or go home with a sweaty young waitress?

SG: Do you use the people and conversations in your work in any sort of direct way?

KG: Sure. I've talked with cops, doctors, politicians, call girls, minor gangsters, soldiers who have seen combat. It's a rich source of material. And it is amazing what people will tell me. I am like a priest who has heard fifty thousand confessions. I always have a notebook in my pocket when I'm working (or when I'm doing anything else, for that matter). They are ordinary three-by-five pads with fifty pages. I divide them in half and staple them at the end so the pages won't come out when I take the notebook out of my hip pocket. I make notes all night. They may or may not lead to something I can specifically use in my writing, but they are always stimulating when I read them the next day. Most of them are transcribed to 8½-by-11-inch lined papers. I have hundreds of pages of these notes, started in Los Angeles in 1967, that will someday be the basis of a novel.

LM: You've experimented with lists and collage forms in your work at least as far back as your first book of poems, *Lydia*. I know the list has a venerable tradition, going back to Homer and Rabelais, Joyce, and so on, but what intrigues *you* about the list as a form?

KG: Lists are an orderly way to present material. As you said, lists have been made by writers for thousands of years. As a form, it's nothing new. In fact, at first glance, a list seems to have little to do with literature, at least not directly. But if you fuss and fool with it, artistically arrange it, a list becomes an interesting literary form precisely because of its orderliness, its economy of form, its aesthetic simplicity. I seized upon it and started doing it because of my educational background, which is engineering, not English literature or the liberal arts. And engineers are often concerned with the most efficient way to do something. To us (and I am still an engineer in many ways) lists are something we feel very comfortable with.

SG: Did you practice engineering at all?

KG: I worked as an engineer in San Francisco in 1959 for a total of six months. It was dreadful work. That was my only office job, and it was like being in prison. I hated it. Five days a week were completely ruined. On beautiful mornings I had to be at that damn office at 9 A.M., dressed in a coat and tie. Two rush hours every day, standing up on the number forty-seven Potrero bus. By the time I got home I was tired and did not feel like doing anything creative. That depressing experience soured me on engineering—and office jobs—forever.

SG: How do these lists seem to accumulate into materials you can shape into a poem or a text?

KG: In one case, a poem consists of selected underlinings that I had made in the course of reading and rereading *Ulysses*, so that what you wind up with is *Ulysses* distilled into two pages of pure poetry. Typically, though, the lists evolve from my collecting words and phrases on slips of paper, which I place into envelopes. Some of these eventually find their way into a list, while others wind up as paragraphs in my fiction. Basically all of my works evolve through a process of accumulation. The words and phrases in them are what I happen to think of while walking or reading or tending bar or whatever, and then I write them down. For example, here is the envelope that preceded my poem "A Few Preferences." It is empty now, but the elements of the poem originally all accumulated on slips of paper that were "filed" in this envelope. And they are, as you've indicated, highly selected. I gathered material for my first book of fiction, *Olt*, in the same way. The procedure is the same in prose as in poetry.

SG: What's involved in the way this "process of accumulation" evolves?

KG: When I first started writing this way in Mexico City, I would make lists of what I would describe as "strong words"—good solid nouns, like volcano, moon, girl, beach, tiger, planet. Eventually I would have a list of maybe twenty words. Then I would accumulate another list of twenty words. By matching these two lists alongside one another, I could make pairs of random words; and if I moved the page down one line, I would have a different matching. I did this for many hours. It's what a cartoonist friend of mine once described as a system of creative thought, a way to get your mind moving outside the familiar patterns.

LM: That sounds like what Brion Gysin and William Burroughs were experimenting with in their fold-in and cut-up methods.

KG: I didn't hear about the cut-up method until long afterward. The person who had the most influence on me was that cartoonist, who was a friend of mine when I was twenty-four and living in Mexico. He did cartoons for trade magazines (the kind you never see on newsstands) and he also had a lot of books on cartoonists. One of these books, by Herblock of the *Washington Post*, said that when you have to produce an editorial cartoon every day, you can't just wait for inspiration to strike if you must have the cartoon on the editor's desk in three hours. So Herblock had devised many systems to help him create his cartoons, systems to help get his imagination moving quickly into the sorts of peculiar realms he needed to do these cartoons. That book and my friend the cartoonist were profound influences on me when I was starting out as a writer. I began devising my own "systems of creative thought" right in that little town in Mexico. What I was looking for was a way to juxtapose words and concepts in interesting ways. The process starts when you join two words together that you have never seen joined together before. Sometimes a two-word bit of poetry results. Other times it can lead to sentences and even paragraphs.

LM: The surrealists and dadaists were doing something similar.

KG: Many people have done this sort of thing before me. Years after I arrived at my particular way of writing, I was amazed to discover that Lewis Carroll had worked in the same way. His method is described at the beginning of the preface to *Sylvie and Bruno*, a little-known book that is usually available only in his collected works. What Carroll says is so close to what I do that it's worth quoting: "As the years went on, I jotted down, at odd moments, all sorts of odd ideas, and fragments of dialogue, that occurred to me—who knows how?—with a transitory suddenness that left me no choice but either to record them then and there, or to abandon them to oblivion. Sometimes one could trace to their source these random flashes of thought—as being suggested by the book one was reading, or struck out from the 'flint' of one's own mind by the 'steel' of a friend's chance remark—but they had also a way of their own, of occurring, *à propos* of nothing—specimens of that hopelessly illogical phenomenon, 'an effect without a cause.'"[1]

SG: What is the *value*—literary or otherwise—of the texts that result from such an operation? Isn't it just a form of jibberish?

KG: At the beginning it *is* jibberish. It's simply raw material. But this is where I part company with a lot of the people connected with the St. Mark's Poetry Project, and even with Burroughs himself. They don't work hard enough once they have this raw material, so that what they write is often sprawling, and reads like an overwritten first draft. They don't cut and edit and organize it to put it into a readable literary form. Their standards are too low. At the other extreme is the so-called "New Formalism" in American poetry, which I find appalling. It is a doomed movement in the wrong direction, going backwards in time. Instead of

---

1. Lewis Carroll, Preface to *Sylvie and Bruno*, in *The Complete Literary Works of Lewis Carroll.* 1889; reprinted, New York: Random House (Modern Library Edition), n.d., 277–79.

reaching out to more readers, this kind of poetry is turning in upon itself. It will never have more than a very small audience.

LM: What about the argument that once you start working this raw material over in an effort to achieve a "finished" effect, you get farther and farther away from that initial flash?

KG: That's true. I'm looking for some kind of middle ground that allows me to retain the flash but still produces something interesting and readable.

SG: Where did you get the title for your book *Corroboree*?

KG: It's an Australian word that is never used in speech in this country, so you can pronounce it any way you want. In Australia it means some sort of wild, all-night tribal dance or celebration. I meant it to apply to language and writing—a wild dance or celebration of words and images.

LM: You've described *Corroboree* as a "book of nonsense and satire." The kind of nonsense you present in that book seems very different from what I would call *real* nonsense—the kind of thing you see in something like "Jabberwocky" or in works by people like Hugo Ball, where the words literally have no "sense" to them at all beyond a certain onomatopoetic quality.

KG: My attention span for that kind of demanding writing (Lewis Carroll and a few others excepted) is no more than thirty seconds. Oh, I can read the hard-core nonsense but choose not to. I find it unappealing to work that hard when I'm reading. Those kinds of absolutely bizarre images seldom mean anything—nothing interesting is happening when the words interact. It's a dead end in the same way that most of the New Formalism is—writing directed to a tiny readership of maybe a few hundred.

LM: You can see in Jack Kerouac's "The Essentials of Spontaneous Prose" that he (and most of the other Beat writers) were also interested in finding ways to uncover the energy and meanings of words that had been covered up by ordinary usage.

KG: Certainly the Beats were an influence once I began writing, which was right at the end of the Beat Generation. I graduated from Rensselaer Polytechnic Institute as an engineer in 1959 and went right out to San Francisco. I was twenty-one years old and spent a lot of time walking around North Beach. But there were several years when I wasn't really writing much. I was reading enormously and becoming interested in being a writer, but not actually doing much writing. I started graduate school at San Francisco State and came to Walter van Tilburg Clark, for whom I had a high regard. He was very patient with me, the rawest kind of creative writing student, right out of engineering school. I studied with him and George Price for one semester and then had to do my military service.

LM: Were there other writers or artists who influenced your sensibility early on?

KG: The French writers of the *nouveau roman*, whose works were just appearing when I was starting out. James Joyce, *Ulysses* in particular. *The Gallery* by John Horne Burns. *Nine Stories* by J. D. Salinger. *Fancies and Goodnights* by John Collier, a collection of fifty short stories, eight of which are superb. What I like about Collier is that he was a poet writing in the short story form, so in his stories there are marvelous nuggets of poetic prose and memorable dialogue. Lewis Carroll, already mentioned. Tennessee Williams wrote excellent prose—his introduction to *A Streetcar Named Desire* is a beautiful piece of writing. *Miss Lonelyhearts* by Nathanael West. *The Big Clock* by Kenneth Fearing. He was a poet, but wrote that one outstanding mystery. Hesse, Rilke, Orwell, Whitman, Hemingway. Nonfiction influences were Emerson, Thoreau, Montaigne, and Darwin (*The Voyage of the Beagle*, one of the great travel accounts of all time). *Enemies of Promise* by Cyril Connolly. My most prized book of poetry is *One Hundred Poems from the Chinese*, translated by Kenneth Rexroth. Two books about writing that were major influences are H. W. Fowler's *Modern English Usage* and H. L. Mencken's *American Language.*

SG: What persuaded you to turn to writing after being trained as an engineer?

KG: I had always been a reader, largely due to my mother. I'm the eldest of four children and grew up in an old-fashioned family system. My father worked in New York City, we lived in the suburbs in Westchester County, and my mother had little to do all day except for the housework, shopping, that kind of thing. I was her first child and she had the time to read to me a lot. It's a shame that this kind of one-to-one relationship doesn't happen as much anymore because so many mothers have jobs—there are nannies and day-care centers and so forth. I was very fortunate to have this relationship with my mother, who was naturally very interested in her first child. From an early age, she gave me book after book—picture books at first, but she also read to me. So in terms of my influences, she was the first, and a very important one. Right away I became interested in books as objects of joy and stimulation, as sources of pleasure. Imagine a small boy climbing up on a sofa and settling down with his children's book, *Babar* or *Pinocchio* or whatever. That early reading experience is invaluable because it opens up a whole other world for the child. Certainly it was that background, and also the excellent schools in Scarsdale, which eventually drew me to writing later on.

Much later, in December of 1958, while skiing in Vermont during a college vacation, I met a man about twenty years old who had sold a few short stories to various magazines. He was the first writer I had ever met, and because we were about the same age, I could relate to him. The authors I had seen on the jackets of books had always been older men. He had published a number of stories in places like *Redbook* for about three hundred dollars, which back in 1958 seemed like a lot of money to a college kid. At any rate, after talking with this young man, it took me about two years of thinking before I actually decided to learn to write. I listened carefully to what he told me, what size envelopes to use when I sent out manuscripts, and other idiotic questions, and he told me what he did, how he typed up his drafts, that you should always keep a carbon (in those days there wasn't any Xeroxing). Anyway, eventually I said to myself, "If he can do it, I can do it."

Another important step in my development was when I discovered modern literature at Rensselaer Polytechnic Institute, where the English Department was outstanding. I had a seminar in which we read Joyce and Conrad and other good writers, mostly Americans, like Faulkner, Hemingway, and Steinbeck. It was all enormously exciting for me. We also read a couple of Malcolm Cowley's books in the Viking Compass editions. His writing was first-rate and endeared the world of books and writers to me.

LM: Do you recall what most impressed you in reading these modernist writers?

KG: What I was most impressed with in those works was very literally the individual phrases and sentences. When I was reading a book I had no hesitation about marking it up, so I would go through these stories and novels and poems, and mark significant lines or phrases that appealed to me. I didn't care about the plot or the "lesson" in the work. I simply cared about the phrase or the sentence—occasionally the whole paragraph, but that was rare. To me these bits were the choicest part of the work, like gems found studded in rock.

When I began writing myself I dreamed of creating a work of fiction that could be *all* like those parts that I underlined. I envisioned a work that would be so compact, so dense, that a future reader, instead of underlining a couple of lines on every page, would be able to mark a line right down the margin. Everything would be worthwhile, the whole thing! That's what I was trying to do with *Olt*: create a book of this very condensed prose, sometimes more like poetry than prose. For me, *Olt* succeeds on this level, although I know that for most readers only portions of it are appealing.

SG: *Olt* is a very slim book. Did you have trouble getting it published?

KG: Oh, sure. For years I was asking people, "Why can't a book of fiction be the same size as a play or a book of poetry?" The manuscript was slightly over ten thousand words. It is remarkable that Marion Boyars agreed to publish it as a separate book. I called *Olt* a cycle of three stories, but for practical and commercial reasons the publishers called it a novel. In retrospect I think they did the right thing.

LM: Except for perhaps *The Interceptor Pilot*, none of your works are very plot-oriented.

KG: I don't believe in plots. A plot is obviously something that is made up by the author. It's artificial, an aspect of form, and for me the form of my books is almost an afterthought. The content always comes first.

SG: Couldn't you say that "characters" are equally artificial and made-up?

KG: Yes, but I find that when a character is described, there are parts of the description that are true and meaningful. But a plot is all fake. Of course, I understand why it is done—plot is the easiest way to move readers from one sentence to the next, to make them want to turn the page and keep reading. I understand that 98 percent of the readers out there love plot and want it and need it. They hang from minute to minute in a novel with a strong plot. I feel the same way when I see a movie, a thriller, for example. I can create plots if I want to, as I did in *The Interceptor Pilot*, and I might do so in the future. But it will be for the simple reason that I will then be able to reach a much larger audience.

LM: Obviously the problem facing a writer who isn't interested in plot is finding a way to move the reader through the text.

KG: One way to do this is by providing a simple time sequence, as I did in *Olt*. Another way is to supply a purely arbitrary organizational sequence, as I did in *The Volcanoes from Puebla*, where the titles of the 175 sections are arranged in alphabetical order. That gives the reader something. It is not much, perhaps, but it is something.

SG: Your work has received considerable attention in France while remaining relatively unknown in the States. Why do you think this is—simply the greater acceptance of the avant-garde over there? Or the fact that a work like *Olt* seems to have such affinities with the French "New Novel"?

KG: Probably it's a little of both. *The Interceptor Pilot* was well suited to be first published there. The French have a love of aviation, a previous involvement in Southeast Asia, and a familiarity with the cinematic novel. It has struck me as ironic that in a way I've done better over there than I have here. In France I've had features in magazines and there was even a symposium about my work at the Centre Pompidou. When the critics spoke I couldn't understand what they were saying, but for the sake of the audience I had to pretend that I did.

Afterwards the publisher, Christian Bourgois, took a large group out to a café and picked up the tab. Earlier he had sent me a round-trip ticket from New York to Paris so that I could come over for the publication of the book. He is a very charming man with a lot of style. One afternoon we walked from his office on the rue Garancière through the Place St.-Sulpice (he pointed out the café where André Breton hung out) to the Café de Flore, his favorite at the time. When he ordered a glass of Pouilly-Ladoucette, the white wine of the Flore, I said to the waiter, "I'll have the same." That was the smartest thing I did in Paris.

LM: Did you start out with the idea that *The Interceptor Pilot* would actually be a film?

KG: Yes. I got the idea about the time the book starts, in 1966. I used to be a pilot, you know, and I was only five years out of the Navy, and I was seeing all these headlines about fighter planes. I was married at the time and my mother-in-law had a summer place up in Canada, on a little island in Georgian Bay. We used to go up there for a few weeks in the summertime. Every day someone took a motorboat and went in to the mainland to get the mail and the newspaper and a bag of groceries. The book started when I saw the headline (which I'll never forget), "Johnson Orders Bombing of North Vietnam." I couldn't believe what was happening. I had no politics at all in high school and college, mostly because I grew up in the Eisenhower era; but I soon became very political. The House Committee on Un-American Activities conducted hearings in San Francisco's City Hall. I wasn't part of the demonstrations that resulted from those hearings, but I had some friends who were there. They told me what had happened, the violence with the cops and the fire hoses. But when I read about it in the papers the next day, the report was totally different, as though the demonstrators, who were peaceful, were at fault. Of course I believed my friends. Why would they lie to me? Meanwhile what I read in the papers, what had gone out on the wire services to the rest of the country, was completely different, a fabricated story. I was astounded, and that event was the beginning of my political awareness. I was also interested in what was happening in Cuba at the time, the stupidity of the U.S. policy, which left Fidel Castro no choice but to seek help from the Soviet Union. The election was also taking place that year. So my political awareness didn't start until 1960. The Eisenhower era was definitely over.

At any rate, I started *The Interceptor Pilot* by writing all the parts of it at once. When I write up the elements that precede a first draft, I frequently use a scissors. I would never write a novel by starting with the first sentence and then going all the way through and ending up with the last sentence. With *The Interceptor Pilot* I immediately sketched out the characters and wrote some of the key lines of dialogue. I started with the Vietnam scene, then the University of Colorado scene, then a couple of flashbacks, then the New York and Paris scenes, the scenes aboard the aircraft carrier, and so on. I made separate running notes at the same time. There are really two types of writing that I do: the material itself, and notes about the book that I am writing. In effect, I produce two manuscripts. If I've published five books at this time, I've really written five books and five sets of working notes that accompany the books. These notes are for my eyes only. I make plans, jot down notes about the form and structure, muse about how I am going to do this or that.

SG: Early on were you still thinking of *The Interceptor Pilot* as being an actual film script?

KG: I thought of what I was doing as *describing a film*, not writing a manuscript. It is fiction that defers to the superiority of film in every paragraph. It was similar to a screen treatment; in a way it was a treatment elevated to a literary form. Someone later described it as "a film you read." A French critic called it *un film de poche* (a pocket film). After a week of intense effort, including a lot of scissoring and organizing, I had a manuscript of eight pages. Then I stopped getting ideas. I had reached the end of that stage of the project, so I put the manuscript away. It was a film idea, and I was vastly inexperienced in the literary world, let alone Hollywood and the film industry. My first story had been published in *Art and Literature* only a few months earlier, and I didn't yet have an agent. The idea for *Pilot* was excellent, but it required a more mature writer. I didn't know what to do with this weird manuscript, so I put it away.

In 1967 my wife and I moved out to California where we lived for about three years in Santa Monica and then in Palo Alto. When we came back to Manhattan, I rented a room at 32 Union Square, an artist's studio on the top floor with a skylight and everything, for only seventy-five dollars a month. *Olt* had just come out and *Lydia* was due to be published in a few months. I had nothing in particular to work on. As I was getting my notes and papers organized, I came across the eight-page manuscript, which I had almost forgotten. I read it and became very excited. Apparently it had been "cooking" in my subconscious during the three years in California. I started working on the manuscript again and wrote *The Interceptor Pilot* in eight months.

LM: Did you find it difficult to work with this sort of a form? Not only was it obviously different from the other work you had been doing but you must have felt you were working in a whole new literary territory.

KG: Attempting to transfer film to the typewritten page was a difficult, almost an impossible task. Every sentence was a struggle and a new challenge. For example, I decided to modify all the film directions in order to make the book accessible for the general reader. I had no guidelines to work with, no models to imitate. My conception of what I was doing changed several times. In the end I had a ninety-eight-page manuscript that was a weird kind of cinematic novel. But it seemed so readable to me, and so relevant. I had never seen anything like *The Interceptor Pilot* before, and neither had my agent.

It took me ten years to get the book published in the United States. This was regrettable because given the history of the Vietnam War, 1970 (when I finished it) would have been an ideal time for it to appear. It would have been another statement against the war, and perhaps widely reviewed. Even if the critics and book reviewers did not care for the style, the book would have given them an opportunity to express themselves on the war, which was an extremely timely subject. But the New York publishers wouldn't touch it because it was not a conventional war novel. It was "avant-garde," "experimental." The technique has an established tradition in French literature, but has seldom appeared in the United States. William Burroughs published a book about Dutch Schultz that is very similar in style, but look how long it took before publishers were willing to take a chance with Burroughs. Anyway, Gérard-Georges Lemaire eventually published a French translation at Flammarion in Paris in 1975; and Marion Boyars published it in England and the United States in 1980.

LM: Has your literary sensibility been influenced by other art forms, other media?

KG: Films are what Americans do best of all. It is a compromised form that is tainted by commerce, and ranks well below art, music, and literature. Nevertheless it is a major influence on my writing. When I see a good film, I am terribly envious that certain things can be done so well, so much easier, than they are in writing. This is especially true with dialogue. In a movie, you are actually hearing dialogue being spoken. And while people are talking in a movie, you see their faces and hear their distinctive accents, and the people talking are trained actors who deliver the dialogue in the proper way. If you look, you'll see that there is very little dialogue in my books—that's because I believe dialogue should be *heard* and not just read on the printed page. But nearly all the conventional novels you see in bookstores are filled with dialogue. Many of these books, of course, are basically nineteenth-century novels, which were also filled with dialogue. A hundred years ago, all that printed dialogue was justified, as there was no radio, film, or television that could present it better.

SG: This relates to what you say in *The Volcanoes from Puebla*: "With film and the proper soundtrack, used together with this book, I could have far better communicated my Mexican experience." But surely there are some things about experience that can be communicated better through writing than through any other medium.

KG: Sure. One important way that something on the printed page is not second best is that something in a book will last in a person's mind, much longer than if he had seen it in a movie. Even if you see a wonderful PBS documentary about Mexico, by the next month it has faded from your memory. With a book, though, you can always pick it up after a time interval and read that section over again. A third reading, after another time interval, and you definitely have it (psychologists say that it usually takes three repetitions over time to really learn or remember something).

What frightens me about all these kids who grow up with television is that they don't really have much in their heads except for millions of vague, nonverbal impressions. Another advantage of using language as your artistic medium is that the printed page requires a more active response on the part of readers—they have to use their imaginations and mental faculties more thoroughly to transform the symbols into words and then make these words make sense, whereas a person watching TV or a movie is more passive, the brain is simply not working as hard. Rilke says something in *Letters to a Young Poet* that strikes me as being appropriate to what we're talking about: "People have . . . oriented all their solutions toward the easy and toward the easiest side of the easy; but it is clear that we must hold to what is difficult."[2]

LM: Should writers apply what Rilke is saying by making the process of reading their works difficult—maybe because many aspects of reality are difficult to understand and relate to?

KG: Rilke was speaking in general terms, not specifically about reading and writing. The way one lives one's life is what he was really referring to. It's one's total existence that needs to be made difficult and challenging. Unfortunately, authors who aim for this type of engagement in their works usually have few readers because too many people are basically lazy. Readers, especially in today's electronic world, don't want to work to engage their imaginations. They want to sit back, turn on the tube, and be entertained. In some ways television is the devil's invention. I much prefer radio and tapes. To people who claim to have no time, I say: get rid of your TV. They usually look at me as though they've just received a death sentence.

That Rilke quote is also applicable to all the young people today who are enrolling in creative writing programs. It all seems so easy: to become a writer, you simply choose the right school. But there's no substitute for the long, hard, unaided search to find your own voice. Rilke would have been the first to agree that what's required to become a writer is the opposite of easy.

---

2. Rainer Maria Rilke, *Letters to a Young Poet*, trans. M. D. Herter Norton (New York: W. W. Norton, 1934; rev. ed. 1954), p. 53.

LM: In an earlier interview you agreed with a comment made that your work often seemed to have more to do with photography, drawing, and painting than it did with, say, music. Is there any sense in which you feel your writing attempts to create an equivalent surface texture to what we find in the visual arts?

KG: Maybe so. I've always felt a deep kinship with artists—for instance, that cartoonist friend of mine whom I mentioned earlier. I could have been an artist at one time—I was the class artist in grade school—but something happened when I was eleven or twelve that drew me away from painting and drawing. I don't know what it was, possibly the negative influence of my classmates and the absence of encouragement. But I still feel that I could have been very comfortable with a life as an artist instead of a writer.

LM: Most reviews of your books wind up saying something to the effect that these books are "devoid of any personal or moral judgment." That seems basically incorrect, not only in regard to books that are obviously full of fairly explicit moral judgments (like *The Volcanoes from Puebla* and *The Interceptor Pilot*), but also even in a book like *Olt*.

KG: *Olt* has been frequently described as simply the recording of experience, one thing after another being presented with no apparent selection (that, of course, is entirely wrong—a great deal of selection went into that book). I suppose *The Interceptor Pilot*, at least at first glance, more closely fits what those reviewers are suggesting. That book has been said to be a "double remove" from the experience it's describing (a novel would be a single remove, whereas a cinematic novel would be twice removed). But I didn't consciously write that book to create a sense of being removed from what I was describing, either morally or from any other standpoint. Actually, the reasons for this seeming lack of judgment in *The Interceptor Pilot* are not that complicated. There is no obvious judgment in the book simply because when you are describing a film, there is no place for it. Take a look at the text and try to find a place where moral judgment could be inserted. I suppose some moral judgments are made clear in the way some of the characters talk about the war (like the French woman and the journalist), and there is a moral judgment implied in my presentation of Commander Richards, who is shown to be very pro-war. I had certain viewpoints I wanted to air, but I didn't want to write a political tract. So I decided to go right down the middle of the road by presenting both sides of the Vietnam War.

SG: While you were working on *The Interceptor Pilot*, were you consciously aiming at creating a commentary on (or contrast to) the epic blockbuster war novel/film that your story seems to refuse to tell?

KG: Absolutely. Readers should be able to tell in a few seconds that they are reading a traditional war novel by observing the way the writing is on the page: the dialogue, descriptions, the way characters evolve as "heroes" and "bad guys"—the same fictional techniques that were being used to tell war experiences a hundred years ago. On one level, *The Interceptor Pilot* was a statement against the conventional nineteenth-century novel.

LM: Beneath the seemingly objective and random descriptions we find in *Olt* about what the character is seeing, we gradually begin to get a sense not only of what this character is like but also of the world he lives in. *Olt* seems to be a very alienated person living in a very alienating environment—which, again, is hardly a nonjudgmental viewpoint.

KG: Robert Olt is alienated, very much so. *Olt* was formed in the early 1960s, a time that created all sorts of alienation, so it's not surprising that alienation is one of its key characteristics. And yet not even a single one of the many reviews mentioned alienation.

SG: You said in the *Gargoyle* interview that Robert Olt is "the transformed author, both a mask and a revelation." Can we then assume that in a certain basic sense you *are* Olt?

KG: Certainly to the extent that the book is composed of these tiny "nuggets" of writing I had been collecting, you could say that it conveys a sense of who I am, what I was interested in at the time I was writing it. I also lived pretty much the way Robert Olt did in the book. I set it in a nonspecific American city because I wanted readers living in Boston, Chicago, New York, et cetera, to be able to adapt the book to their own cities. But the city I was using as a model was San Francisco, the first real city I ever lived in. After graduating from college when I was twenty-one, I had a wonderful year living there in a little room that cost twenty-six dollars a month. I had lots of free time and the whole experience was glorious. As for the way the book was written, it was really a device which permitted the presenting of all those striking, unusual images I had been accumulating.

LM: In the *Gargoyle* interview, you also said that "characters are essentially false, the only character is the author." Does this mean that you aren't interested in "inventing" characters?

KG: Constructing characters who are totally invented, not like me at all, doesn't seem to be the way I work. For example, if you look at my story "Greenbaum, O'Reilly & Stephens," I should confess that there is a little bit of me in every character. Sam, the complete New Yorker, the honest Polish cop, the woman lawyer (Kathy O'Reilly), her tough Irish father, the widowed accountant, the hardworking Italian landlord, Bob, the athlete who loves history, the little old lady who lives out on Brighton Beach—they're not me in any literal sense, but there's something of who I am in all of them. That's pretty much been true with everything I've ever written.

LM: What were the origins of *The Volcanoes from Puebla?*
KG: I was twenty-four when I first went down to Mexico in 1962 to live, and was married at the time to an artist. I was out of the Navy and we just wanted a cheap place to live. We had heard a lot about Mexico while living in San Francisco, mostly from two artist friends, and it sounded very appealing. I had never lived outside the United States, and going to Mexico sounded like a good idea. I went down first on a motorcycle, kind of an exploration. I found a place to live and my wife came a few weeks later and we set up a household. At the time I hadn't written anything yet, and had no intention of ever writing a book about Mexico. But I already had my pocket notebooks and wrote a lot about what I saw and felt and thought, especially about my travels riding around on the motorcycle.

After a year I came back from Mexico with about a dozen notebooks, which wound up sitting in a box for five years. Then when I was living in Palo Alto on the Stegner Fellowship, some free time came along. At this point I had written my first two books and was looking for something to write next. I started transcribing my notebooks because I felt that something would come from them. I produced a lot of new material during the transcription. Sometimes a sentence in my notebook would remind me of what happened, and then I would go on to write a whole paragraph or two. When I was finished, I had many pages of material. And I thought, "Hey, I've got the beginnings of a book about Mexico here." I scissored the transcriptions, classified them into envelopes with subject titles, and then wrote up the material in an obvious, efficient form that appealed to me—individual sections on the various subjects. I ended up with a sixty-five-page fragmentary manuscript. Several years later, when I was back in New York, that manuscript got me a contract and an advance, which was encouragement to take another long trip to Mexico for more material.

SG: What gave you the idea of structuring the book along an alphabetical arrangement? This is a very peculiar way to organize a book because the headings appear so arbitrary.
KG: The efficiency of the form appealed to me. As with all my work, the material came first and the form worked itself out later. I found, for example, that I would have a lot to write about mangoes, two or three pages. I know it is hard to believe that anyone can write that much about mangoes, but I could. When you are living in Mexico you discover that mangoes are very important, not just the fruit but the trees also. So two or three pages is not much at all. It didn't occur to me to present this material as part of a time sequence because my notes about mangoes were combined from dozens of separate notebook entries that I had made over long stretches of time.

In real day-to-day travel there is a lot that is not interesting to read about. For example, the trip I took from Guaymas to San Blas, with stops along the way at Culiacán and Los Mochis, was not all that interesting. So I removed what happened during the trip from the time sequence, edited the material, and combined it with similar experiences that provided the basis for miniature essays on specific topics. If something happened to me in Mexico City, but was the kind of thing that would have taken place more logically in Oaxaca, I set it in Oaxaca.

Eventually I had to decide how, then, I was going to put these pages about, say, "Mangoes," into a book. Since the section title was "Mangoes," I put it after "Machete" and before "Margaritas," in an alphabetical order of the section titles. Actually I arrived at that order by pure accident. After I had written all my 175 sections and was organizing everything into the beginnings of a first draft, I put everything into alphabetical order so that I could find each section in the manuscript. It was at that point that I saw this was a logical method of organizing the material that worked. The alphabetical order gives it unity, structure, and a sense of progression. It also provides easy reference.

LM: You once wrote me and said that it was only after talking with certain writer friends, and then reading Charles Caramello's essay about *The Volcanoes from Puebla* in his critical study, *Silverless Mirrors*, that you came to realize that your book should actually be seen as a form of fiction rather than nonfiction.

KG: Right. The book is the account of a young American living for the first time in a Third World country and being profoundly changed by the experience. I definitely thought that *Volcanoes* was nonfiction after I finished it. And so did the publisher, Marion Boyars (who has reissued the book in paperback as fiction). What people like Charles Caramello and my friend Michael Stephens suggested to me was that what I had been doing all along—changing the names and characters, changing where things took place, combining episodes and observations when that seemed a more credible way to present something—was actually more like writing an avant-garde novel than writing a conventional travel book. Caramello described it accurately as a postmodern *Bildungsroman*.

SG: Are there any contemporary writers you feel particular affinities with?

KG: I identify with those who write *both* poetry and fiction, especially those who write both innovative fiction and poetry in open forms. I get a big kick out of Charles Bukowski's total irreverence towards institutions like *The New Yorker*. You know I admire Evan Connell for the independent road he has taken. Like me, he has stayed away from the crippling influence of academia. Ferlinghetti is another iconoclast, and very political. But in general it seems pathetic that a country of this size and importance has so few living poets and fiction writers who are truly outstanding. For years I've been asking myself: Why is that? We are much better at producing men of letters like Edmund Wilson and Kenneth Rexroth and Guy Davenport. Some say that nothing more can be expected from this culture and society, that we have exactly what we deserve. But the United States has millions of sensitive, intelligent people who know the truth about popular culture and who are eager to read good books. Perhaps the profound changes that are ahead of us will produce the proper conditions for a more vital literature.

A Sudden Obsession
An Interview with Marianne Hauser

Larry McCaffery
Sinda Gregory

All my life I have been called a fraud and a liar. A few of my detractors went so far as to spread the rumor that I was never born. But if I should die, as is bound to happen, those very same people are likely to accuse me of trickery all over again.
— *Prince Ishmael*

Marianne Hauser's life reads like a story she's spent eighty years dreaming up. Born and raised in Strasbourg, Alsace, dancing on graves to prove her mettle while World War I and epidemics roared through; at seventeen, fluent in German and French, hired by a Swiss newspaper to write and travel through China and India; at twenty-six, adopting the United States and finding a home for her voice in English. After several years involved in the artistic and intellectual life of New York City, Hauser moved with her husband and son to Kirksville, Missouri, where she spent the next decade as a faculty wife at a state college where Frederic Kirchberger taught music. In the 1960s, Hauser left the Midwest and her marriage, moved back to New York, and plunged into the cultural and sexual revolution. As a writer and a teacher at Queens College and New York University, she participated in the excitement and derangement of the times, the anarchy of her own spirit responding to the radical transformations happening all around.

Nearly three decades later, there is still something wild and sexy about Marianne Hauser—about her person and her imagination—that has survived the intervening years that have left too many people saying no to everything but money and invasions. Her fiction has evolved over the last five decades to a remarkable degree. The precise, classical prose of *Dark Dominion* (1947) has loosened, and Hauser has increasingly incorporated American idioms, slapstick, and absurdist humor; she has also been more adventurous in devising experimental formal strategies suited for portraying her sense of the permeability of dream and waking reality. The obsessions explored in *Dark Dominion*—the role of the imagination in shaping one's response to life, the difficulty in inhabiting a coherent "self"—continue through her next three books, *The Choir Invisible* (1958), which is set in a small town in the Midwest, *Prince Ishmael* (1963), a fictional account of the Kaspar Hauser legend which was nominated for a Pulitzer Prize, and a collection of stories, *A Lesson in Music* (1964).

Yet while thematic concerns remain somewhat consistent, the language, style, and tone of her work has undergone significant transformations. Her more recent novels, *The Talking Room* (1976), *The Memoirs of the Late Mr. Ashley: An American Comedy* (1986), and *Me and My Mom* (1993) all display a command of American lingoes and cultural references that range effortlessly from urban to rural, straight to gay, high brow to low, all the voices a chorus of pathos, absurdity, lyricism, and beauty that sing the bittersweet song of the America Hauser found. From her earliest work, Hauser has explored how dreams, the unconscious, the irrational affect our perception of the "real"; but with her last three novels (as well as her more recent short stories), this notion is no longer so much an element of "theme," but rather finds its expression as a fully integrated aspect of her style. Thus, to enter her recent fiction is to find oneself in an unsettling landscape where the strange becomes familiar and the familiar, strange—a realm of people and events, associations and "rightness" that we sense in dreams just after we awaken. Partly this effect comes from connections that make no logical sense being brought together with Hauser's powerful and evocative particularity—her ability to ground her fiction in details that are vivid and sensual—but it arises too from the playfulness of her language, her willingness to let go of the linear in favor of something wilder and less predictable.

The following interview was conducted at Marianne Hauser's Manhattan apartment during several taped sessions. Throughout our conversations, Hauser talked animatedly—her voice still bears a trace of the Alsatian region she left behind for good sixty years ago—while sitting in the lotus position she has favored since taking up t'ai chi several years ago. In response to our questions, Hauser improvised stories and explanations that continually digressed, progressed, and regressed in a whirl of laughter, puns, free association, and illuminating anecdote. For

Marianne Hauser, the next word, just like the next moment, comes best unannounced by context or convention.

* * *

Marianne Hauser: Selected Bibliography

Novels and Collections

Indisches Gaukelspiel (*Shadow Play in India*). Vienna: Zinnen, 1937.
Dark Dominion. New York: Random House, 1947.
The Choir Invisible. New York: McDowell, Obolensky, 1958. Published in England under original title, *The Living Shall Praise.* London: Gollancz, 1957.
A Lesson in Music. Austin: University of Texas Press, 1964.
Prince Ishmael. New York: Stein and Day, 1963. Reprinted, Los Angeles: Sun and Moon Classics Series, 1991.
The Talking Room. New York: Fiction Collective, 1976.
The Memoirs of the Late Mr. Ashley: An American Comedy. Los Angeles: Sun and Moon Press, 1986. Trans. in German, Suhrfkamp, 1992.
Collected Stories. Los Angeles: Sun and Moon Press, 1993.
Me and My Mom. Los Angeles: Sun and Moon Classics, 1993.

Uncollected Stories

"The Colonel's Daughter." *The Tiger's Eye* 3 (March 1948): 21–34.
"The Rubber Doll." *Mademoiselle* (1951).
"The Sun and the Colonel's Button." *Botteghe Oscure* 12 (Fall 1953): 255–72.
"The Seersucker Suit." *Carleton Miscellany* 9 (Fall 1968): 2–14. Reprinted in *American Made: New Fiction from the Fiction Collective*, ed. Mark Leyner, Curtis White, and Thomas Glynn, 93–106. New York: Fiction Collective, 1986.
"Heartlands Beat." *Fiction International* 18, 1 (Spring 1988): 11–22.

Nonfiction

"Marrakesh: Descent into Spring." *Harper's Bazaar*, 3054 (May 1966): 188–203.
"Mimoun of the Mellah." *Harper's Bazaar*, 3061 (December 1966): 114–82.
"My Life So Far." Autobiographical essay. *Contemporary Authors.* Detroit: Gale Research, 1990.

Essays, Reviews, Interviews, and Miscellaneous Commentary about Hauser's Work

"Marianne Hauser" (unsigned entry). *Encyclopedia of Short Fiction.* Salem, MA: Salem Press, 1981.
McCaffery, Larry. "The Fiction Collective." *Contemporary Literature* 20 (Winter 1978): 99–115.

McCaffery, Larry, and Sinda Gregory. "An Interview with Marianne Hauser."
Mississippi Review—Interview Issue, 20, 1 and 2 (1991): 120–30.
Morris, Alice S. "Marianne Hauser." *Dictionary of Literary Biography 1983*, 238–42. Detroit: Gale Research Company, 1984.
Nin, Anaïs. "Anaïs Nin on Marianne Hauser." *Rediscoveries*, ed. David Madden, 115–20. New York: Crown Publishers, 1971.
Tytell, John. "666 Words on Marianne Hauser." *Critical Ninth Assembling*, ed. Richard Kostelanetz. Brooklyn, NY: Assembling Press, 1979.

*   *   *

LARRY MCCAFFERY: You published your first novel, *Shadow Play in India*, nearly sixty years ago. Could you tell us a bit about the circumstances that produced it?

MARIANNE HAUSER: I wrote *Shadow Play* when I was twenty-three or twenty-four. I had done travel pieces in India, and this novel, which was my first "serious" novel, was born there and came out of that experience. It appeared with some obscure underground press in French, and with Zinnen in Vienna. A few years ago, John Hall Wheelock, a senior editor at Scribner's, wanted me to translate it for publication. But I couldn't do it. I am such an idiot. I do things you wouldn't believe—like burning the first draft of *Dark Dominion*. Anyway my early stuff isn't worth much. It was silly, childish work, you see. I started writing young but I grew up late up here [points to her head]. I was smart, but without values as to my writing. In fact, I didn't want to *be* a writer. I wanted to be a dancer or a missionary because both get to travel a lot. My dream was to travel all over the world.

SINDA GREGORY: Why did you come to the States the first time?

MH: I came on assignment from a Swiss newspaper, the same paper for which I had written feuilletons on Asia. (A "feuilleton" is comparable to a vignette or column.) I was in my early twenties, an age when you were unlikely to get a responsible job, not in those days! But I was lucky to meet the late Dr. Kleiber, literary editor of a Basle paper, progressive, with an eye for new talent, and high standards. My feuilletons were not "journalistic" in the accepted sense. They were centered in specific, personal observations. And they taught me craft. I'd never written more than one draft of anything in those earlier juvenile works. Now it took me all week to finish a piece of maybe three typed pages. Traveling and writing for a living—and I wound up getting to visit magical places like China, India, and Egypt—I learned to organize my work, to cut, to revise.

SG: So when you first came to the United States, it was for a specific assignment and not because you intended to stay?

MH: God, no! This was the last place where I wanted to live. It's the language that caused me to stay. You might say I fell hopelessly in love with it. Not that English was new to me. At home, my parents often entertained friends from the States or Britain. And when I was little, I had a British nanny for a while. In school, I found I did my best compositions in English. Still, I wasn't aware how strong the affinity was until my first year in New York. I was suddenly hit by a sense of urgency: I absolutely must write in English. And that realization literally forced me to stay on, indefinitely. I once read somewhere that English was ideal for either a perfunctory business letter or great poetry. I agree. English lends itself to great variety of expression. It can be concise or flexible. It's wonderful for verbal acrobatics. The sound can get you drunk. I used to read out loud to myself, indiscriminately, the tabloids, Ford Madox Ford, Conrad, what have you. My small furnished room was high up on Riverside Drive and 116th Street, with a broad view of the Hudson and Bear Mountain, and I'd sit by the window and read to that view. The view was my audience.

SG: That sounds like the view from *Dark Dominion*. Was that where you began that book?

MH: The actual writing of *Dark Dominion* came later, but the *need* to write that novel came out of there after a brief, intense affair with a psychotherapist. He was an eternal patient of Otto Rank, and it was via his analysis with Rank that he broke off with me. You can see how these facts relate to the plot of *Dark Dominion*, at least superficially. In most parts, the specifics you find in that book are substantially reversed. When my lover split, I decided to kill myself. There followed a comedy of confusion—it took me forever to find my pulse, I had to search for a sharp razor, I wished to die in a hot tub, but the communal bathroom was occupied! So there I was, waiting for my bath, when an unexpected phone call finally rescued me from further delays. It's clear to me now that my "suicide attempt" was a pose I had to assume to save face. I'd never been the loser in love games before, and suicide seemed like the obvious pose for a young lady to adopt in such circumstances. In *Dark Dominion*, Beatrice's suicide results from a vastly different situation. She had sacrificed her ego when she married her analyst. And whatever face she may have saved was destroyed by a double betrayal—her lover's and, by indirection, her husband's.

LM: In *Dark Dominion* you present a psychiatrist who doesn't dream— which is why he is particularly interested in dreams as an alternative form of language. In a lot of your books, there is an implicit criticism of logical, rational discourse, an ongoing interest in waking logic versus dream logic.

MH: I can't make that distinction. In this space age, it seems futile to think in terms of dreams and reality. *Ever.* It is all one experience. Perhaps that's why I have no faith in Freudian dream surgery. I never underwent analysis and trust I never will. *Dark Dominion* was written without my having read Freud (not even his *Interpretation of Dreams*) or any other soul technicians. Yet some reviewers have praised the novel for "the author's clinical know-how." Funny. Actually, though, after I'd done the first draft I was worried over my lack of background in these matters, so I gave the manuscript to Rank to read for "mistakes." And he found none. He said an artist knows the human psyche by instinct. Still, it took me many further drafts before I was satisfied.

LM: Have you been approaching writing in recent works differently or is the process still basically the same as it was in the books you were writing back in the 1940s and 1950s?

MH: One develops. My writing has become freer, more like myself. I got rid of a certain formality in style. The big break came with "One Last Drop for Poor Abu"—a short story from my collection *A Lesson in Music.* In the mouth of Abu, the formality becomes comedy, a guise to be undercut. I let my humor work for my writing. I had learned to play with the language.

SG: Was this break in your style the result of something happening in your life, or was it mostly just an evolution in your fictional technique— say, a greater familiarity with the language that allowed you to play with it more easily?

MH: Both. I was going through a lot of personal changes in my life that must have somehow seeped into my work. For one thing, after many separations, my marriage to Fred came to an end. It had been a long and strange marriage, but once I had made the break I had an exhila- rating sense of freedom—a feeling (or maybe a fantasy) that I didn't have to account to anybody or anything. This sense of independence certainly affected all the writing I've done since, although it's impossible to say exactly how.

LM: The wider social and political disruptions of the sixties are often seen as providing an impetus for the various radical features associated with "postmodern fiction." Was this at least partly true for you?

MH: Absolutely. The sixties and early seventies were among the most decisive years in my life. The Vietnam War and the political/social up- heavals had an enormous personal impact on me and consequently on my work. The hippies confirmed my own lifelong distrust of the bour- geois establishment. Though I was middle-aged, it was only normal for me to become part of the youth movement. At Queens, where I taught, I joined my students in sit-ins and peace demonstrations. And my son was heavily involved in the 1968 uprising at Columbia University. So I got pretty thoroughly into the struggle for what we naively hoped would be a juster society. But naive or not, those experiences were bound to change the way writers were feeling about a lot of things that seemed part of the "established order"—including books.

LM: Was your work influenced by any of the postmodern writers who were emerging during that period—Barthelme, Coover, Pynchon, and so on?

MH: I went to poetry readings in those days, but I wasn't reading much fiction. Paul Krassner's *Realist*, for instance, or Abbie Hoffman left a sharper imprint on my mind than did the fiction of that time. I am not too aware of what's happening as to new trends in literature. To speak of my early readings, my mother was very well read and so I knew Tolstoy and Ibsen and Flaubert, et cetera, but I wasn't an observant reader. I went to a horrible school and so I skipped classes all the time. My son is probably more responsible than anyone else for deepening my understanding of literature. Partly this had to do with my going to those poetry readings with him and his hippie friends in the 1960s, when he was at Columbia. But his education of me started when he was a baby, where I read him things I had missed as a child in Europe—nursery rhymes, all that stuff at first, and then later things like *Great Expectations* (I had refused to read Dickens in school), the *Iliad*, and the *Odyssey*. It was only while he was attending college at Kenyon and Columbia and bringing home these learned papers on literature that I came to see how people could *talk* about literature. In school I had skipped all that.

LM: Were there really no writers you would point to as having affected your work, either early or more recently?

MH: Perhaps Stendhal, in my early youth. And always Gogol. And certainly Beckett. The way books "influence" other writers is often a matter of coincidence. Every great writer leaves a distinctive mark, but even a minor book may become substantial if it hits the right key at the right time. My involvement with Kaspar Hauser may be linked to a childhood story, Hector Malot's *Sans famille*. It's the tale of a foundling who journeys all over France with an old street singer and his little circus of performing animals. It's a real tearjerker, but with truly fine descriptions of the French countryside. And of course there is a happy ending—the street singer turns out to be a once world famous tenor, and the foundling, a poor boy, is reclaimed by his rich and noble parents in Italy. I loved that book. I still do.

SG: Influences aside, who are the writers that you especially admire?

MH: That's a tough question because my taste never stops changing. Twenty, thirty years ago I was deep into Henry James and Faulkner, to single out the two writers I loved for their complex and lucid style. I still respect those qualities, though my enthusiasm has cooled. Change in tastes is a positive thing. One thing that hasn't changed for me, though, is my admiration for Melville. *Moby-Dick* remains for me the greatest book in the entire world.

LM: What about more recent writers?

MH: Beckett, of course. But he is futuristic, not recent. To me he is a visionary—superior to any contemporary writer I've read. And Nabokov. I'm still enthralled by *Lolita*. And by *Pale Fire*—that phenomenal tour de force. I'm still hoping to finish *Ada* some day. But his game playing at the expense of the reader puzzles and bores the hell out of me. Again, it's possible I may change my mind, but I doubt I'd ever turn away from *Lolita*, his crazy, wonderful evocation of America—the stars, the bars, the endless motels and the endless roads and the landscape. If there are others, great new writers I've missed, I'm confident they'll come my way eventually. I've never bothered to "keep up," as I said earlier. And now, in my old age, I refuse to spend time on fads. When students ask for my opinion on this or that best-seller, I must claim ignorance. Of course, you have to remember that I spent many years in a small town in the Midwest, light years removed from the literary cocktail or P.E.N. Club scene. I'm sure it hurt me businesswise, but as a writer, I learned; I found time or space to improve.

LM: Is there any consistency about what gets you started with a story or a novel?

MH: There is a sudden obsession. An image; something that is based on photoreality, the mirror. I'm not talking about parapsychology, but the image persists, pursues me; it becomes very centralized until I feel almost physically pushed into writing. I have to feel driven in order to write at all, which may be the reason my output is small.

SG: Could you talk about the particular "photoreality" that eventually compelled you to start work on *The Talking Room*?

MH: Rather than "photoreality," I should perhaps say "mirror image": a recurring symbol in *The Talking Room*. I'm androgynous by nature, and the mirror fits the lesbian theme. For a long time I'd hoped to find the impetus to integrate Sapphic love (one manifestation of many different loves) into a novel. The impetus finally came about by way of a child, a little boy. Two lesbian women, both good friends of mine, had adopted him. Shortly after my divorce from Fred and my move from the Midwest back to New York, I was for some weeks a guest at their house. An old brownstone near the waterfront. The place and the silent, thin little boy they had adopted were the catalyst. Obviously, there's no similarity whatever between that real child and fat, thirteen-year-old B. Nor between my two marvelous friends and B's tough "aunt" or her crazy "mom." The *neighborhood*, the *waterfront*—that's where the novel germinated. And the *idea* of adoption into an unconventional household stirred up quite unrelated childhood memories. But how all these things come together in the process of my actual writing can't be rationally explained. It just happens. A few months later, when I was visiting a cousin in Paris, I wrote most of the first draft of *The Talking Room* in a matter of weeks. The speed, unusual for me, was maybe produced by the bottle of good red wine she put on my desk each morning. In those days I still drank a lot, though never when I was writing. As my son puts it: I must have been born with a natural "high." At any rate, *The Talking Room* was born in the bottle.

LM: And I take it that in this case the bottle was an agreeable midwife?

MH: Drinking made the whole initial writing process of *The Talking Room* seem *wild*—and a lot of rewriting was required later on. The first paragraph of the draft is nearly identical with the final version, but outside of that fluke, the rewrite took reams of paper. I'd never written at such a fast tempo as I did in Paris, except perhaps as a kid. I wasn't *smashed* while I was writing, you understand—just drunk enough to keep my brain in an agreeable haze. In which state I did about three-quarters of the opus-to-be. On the flight home I looked over the disheveled pages and I was appalled but for some reason didn't destroy the manuscript. In New York, I stashed it away and started on some short story. There's no telling if I'd ever have returned to the novel if my longtime friend, the late William Kienbusch, had not urged me to. He was a great painter and one of my most discerning critics. So it was upon his insistence that I let him read the draft which I had already dismissed as a piece of junk. And he disagreed with me. He felt sure it would be one of my best novels. It just needed work. Most of the final rewrite was done with my leg in a cast after a busted ankle.

SG: *The Talking Room* is one of the most feminine books (as opposed to "feminist") I've ever read. All those recurring images—the moon, water, rings, blood—make up this unifying logic that is remarkably coherent and yet still so mysterious. How conscious were you in the writing process that you were turning again and again to those images?

MH: The writing process just seems to happen. Usually my writing is not "designed." I don't plan recurrent patterns or images—not even the plot. For example, when I start out, I don't have an ending in mind. With *The Talking Room*, the beginning was there. Complete. But not the end. In fact, I considered various endings. I thought to finish with a masked ball. But I had no blueprint. I didn't even know ahead of time about the disappearance, the constant disappearances of J and her constant returns. The "movements" formed themselves in the process of writing.

SG: Like several other contemporary artists, you've obviously been haunted by the Kaspar Hauser myth. Eventually you even wrote your own version of the myth in your novel *Prince Ishmael.* What got you interested in pursuing this story in your own work?

MH: My preoccupation with Kaspar Hauser started as a puppet play. My uncle, this remarkable man who influenced my life in so many ways, was the first to acquaint me with the legend. He gave me a book about Kaspar—a collection of documents, police records, letters, et cetera, and I marked up the pages, underlining, making notes on the margin, question marks. I totally identified with his fate. When he took his first bow as a puppet, his adversary was the devil, a real devil with horns.

LM: What was the source of this strong sense of identification?

MH: Perhaps initially I identified with him simply because we shared the same name. Hauser is a common name, which may be the reason why it was given to him by whoever had let him out of his prison hole. Also, children of my generation were swamped with tales about Gypsies dropping a baby by a stranger's door. I know of many kids from solid, middle-class households who fantasized about being parentless. Perhaps it's a quest for a special self by rejecting one's parents. Even today a whole lot of middle-class kids can't imagine that their parents have sex. There must surely be countless reasons why I was captivated by the legend, though such "explications" are essentially foreign to my instincts as a writer. One can try to x-ray the motivations behind a book. But the author may be the least reliable interpreter.

LM: You return repeatedly in all your books to the idea of people's personality or persona as possibly being a fraud, an illusion. Why is that?

MH: Maybe because my own profession constantly requires me to be a fraud. Writers are frauds. There is no question that Plato was right. Artists pretend, we have to make people believe the illusions we create. The fraud, the double, fascinates me. You can find him repeatedly in my use of the *acteur manque*. Come to think of it, instead of fraud, I'd prefer: illusionist.

SG: I was curious about the fact that you so frequently use male narrators. Is your choice of male narrators maybe a way of distancing yourself from your material, putting on another mask, exploring another kind of self?

MH: In fiction, the author's gender is irrelevant to the narrator's. The point of view *should* be dictated by the theme. It wouldn't have occurred to me, for example, to tell the story in *Dark Dominion* from Beatrice's point of view. In many ways I find it difficult to adopt the persona of a grown-up woman. I could do the girl in *The Talking Room* easily because I have this basic childishness in me, but somehow telling something from the perspective of an adult is harder. But, really, I don't see my choice of male or female narrators as being essentially tied to my own "real" psychological makeup. To feel a person's character, you have to identify with it, yes; or to paraphrase Dostoyevsky, Raskolnikov is the killer he (Dostoyevsky) might have been. But perhaps we also explore a new self each time we write a new story. Besides, I'm convinced that *all* of us have both sexes inside (especially writers!). It's crazy how that's denied by most of our society, how desperate we are to keep our sexuality in simple categories when it's so enormously complicated. I see nothing weird about slipping into other personas, regardless of gender, though I'm afraid society is still suffering a hangover from overindulgence in realism or naturalism which demand a so-called unified narrative perspective—a concept which was exploded at the start of the century. Popular taste, of course, usually lags behind innovation. To me, the male perspective poses no more of an obstacle than any other focal point. As to distancing myself—one has to be distant from one's material *and* totally wrapped up in it. In writing, contradiction is the name of the game. Call it a magic trick. Without it, the work will be flat. That's how I see it. Flaubert achieved the trick most gloriously through *Madame Bovary*. But there are stranger examples from a more remote past. In La Fontaine's *Fables*, the birds and beasts, yes, even the fish address us convincingly. But to return from the animal kingdom to our own endangered species, the "choice" of male narrators for some of my novels is, once again, not really a choice. It *happens* because it's inseparably woven into the fabric of the whole.

SG: You subtitle *Mr. Ashley* "An American Comedy." Why do you think your books have gotten so much funnier? Your earlier writing was somewhat solemn, but now everything seems more open and wild and comic.

MH: As I get old, I see more and laugh more. And I think when you are old you are able to take in more, you learn and you change. One of the results of these changes is that I see now how funny or ridiculous many events are that I used to take very seriously.

SG: But I don't think that happens with most people—usually as they get older everything about them sort of shuts down, becomes less likely to change. And more serious.

MH: It's mostly a matter of genes—"designer genes," you might say. The comic has always been a part of me. I just get better.

LM: You spent a number of years living in the Midwest and South. This must have seemed like a radical change for you, but my experience has been that being forced to adapt to a very different environment often serves to stimulate our imaginations. I gather that this was partially true at least for you, so that Kirksville, Missouri [where Hauser lived for four years], partially inspired *The Choir Invisible* as well as your wonderful story, "Heartlands Beat." And maybe by now you feel more comfortable in this role of perpetual expatriate than most people would.

MH: Keep in mind: I was *born* an expatriate. I have no country, you see. I never had a country. Many Alsatians feel that way. But having no roots isn't necessarily a bad thing. To me, the move to the Midwest was an adventure into the unknown. Besides, I had no choice. Fred Kirchberger (then my pianist husband) had accepted a teaching job at the Northeast Missouri State College. We were picked up at the Quincy, Illinois, airport and driven to Kirksville, past those endless cornfields. I remember how our driver (a part-time farmer) pointed toward a shack in the corn and said with that Midwestern twang, "That's where the James Brothers hid out." I couldn't believe my ears and I cried, "What? How can this be possible? Not the James Brothers!?" And my son Michael, almost a first grader, piped in, "Where have you been? Jesse and Frank robbed every bank in Missouri." So much for my first recollection of the Show Me State.

What strikes me as odd in America—especially the Bible Belt and the South—is a certain narrowness, despite the vast spaces. You find provincialism in other countries, but the Puritan brand of provincialism you encounter here is unique. That pretense at Christian values and equal opportunities when the big buck is all that counts—it's hard to believe that the hypocrisy could quite be doubled anywhere else in the world. When I first arrived, I was shocked by the blatant discrimination against blacks in this "Land of the Free"; and by the phobia of socialism, the lack of political vision across the board. And that absurd Victorian reticence about sex, or the human anatomy in general. In the Midwest, and the South where I spent some years also, those traits—a sad denial of the self, really—surfaced even more directly. That solemn facade of democracy and human rights . . . you got to look behind it, to find— what? Maybe the National Rifle Association.

SG: You were a young child when World War I was taking place. Do you remember much about it, did it have much of an impact on you?

MH: I was four at the start of the war, and close to eight when the senseless mass murder finally stopped and the ominous peace treaty was ratified. We Alsatians were smack in the danger zone and so got the worst of the horror. Small children are extremely vulnerable to disaster. In "Allons Enfants" (the lead story of my collection *A Lesson in Music*) I have a seven year old tell of the war years. Though it's fiction, it is autobiographical in feeling. It gives you a good picture of what happened in those days—to me and my family. And to Strasbourg.

LM: Being raised in a different country and culture could be an advantage for a writer in a certain sense—like we were saying about your experiences in the Midwest, being an outsider allows you to see how strange many things are that we take for granted.

MH: Yes, or take the American South, for instance, that far-out preoccupation with an aristocratic past. Or our peculiar notion of sin. Like pleasure is sin: a particular brand of ice cream touted as "sinfully good"— that sort of misplaced virtue. Coming out of a different value system, you are likely to see things in a fresh light, provided you haven't been brainwashed by TV or patriotic propaganda about the starved immigrant swooning with gratitude at the sight of Our Lady with the Torch. Certain aspects of American culture are more baffling, more genuinely strange, to me than, say, Peru, or at this stage Europe, which of course is rapidly becoming a photocopy of the States.

LM: You display a marvelous ear for American idioms, especially in your recent works. Is this something you've worked to develop or does it come naturally, like perfect pitch?

MH: Perhaps it is the result of my obsession with the English language. When I came here, for better or worse, I would read and speak only English. But there was a negative side to my lingual love affairs, as I learned on a trip back to Paris. I found myself groping for words. My syntax had become Anglicized. And French used to be my first language! I was really embarrassed. On another occasion, on a visit to the Black Forest, my German sounded god-awful. My French and German friends can't be blamed for thinking I was putting on an act. They couldn't know that my obsession with English had robbed me of my native languages. Being the extremist that I am, I guess I had it coming to me.

LM: One of the things I've wondered about writers like Nabokov, Beckett, and Federman who write literature in a language other than their native tongue is whether or not they ever lose a certain self-consciousness about their adopted language—that sense that, no matter how immersed they are in another language they still regard it as an artifice. Do you feel any of this when you're writing in English?

MH: The idea of language as a manipulator? I don't know. Especially at this point in my life it's difficult for me to think of myself as "self-consciously" using English because by now I have been in this country over half a century, speaking and writing English. A longer time than my life in Europe. And yet there must be something "foreign" to me about English, if only because I have kept my Alsatian accent, which is difficult to define and which I want to keep. Ray Federman seems admirable to me in this regard (I love his writing by the way) because he writes in French and in English, with equal ease I'm sure. But he still has kept his accent.

LM: I would describe a lot of your writing as having "poetic qualities," but your story "Heartlands Beat" contains a lot of materials that are presented more directly as poems—prose poems, or whatever. Have you written much poetry in your career?

MH: No, not really, except for a few, not too serious tries. But, as you say, "Heartlands Beat" does have poetry in it. The story derives from a brief article in a Kirksville, Missouri, paper: a local high school boy hanged himself in his parents' garage because they wouldn't lend him the family car to go to the movies. The situation struck me at once as uniquely American, with vast resonances beyond it. I clipped the article and typed out some notes in the form of a poem. That procedure wasn't new, and is almost automatic. My notes often turn out in shape or beat like breathless, nonprofessional poems. In this case they started, "Johnny J. Upjohn, Jr."—just the way my story was to start decades later. The notes had got stuck in my disorganized files and may have forever remained stuck if I hadn't searched through them for something quite different. So there, almost falling apart in my hands, were two yellow, crumbling "second" sheets. And that's how "Heartlands Beat" came to life—by sheer accident. But I knew instantly I had a story I must write. The Midwest had, oddly enough, become part of me.

SG: Do you know from the start what form a particular piece of writing is going to take?

MH: For quite a while whenever I was contemplating a new story, I used to see it as a play. *Dark Dominion*, for example, was originally to be a play. I had the framework for it in mind, the sets, the actors. Something of that has survived in the novel, I think, because despite the often abundant images (dreams), you have a certain hard-edged sparseness. But that was a good while ago. Now usually right from the start, form and content are inseparable.

SG: Could you talk a little about your work habits? Do you work at the same time every day or have other daily writing routines?

MH: I write best in the morning when I am still connected to my dreams. Dreams are important to my work because they're important to my soul, to what's going on inside me. I have a very rich dream or night life. Before I learned t'ai chi, my days started at the typewriter; now they start with "the form." The t'ai chi, combined with the usual distractions, means that I now work at different hours, whenever I have time.

LM: What got you involved in t'ai chi—it seems like an unusual thing to have taken up relatively late in life.

MH: My close friend Carol is married to the t'ai chi master C. K. Chu. I studied the form at his center after I had recovered from a fractured ankle. I had recently returned from Peru when I slipped on an oil slick during a brisk walk in between work on *The Talking Room*. I had a multiple fracture. And I was sober! If I'd been drunk, or already trained in t'ai chi, my muscles would have been relaxed and the fall may have been less severe. Or it may not have occurred. At any rate, learning the ancient Chinese discipline was great for my head and my body. Chu is an outstanding teacher, probably the acknowledged expert of Chinese martial arts. Though I never made it into the *martial* act. He never suggested that I should. Physically, I'm a coward. He could tell. I'd rather run than fight.

LM: From what we know about your fiction and what you've been telling us about your life, the last twenty years have been a period of tremendous growth and change for you. How have you managed this?

MH: Most people have too much respect for the past. That can be a dangerous handicap. When I taught creative writing (God, that expression!), I couldn't figure out why some of the young, intelligent students wrote as if they were living in the nineteenth century. It occurred to me that they must be so awed by the written word, they'd already closed up to the language that's alive all around them today. To many, writing had no connection with their real existence. They structured a sentence and used words nobody in time or space would use today. This weird attitude must be the fault of our stupid educational system.

LM: Especially since *The Talking Room*, your own approach to language seems much freer, wilder, more playful and experimental. These different textures allow you to get inside your characters and the worlds they inhabit in ways that your earlier prose, wonderful as it is at times, didn't permit.

MH: I feel that myself. I feel I'm writing better now than I ever have, though the process is just as slow as it's been all along. It has always taken me forever to write a book (and usually even longer to get it published), and the same is true of short stories. I write very slowly, and I'm constantly revising; unfortunately, nothing has speeded up. But that's how it goes.

LM: Obviously the point of view in *The Memoirs of the Late Mr. Ashley* is very peculiar, because it is narrated by somebody who has died. Did you begin by having Drew narrate the book and then only later decide that he would die?

MH: First of all, the narrator in a work of fiction has the power to take on any voice. (Look at Tristram Shandy, who isn't even born until book three.) With Ashley, I did know in advance that Drew would die because my main inspiration for his temperament came from an acquaintance who had died in the sixties, I think. I learned about his death from one of his gay friends who joked that the widow of the deceased would most likely mislay the ashes. That's how my prologue originated—from a joke. It made a fitting introduction to the Ashley saga. Generally, though, I don't worry over technicalities. They solve themselves as I write. I am not an intellectual person. I am not a logical person. As a kid, I regularly flunked math. I remember how the teacher consulted with my parents to find out if I was retarded. And this wonderful uncle I've already mentioned (he was a math professor) was outraged when he heard this. He blamed the teacher and offered to tutor me in basic math. But after only a few sessions, he threw up his hands and cried, "It's hopeless! She won't even listen." And I loved this man, right? I still act in peculiar ways, you see, and it is terrible.

LM: You mentioned the importance of dream or nighttime life to your work. Do you consciously draw upon specific dreams when you are working, or is it much more diffused than that?

MH: Since I was a child, I've always known that dreams are real. I've never believed in that line that's drawn between our waking life and our dreaming life—that one is "real" and the other isn't, that one is "true" and the other isn't. Life as we feel it *is* unreal, life is a dream and through time, I see this more and more clearly. Yet only two of my stories are drawn directly from dreams. "The Seersucker Suit" in the Fiction Collective *American Made* anthology is an example: it was based on a dream I had at Bill Kienbusch's house up in Maine. He had old fairy-tale illustrations tagged to a wall, and one of them—a doberman on his hind legs and dressed in an outmoded suit—must have caught my fancy because that night in my dream the dog reappeared and talked with the voice of my son. I "dream figured" how a talking dog would yield a fortune if I'd sell him to science. And here the dream stopped—on a note of acute guilt *and* horror. I have to point out that both dream and story happened at the height of the Vietnam War when I was extremely concerned over Michael's draft status. Basically, "The Seersucker Suit" can be read as a mother's fear for her son's life. She and the son are fated to be the inevitable victims of science and computerized war. The coarseness or disloyalty of the mother's common lover is perhaps an omen for more concrete suffering. It's a comic-tragic tale, a political allegory, like another much shorter piece, "It Isn't So Bad That It Couldn't Be Worse," which also originated in a dream. In fact, the title comes verbatim from a dream speech Jane Fonda delivered from atop a closed coffin draped with the American flag.

SG: It's interesting that you create a character like the inspector in *Prince Ishmael* who has this rational, investigative mind, who believes facts are facts and only facts; then you have Hauser, the writer, who is this associative person who has no trust in cause and effect. In that book, and your others too, there seems to be a kind of swinging back and forth between the two.

MH: Maybe the "back and forth" means simply the eternal conflict between emotion and reason. Here again I must stress that my characters aren't conceived to represent predetermined notions about the human psyche.

SG: What draws you to writing about sex and cemeteries in your books so often?

MH: Back in Europe, and much more so in the Bible Belt, a lot of kids make love in the graveyard. Maybe there's an erotic thrill in keeping company with the dead, though, more important, there's privacy. I myself never felt a yen for such pursuits. Instead, I enjoyed doing handstands on the tombs to prove to my school chums that I wasn't scared of ghosts. Today, when I visit a strange town, I like to take a walk through the cemetery. It's one of the rare spots in the United States where one can experience history of sorts by reading the tombstones or monuments, to use one of the many euphemisms in reference to death. Death may have preoccupied me as a writer, to some extent. My oldest sister died of meningitis when I was about seven. Her death affected me so deeply, so directly, that I couldn't write about it for forty years. Not until I let go of that pent-up misery in my story "Allons Enfants." My mother's protective attitude (she wouldn't let me attend the funeral so I wouldn't think too much about death), her pretense that all was well had, of course, the opposite effect on me. So, by default, her denial of reality may well have stirred up the artist inside me. One never knows.

SG: In both *The Talking Room* and *The Memoirs* there is a sense that love is a continual problem that has to be wrestled with. Love means pain.

MH: It does, occasionally. I told you how I wanted to cut my wrists due to love—what else can one say? But in the novels you mention, love is one of many other problems, like Mims' awareness of self in *Memoirs* or J's mysterious absences in *The Talking Room*. If one equals love with pain in the sadomasochistic sense, then, yes, there is quite a bit of S and M in both novels. Why? Only the characters themselves have the answer. If I can touch the reader with their humanness or inhumanity, I've done a credible job. I refuse to play the soothing, pigeonholing role of the psychoanalyst because that role can't ever be done to my satisfaction. What is going on inside of people is all one vast, fantastic fusion of things. One of the things I tried to show in both novels is that there's never only one problem with love and never only one solution. It depends on the characters. Each must have his/her motivation. If I started psychoanalyzing my characters, I (or they) would be on the couch forever.

SG: What is your view about feminism? Everything you've told us about your life makes it seem as if you have probably been a feminist since you were a little girl.

MH: Well, my mother was a feminist, so feminism came to me by osmosis. Of course, today's society gives women token recognition, as it does for blacks. But in both the women's and civil rights movement, a fundamental master-slave tradition hasn't only survived but is reinforced by the far right, not to mention the lethal shenanigans of the antiabortionists. It looks like when we take a step forward, we're kicked back into the maternity ward. Margaret Atwood's *The Handmaid's Tale* presents a scary picture. The writing isn't all that good, but I was shaken by her metaphor of women as birthing *machines*. I'll never understand how any woman in her right mind can reject feminism. If the movement had some excesses, they were necessary to drive home the message. Remember the slogan, "Black is beautiful"? Black isn't more beautiful than white, but the phrase was needed to foster personal pride, "Black pride."

SG: Certainly *The Talking Room* and *The Memoirs of the Late Mr. Ashley* are very much concerned with gender roles. And there's a number of funny moments in both books where you parodically confound sexual role playing—like the woman in *The Talking Room* who dresses up like a man dressing as a woman to go into a transvestite bar . . . all the variations on a theme.

MH: Yes, that scene may well be a parody on sexual role playing. Aunt V's secretary, U, dreams she's in a tunnel—an immaculate subway tunnel—and also in a pissoir, a man's urinal where she encounters a row of guys in business suits, their flies open, but no genitals. (When she wakes up, she crossdresses and plays the queen at a gay bar on Queens Boulevard.) I had a similar dream which worked itself into the text without my planning it ahead of time.

LM: What you're aiming for when you're writing seems to be mainly leaving yourself open to a kind of improvisational incorporation of associations. And yet when one finishes your books, the pattern of imagery, associations, dream materials, and so on somehow seems coherent— though not necessarily *logically* so.

MH: I hope so. What I've been trying to say about the way I write (which can't be expressed in words) is that the process has more to do with my temperament than with any abstract idea that this or that approach to writing is "right." Each writer has a different way of doing things. My writing reflects how I am, how I relate to the world and the people in it. But the beauty of writing is that there are so many possibilities, so many variations. That's why I don't like any of these catchwords—realist, postmodernist, surrealist, et cetera—that try to squeeze art into a pigeonhole or an academic niche.

SG: In the very first paragraph of *Prince Ishmael* you say, "This may, or may not, be the truth." So from the beginning we don't know if that book is a work of fiction or nonfiction, history or legend. And, of course, it further resists pigeonholing because it's a mystery novel that refuses to supply any final explanation.

MH: It's the ambiguity that is paramount in this mystery book that has no solution. I was hung up on mystery stories for a while, especially trash ones like Erle Stanley Gardner's. Agatha Christie was already too intellectual for me. My way of reading those books probably tells you a lot about my head: no matter how engrossed I became, I usually didn't read the ending. I didn't want to know "who did it." I wanted to leave all the possibilities wide open.

SG: It's partly your refusal to provide the usual sorts of reductive explanations about Prince Ishmael—your refusal to solve his mystery—that makes that book so sad and moving. All his life he wants to hang on to things, even the junk. And yet his whole life is denial, loss, deprivation.

MH: It's true in that book, and it's also true of life. I mean, look at mine: nobody believes it. My life has been ridiculous, really. Spatially speaking—and geographically, intellectually, sexually, linguistically, you name it—my life makes no sense. Maybe that's why enigmas have always intrigued me so much more than solutions.

A Local Strangeness
An Interview with Lyn Hejinian

Larry McCaffery
Brian McHale

> If reality is trying to express itself in words, it is certainly taking the long way around.
>
> — *My Life*

If your local bookstore carries Lyn Hejinian's *My Life* (1980, 1987), it will most likely be shelved with the poetry. But open it, and you will find what looks to be prose—Lyn Hejinian's prose autobiography, evidently. Now open Hejinian's *Oxota* (1991), identified right there on the cover as "A Short Russian Novel," and likely to be shelved with the fiction; what do you find? Poetry, or so it would appear: a series of some 270 sonnet-length poems ("free sonnets," according to the jacket blurb), each purporting to be a "chapter" in this "novel." And indeed, the more closely one scrutinizes this text, the more it appears that there might, after all, be something like a novel here, though a strange, elusive one. Characters swim in and out of focus; shards of setting—cityscapes, interiors—seem to flicker just at the edge of our peripheral vision; narrative fragments slip past without ever quite cohering into *a* narrative. . . . What is going on here?

One is tempted to adapt William Carlos Williams's anecdote about the painter and poet Marsden Hartley. Asked by a visitor to the gallery at which he worked to identify something in the corner of one of the pictures, Hartley is supposed to have replied, "That, madam, is paint."

What is this here on the page of Lyn Hejinian's book? Poetry or prose? Autobiography? "Short Russian novel"? Or what? That, madam and sir, is *sentences*: language.

Which brings us to Lyn Hejinian's affiliation with the group of writers variously called "New Sentence" or "Language" poets. The institution of the literary "school" or "circle" does not have much in the way of historical precedent or sanction in American culture—the legacy of Emersonian self-reliance and rugged individualism is too deeply ingrained for collective literary identities to flourish here. Schools of poetry in America have tended to be short-lived, gone almost before their existence could be registered, occasions for nostalgia more than active players in the game of cultural intervention (think of the Beats, Black Mountain); either that, or they have been dummy schools fabricated for the convenience of book reviewers and English professors (think of the confessional poets). The Language school is neither of these things, but more like a literary school in the European sense, with its own collective identity, institutions, and forms of solidarity—its journals, small presses, manifestos, collaborations, collective interventions. Lyn Hejinian has been, from its inception, a member in good standing of the Bay Area "cell" of Language poets (there is also an East Coast group), numbering among her colleagues Ron Silliman, Barrett Watten, Carla Harryman, Michael Palmer, Bob Perelman, Steve Benson, Rae Armantrout, Robert Grenier, and a half-dozen others. Hejinian has not only contributed writing of her own to the collective Language school project, she has also—as publisher of Tuumba, one of the Language school presses, and coeditor with Barrett Watten of *Poetics Journal*, its main theoretical organ—helped to stimulate, circulate, promote, defend, and explain the work of others in the group.

The Language group has received a certain amount of critical attention, but more for its radical political agenda than for its aesthetic agenda, though, in fact, the two are inseparable. For the Language poets, the essential tool of cultural critique, resistance, and intervention is *writing*: they have designs on the language, and on the social reality of which language is the medium. They share with the European avant-gardes of the early twentieth century—the Russian Formalists, the Russian and Italian Futurists, the Dadaists—not only forms of school solidarity, such as collaborative projects and manifesto-writing, but also the key aesthetic principle of "alienation" or "estrangement" (the Formalists' *ostranenie*). "Make it strange" could be the Language poets' motto, where "it" embraces poetic convention, literary institutions, social life, language itself.

In Lyn Hejinian's writing, we can discern two grand strategies of estrangement. One is exemplified by the prose book *My Life*, where

Hejinian takes the banal genre of autobiography and the equally banal outlines of a midcentury, middle-class life—her own, presumably—and passes them through the filter of an alienating form. The subject matter of *My Life* is the experience of growing up American, middle-class, and female—a forties childhood (Hejinian was born in 1941), a fifties adolescence, coming of age in the sixties, a life lived on both coasts (born in California, Hejinian was schooled from age thirteen on in Cambridge, Massachusetts, returning to the West Coast after having graduated from Harvard). But this perfectly "normal" experience is transmitted to us not through the normalizing discourse of conventional autobiographical narrative, but "cinematically," as a series of distinct "frames"—one sentence per frame—that flicker across the page, somehow producing the illusion of movement—a life lived in time—without ever falling into the all-too-predictable, prefabricated sequences of a "life-story." As a further estranging device these sentences appear in arbitrary (or, from a different perspective, totally determined) groupings—thirty-seven groups of thirty-seven sentences each in the 1980 version of *My Life*, forty-five groups of forty-five sentences each in the revised and updated 1987 version; in other words, a group for each year of Hejinian's life at the time of writing, in every group a sentence for every year. Strange, yet familiar; familiar, yet estranged.

The other grand strategy involves not subjecting a "normal" experience to an estranging form but rather courting strange experience and then finding a form appropriate to that lived strangeness. This dimension of Hejinian's poetics—or is it a dimension of her biography? for here poetics and biography converge—is manifested most clearly in her ongoing, profoundly estranging experience of Russia. Hejinian first encountered the irreducible strangeness of Russia (for an American, that is) when she accompanied her husband, Larry Ochs, there on a tour by the avant-garde musical ensemble ROVA Saxophone Quartet (Ochs is the O of ROVA). A number of visits later, Hejinian continues to experiment with means of capturing and voicing her experience of Russia: through her translations (with Elena Balashova) of the poetry of the Leningrad (now St. Petersburg) poet Arkadii Dragomoshchenko (*Description*, 1990; *Xenia*, 1994) and her collaboration with him in translating her own poetry into Russian; through her collaboration with fellow Language poets Michael Davidson, Ron Silliman, and Barrett Watten on a prose work, *Leningrad: American Writers in the Soviet Union* (1991); and finally, through her "short Russian novel," *Oxota* ("The Hunt"). In *Oxota*, Hejinian finds a counterpart for the strangeness of her Russian experience in the strange literary model of Pushkin's "novel in verse," *Evgeny Onegin*, a text whose unstable compound of genres, attitudes, tones, styles—novel and verse, sentimental and cynical, cosmopolitan and provincial, colloquial and artificial—has never been successfully naturalized in English. These two grand strategies are to be found, in various mixtures and dosages, not just in *My Life* and *Oxota*, but in all of Hejinian's other writings as well, including *A Thought Is the Bride of What Thinking* (1976), *Writing Is an Aid to Memory* (1978), *Redo* (1984), and *The Guard* (1984).

This interview was conducted at Lyn Hejinian's home in Berkeley, California, by Larry McCaffery and Brian McHale. We had just spent several days at the annual convention of the Modern Language Association in San Francisco, hearing (among too many other things) talks and readings by various members of the West Coast Language group, including Ron Silliman, Barrett Watten, Michael Palmer, Douglas Messerli, and Fanny Howe. Hejinian, too, had been in attendance at some of these events, so all parties were primed to discuss matters Language-poetical. We rendezvoused with Hejinian, appropriately enough, at Small Press Distribution in Berkeley, one of the outlets through which Language poetry finds its way into the world. The first item of decor to meet our eyes upon entering Hejinian's living room was the oil painting by the Leningrad artist Ostap Dragomoshchenko that appears on the cover of *Oxota*. Midway through our conversation, Larry Ochs arrived home and, after introductions all around, ducked out again. So, one way and another, nearly all of the elements of our conversation were actually present, physically or through some delegate or surrogate, in the time and space in which this interview transpired.

*　*　*

Lyn Hejinian: Selected Bibliography

Books of Prose Poetry

My Life. Providence, RI: Burning Deck Press, 1980. Expanded edition. Los Angeles: Sun and Moon Press, 1987.
Leningrad: American Writers in the Soviet Union (with Michael Davidson, Ron Silliman, Barrett Watten). San Francisco: Mercury House, 1991.
Oxota: A Short Russian Novel. Great Barrington, MA: Figures, 1991.

Books of Poetry

A Thought Is the Bride of What Thinking. Willits, CA: Tuumba Press, 1976.
A Mask of Motion. Providence, RI: Burning Deck Press, 1977.
Writing Is an Aid to Memory. Berkeley, CA: Figures, 1978.
Gesualdo. Berkeley, CA: Tuumba Press, 1978.
The Guard. Berkeley: Tuumba Press, 1984.

Redo. Grenada, MS: Salt-Works Press, 1984.

Individuals: A Book of Twenty-four Poems Written Individually in the Fall of 1986 (with Kit Robinson). Tucson, AZ: Chax Press, 1988.

The Hunt. La Laguna, Tenerife, Canary Islands: Zasterle Press, 1991.

The Cell. Los Angeles: Sun and Moon Press, 1992.

La Jour de Chase. Trans. Pierre Alferi. Cahiers de Royaumont, 1992.

The Cold of Poetry. Collection of Hejinian poetry books now out of print: *The Guard, Ground, The Flying Statues, Gesualdo, Punctual, Redo, The Composition of the Cell, The Dream, The Person,* and *Oblivion.* Los Angeles: Sun and Moon Press, 1994.

Two Stein Talks. Sante Fe, NM: Weaselsleeves Press, 1995.

Translations

With Elena Balashova, *Description* (poems), by Arkadii Dragomoshchenko. Los Angeles: Sun and Moon Press, 1990.

Arkadii Dragomoshchenko selections in *Third Wave: The New Russian Poetry,* ed. Kent Johnson and Stephen Ashby. Ann Arbor: University of Michigan Press, 1992.

With Elena Balashova, *Xenia* (poems), by Arkadii Dragomoshchenko. Los Angeles: Sun and Moon Press, 1994.

Essays and Reviews

"An American Opener." *Poetics Journal* 1 (1982).

"If Written Is Writing." In Bruce Andrews and Charles Bernstein, *The L=A=N=G=U=A=G=E Book,* 29–30. Carbondale: Southern Illinois University Press, 1984.

"The Rejection of Closure." *Poetics Journal* 4 (May 1984): 135–43. Also, in *Writing Talks,* ed. Bob Perelman, 271–91. Carbondale and Edwardsville: Southern Illinois University Press, 1988.

"Aesthetic Tendency and the Politics of Poetry: A Manifesto" (Ron Silliman, Carla Harryman, Lyn Hejinian, Steve Benson, Barrett Watten). In *Social Text* 19/20 (fall 1988).

"Line." In *The Line in Postmodern Poetry,* ed. Robert Frank and Henry Sayre. Urbana: University of Illinois Press, 1988.

"Strangeness." *Poetics Journal* 8 (1989).

"Strangeness" and "Two Stein Talks." *Revista Canaria de Estudos Ingleses* 18 (April 1989).

Sound Recordings

Chronic Ideas. 80 Langdon St. talk series. San Diego: University of California at San Diego Special Collections, 1977.

UCSD New Poetry Series (with Carla Harryman). 30 April 1980. UCSD Special Collections.

New Writing Series. Poetry reading, 30 October 1985. UCSD Special Collections.

Interviews

Georgeson, Alison. "An Interview with Lyn Hejinian." *Southern Review* 27, 3 (1994).
Miller, Tyrus. "An Interview with Lyn Hejinian." *Paper Air* 4, 2 (1989).
Schelling, Andrew. "Interview with Lyn Hejinian." *Jimmy's and Lucy's House of K* 6 (May 1986).

Reviews and Essays about Hejinian's Work

Abbott, Steve. Review of *Writing Is an Aid to Memory*. *American Book Review* 4, 2 (January/February 1982).
Armantrout, Rae. "Lyn Hejinian." In *Postmodern Fiction: A Bio-Bibliographical Guide*, ed. Larry McCaffery, 400–403. Westport, CT: Greenwood Press, 1986.
———. Review of *The Guard*. *HOW/(ever)* 2, 2 (February 1985).
Bernstein, Charles. "The Dollar Value of Poetry." In Bruce Andrews and Charles Bernstein, *The L=A=N=G=U=A=G=E Book*, 138–40. Carbondale: Southern Illinois University Press, 1984.
———. "Hejinian's Notes." In *Content's Dream*. Los Angeles: Sun & Moon Press, 1986.
Greer, Michael. "Ideology and Theory in Recent Experimental Writing, or The Naming of 'Language Poetry.'" *Boundary* 2, 16 (1989): 2–3.
Grenier, Robert. Review of *Writing Is an Aid to Memory*. *Language* 8 (June 1979).
Higgins, Dick. Review of *A Mask in Motion*. *Stony Hills* 1, 2 (1977).
Lazar, Hank. Review of *My Life*. University of California at San Diego *Archive Newsletter* (Winter 1988): 31–36.
Jarraway, David. "*My Life* through the Eighties: The Exemplary L=A=N=G=U=A=G=E of Lyn Hejinian." *Contemporary Literature* 33, 2 (Summer 1992): 319–36.
Mayer, Bernadette. "Mayer on Hejinian." *L=A=N=G=U=A=G=E*, 13 December 1980.
Mulford, Wendy. "'Curved, Odd . . . Irregular.' A Vision of Contemporary Poetry by Women." *Women: A Cultural Review* 1, 3 (1990).
Naylor, Paul Kenneth. "In Process/On Trial: Lyn Hejinian and Julia Kristeva." In *The Moment of the "I": Self-Portraits in Poetry and Philosophy*, 263–310. Ph.D. thesis. University of California at San Diego, 1990.
O'Brien, Geoffrey. Review of *The Guard*. *Village Voice Literary Supplement* (December 1984): 6.
Parsons, Marnie. "What Then Is a Window." In *Touch Monkeys: Nonsense Strategies for Reading Twentieth-Century Poetry*, 206–14. Toronto: University of Toronto Press, 1994.
Perloff, Marjorie. "The Word as Such: L=A=N=G=U=A=G=E Poetry in the Eighties." *American Book Review* (May/June 1984).
Quartermain, Peter. "Syllable as Music: Lyn Hejinian's *Writing Is an Aid to Memory*." *Sagetrieb* 11 (1992): 17–31.
Ratcliffe, Stephen. "Private Eye/Public Work." *American Poetry Review* 4 (1987): 40–48.
———. "Two Hejinian Talks." *Temblor* 6 (1987).
Wakowski, Diane. Review of *My Life*. *Sulfur* 8 (1983).

Watten, Barrett. "The World of Work: Toward a Psychology of Form." In *Total Syntax*, 146–49. Carbondale: Southern Illinois University Press, 1985.

As Editor or Publisher

Tuumba Press (editor and publisher), 1976–84.
Poetics Journal (coeditor and publisher with Barrett Watten), since 1981.
Logos (Leningrad State University Press) (corresponding editor), since 1989.

*   *   *

LARRY MCCAFFERY: The title of *Oxota* can be translated as "The Hunt." And, at least on one level, the book seems to be a record of your own hunt, as a writer and as an individual, to give expression to your experiences in Russia.

LYN HEJINIAN: I've spent a lot of time in the Russian part of what used to be the Soviet Union during seven different trips there, including two extended visits there by myself. At first I had a sense of familiarity with what I was seeing—the landscape, the city (primarily what was then Leningrad), objects in friends' flats, how people behaved. At that time, the Soviet Union was the other great superpower, that is, not a so-called Third World or "underdeveloped nation" but a nation in the same condition as the one I come from. I arrived with that assumption and saw things initially from that point of view. But I very soon began to realize that they were, in fact, utterly unfamiliar, and not only unfamiliar but different in a profound way.

Meanwhile, I have for a long time been a student, so to speak, of the writings of William James. I'm especially interested in his approach to the psychology of consciousness and cognitive perceptions. The radical introspecting and the descriptions of the results that are his investigative instruments are not entirely unlike Freud's, but James's interest is in consciousness and perception, rather than in the unconscious. And as a writer, I'm particularly interested in consciousness, or in the consciousness of being conscious which seems central to poetry. I've also been interested in various experiences of what I'd call strangeness—really no more than a heightened awareness that results from radical introspecting (a simple example would be an experience of staring at your hand so long it no longer looks like a hand and no longer seems a part of you). I'm interested also in the experience of strangeness in other contexts, particularly philosophical contexts. But actually to experience strangeness in a situation of daily living as I did in Russia was deeply moving and disturbing; I wanted to understand it better, and the wanting to understand better is always my motivation for writing.

When I started writing *Oxota*, I wanted to recreate in writing the *Russian-ness* of what I experienced as a kind of strangeness and to experience it again but intentionally. Wanting to understand what I'd experienced better was the real origin of the book—not just understanding what I experienced in Russia but also the profound sense of being creatively estranged. Taking alienation as a perceptual device.

LM: I experienced a similar sense the year I spent in Beijing (1988–89)—the utter *strangeness* of everything separated me from what I had taken for granted (my "cultural self," I guess you could call it); seeing other habits and ways of thinking clarifies your understanding of who you are, where you're from, how these are related.

LH: Right: it helps put the strangeness of *home* into relief—a strangeness which is obscured by familiarity and disappears from most people's awareness when they're "at home." To me the sense of "local strangeness" is essential—the strangeness of oneself but also the more fundamental and pervasive strangeness of having a life, with its various parts, the seeming randomness of one's encounters with events, the unpredictability of the ways in which it unfolds.

LM: At what point did the title occur to you?

LH: It came from something that Zina Dragomoshchenko said. Zina is a friend of mine and the wife of the poet Arkadii Dragomoshchenko (I'm the translator of his works into English and he is the translator of mine into Russian). I lived with them in both of my extended visits to Russia. Zina often referred to herself as *oxotnitsa*, "the huntress." It's the epithet for the Roman goddess Diana, and Zina took it somewhat facetiously but also accurately for herself, since like most Russian women she spends much of her time out in the city in an endless hunt for food for her family. I liked the literary connotations of the word—the possible allusion to Turgenev's *Hunter's Sketches* and the notion of a landscape through which one moves guided by something outside oneself.

LM: Was the free sonnet form part of your conception of the book from the beginning?

LH: No, I began the book as a prose book, which was a disaster for a number of reasons. Basically I made two major attempts to write the book before I ended up using this fourteen-line form—in which, by the way, I wasn't thinking at all of sonnets but of the fourteen-line stanzas of Pushkin's *Evgeny Onegin*. To think of the "chapters" as sonnets is very misleading.

BRIAN MCHALE: When you say it began as a prose book, do you mean as prose poetry or regular prose?

LH: It began in prose as "regular" as I could write. I couldn't use a conventional narrative logic (grounded in chronology, evolving from causes and effects) because it was precisely the inscrutability of effects and the apparent loss of causes that was defamiliarizing my Russian life. The prose was inevitably full of jumps and I couldn't find other logics. The work was uncontained and as a result sentimental. It became obvious that this was the wrong way to write what I was trying to do. The formal structure I ended up using was largely influenced, as I said, by Pushkin. His *Evgeny Onegin* is commonly known as "the first Russian novel," and is written in a continuum of fourteen-line stanzas. They haven't the finish of sonnets—it's a far looser form. And once I decided to use it, the book just took off. It seemed like the perfect vehicle for what I was trying to do—it is concise (elegant, even) but allows room for speculation and digression. And it rhymes with Pushkin's Russian work, which I wanted to imitate in other ways as well—by including social commentary, self-examination, literary discussion, by writing a "comedy of manners," and all the while indulging in metaphysics.

LM: When you began work on the book, did you have a clear sense of where the book was heading? Or did things just start accumulating?

LH: Essentially, I had no plan—no plot outline, for example. There were, however, certain elements that I knew from the beginning I wanted to include—a violent act, for example. That wound up being a stabbing of the painter Gavronsky. That stabbing actually happened, only it happened in San Francisco to a young American musician—my nephew, a drummer with a metal band. He recovered—he's fine now; but the event was terrifyingly traumatic and it was very much on my mind when I was starting the book. I had seen enough violence in Russia that I knew I could transpose this incident and intertwine it with the rise of nationalism that appeared in the wake of *perestroika* and with anti-Semitism, which is one aspect of nationalism. I am very troubled, of course, by the nationalistic sentiments that are emerging all over the world, and I wanted to address this—to present it, at least, as part of a context of something awful. And there were other things I knew I wanted to include—the colonel, for example. The Russian equivalent of our urban myths almost always includes a colonel. When I mentioned to Russian friends that I was going to write a Russian novel, they understood that this was a trope, but they also wanted to make sure I included the appropriate and accurately Russian elements. So they told me many stories, true and apocryphal—but all of them typically Russian stories that "had" to be included in a Russian novel. There were a number of stories that had a colonel in them—not just because of the colonel's prominence in urban myths but sometimes because so many men of the generation just before mine were in the military and ended up as colonels. Some of these stories were tragic, some bathetic, some comic. I was told a racist story about a Chukchi colonel (the Chukchi are a northern native people) in which the Chukchi is "typically" stupid—I used the story, though without the ethnic element (curiously enough I just recently heard the story in a version in which Dan Quayle plays the role of Chukchi). While writing down these stories, I also made a series of notes on "themes"—nationalism, light, snow, apathy, stubbornness, et cetera—qualities I observed in myself or in my surroundings. As I began writing, I would just pull pieces from all these notes, keeping the materials diffused and dispersed because that's the way I experienced them. One simply doesn't experience most events with the kind of clarity that most accounts of them imply. The stabbing episode, for example—what led up to it, the reasons for the attack, the emergency, Gavronsky's stay in the hospital, the role his mother played, the arrest of the assailant, and so forth and so on—all this took a long time to unfold; meanwhile other things were going on as well. I wanted that episode to take place over a large part of the book rather than just to explain it all at once. So I kept pulling in fragments from many elements, and I never really knew when any one theme or story might be complete.

LM: This deliberate "diffusion" seems present in *My Life*, as well. There's a very general chronological structure to it, but also a sense of this "all over" quality, where different aspects of different experiences appear in different parts of the book. How did you conceive of the movement of the book, or the relationship of the different sections, as you were writing it?

LH: It built. As I wrote one section it then led me to think about the next. I did very little rearranging of the materials—really almost none at all. There are maybe three chapters I moved before I sent the manuscript off to the publisher, but that's all. What you see in the book is more or less presented in the order I wrote it, which is the order in which I was thinking it.

LM: Could you talk a bit about your interest in presenting your "self" in your writing—as opposed to developing more obviously fictionalized versions of other selves (the way most novelists or story writers do)? I would describe the self that emerges in your books as being a fictive construct owing its existence to language and narrative.

LH: There's an important distinction I like to make between the "self" and the "person." The self is thought of as one's inner, irreducible essence—the real, permanent, unchanging "you." It's very hard to locate this kernel essentially. Basically I think one has to disregard it. What's more interesting to me than the concept of this ineffable "self" is the concept of the person, which has to do with activities, our daily and nightly being in the world. The person exists in context—or in an array of contexts enabling and/or requiring us to make choices, act on intentions, make the decisions which move us through life. To that extent, a person is self-creating, a construct or a construction, while at the same time being that which does the constructing. Thus an autobiography is always written not by a self but by a person. So, yes, the book *My Life* is a *written* life. This doesn't mean it's untrue or inaccurate (every sentence in *My Life* is true) but the end result is as many truths as there are sentences.

BM: *Oxota* struck me as being almost a calculated display of how fragile and "contextual" the construction of ego or person actually is—certainly you show how easily disintegrated (and reconstructable) identity is here . . .

LH: In some respects I can see now that *Oxota* is a continuation of some study of identity, of personhood and its boundaries. My experience in Russia was in a certain way transgressive—or more precisely it was "auto-transgressive" in that my ego seemed to disintegrate under the impact of thinking I understood what was going on but then realizing that in fact I didn't. In effect, I was losing the boundaries of myself. Of course Russia—both Soviet Russia and the centuries-long czarist feudal Russia before it—have an entirely other concept of self and person. There isn't, for example, a Russian equivalent to our word "self."

I should say that altering my sense of the boundaries of self was transgressive in a positive way. Subtitling *Oxota* "A Short Russian Novel" was intended to be somewhat similarly transgressive, but of genre boundaries. Seeing the book shelved under the heading "Fiction" in a number of bookstores has secretly delighted me.

BM: But *isn't* the book really a kind of novel? There's this sense of a narrating that readers gradually realize can be recovered from the text—that is, the "characters" begin to take shape as you read more, and the anecdotes that you distributed throughout begin to emerge in a chronological fashion, so when readers encounter the colonel again, they can flip back a few pages and find the beginning of the anecdote. My point is that you're not just playing off of the name "novel" but off of its conventions as well—"big narrative," having characters, and so on.

LH: I should mention that while some of my "characters" are real, others are constructs or composites—Misha, for example. I knew several Misha's and I used the name to gather material together. Often when I wanted to say something—when there was something I wanted said—I'd just say Misha said it.

LM: Even your use of the fourteen-line chapter form could be seen as a kind of experimental novelistic convention—an elliptical presentation of things that the reader could use to fill in or anticipate other aspects of the overall narrative. How would you describe the differences between your approach to exposition and more conventional modes?

LH: For one thing, I leave out all the background exposition and explanations of materials or events that I already know, so that the writing always begins at a point after the basic setup, so to speak, at the point where I don't know what's going on until I am writing it. That's not really an artistic plot, however. My reasons for writing are inquisitive—writing is the site of thinking, and in that sense I'm not interested in storytelling or in recapitulating what I've previously figured out. I've found, in fact, that when I attempt to keep a journal or even when I write letters describing something that is now over, I am almost instantly too bored to continue.

LM: Have you ever written traditional fictional stories?

LH: No. Poetry seems a more direct medium for scrutinizing and philosophizing. I don't seem to feel a need to populate my metaphysics.

BM: You attribute to Arkadii a kind of *ars poetica* having to do with a distinction between narrative and adventure—the latter implying a resolution. Is this your own *ars poetica* for *Oxota*? That is, even though there is indeed a narrative in *Oxota*, it's not as though you're shaping these materials toward some kind of inexorable novelist resolution.

LH: I'm considerably more interested in the "experience of the experience" than in recounting the experience itself (if that makes sense). The consciousness of being conscious is what I think writing is finally all about—bringing into consciousness the fact that you are conscious of what you're doing and seeing, witnessing, thinking, and so on.

LM: You and most of the other Language poets seem to have been majorly influenced by some of the early Russian Formalists. What sort of an impact has being in Russia and meeting Russian poets and artists had on your literary sensibility?

LH: You're basically asking about two sources of the influence of Russian experience on my work—one is the Russians and Russia I know, and the other is the reading in Russian theory and Russian literature which is really independent of the Russia and Russians I actually know. It's obvious that I've been influenced by Russia. It's become a part of my life in a profound way. I feel as if I have lived another life in Russia, partly because I've been there so many times, but more because the profundity of the experience of being there has been so great that it was like having lived a parallel life—and because when I've been there I necessarily interrupted my life here in many ways. Life here is so far away while you're in Russia. You can't telephone. You lose the sense of connection. It's a sensation of complete dislocation and relocation.

In terms of my actual writing practices, the major change comes from knowing that Arkadii Dragomoshchenko might translate what I am writing. I now sometimes write more clearly towards his anticipation of what I might say; for the same reason, I also find myself using less local topical references than I might ordinarily use because they would be irrelevant in Russia. In that sense, I'm sometimes writing *for him*. Nonetheless, even though I've translated so much of Arkadii's work and even though we're both interested in perception and description and the value of shifting point of view, he writes so utterly unlike the way I would that I feel quite free from him.

In terms of the question about the influence of the Russian Formalists—Viktor Shklovsky and Yuri Tynyanov, Boris Eikhenbaum, and that circle—yes, my thinking is profoundly indebted to them. With significant corroboration from this side of the Atlantic. Earlier I mentioned William James's approach to descriptions of the self. He writes a great deal in his *Principles of Psychology* about language as instrumental in forming consciousness. The Formalist concept of strangeness (*ostranenie*) and the role poetic language plays in a system of alienating devices is also in James, although that's not the vocabulary he uses. The Formalists, by the way, were talking more about culture than about the self—that is a major distinction—but conceiving of language as a tool for understanding and for making the world palpable is very Jamesian, or James is very Russian in this. I also think the Russian Formalists' sense of the availability of the whole history of literature for immediate use—that all of this has immediate value—is very important. There's a way in which the Russian Formalists' view of literary history allows one to read anything as of one's moment at the same time that it acknowledges the specific historical and socioeconomic conditions that produced it.

LM: Could you supply an example of their particular view of literary history?

LH: Shklovsky's discussions of Sterne or of Dickens isolate the devices or techniques or methods in their works while simultaneously bringing them into current use. And by implication anything one can read can demonstrate something that's pertinent to current use.

LM: Again, it's easier to be idealistic about these things when one hasn't had any experience with the realities involved in totalitarianism. People did what they had to do.

LH: Right. Nadezhda Mandelstam talks about Shklovsky and his wife as being incredibly courageous, the only people that she and [Osip] Mandelstam could go to in Moscow who would protect them; the Shklovskys would stay awake and take turns listening in case anybody was coming.

BM: As I was reading *Oxota* I kept being reminded of a note that Arkadii Dragomoshchenko wrote to your translation of *Description* where he says that this entire poem emerged from a misreading of a sentence from your letter to him. It was something about "everything begins in an error of vision" (a lovely self-referential line). It strikes me that over and over again your materials are those of mistranslations back and forth—your misunderstanding of them, their strange versions of English, and so on, which throws up a lot of seminonsense or comical phrases: a "sheep thriller," a "heavy mental," et cetera. I wonder if there's not here almost a conscious practice of *mis*translation, or a theory of mistranslation—mistranslation as a norm of language or as an alternative to a communication theory. In a sense we're always mistranslating; we never get in our context of reception what was intended in the context of transmission and consequently new meanings are constantly produced.

LH: Absolutely. There are two important things about mistranslation. One is that it's tantamount to invention (that's very important, of course), and the other is that it's inconclusive, which is equally important. I mean that mistranslation is not the final translation, by definition, because it's "wrong"; thus, it leaves phrases open to reinterpretation—it demands retranslations—whatever it is that's been mistranslated. In fact, that's true of all translation—something is left open whenever you take the work of somebody from another language and put it into the language of your readers. "Mistranslation" might be too strong a word; it's almost coy to say I've done a "mistranslation of Arkadii's work"—but in fact this seems part of its legitimacy.

LM: This general area of translation seems related to a topic that's come up with several of the writers included in this volume: namely, the rejection of this whole Western-oriented notion of artistic originality, the romantic individual inventing something original out of his or her unique experience—and the replacement of this with writing that emphasizes various types of collaboration, or that foregrounds intertextuality in some fundamental sense.

LH: This seems to be very much in the air these days. The work that Arkadii and I have done is virtually a collaboration since we've always been able to check our texts with each other; maybe more revealingly, we've also both rewritten our "originals" to more closely correspond to the translation when the translation seemed better. Both of us have been repeatedly told that our "translations" are better than the "originals"—so Arkadii has been told that his Russian versions of my work are better than mine and likewise I've been told that my translations of his work are better than his in the original. This is really funny.

LM: Lydia Davis described working with Blanchot and sometimes having the urge to "correct" the original in some sense. Have you felt that?

LH: I wouldn't describe it as an urge to correct so much as sometimes to clarify. Or to render the vernacular equivalent of something originally not in that vernacular.

LM: Why do you think there's been so much recent emphasis on generative writing or collaboration? What's "wrong" with the romantic conception of the artist? Why not strive for artistic originality, develop your own voice?

LH: Because the romantic version of the poet is not very exciting anymore or at the moment. It seems extremely limited, solipsistic. The question that I often ask myself, that I feel I *have* to ask myself is, "Are you contributing something with all this writing?" And if I just felt I was contributing "me," the answer would be no, that's not a relevant contribution. It would be stupid and limiting to enshrine myself as some unitary voicing of the world as if I were a representative person, which I'm not; *nobody is* living in such a complex culture as this. It seems as if anything that I would say as me alone is simply not very novel. Anybody could say it. What makes the idea of the collaborative person, or collaborating persons, so appealing is that it opens up enormous possibilities for diffusion and multiplicity of points of view. It's just more interesting than the romantic, unitary voice. And beyond any sort of aesthetic appeal that collaborative strategies might have, it also seems undeniable to me that in a funny way feeling oneself as many selves or as many persons is more *accurate.* The other thing is that I would encourage anything that decommodifies. Like the *Leningrad* book that Michael Davidson, Ron Silliman, Barrett Watten, and I wrote together. I love going to bookstores and seeing that they can't figure out where to put it—under Davidson, Hejinian, Watten, or Silliman. I saw one bookstore where it wound up in four different places!

LM: This self-conscious intertextuality on the part of authors—this refusal to pretend you're presenting this objective, solipsistic "original" text—coincides with the appearance of critics like Barthes and Bakhtin, who are arguing that this was always a pretense.

LH: Your use of the word "objective" is interesting in this context because most people think of the romantic individual purely in terms of presenting itself as being highly subjective—whereas in fact, an equally important aspect of this is the claims for objectivity. It represents the lone pioneer, the single scientist, the hero/explorer coming to grips with the role and yet somehow claiming objectivity. Collaboration also *radicalizes* or highlights subjectivity, partly I guess because the reader wonders who wrote which word. This confounds the reader's sense of a text's wholeness in a most basic way; certainly having two observers puts objectivity into question.

BM: Would it be fair to say that a lot of the things you do—not just collaborative strategies but the others you use—have to do with throwing into question the wholeness in a text, continually forcing readers to be asking, "Just who is this 'I' here?"

LH: Yes, and equally important, "Who am I reading?"

BM: Right. Using external forms as templates for shaping writing is one way of throwing readers off balance so that we ask, "Is this form that's been invented responsible for this work?" For instance, I had to have a student point out to me that there were seven more sentences in the

1987 edition than in the 1980 edition of *My Life*—you know, I didn't get it! Was the choice of that mechanical procedure meant to shift responsibility or authority away from you, the one who produces the sentence, to some kind of external machine for shaping sentence into text?

LH: Not really, although I could see that argument. Because I consider one of the important things that form suggests is decision-making and choice, what I actually want to do is to *foreground* that responsibility. And the creating or inventing of artistic form would hopefully suggest the possibility of making choices and decisions in other experiences in life, too. In other words, I want to suggest that we can make our lives. So what I was really trying to do with the form of *My Life* is emphasize that what you have here is a made life—a written one, but a made one. If there's any hope at all for people, it's that we can make our lives rather than just sort of be dragged along by them.

BM: How come your autobiography is so unlike all those autobiographical poems, the expressive lyric, which are really the staple of American poetry? As far as I'm concerned, once you've read one of these, you've read them all.

LH: My overriding concern as a writer is *epistemology*. My work is nearly always concerned with the question, How do you know anything? Whereas the conventional beginning point is, I know something and want to express something about this. Well, in *My Life* I wanted to write a work in which "I" is tremendously mediated by knowing prior to being "I." I tried to do this with all the snippets of language that are in quotes which are a kind of ambient constructing of the I or contextualizing of the I: social, parental, and familial contextualizing, even things that go through my head, like chronic ideas, all those things that modify and mediate the I that's knowing. I wanted this sort of tumbling effect in which context and I roll along, an effect that would be to some extent cumulative, to some extent fragmenting, dispersing. I don't know— maybe the postmodern era produces postmodern people.

LM: There's a lot of talk in the air these days about the way that postmodern texts reflect, say, the fragmentation of life or the lack of linearity, causality in people's lives. But it doesn't seem to me that many writers who set out thinking to themselves, Okay, my experience feels fragmentary and doesn't hold together and have resolutions, so therefore I will write this way.

LH: Despite all this talk about fragmentation and discontinuity, a vast majority of the so-called postmodern writers write long works. We're not a generation of short poem or short story writers by and large. One would think that in a fragmented life, one would write little fragments, but actually that's not true at all. Many of us feel the necessity to take time and space in order to figure and consider and allow a lot in.

LM: It seems to me there's a difference between the kind of gathering of fragments we find in Eliot's *The Waste Land* or Joyce's *Ulysses*—where these fragments are meant to add up to something whole—versus more of an acceptance of the fragments, the way you see in Burroughs's work or Donald Barthelme's "fragments are the only form I trust" idea.

LH: I'm not sure that it's exactly "fragments" we find in postmodern works. Its discontinuities don't isolate its parts; they are like things momentarily pausing in their existing and then picking up again. Whereas the term "fragments" suggests that someone has simply gathered a little bit of this and a little bit of that without any of it really going together. My work isn't at all collagist, for example. I'm not taking a snippet of something here and a snippet there and then randomly juxtaposing them—or juxtaposing randomly simultaneous things. There are specific themes that I'm working on, things I'm thinking about that are related. I don't think about everything in any one work. I'm really trying to concentrate on a problem, or on a range or a matrix of issues.

BM: Belonging to a circle of writers with an acknowledged collective identity, as you do with the Language Poets, is something rather atypical of American writing, though of course there is a strong European tradition of "circles" or "schools," of writers supporting each other, bouncing ideas off of each other, inspiring each other. What has being a Language Poet meant to you? What have you gotten out of belonging to this collective?

LH: It's essential to me. I'm just going to talk about the Bay Area scene, although East Coast people and their books have certainly been important: Charles Bernstein, Bruce Andrews, Alan Davies, Diane Ward after she had gone to the East Coast; also a number of other East Coast writers who are not always regarded as belonging to the Language group—Clark Coolidge certainly, Bernadette Mayer, Alice Notley. I moved back to the Bay Area in 1977, but by then I'd already been in correspondence with Barrett Watten, Ron Silliman, Bob Perelman, and slightly with Rae Armantrout (I guess I'd met both Ron and Barrett at a book fair around 1976). The economy was healthier then than it is now, so that people could get by on part-time jobs, which gave everybody more time for hanging out. It was also easier to find money to publish magazines and books. So there was this moment of enormous activity, lasting for about ten years, although things changed over that time. It's really in the crucible of that activity that I developed some major sense of what writing was and what I could do with it.

This had something to do with a reassessment of what social structure was in the light of the political challenges that were occurring in the sixties. Collective action for me began with the civil rights movement—the early boycotts of Woolworth's, for instance. My earliest stage came when

I went to Harvard; there was a Woolworth's in Harvard Square, and we marched around it endlessly. Next came the women's movement, and then the antiwar movement. All three of those called for a reassessment of the structures of understanding and opinion—which are both partly language, or largely language—and through language, a reassessment of the social structures themselves. We certainly weren't afraid of or repelled by having a social structure of our own, hanging out together, doing things together, challenging each other and being contentious, pushing each other. We did do a lot of pushing each other, which is probably where we got our reputation for being aggressive and impossible, which is current here and there. It wasn't at all unusual for people to shout at each other, but the energy behind it was the energy of the ideas, not hostility or enmity, certainly not as I experienced it.

There's a tendency in capitalist culture to lump a lot of things together and regard them as all the same because they've been lumped together, and then to illuminate the "best," the stars. The whole system of publication and creating "news" about artistic production is more efficient that way, and you don't have to go to the trouble of reading all the other stuff that might be more awkward to lump together or find a label for. This happens to African-American writers much worse than it ever happened to us. The system finds and promotes a black woman writer, it doesn't have to bother publishing any more black women writers. You've got your Alice Walker and your Toni Morrison, sure, but their success doesn't necessarily open doorways for women not writing a certain kind of "black woman's novel."

LM: There's an illusion about literary movements, including the Language group, that everyone magically achieves some kind of monolithic consensus about issues and actions. But every movement passes through something like this period of contentiousness that you've described. Can you give us some sense of the different positions you were all coming from, and how, out of all this arguing and shouting, a consensus finally emerged?

LH: One would be the notion of nonreferentiality that somebody threw out at some point—it might have been Ron Silliman, but I say that with some trepidation because I'm not sure. I vehemently disagreed that there could be such a thing as nonreferentiality in language. It seemed to me that every word, even every word-part, is screaming, calling out to its referent and grabbing as many referents as it can. You can't make nonsense with words, in my opinion. There's always some kernel of sense that somebody will extrapolate from the words, even if you don't want it to be there. It's as though language were always constructing meaning around itself, and meaning is reference and contains reference. So here, let's say (I'm making this up), we might have Ron in conversation referring to the nonreferentiality of Bruce Andrews's sonnets, and someone saying no, Ron, no, you're wrong, and then everyone getting into it. This would be a typical situation with Ron, or whoever it was, testing a term and a concept, and everybody else jumping on it and tearing it apart. Nevertheless, "nonreferentiality" stayed in the vocabulary. I still find people saying I'm a nonreferential writer, which always makes me feel uncomfortable.

BM: What about the way the Language group has gone about explaining itself? Part of the practice of Language poetry has been to surround the poems with manifestos, explanations, commentary and so on, in a way that, once again, is somewhat anomalous in America, though not so strange in Europe.

LH: I can't imagine why people *don't* write polemics! If I have an idea and I am a writer, the only way that idea gets interesting and goes any place is by my writing it out. If I feel polemical about the idea, then I write polemically. The rhetoric of polemics is often very beautiful. Anyway, polemic is not interesting to me so much for its persuasive value as for its exemplary value, the way it serves as a means of encouraging other positions or the life of ideas itself, which seems so exciting. Our interest in theory exemplifies an interest in the life and value of ideas, and the value of elaborating and pressing ideas forward to the very farthest point they can go.

LM: I take it, though, that your goal in exerting this kind of pressure on ideas has more to do than merely furthering intellectual development—ultimately, you hope to change the world, right?

LH: The ultimate goal is to improve the world, yes. Polemic also puts us in the world with much more efficacy than the isolated lyric poet can have. It's important for artists to be efficacious. During the Gulf War, in the Bay Area, there were enormous protests and demonstrations, and what was characteristic of these demonstrations and unlike the ones during the Vietnam War, or even the U.S.-out-of-Central-America demonstrations, was the tremendously self-conscious use of art in them. Street theater, posters, literary graffiti, costumes, installations—it was amazing. Since the mass media were projecting a highly modified version of the events and expressing a very narrow band of opinion—just to the right of center, and then a few voices on the far right and virtually none on the far left—the only people who had the critique and the means for publicizing the critique were the artists. And not just the critique, for that matter, but the facts of what actually was going on—how many people had died, for instance. You learned that at the demonstrations, not on CNN. The whole situation made me feel terribly depressed about our world, but very heartened about the role of the artist.

LM: But for a lot of people today (my students, for instance) everything—demonstrations and television alike—seem to be all just part of Guy Debord's "Society of the Spectacle." This makes me worry that the avant-garde, or artists generally, may have lost the ability to genuinely affect things, to genuinely outrage.

LH: I don't know about "outrage," although the Language Poets at least certainly have generated a lot of hostility. Some of the art I've seen that could be taken as spectacle is work that posits something everybody already knows and then ironizes it slightly, for instance with a motto. That's a typical postmodern device. One of the curious and notable characteristics of my work, Barrett Watten's, Carla Harryman's, Ron Silliman's, Rae Armantrout's, Kit Robinson's, Steve Benson's, is the tremendous degree of sincerity in all of it. It's not ironic work. I myself certainly don't feel ironic about what's going on around us. I feel tragic, angry . . .

BM: Is having people thinking of you as belonging to the school a problem for you?

LH: Not at all. It's not like a collective consciousness, more like a social group. Besides, it's probably not even a school anymore. These things have a lifespan, and the Language school is not really functioning anymore, partly because we just don't have the means or the time. I have at times even felt nostalgic for it. But then again, Carla Harryman and I have been working on a long collaboration for a few years; the *Leningrad* book is a collaboration; so is *Identical Irish*, a book I've done with Ray DiPalma. I've done a sort of collaboration with Kit Robinson. All of this keeps our contacts extremely active, at the forefront of what we're doing.

All in all, I've gotten enormous pleasure from the radicalness of there being a school. I think it's really valuable. There's nothing wrong or anti-human in having a circle of people who collaboratively and individually push literature.

BM: The use of external devices for generating form seems to be a shared technique among your circle. Larry and I were talking about this with Sorrentino the other night, and he says he actually uses this as a pedagogical strategy in his writing classes—he asks his students to use it as a means of inventing a way of generating texts. What's the interest or advantage in such forms?

LH: At a practical level, it provides a container for this great wide swath of potential experience that's going by. Since you're always born in the middle of this and you stay in the middle of it, the question of where to begin and where to stop raises itself as a problem. An invented form allows one to begin anywhere—the form says begin now and then the form says stop now. You're always already writing, and it's always already going on when you stop and you're not making any particular claims on that particular moment as being divine or a moment of transmission or anything. It's just part of what's going on. There are also some forms that are metaphorical, or which are in some way exemplifying what the work is about.

LM: Like using thirty-seven sentences in a book about someone who's thirty-seven years old?

LH: In a way that device was almost like a joke—you know, squaring off with your life or something, forty-five sections with forty-five sentences. I was also interested in paragraphs, the arbitrariness of paragraphs. Sentences get a lot of attention from writers, but Gertrude Stein really is the only one who ever talks about paragraphs. In writing *My Life* I wanted a steady length that was a paragraph, and using thirty-seven seemed to be as logical as anything else I might use.

LM: Of course, the thirty-seven- or forty-five-sentence paragraph structures used in *My Life* have very different parameters from the fourteen-sentence forms used in *Oxota.* Did you find that the compression of this shorter form made the writing process in *Oxota* more difficult for you?

LH: Not at all. It was a pleasure actually. There was a lot of room to maneuver within the overall format. For instance, I could write lines whose sentences could be very long—as they are in chapter 109, the one called "The Change of Seasons," which almost looks like prose. There was plenty of space in the fourteen-line form, but it was also short enough that the rhythms of thinking that go on when you're noticing or contemplating something are clear; whereas in a longer space, like the one in *My Life*, you begin to lose the palpability of that rhythm of sort of turning and glimpsing something, or whatever the thought equivalent of that is. In *Oxota* I wanted that process to be made palpable, to be like thinking. Fourteen lines seemed to be exactly right, whereas in *My Life* the longer space is more like a whole year.

BM: Does it matter if the forms are invisible to the reader or if the reader never picks up on it?

LH: If I really cared about it, I would have written a little preface and pointed it out. Some readers will notice, and others will have this interview in which I'll get to tell them! [Laughter.] But really, if the reader has to have it pounded into his or her head that this is what they're experiencing, then probably the writing isn't that good. I mean, who would go around counting sentences? I know I've never counted how many sentences are in a George Eliot chapter, and there's no reason to expect my readers to do this.

LM: What kind of experience was it for you to go back and add these extra sentences for the later edition of *My Life*? And what was the impulse to do this?

LH: As I said earlier, I don't like commodification of texts—certainly not commodification into a finished product of something called "My Life," to be concluded when I'm still alive! So I thought the best way to foreground the notion of nonclosure, the ongoingness of writing, writing as thinking, was to add to it—which would sort of decommodify the other book. The second thing is that doing this makes a case for the ongoingness of living and writing by showing that thoughts are always adjusting themselves, that thinking is always reinventing what's already been thought. Adding more makes each section at least somewhat different. I actually have been adding to it . . .

BM: A general problem with long poems that are life works is that there's no formal ending to them—or maybe, as Ron Silliman says, *death* becomes a formal problem in such cases. Is *My Life* that kind of poem? A life work? Or are all your works like this, in a sense?

LH: Potentially they all are. I don't know for sure. I'm just starting a new work now called *Sleeps* that's inspired by the *The Thousand and One Nights*, and I want there to be a thousand and one poems with each of the poems being different from each other in the way that the tales are different (I don't think the poems will be tales, although I might invent some, I don't know). Anyway, I just started—I'm on number one—but I figure it's going to take twenty years, if I write one poem a week, which would be really a lot of writing. Isn't that right, twenty years, a thousand and one weeks? Somehow I find that's extremely comforting. At least I won't have to face the panic I feel when I'm between works until twenty years from now.

LM: How would you describe the chief differences between the two versions of *My Life*—and the sources of these differences?

LH: It's a fuller account intellectually. Those seven years coincided with the beginning of the Reagan era, and I concurrently experienced an enormous increase of skepticism and critical abilities. Everything was again open to examination but not as it had been in the sixties, which is where I built my social consciousness and my aesthetics. Then there was this lull during which Larry and I and our children lived in the country; we were certainly not out of touch, but somewhat removed from difficulties. And now we've come to this extraordinarily difficult time that's so unchallenged, whereas in the sixties we were all out there challenging everything, full of optimism, almost as a kind of unit. Now we challenge it, but more on an individual basis; in a general way the culture isn't challenging what's going on. I think I made *My Life* a better book by having refined my abilities to challenge and to critique what was going on, including a lot of my own assumptions. It's being able to go back and say, no, was it so easy as that? Try again.

BM: You have a painting by Ostap Dragomoshchenko on the cover of *Oxota*, and on the copyright page you thank him for the "many real and imaginary paintings" in the book. And in fact, there are a good many paintings described in the course of the book, which suggests that paint-

ing must have some importance for you as a tool or material for writing.
LH: Although I love painting, I'm not sure how much it has influenced
me, apart from inspiration. Film has influenced me more, not actually as
I watch it but as I imagine how it's constructed. The idea of a sequence
of single frames is an exciting notion to me from a compositional standpoint: you get this, then you get this, then you get this, then you get
this. . . . It's the stopping between that's really interesting, exhilarating
to me, and makes me want to write something (though not something
about film!). The influence of music is more complex because of my
being married to a musician, Larry Ochs, who both plays and composes.
He plays in a quartet and a trio, and the nature of those collaborations
is an ongoing inspiration to me. In the case of ensemble playing, the
thing doesn't even exist except collaboratively. Larry playing a solo is
not at all the same as the ROVA Quartet playing a piece, even if his solo
is in it. There's also the dimension of improvisation, as in jazz. Larry's
not really a jazz musician, though; what he plays is avant-garde improvisational music. The process of improvisation is different in poetry, of
course, because once it's on the page it's not being improvised, so it
doesn't exist improvisationally the way a concert of improvised music
does. But the process of not knowing where you're going to end up, and
knowing to avoid your habitual patterns because you just keep doing
the same thing if you don't avoid them, pushing yourself in directions
you can't anticipate—that kind of unpredictability has definitely had an
influence on me.

There was also something liberating for me in recognizing that with
improvisational music, the end result can be okay even if it's not perfect.
Responding to that has been a big release, because otherwise I would
tend to rewrite forever, trying to make something perfect. The improvisation model freed me from the notion of perfection, which in turn has
liberated me from the notion of the commodified final product. There
is no final product in improvised music. There are tapes and CD recordings, but that's like a record of an event rather than the event itself.

Music also undoubtedly shapes other aspects of my writing in ways too
deeply intuitive to talk about very clearly. Among the logics by which I
move from step to step in writing are logics that have to do with either
the sounds of words or associations that are music-like; these logics are
music-like in themselves—or at least they're a poet's interpretation of
music-like logics. The truth is, though, that there's not much relationship between poetry and music, and I'm skeptical of attempts to force
an analogy between them. A musician's mind is utterly different from
the mind of a language-using artist. I've asked Larry sometimes, "What
are you thinking?" and he'll say something like, "I'm listening to the
street." It's utterly alien to me not to be thinking in words.

LM: What kinds of writing interested you in the years before you became associated with the Language school?

LH: I started writing when I was nine or ten, on my father's typewriter.
Actually, a lot of what I wrote were radio dramas, Gene Autry mostly,
dictated to me by my best friend, and it was the typing that felt like writing. So I began my writing career as a typist. The materiality of writing
was already very important to me at a very young age.

BM: Wasn't it a problem that it was your best friend's voice speaking to
you from the page?

LH: No, in my own mind, I was the principal author, and I unabashedly
claimed so because I had typed it, right? So it was my paper. Basically,
though, I always wanted to be a writer. My father had been a writer (but
an unpublished one), and then became a painter and did have some
shows. He was a pretty good painter, though never famous. But he died
young, at age fifty. His favorite writers in the world were Gertrude Stein
and Willa Cather. It was significant that his favorite writers were both
women, and that my father would value writing and especially writing
by women—and of course two such different women, both exemplary
in their own ways. Although I've learned more from Stein than Cather,
I certainly *enjoyed* Cather as much as Stein; in fact I have all my father's
Willa Cather right over there on the shelf. My mother had known Langston Hughes. He had been a close friend of her aunt's, and she had lived
with her aunt during part of her childhood. My parents read poetry
aloud to us, and took me to hear Robert Frost and E. E. Cummings
read. I never was really interested in the more conventional figures. I
liked T. S. Eliot, partly due to my uncle Morse (the husband of that aunt
who was a friend of Langston Hughes). He was a lawyer but his true
avocation was memorizing poetry. I used to go for long walks with him
and he would recite Eliot's *Four Quartets*. He was dashingly handsome; I
thought that was the summit of manhood. It was certainly an environment that encouraged me to be interested in poetry.

LM: Did you study writing in school?

LH: No. I went to Harvard and took one half-year writing course which
was viciously destructive; I stopped writing for a year and a half after
that. I probably wasn't writing very well, I should say by the way, but
anyway this writing course was just vicious. So I decided to become a
painter for about a year and a half. I painted vast oil paintings that are
long gone.

I graduated in 1963, the first year that women were given Harvard degrees, and it was a very sexist atmosphere. The Lamont Library, where
the poetry room is, was still closed to women then, so I never went to the
Lamont poetry room. When I went to Harvard the works that we read
all dated from before 1900, so I started reading Kenneth Patchen and

Lawrence Ferlinghetti on my own, and then Robert Creeley. Kenneth Irby, who was there then, gave me Creeley's *For Love* for my twenty-first birthday. So there I was: in the thick of it.

LM: Were there any fiction writers that you were particularly drawn to?

LH: Proust. If I could have written Proust's work I wouldn't have had to write any of those other things. There are a few places in *My Life* where I took the Scott-Moncrieff sentences, especially from the prelude to *Swann's Way*, and just replaced all the words: the words are different, but the rhythms are identical. John Ruskin is also a big favorite of mine, and Proust developed his prose style translating Ruskin into French. And Scott-Moncrieff of course translated Proust back into a Ruskin prose.

BM: It's obvious that Stein has been important to you.

LH: Of course, I'm not Gertrude Stein so I'm not doing the same thing Gertrude Stein is doing. But what she did was remarkable. If I could do something as good as that, that's fine with me. I read some of Stein early on, and then I didn't read any for years and years until Marjorie Perloff wrote an article pointing out how obviously I was influenced by Gertrude Stein, and I decided to get influenced. Coincidentally, about two weeks later I was invited to give some lectures on Stein, so then I really had to read it all. I don't think I was so much influenced as intensely respectful—with some reservations, too.

LM: Were there any other figures later on in your career who played a similar role for you?

LH: Louis Zukofsky. And I read Wallace Stevens with great passion when I was in my twenties. Where does one stop? George Eliot, Dickens, Melville. I read detective novels, Ruskin, Sir Francis Bacon. I read a lot of books about exploration, the classics, and I'm moving more and more to readings in the history of science.

I've also been reading about the West a lot recently, and that's going to influence my ideas, in the sense that that's something I want to address directly. I thought I was going to write a Western poem, as a counterpart to my Russian novel. I may still, but it hasn't been going very well. Meanwhile I'm supposed to give a talk in Colorado in the summer, so I think I'm going to talk about Western knowledge, from the Western concept of how you get knowledge, with some discussion of clinical medicine— maybe even clinical anatomy. Since my daughter is in medical school, I've been able to go to the anatomy lab a few times. Seeing a cadaver and everything inside it is intensely interesting and revelatory, although of what I'm not quite sure yet.

BM: Having already done a second version of *My Life*, do you plan to do another version again sometime?

LH: Yes. But I won't publish it for a long, long time!

Photograph by Maggie Jaffe

Swallowing the Poison
An Interview with Harold Jaffe

Larry McCaffery

The decal on my left thigh reads Adolph, on my right, Coors. I have Manville on my chest, the good-hands folks who brought you asbestosis. On my big but not big-big: the boycotted grapes of Gallo, rich red wine, you can cut it with a knife. Futures brokers' salaries run up and down my spine, like sutures, like the Frankenstein monsters of the old black and white flicks, recently colorized, a fine example, if you need one, of state-of-the-art technology addressing itself to art and entertainment. I've been places . . .

— "Eros/Calvin Klein"

Judging from his last several books, Harold Jaffe is horny as Warren Beatty, melancholy as Hamlet, and furious as an Old Testament prophet. For example, his collection *Eros Anti-Eros* (1990) is an outraged and outrageous denunciation of the current status of eros, free expression, and bodily sensuality in the time of AIDS, Jesse Helms, Madonna, and legal harassment of rock stars, performance artists, gallery directors, and college professors. During the past fifteen years, Jaffe has published a series of books whose innovative formal strategies are designed to counter the political and sexual repressions associated with late capitalism's expansion into our culture's most intimate reaches.

Jaffe has written two novels, *Mole's Pity* (1979) and *Dos Indios* (1983), the latter an evocative portrayal of the life of a crippled Peruvian flute player. While *Dos Indios* deals with some of the themes and character types found in Jaffe's other work, it is also notable for its surface realism, quiet tone, and straightforward narrative structure—features that contrast strikingly with the oblique, multilayered approaches, the rage, and razor-sharp humor found in his short fictions.

Jaffe's first collection of fictions, *Mourning Crazy Horse* (1982), focused on the victimization and alienation of socially marginalized people—blacks, Native Americans, drug addicts, criminals. In *Mourning Crazy Horse* Jaffe often created jarring intellectual and emotional resonances by juxtaposing slight narrative episodes with fragments of literary and other cultural references (some "real" and some invented), most of which were drawn from "high culture."

But while analogous formal strategies are evident in all his subsequent work, by the time of his next collection, *Beasts* (1986), the range of reference and allusion broadened to include pop culture—a realm Jaffe increasingly began to draw upon and reconstitute in order to analyze and interrogate its hold over people's imaginations and value systems. Like all of Jaffe's collections, *Beasts* is so unified in theme and structure that it can almost be regarded as an innovative novel. Modeled on a medieval bestiary, each fiction in *Beasts* has a beast as its title, and in each case the particular beast (Sheep, Monkey, Pelican, Crow, Salamander, Sidewinder, and so forth) is employed variously as the name of a parlor game or a prison, purely as a metaphor, as a "character" in the story, and so on.

One of Jaffe's best-known books, *Madonna and Other Spectacles* (1988), displays the deepening influence of recent critical theorists (notably Fredric Jameson, Jean Baudrillard, and Guy Debord, whose pioneering postmodernist study, *Society of the Spectacle*, figures in the collection's title). Here Jaffe uses the names of various well-known pop figures (Madonna, the Three Stooges, Lightnin' Hopkins, Boy George, Tonto, Hurricane Carter) as the basis for improvisational forays into the sources of racism, the denaturing of the body, and the substitution of real desire and appetite by media images. With these works and more recent works—*Eros Anti-Eros, Straight Razor* (which includes fifteen computer-generated visuals by Norman Conquest [a.k.a. Derek Pell], 1995), and *Othello Blues* (1996)—Jaffe has created a body of what he has termed "guerrilla writing," which, like Kathy Acker's work, defamiliarizes familiar narrative materials as a means of relentlessly interrogating our society's underlying assumptions and obsessions. Jaffe is of course keenly aware of the current resignation and impotence among artists who have forfeited their imaginings in the manipulated hyperspace of contemporary America.

Nonetheless, Jaffe's stubborn, though carefully analyzed insistence is that art still has the capacity not only to defamiliarize but to destabilize institutionalized oppressions. Hence Jaffe's poetic dictum both in his manifesto-essay "Guerrilla Writing" and in *Eros Anti-Eros*: "find a seam / plant a mine / slip away."

The highly unusual formal features of Jaffe's fiction are unified by his desire to find ways of bringing together planes of cultural discourse that would normally be separated, in the hope that their intersection will reveal deeper patterns of prejudice, ignorance, and repression. But while undeniably deeply engaged with the wonders, banalities, and absurdities of our postmodernist "Society of the Spectacle," Jaffe's work to date has, curiously, received little attention in the United States outside "serious" literary circles. This is in interesting contrast to Japan, Germany, Cuba, and elsewhere, where Jaffe's work has been translated and is receiving considerable attention.

In any case, Jaffe's relative anonymity in the United States is undeserved, despite the occasional difficulties readers are confronted with in responding to the disquieting aesthetic and thematic collisions one finds in his fictions. True, when readers pick up, say, *Eros Anti-Eros*, they are going to find collage-like "texts" (rather than "stories" in the usual sense), oblique angles of presentation, unsituated bits of dialogue, skewed narrative fragments, and pastiches of forms and discourses drawn from a bewildering array of sources. Madonna and the Meese Commission *Report on Pornography*, MTV and Derrida, inner-city vernacular and poststructuralist jargon, scenes of skinheads, serial killers, and Reagan—just about any image or sound bite can appear in a Jaffe fiction. On the other hand, this stunningly discontinuous barrage of "information" mirrors—and models—the way we First Worlders experience "reality" these days. The point is that Jaffe sees, mimics, and interrogates what most of us experience only dimly. "Analyzing" Jaffe's fiction may be as much beside the point as trying to analyze the discontinuous media onslaught we are all subjected to daily.

And that is also Jaffe's point. Like Kathy Acker and Mark Leyner—two contemporary writers whose innovative works are similarly strange and formally "difficult"—Jaffe is one of the new breed of postmodern writers creating fiction whose "experimental" features actually follow old-fashioned realism's dictum to "tell it like it is." This realism, however, reflects the experience of postindustrial capitalism—the "realism" of fifty-seven-channel televisions and remote controls, of an infinitely reproducible series of images that "stand in" for the real.

Jaffe's work has always been overtly political, inflammatory in its rage at racial and social repression. What is new in Jaffe's recent work is its explicit focus on all manner of sexual repression and censorship, the denaturing of the body, the replacement of bodily gratification by erotic simulation and image, the replacement of the sixties' "polymorphous perversity" by the "safe sex" eighties' sense of shame and guilt. According to Jaffe, the body in the time of AIDS is the site both of ongoing social repression and of passionate, principled resistance to this repression.

The following interview was initially conducted on the back patio of Jaffe's home in San Diego and was emended on several occasions. Following an earlier stint as a university professor (at Long Island University during the early seventies), Jaffe had moved to San Diego in the early eighties after having spent several years traveling extensively in Asia, Central and South America, and the Caribbean. A professor of creative writing and literature at San Diego State University, Jaffe is also editor of *Fiction International*, a journal notable for promoting writing that combines formal innovation and radical politics.

*   *   *

Harold Jaffe: Selected Bibliography

Novels and Fiction Collections

Mole's Pity (novel). New York: Fiction Collective, 1979.
Mourning Crazy Horse (fictions). New York: Fiction Collective, 1982.
Dos Indios (novel). New York: Thunder's Mouth Press, 1983.
Beasts (fictions). Willimantic, CT: Curbstone, 1985.
Madonna and Other Spectacles (fictions). New York: PAJ/Farrar, Straus, and Giroux, 1988.
Eros Anti-Eros (fictions). San Francisco: City Lights Books, 1990.
Straight Razor (fictions, with visuals by Norman Conquest). Normal, IL: Black Ice Books, 1995.
Othello Blues (novel). Fiction Net, 1995.

As Editor

Walt Whitman. Facsimile edition of the 1883 biography by Richard Maurice Bucke. New York: Johnson Reprint Corporation, 1970.
The American Experience: A Radical Reader (coeditor). New York: Harper and Row, 1970.
Affinities: A Short Story Anthology (coeditor). New York: Crowell, 1970; revised and expanded, 1976.
Fiction International (coeditor, 1983–93). Special double issues on Writing and Politics (with Larry McCaffery, 1984); Central American Writing (with Larry McCaffery, 1986); Third World Women's Writing (with Larry McCaffery, 1990); Sex, Pornography, and Censorship (with Larry McCaffery and Melvin Freilicher, 1992).

Uncollected Fiction

"Desert Hare." *Another Chicago Magazine* (Summer 1983).
"Broken Glass." *Minnesota Review* (Spring 1987).
"Man Ray." *Boundary* 2, 15 (Spring 1987).
"Foucault the Cyberpunks." In *Mississippi Review: The Cyberpunk Controversy*, ed.
    Larry McCaffery (Fall 1988).
"Blackface." *Bakunin* (Summer 1991).
"Dartman." *Asylum Annual* (Winter, 1992).
"Bad and Personal." *Asylum* (Winter 1992).
"War Couture." *Black Ice* (Winter 1992).
"Kong." *Bakunin* (Spring 1993).
"Gender." *Collages and Bricolages* (Fall 1994).
"Drug Addict." *Witness* (Winter 1993).
"Prison Ferries." *Asylum Arts Annual* (Winter 1994).
"Innocent Language." *Black Warrior Review* (Fall 1995).
"Queen of Hearts." In *Loompanics Unlimited: Live in Las Vegas*. Port Townsend,
    WA: Loompanics Unlimited, 1996.
"Bondage." *Nobuddies* (Summer 1996).

Essays and Reviews

"Bucke's *Walt Whitman*: A Collaboration." *Walt Whitman Review* (September
    1969).
"Richard Maurice Bucke and Walt Whitman." *Canadian Review of American Studies*
    (Spring 1971).
Review of *Diane Arbus: An Aperture Monograph. Psychocultural Review.* (Winter
    1977).
Review of *The Face of Madness: Hugh W. Diamond and the Origin of Psychiatric Pho-
    tography. Psychocultural Review* (Spring 1977).
"John Gardner's *On Moral Fiction*." *Fiction International* 12 (1980).
"The Minnesota Review." *Literary Magazine Review* (Fall 1982).
Review of *From Sand Creek* and *Fight Back: For the Sake of the People, for the Sake of
    the Land*, by Simon Ortiz. *The Nation* 3 April 1982.
Review of *The Partisan Review Reader: Writers and Politics*, ed. William Phillips and
    Edith Kurzweil; and *The Truants*, by William Barrett. *American Book Review*
    (Fall 1983): 5.
Foreword to *Fiction International—Central American Writing Special Issue.* (Spring
    1986): 1–2.
"Chester Himes's Harlem Novels." *American Book Review* (Spring–Summer 1986).
"John Wideman's *Reuben*," *American Book Review* (1988): 3.
"Fiction-Writing in the Space-Time of Late Monopoly Capital." *Cream City Re-
    view*, special fiction issue (Winter 1989).
"Guerrilla Writing." *American Book Review* (Spring 1990).
"Harold Brodkey's *Runaway Soul*." *Los Angeles Times Book Review* (November
    1992). Reprinted, (expanded version), *Fiction International* 23, (1993): 176–91.
"Introduction." *Fiction International—Sex, Pornography, Censorship Special Issue* (Fall
    1992): 1–2.
"Letter to the Shade of Hemingway Concerning the Current State of Fiction."
    American Notes and Queries (February 1993).

"That's What Zipper-Bustin' Avant-Pop [Mom] Is All About." In *In Memoriam to Postmodernism: Essays on the Avant-Pop*, ed. Lance Olsen and Mark Amerika. San Diego: San Diego State University Press, 1995.

Reviews, Interviews, and Essays about Jaffe's Work

Filas, Michael, and Andrew Koopman. Review-essay on *Straight Razor* and *Queen of Hearts*. *Central Park* (Fall 1995).
Krekorian, Michael. "Harold Jaffe." In *Postmodern Fiction: A Bio-Bibliographical Guide*, ed. Larry McCaffery, 413–15. Westport, CT: Greenwood Press, 1986.
McCaffery, Larry. "An Interview with Harold Jaffe." *Pacific Review* (Spring 1991).
———. "An Interview with Harold Jaffe." *Central Park* (Fall 1993).
Miller, James. "Contesting the Spectacle: Harold Jaffe's 'Guerilla Writing.'" *Postmodern Studies* (Spring 1995): 227–49.
———. "An Interview with Harold Jaffe." *New Novel Review* (Summer 1996).

*   *   *

LARRY MCCAFFERY: This would seem to be a good time for radically innovative writers like you, Mark Leyner, and Kathy Acker—"good" in the sense that you're able to get your books published and attract reasonably wide audiences. But isn't there a flip side to this—a weakening of the ability of even truly radical, revolutionary art to affect anything simply because it can be appropriated and commodified so easily? We saw this, for example, with punk . . .

HAROLD JAFFE: Commodification is probably the most intractable problem facing resistant or oppositional art today. Can you rupture something with which you are, willy-nilly, in complicity? Can you destabilize institutions like Random House and its parent corporation if in fact you are published by Random House?

LM: And that dilemma is further complicated when Random House is only an extension of Standard Oil. What you really want to destabilize isn't so much Random House but the entire web of corporate patronage and what sustains *that*.

HJ: A number of artists, particularly visual artists, have theorized about this question of complicity. Many of them are unhappy about it, but others have accepted that this is simply the way it is. The patronage of the wealthy in the arts has long been accepted; well, now it is *corporate* patronage. This is a particular problem if you see yourself as an oppositional artist. Can you both be sucked up into the vortex, and yet retain some autonomy and disruptive charge in what you write? And even assuming that you can retain some disruptive charge, what about your readers? Can your readers react in any meaningful way to oppositional notions if they recognize that the frame around you is Random House and the conglomerate that frames Random House? It's like seeing Hans Haacke in a museum, or like seeing Duchamp. When you see the Paris urinal in the fancy museum, you are obviously not reacting in the same way as you would seeing the urinal on the Left Bank. Can you, then, make a deal with "The Man" and still retain some semblance of integrity? One would think no, but it might be too early to tell. Maybe if there is enough oppositional art being created and bought up because it is there, because it somehow reflects the zeitgeist, then willy-nilly it may have some influence.

LM: What got you started with the pieces collected in *Eros Anti-Eros?*

HJ: Because my disposition is subversive, and because physical love has been re-stigmatized now in this time of the renewed elevation of Helms, I felt moved to recuperate desire, to reinsert polymorphous pleasure into the commodified nest of leisure. That was the original impulse, then one thing led to another.

LM: Your original title—"Eros in the Time of AIDS"—seemed to suggest that the AIDS hysteria is one of the specific sources of this devaluation of bodily love?

HJ: Yes. The AIDS rhetoric fell right in line with the governing Zeitgeist of the Reagan years, and with the convenient capitalist puritanism we see today. The AIDS propaganda not only further marginalized any kind of physical love thought of as deviant between men, but at the same time it's been used to marginalize even heterosexual love which appears to be even in the smallest way "deviant," which is to say, not entirely monosexual, missionary, segregated from desire. Even *thinking* sensually has been made suspect. One of the typically opportunistic capitalizations we see these days is sexual counseling. Ten years ago sex therapists were encouraging people to go for it, fuck, suck and muck all night long. Now, sex therapists and other self-styled "counselors" are treating these same zesty lovers as "sex addicts." Because that's the direction the Zeitgeist is blowing.

AIDS is the largest "objective" phenomenon to have played into that. I use quotes because it is very difficult to understand what AIDS is, particularly its etiology, and the facts of its transmission, which have been deliberately obscured by the dominant culture.

LM: You had previously used AIDS as one of the key tropes in your title piece from *Madonna*—as yet another media production that has managed to infiltrate even the deepest parts of our imaginations and desires.

HJ: It was one example of something I wanted to present in various ways throughout the *Madonna* texts: namely, the official culture getting between people and their most intimate desires. In "Madonna," the fiction, I metaphorized this infiltration as the torturer's electric wires that are attached to our genitals. I continued working with this general idea throughout *Eros*. When you asked about what got me started with the *Eros Anti-Eros* texts, I should have added that part of what was involved has to do with my own situation of being indisputably middle-aged and yet feeling probably more sensual than I've ever felt. My psychophysiological reading underscored my ideological reading.

LM: There is an interesting way in which all your work can be interpreted (at least in one reading) as being a kind of displaced, ongoing autobiography. Do you yourself consider your work to be autobiographical?

HJ: Only in part. And not deliberately so. For example, when I wrote *Dos Indios* I thought that my perspective was largely objective, that I was writing about people who were as far away from me as any people could be. Even in that case, I guess you might say that my year in India and my close reading of Buddhism and anthropology and comparative religion had moved me in a direction where I was susceptible to the kinds of ideas in that book. But still I felt that what I was presenting there had almost nothing to do with me personally. It was only after I wrote it that I recognized a number of aspects of myself in both characters, particularly the legless character, Manco. Specifically, Manco's grievous wound corresponded to an emotional isolation I've always felt. His overwhelming compassion and bitter anger toward those responsible for unjust suffering; his stubborn persistence in his art. These corresponded in important ways to my own circumstances, though I hadn't consciously intended it that way.

LM: In various ways your fiction has always not only dealt with sexuality but with the ways we *talk* and *write* about sexuality. I wonder, though, if foregrounding technique might not seem somehow to interfere with this expression?

HJ: Well, there are different ways of foregrounding, or seeming to foreground, technique. In visual artists like the constructivist El Lissitsky or Picasso of the Guernica period or even Mondrian, or in music, Scriabin, Messiaen, or, say Tom Waits, the formal aspects weave in and out of the sensuous content, shaping it, charging it. It is in fact the energy and technical adornments *in combination* which equal passion.

Regarding writing, there are certain things which, at this historical juncture, can't be spoken about plainly. *Madonna* was very much about that. In "Boy George," for example, virtually no thought is complete without two or three intervening kinds of thoughts or tropes. You see these same kinds of confusions and difficulties being suggested in *Eros*. I don't know how clear it was in "Eros/Calvin Klein" that the two people were actually changing into each other's underwear while this scene was going on. But there too, even though it's sensuality that the male character is principally interested in, his mind didn't let him stay there entirely. Part of what I'm driving at with different verbal interventions is that people are in good part prohibited from realizing their sensuality, or even their sensual fantasies in an unadulterated or uncontaminated way. These dominant-culture-generated contaminations are more obtrusive now than ever before.

LM: Throughout *Eros* you imply that as contemporary life tends to diminish eros more and more, we also find ourselves elevating thanatos, so that the tenuous balance between the two is thrown out of whack.

HJ: We're witnessing the death of *real* desire. In its place we're given this simulacrum of desire—which is really a form of pseudo or formatted desire. In the United States before AIDS, the formatted desire had to do with outsize genitals, sexual avidity, and heroic bodies. Marcuse would have called this repressive desublimation. That is, on the one hand we have something (frank sexuality) that pretends to desublimate, to rupture sexual repression. But when you look at this "frank" sexuality carefully, you see that it is just another form of repression and consumerism because its version of sexuality is mediated by class and heroic fantasies which are contingent on abundant dollars and ample leisure. This "repressive desublimation" is not happening so much with AIDS. It needn't be, since AIDS is made to order. And so it has been harnessed by institutionalized rightists and opportunists.

LM: To what extent is there an actual relationship between these right-wing, repressive racial and political attitudes and the interests of consumer capitalism? For example, is it in the interest of consumer capitalism to normalize and regularize everything so that they can sell things?

HJ: This relationship has to do with the leveling, or flattening tendency, which renders citizens much less susceptible to "deviancy" in their actions. Deviancy in *action* presupposes a kind of deviancy in *thinking*, which is counter to consumer capitalism. On the face of it one would think that if sexuality were being devalued consumer capitalism would be gravely wounded. But what consumer capitalism has done very rapidly is erect a kind of Xeroxed sensuality which can be replicated, packaged, and sold more readily.

LM: This sounds like a Baudrillardian simulation . . .

HJ: It's a simulacrum of sensuality which privileges the representations of sexuality. Miniskirts have come back, sadomasochism is mainstream. Calvin Klein ads jerk around our fantasies. All these reductions work somewhat the way Busby Berkeley musicals operated in the Depression. They have nothing to do with what ordinary people can realize; they are given to people (sold to them, really) as a kind of long-term investment, a fantasy. Obviously, when people are flattened and undeviant, they are more susceptible to buying into these marketable fantasies than if they were doing their own thing, spending long, languid hours making love, acting autonomously. Hence, leisure-sex is sold even as pleasure-sex is prohibited.

LM: Your work, like that of the cyberpunks, implies that there is a key difference between the Busby Berkeley presentations of the thirties and what we see today—the media industry now is able to inundate us with these kinds of definitions and meanings and images much more often (and more effectively) than it could back in the 1930s, when it was just coming into existence.

HJ: Yes: information capital—meaning that the blandishments and manipulations happen much more rapidly and insistently. The dominant ideology is, as James Scully puts it, transparent. At the same time there's also a real sense in which this system and its values are more susceptible to subversion by the same media proliferation. One crucial problem is that the subversion itself can be *consumed*, and thus marginalized—it winds up being sucked up and spit out and forgotten about because it's just another product.

One sees this provocatively in terms of sexual deviation. There's a strong current of mostly young, marginalized people who have lived their entire sexual lives under the AIDS ideology umbrella. Well, they are fed up with the lies and disinformation, with having the federal government's rubber-gloved fist stuck up their ass or womb. And these proud, young deviants have broken out in fundamental ways: by defying gender roles (cross-dressing, validating transsexualism); by piercing and tattooing their bodies (that is, employing their bodies as canvases or laboratories, against the Judaic-Christian dictum of the despised, submissive flesh); by validating sadomasochism (which among other things mocks the organized, institutionalized mayhem under the veneer of capitalism); by publishing violently dissenting fanzines.

Pretty funky stuff, right? Interestingly, many of these impulses of subversive intent have already been mediated and consumed. Postmodern capitalism moves with blitzkrieg speed. Cross-dressing, androgyny, and transsexualism have made the talk programs and the tabloid columns. Sadomasochism has found its way into TV and couture, where you can buy rubber items, Velcro leg restraints, "fetishwear." Tattooing and body-piercing are consumer happenings. Death Herself is in the process of being packaged, sold, and eaten by our white nuclear American family.

LM: Like many other major postmodern writers, you regularly incorporate elements of popular culture into the textures of your fiction. Obviously in your case this tendency has in part to do with what Robert Coover says in his "Dedication" to *Pricksongs*—the need to confront myth on its own ground. And clearly the myths governing people's lives today are derived from pop culture.

HJ: True. Those distinctions (so crucial to modernism) have virtually disappeared, at least in so-called First World countries. It's astonishing how rapidly this has taken place. Almost every American artist I can think of—writer, musician, or visual artist—is as involved with popular culture as she/he is with high culture. Usually more so. Pop culture is the paradigm, the vortex. We're in it.

LM: Is this a loss of seriousness, an indication of decline the way that a number of people have suggested? Or is it simply that contemporary artists have a different relationship to our myths and our information?

HJ: It's a complicated issue. It has to do with the flattening of consciousness that Jameson cites. This flattening, the inevitability of it, is inextricably tied to the various social paradigms. For example, the computer, which has replaced Henry Adams's industrial dynamo, is a paradigm without profile and thus subject to any number of imposed profiles. Unlike the dynamo or any of those other modernist paradigms, the computer's gears and levers are now invisible, replaced by integrated circuitry. In accord with the dominant image of the computer and related storing and replicating devices such as the copier and fax machine, the whole notion of originality has been modified in ways that are perhaps irreparable. With originality flattened, with density suddenly made hollow, it is very difficult to think of yourself, as artist, as having a particular kind of calling, as having a particular kind of knowledge, of having the kind of aura that has, since the Enlightenment, been associated with high thinking kinds of art. For better or worse, these movements are inevitable, they have already taken place, they're part of the way advanced technology infects its users, and also of the way in which consumer capital processes images and representations in order to flatten and commodify. So I don't think we have any choice but to acknowledge and valorize popular culture. But we should also interrogate it, examine the way it operates, not merely blindly embrace it.

LM: Writers today have to take into account the fact that their readers have different cultural touchstones, frames of reference, and artistic allusion.

HJ: The frames of reference have changed radically. For one thing, younger people, even the brightest younger people, aren't in a position where they can read much. This isn't necessarily a fall from seriousness, or even an indication that young people aren't educated. People don't read today because information is conveyed in other ways. Much more shorthand ways. And there is a different valuation put on time. You generally don't have the kind of space and silence people need for contemplative reading, the way we and other people of our generation did. So important-seeming literary references are often closed off to writers.

One particularly troubling aspect of the separation from literacy has to do with young people not reading history, instead learning their history from sound bites and infected movies or docudramas. The period we are now living through resembles Weimar Berlin between the First and Second World Wars. Transgression, delirium, abject poverty, death lurking in the form of brutal violence, or, today, AIDS and "hot zone" viruses. One important difference between now and Berlin in the twenties is that people had a better sense then of historical fascism than they do now, when young people are segregated from their history, which capital has transformed into consumer ambiance and "life-style."

LM: Certainly the range of reference in your recent works seems to have changed since *Mourning Crazy Horse* to reflect this proliferation of pop culture—this filling up of all intellectual and literal space with pop cultural commodities. Previously most of your references were to high culture . . .

HJ: Though I have always been interested in pop culture, it's true that the referentiality in *Mourning Crazy Horse* was more "modernist" in its use of high culture than it has been since. The changes I've made in this regard haven't come about because I necessarily embrace pop culture now more than before but because there's been a paradigm shift that makes the earlier approach anachronistic, hence less useful.

LM: Has living here in California had any specific effect on your writing?

HJ: Yes. It's the fast track leading to . . . well, it doesn't much matter where it leads to, right? I'm currently writing out of California. At the same time I am conscious of what it means to be an innovative writer. Historically, when you think of innovative or cutting-edge kinds of art, many have been pro-fascist, or at least in complicity with a repressive ruling system. Italian Futurism was pro-fascist in the main; one thinks of Royalist Eliot and the more complexly fascist Pound's free verse response to the traditional Georgians; there were the Imagists, who were, in a sense, apolitical, verging on antidemocratic. On the other hand, there were the German Expressionists, the surrealists, the existential writers in the Sartre group, the Situationists—all of these artists determinedly antifascist. What *I'm* relating to is the intersecting traditions of homegrown subversives, like John Brown, Nat Turner, the American Indian Movement, the early Quakers, and antinomians. I've done this mostly intuitively by combining my interests in subversive, dissenting movements with various current realities, including my living on the fast track in California. I am swallowing and processing very rapidly, and that rapidity, or charge, is in my recent writing.

LM: Rapidity, charge. That brings us to your current interest in what you call "crisis writing."

HJ: Yes. I've always been interested in crisis visuals, such as the *affiches* that were posted during the May '68 period in France, or the revolutionary posters in Nicaragua during the Sandinista insurgency. More recently, Queer Nation and Gran Fury have executed crisis art on behalf of ACT UP. And for the last several years the Canadian Krzysztof Wodiczko has been projecting his counterinstitutional image bites on public buildings.

During the Persian Gulf War, I decided to put together a volume of texts generated by the war. Crisis texts, executed quickly, without fuss. Well, the war, like all things postmodern, ended rapidly, and was even more rapidly packaged and consumed. So I decided to expand my conception to war between races, between classes, between genders. The result is a manuscript I've been working on which contains a number of crisis texts, based on the representations of the Persian Gulf War, on the beating of Rodney King, on the representations of the Jeffrey Dahmer killings, on the uprising (I refuse to call it "riot") in L.A., on the so-called war on drugs, on the female serial killers in Florida, on the reinforced repression of sensuality, and so on. Most of these texts are minimalist: unsituated dialogues or monologues.

Among other things, I want these rapid crisis texts to stand in opposition to the perfectionist workshopping mentality pervading creative writing programs and the Associated Writers Program, which naively suggests that serious writing can still exist outside the loop of infectious politics.

LM: Your distinction between pop culture and works which are *about* pop culture raises an important point about the ongoing need for some sort of "resistance" art in creating works that don't simply incorporate the reigning paradigms but that question them, subvert them, confront them on their own grounds. That's the basis of my "avant-pop" concept.

HJ: Which is well conceived. I think of my work as a kind of resistance, or oppositional writing. I like to get inside the culture's systems and metaphors and discourses so I can oppose them—but from the inside out. The point is that all the different elements of power that compose our culture appear to be seamless; you know, this web of interfacing ideology which keeps us from being ourselves, which gets between us and our most intimate desires. But it is *not* really seamless, it can be ruptured in various ways. Computer hackers are doing it in terms of technology. It is done by various kinds of terrorism, though not by institutional terrorism, which is transparent and enlisted to protect the dominant ideological web.

My contention is that this sort of terrorist, guerrilla response can be employed in writing, but there are lots of things to keep in mind. For example, if you telegraph your dissent too obviously, you are not going to get the work published; or if it is published, it is going to be marginalized in particular ways. The notion, as I put it in "Guerrilla Writing," is to find a seam, plant a mine, slip away. To disrupt along the fault lines of a system. Guerrilla art mimics institutionalized discourse and commodity art in order to *turn* it, defamiliarize it, thereby revealing its ideology in order to destabilize it. Destabilization in this sense means empowering readers/viewers/listeners to see through the official culture's blandishments and mediations.

LM: This "guerrilla writing" approach seems related to what you've referred to as a "bulimic aesthetic"—the artist as a kind of shaman who publicly swallows all these ideological poisons and then, in an exemplary act of creative transformation, vomits them back out. And of course, what emerges is often not particularly appetizing . . .

HJ: What I have in mind by "swallowing" the poisonous culture is to reconstitute it, transform it into something that will serve as an adversarial force. When I see virulent bits of language or data, or the sinister associations or physical alignments on TV or in the newspapers or online, I extract them and recontextualize them so my readers can *really* see them. At the same time, I mean to show the dominant ideology at work, to isolate it in order to display its virulence.

LM: Your works often have narrators who display language and erudition with a kind of bravura and exuberance; but I sense something else going on inside them, something fearful, a sense that they are using their verbal displays and erudition as a shield between themselves and the world that is out there, that is threatening.

HJ: I've thought about this, tangentially, and after the fact. Part of that division you cite has to do with the various divided impulses I feel when I am writing. There is often a sense of rage inside me when I write, but connected with the rage is a sense of disgust, which tends to move me in a different direction. The rage moves me to confront while the disgust moves me away. Disgust brings with it this deep, negative feeling that there's no sense in confronting anything, it's useless, so you might as well trope it, play with it, laugh raucously, become delirious, dance naked on the abyss. Those impulses—anger/delirious disgust—often seem to overlap when I'm working, and to some extent they are in conflict. But it is important to say that my negativity means to be dialectical, my No! in thunder is a no which posits a yes. It is a no to institutional denial, and so implies a yes to eros and fundamental life.

LM: For all the rage and disgust that are present in your creative process, there is also often a peculiar distancing in your work, a lack of obvious affect in the surface textures.

HJ: That neutral tone is meant to simulate the kind of numbness that attribute to the postmodern condition. So the lack of affect you find in a text like "Max Headroom" mimics the way the culture operates to seduce us into feeling, but then curtailing the feeling, positing desire,

but preventing us from consummating the desire—particularly not letting us consummate it in ways that are independent of institutionalized
notions of desire. Consuming the desire without consummating it.

   This cooler, harder tone is in contrast to the way I was working in
Mourning Crazy Horse, which I wrote in virtual isolation in Sag Harbor fifteen years ago. My connection in *Mourning Crazy Horse* with the people
that I thought of (and still think of) as oppressed was almost dangerously close.

LM: How do you mean "dangerously close"?

HJ: In the sense that my imaginative involvement with these people became emotionally or mentally dangerous. This narrative empathy allows
me an imaginative entryway into another realm, so that I get away from
myself, while still being in myself. A lot of my work has to do with various voices emerging, colliding. But when you stretch your mentality like
I was doing, it becomes like the situation in the Chekhov story I refer
to somewhere in *Mourning Crazy Horse* ("Ward Six") about the physician
who becomes so taken with a schizophrenic—in love, in a sense, with
him, a kind of Christ-like love—that he is finally sucked into the vortex,
and then loses everything. But I'm never really worried about control;
in fact the more dangerously out of control, while being *in control* you
are, the more tensile and interesting the art is liable to be. Like Van
Gogh, Little Richard, the Sex Pistols, Robert Johnson, or N.W.A. The
point is that you have to maintain, finally, a certain emotional distance,
while at the same time merging, or suggesting merge. I'm talking about
a felt distance; Hindus call it disinterest. Well, as I cultivated that disinterest, I started decorating it, as one decorates the figure of Shiva the
Destroyer in the temple, playing with it, making music with it.

LM: Your recent fiction seems more playful than your earlier work. Has
there been a conscious shift in your writing (or yourself)—maybe the
influence of living out here in "laid-back" California?

HJ: I don't know about the "laid-back" part, but, yes, the fictions in
Mourning Crazy Horse are probably *fiercer* than my work today. There's
considerable anger and rage in *Madonna* and *Eros* and *Beasts* and *Straight
Razor*, but it is somewhat modulated. I don't think you can keep dis-
charging as much energy as I was in my earlier work without some sort
of return, or emotional recompense. Otherwise those emotions begin
to circle around and come back at you—no sense of purge. Imagine
Beckett writing that prose without publishing it. You get the sense of
all that energetic despair falling into a vacuum. Even if the response is
not commensurate with what you've done or not really on target, the
response helps. So I guess you could say that I turned away from that
fierceness partially in self-defense. It's not possible to bleed constantly as
a writer without eventually bleeding yourself dry. Moreover, bleeding art

is not effective oppositional art at this po-mo, techno-smug juncture. My writing combines calculation and intuition now, whereas earlier it was fundamentally intuitive. In respect to combining calculation and intuition, I follow the examples of Brecht and Blake, B. Traven, and others.

LM: Do you consider yourself a Marxist?

HJ: My impulses are closer to anarchism.

LM: Do you see anarchism as a possible pragmatic political solution?

HJ: In the long term, no. Something more organized and collective would seem to be necessary. I was very moved recently when I saw a documentary film about Neruda, which dealt with his commitment to communism. Here was one of the most singular poets of this century, going to communist functions, deliberately subsuming his individuality to the larger cause. A heroic commitment; I admire it, but I don't think I could do it.

LM: Why not? Are you suspicious of seeing yourself primarily in a relationship to a collective "other," rather than as an individual? Or are you suspicious of any collective organism?

HJ: My platonic version of myself would be prepared to subsume its creative impulses to some principled collective response. But another aspect of myself is skeptical that any collective response can—after the first thrust—resist mediation or commodification. In this respect I identify with some of the Frankfurt school, Adorno, say, whose persistent denial of constructive long-term change, was, as I see it, a principled "no" to blandishments and shallow idealism. Still another aspect of myself is a kind of closet Buddhist who believes that stripped-down humankind is not unbenign.

LM: Fredric Jameson argues that both modernism and postmodernism can be seen as ideological and aesthetic expressions of different stages of capitalist development. Do you agree?

HJ: The theorization of postmodernism is still largely in its adolescence (though it's proliferating hourly) and so there's a kind of myopia and megalomania about it. As with psychoanalysis in its early period, adherents take postmodernism very seriously and see it as a unique juncture in our epoch. But basically, yes, I agree with some of what Jameson has been saying about p.m.—the notion that capitalism has now entered a post-corporate, or late-corporate stage that produces a different kind of alienation than the nineteenth-century industrial or monopoly capitalism. Technology, the way information operates, the "music" of billions of bits of information interfacing with each other, the particular mechanics of the electronicized universe that we occupy—all this forces us to hear differently, see differently, forces us obviously to *feel* differently. We can't really think safely at all, in linear terms. We can't easily posit any kind of inwardness which isn't corruptible, which isn't infected by some aspect of the dominant culture. In other words, we can't assume there *is* any kind of personal inwardness which is unmediated by cultural production. This means that the idea of fantasy, so dear to modernism—the idea of the unique, secret, inner self—has to a large degree been problematized. We have been compelled by the transparent, intrusive, dominant culture into a kind of collective commodification of the unconscious.

LM: Hence postmodern art's emphasis on surfaces and the irrelevance of depth.

HJ: Yes, though there are different methods of interfacing surfaces. The method employed by the language poets is to "make strange" or defamiliarize infected language so that we can see it freshly. This is important, but, in my view, only a first step, at least in terms of real opposition. Destabilization is the crucial, though obviously difficult, second step. I think of postmodern visual artists like Wodiczko (the Canadian guerrilla-projectionist I mentioned earlier), Hans Haacke, and Jenny Holzer. It's somewhat easier for a visual artist to defamiliarize in order to destabilize because the impulse to infiltrate the macroculture is functional to their intention, which is often public, as Diego Rivera and the Mexican muralists' art was public. When Wodiczko projects subversive messages onto public buildings, he compromises them, forces people to see the ideological subtexts of public buildings. His art is "postmodern" because it emphasizes that these images are just images. There is nothing permanent about them, they are copies. Nothing remains after the guerrilla projections. If somebody photographs them, they leave a trace, or afterimage. But they have no aura.

LM: How do you reconcile being a "difficult, avant-garde writer" with the desire to have some *real effect* on people's political awareness?

HJ: On the one hand you want to be exploring new grounds, or combinations, in new ways, yet you want to affect people who generally aren't in a position to read difficult kinds of literature. In my opinion, writers like Gass did not, early on, think about the full implications of mediation, about "apolitical" stances being a species of political stance. In other words, they didn't recognize that by virtue of stepping back and saying, "What I am doing is purely aesthetic, divorced from politics," they were making a gesture that was, in effect, complicitous with the dominant culture. Deliberately disengaging your constructed language from the areas where language can operate usefully is *not* an apolitical act. Doing this also reinforces the long-standing institutionalization of the avant-garde, in which the official culture permits, actually encourages, legislated bad boys and girls to pee and pirouette in the corner.

In fact, it's easier to posit non-elitist innovative writing than it is to realize it. How can one affect ordinary people's consciousnesses while at the same time making use of the extraordinary linguistic structures with which Gass was involved? Brecht addresses this question. He said it is easy to undervalue what ordinary people can relate to. Ordinary people apparently related to *Potemkin*. Ordinary people have responded to abstruse passages in the Bible. Ordinary people respond to the Koran. Ordinary people can relate to any number of things if they feel it addresses them and their needs.

Part of the reason ordinary people don't respond to seemingly difficult art is that the dominant ideology forces certain kinds of dietary restrictions on ordinary people. People don't have refined palates because they are constrained to eat fast foods, because those are the only kind of foods around them, and because they work hard and don't have much time to prepare nutritious foods. Similarly, they are separated from the kinds of "difficult" art which *might* matter to them if only they were permitted to access this art. Whitman was addressing this early on, but even with Whitman one might reasonably ask: how many "ordinary" people have actually read *Leaves of Grass*? An important part of our obligation, then, is to get our art to people whom it might impact.

LM: Were there writers in, say, the mid seventies who had some influence on you? I'm wondering about writers who posited the need for fiction that suggests the glut and overdetermination and bombardment— and the need to reconstitute this. Burroughs, for example . . .

HJ: Burroughs *is* central to this whole project of deconstruction and reconstitution. The early Burroughs especially, with the cut-ups and so on, was an important figure for me. It's hard to know about this question of influences. A lot of the people I liked (and like) aren't people who write like me, but people with whom I share certain inclinations, or whose consciousnesses interest me. Alberto Moravia, for example. I like him because of the precision and courage of his sensuality. I like Max Frisch, particularly late Frisch after the modernist period, because of his particular blend of rage and melancholy, a certain emotional recklessness that I identify with. I like the desperate self-consciousness of the Brazilian writer Clarice Lispector. I admire the courage and dark grace of Primo Levi. Among North American writers, I got lots of technical ideas from Barthelme, Barth, and Coover and from several of the writers associated with the Fiction Collective.

LM: Most of your work can be seen as politically engaged, as ideological in nature, even self-consciously so. And you seem to be sympathetic to the postmodernist notion that artists should be creating genuinely open-ended forms that don't manipulate audiences toward specific conclusions. But how can you create ideological art that isn't didactic?

HJ: Some cunning person said recently that the meaning of art in the future will be outside the art—it will have to do with who bought it, where it is situated, which corporation is displaying it, rather than with any intrinsic quality in the art. The point is that there is no longer any way to segregate art from any number of elements contaminating it from the outside. The head of the NEA said recently that artistic excellence, far from being an intrinsic category, cannot be separated from the views of Congress and the American taxpayers. She speaks the gospel. In short, I don't think we can separate didacticism from an art which, no matter what its intentions, is already pocked with ideology.

LM: Your collections of fiction are more unified than most collections— *Mourning Crazy Horse, Beasts, Madonna,* and now *Straight Razor* can almost be viewed as innovative novels. Did these books evolve with specific unifying tropes in mind?

HJ: I wasn't looking for any specific point of departure when I began them, although when I hit on something like the bestiary in *Beasts* there was an immediate structure built into it from the outset, which made it more accessible to being viewed as a collective text. The fact is that when I'm in the middle of something and thinking about what I am doing, I feel that almost everything I pick up relates to what I'm doing and can be incorporated in it. For example, with *Madonna* I wasn't particularly looking for a unifying principle. One thing followed another. I knew from the outset that I wanted to deal with spectacle, and how spectacle has been made "real," whereas real experience has been spectacle-ized. I started writing this in '85, around the time that plane was hijacked by the Shi'ite Muslims, who were on TV every evening playing up to the media. The whole event was transformed into a sitcom spectacle. This was also the time of *Rambo* and all the rock festivals for peace. On the one hand you had these purely media spectacles being made into something which appeared real; on the other hand, there were real events, like the skyjacking, which were framed and fictionalized. And the way they were exchanged—so that you couldn't tell one from the other—obviously had to do with forcing particular kinds of thinking patterns on people.

In terms of the specific pop cultural figures I wound up being drawn to, what interested me about these figures (although I didn't analyze it initially) was the complex resonances they had, though it's hard to put into words what drew me to this figure rather than another one. In the case of Madonna, it wasn't only Madonna, the woman who was really Louise Ciccone, I wanted to deal with. It was how she was imagined, how she was *imaged*, how we were obliged to consume her—a forced consumption I related to torture (that is, to the way the official culture formats Madonna, compelling us to access the *simulacrum* when what our bodies and psyches need is the *real*). Hence the image of the electrified wires on our genitals: the dominant culture getting between us and our most intimate desires. I wove a Medusa's head of signifiers about

Madonna, from the obvious Marilyn Monroe to adolescent girls in Edin-
burgh to the doubloon in *Moby-Dick* to Sikh exiles in London. Here I
was mimicking, confiscating, appropriating the way the dominant culture floods us with signifiers while denying us purchase.

LM: Your work displays a strong sense of empathy with dispossessed or
marginalized people. Was your Jewish background growing up one of
the sources of this?

HJ: My being Jewish is a very aggrieved aspect of my self. I never felt
on easy terms with being Jewish, even from a very early age. My real
affinities always seemed to be with black people. One of the reasons I
relate to working-class black people more easily is because of their mar-
ginalization. They are obviously less mediated by property and by the
other concerns that middle-class white people would have. They seem
in a sense exiled, the way I've always felt myself to be. I respect their
long suffering and I admire their grace. Again, I'm referring to the
vast underclass and not to the small percentage of middle-class blacks.
When I hear some chords in Lightnin' Hopkins or Robert Johnson or
Nina Simone or Gil Scott-Heron, I feel a closeness to them that I've
never been able to feel with Jewish writers. There are of course Jewish
cultural figures I've identified with: Walter Benjamin, Primo Levi, Heinrich Heine, Lenny Bruce . . .

LM: You didn't feel that sense of intimacy with the New York Jewish
writers who were so prominent in the fifties—Bellow and Mailer and
Malamud and Roth and so on?

HJ: I admired some of the writing, but I never identified with it. When
I'd read Malamud or Bellow or Philip Roth, the occasional shock of recognition was never like what I experienced reading Richard Wright or
Ellison or Chester Himes or some of LeRoi Jones or listening to Lightnin' Hopkins and Lester Young. I did like Edward Lewis Wallant and
Nathanael West and Wallace Markfield's *To An Early Grave*, the quirkier,
less institutionalized-seeming writing.

LM: There's a striking number of very radical postmodern Jewish writers
—people like you, Kathy Acker, Steve Katz, Ray Federman, Ron Sukenick, and so on. I'm wondering if this radicalness might be a reaction to
the confining notion of "the Jewish writer."

HJ: There are several aspects of the basic paradigm about Jewish writers
that I resisted, although it is difficult to escape them. I suspect that
all the people you've mentioned have resisted the paradigm. For example, the notion of the male Jewish writer as being feminized, of not
being a *mensch*. Philip Roth, especially in his earlier work, contested
this stereotype, and I've always fought against that in my mind. Other
coded rules of behavior read: You are first- or second-generation Jewish,
certain things you can do, and other things you can't. My responses to

these inhibitions were subversive; that is, I've acted out a great deal in my life. I've done and imagined things that other people wouldn't allow themselves to do. Harry Crews once said something that I understood immediately. He was talking about Charles Whitman climbing the tower and shooting people in Texas about thirty years ago. He said that other people wouldn't allow themselves to imagine what it would feel like to be Whitman, to actually climb that tower and get up there and start firing. Well, all my life I've been moved to feel what the alleged criminal feels. That time between the person shooting somebody and then being actually incarcerated or executed is a period that seems very vital, very charged to me. And it is not just the aesthetic state that compels me, it is marked by empathy for the marked killer, Cain.

That's why I think of my imagination as being naturally violent. When I first recognized this, I tried to cultivate it and get as much imaginative charge as I could. I can recognize this same sort of violent, compelled imagination in other writers—Dostoyevsky as opposed to Turgenev, say, or Emily Dickinson as opposed to James. Among contemporary writers, Clarice Lispector, Pierre Guyotat, Baraka, John Edgar Wideman, Jayne Anne Phillips, Ishmael Reed, Kathy Acker, Gayl Jones, Monique Wittig. Not that I like all of these writers equally, but this is an important aspect of their imaginations.

LM: At first glance, it's hard to reconcile the kind of inner peace and serenity you find in *Dos Indios* with the anger and rage (and bitterly black humor) in your other books.

HJ: It's not as contradictory as it seems. Buddhism has also to do with principled action. And there is, dialectically joined to the peaceful Buddha, the wrathful Buddha, a trope perhaps inherited from Hinduism and Shiva the Destroyer. Think of the monks who immolated themselves in Vietnam. And the crucial (to Buddhism) idea of the Bodhisattva (which I refer to in several places, starting with *Mole's Pity*), an enlightened being who has vowed to undergo human suffering until humans themselves can exit and emerge into a kind of nirvana. The motto of the Mahayana Buddhist Bodhisattva is "the void and compassion." Well, compassion, in the nineties, implies being in the world. And the void, obviously, suggests being beyond the world. But Buddhism stresses the importance of *both*, an integration of the two. I don't claim to be so highly evolved that I've arrived at that integration, but the sense of Buddhism in my work has to do with an active compassion and an angry, relentless analysis. It doesn't make me feel at peace, but when I sit down to write I often feel that everything that is disorganized around me immediately unfolds itself in configurations that have a natural harmony about them in one way or another, even in collision. It's rare that I sit down and I don't have that sense that this is a natural place for me. It's almost like sitting down for zazen meditation.

LM: You seem to have been influenced as much by things outside fiction or poetry—painters, musicians, and literary theorists—as by literature.

HJ: True. For example, right now I don't read fiction as much as other things. I read art history, natural history, anthropology, critical theory. I read genre fiction like detective stuff, science fiction. Some poetry. Recently, my work has been affected by aspects of visual art. The postmodernist work being done by people we mentioned before—Jenny Holzer, to some extent Christo, but less him because he defamiliarizes without destabilizing. Artists like Haacke, Wodiczko, Robert Gober, who in his installations recuperates desire in subtle, insidious ways. Leon Golub, who deals with terrorism and fascism, but in a kind of faceless commodified way, so that his figures are all merely signifiers in a sense. Orlan, who mutilates and reconfigures his body. Among older artists, I've been affected by a wide range of people, including Man Ray, Duchamp, Giacometti, Artaud's drawings, Magritte, the photomontagist John Heartfield, some of the German Expressionists, the situationists, Joseph Beuys and the Fluxus group. The filmmaker Robert Bresson. The composer Messiaen, but also Stockhausen and Cage.

LM: Many of the best known postmodern authors began writing during the sixties, when the whole counterculture thing was emerging. Did you share any of that sense of being in an era when conventions were opening up?

HJ: I felt very much at home in the ethos then, but overall I don't think of the sixties as a notable time in literature, in part because it lacked tension, was too easy a gig for the middle class. It's true things were going on in France and elsewhere with structuralism and semiotics, but, critically speaking, it was a myopic time. Leslie Fiedler, for example, who always tried to be a step ahead, wrote what he hoped would be a seminal essay in *Playboy*, arguing that criticism should involve interpretation from the inside out, rather than analysis from the outside in— that is, getting into a work and imagining it in the way the writer wanted to write it. A kind of applied Buddhism in a sense. A generous impulse which suited my inclinations: the anarchism, the gender interface, polymorphous sexuality, visionary inwardness.

LM: You mentioned the peculiar "charge" or energy involved with figures like rapists and serial killers. Isn't your use of such people also a commentary on normalcy?

HJ: Certainly the criminal or outcast figure indirectly interrogates institutionalized normalcy. I can't say that I condone antisocial violence per se, but I tend to feel closer to the serial killer than to the authorities who apprehend him.

LM: One unfortunate result of postmodernism's emphasis on "pluralism" is the conclusion that all systems and meanings are equally valuable.

HJ: Pluralism is a potentially liberating concept, but it can be interpreted variously, plurally. As you say, some of it can be seen as a reflection of many different kinds of possibilities of truth existing. But other aspects of it have been interpreted as a failure of nerve—the idea that in the seeming absence of objectivity and even infrastructures, we are compelled to accept that "this is what it is" and go with it. I resist the idea of simply allowing these things to pull us and take us for a ride. It is a *nice* ride for the solvent middle class—this dizzying media-infected roller coaster—but it can and should be interrogated. As with other seminal, apocalyptic-seeming changes—the movement to industrialism, the inception of psychoanalysis, the Russian revolution—we are sort of awestruck by the po-mo landscape, but after the initial future shock, the contours become clearer, it becomes accessible to analysis.

LM: One of the keys to being able to have your work really operate oppositionally would seem to be the willingness to really be on the edge, but to have an integrity about that desire to relentlessly interrogate things, consequences be damned. I associate this with writers like Burroughs and Acker, or musicians like the Dead Kennedys and Eugene Chadbourne.

HJ: Those are all good examples, although with some of the punk people, like the Survival Research Labs, you also have a sense of martyrdom. There is a strong martyrdom impulse in the punk movement because of the great discharge of rage along with the realization that unchanneled, uncollective rage is finally impotent. In any case, martyrdom is an easy impulse to appropriate. It is in fact the most familiar association we have with the high modernist version of the tragic artist. Keats, Van Gogh, Virginia Woolf, Artaud, Janis Joplin, Hendrix, Sid and Nancy, Kurt Cobain. You're right: this extremity of feeling and willingness to sacrifice everything is an arresting notion. But it's potentially useful only when it's combined with keen-witted analysis. Really, the official culture can process any number of martyred artists, but they have much more difficulty with passionate, living artists who contest and create and spit and think.

LM: Rimbaud would seem to fit in here. He embodies a kind of calculated, irrational, suicidal response (hence the connection to punk and people like Kathy Acker) to the imposition of rationality and control that he could see very clearly, even a hundred years ago.

HJ: The systematic derangement of the senses. Willful delirium. Very attractive. And when I turn on MTV or listen to some of the articulate young people, I hear them talking in Rimbaud-like terms. I don't know to what extent they've thought it out, but they're saying, "Yeah, negativity is bad, but what if it is done deliberately to confront something which appears to be a greater negativity?"

LM: Among some of the punk people, like Patti Smith and Jello Biafra (and this is true of the cyberpunks a decade later) there was some genuine critical intelligence there about what they were doing. Even somebody as manipulative as Malcolm McLaren, who managed the Sex Pistols, was well-versed in dadaism and was consciously incorporating the gestures of the anti-art aesthetic, which becomes a commentary about conventions and so forth. Now whether Sid Vicious was aware of any of this . . .

HJ: Another question is how far intuition can carry you. In relation to Rimbaud, when I talk with younger writers, I tell them that I know a lot of you think of yourselves as being intuitive writers. But now more than anytime in our lifetime, you have to train yourself to develop a critical intelligence. There is so much information/disinformation out there which has to be sorted out. And just as importantly, that information is potentially art. It can be appropriated in many ways even as much of it was based on appropriation in the first place. Lyotard said in *The Postmodern Condition* that in the near future knowledge will be entirely instrumental and will be contained in data banks. The system or entity that has the instrumental knowledge—the knowledge that can be cashed into money and power—will be the system that has access to the data banks. If Rimbaud is the romantic emblem of modernist intuition, an appropriate emblem for our time is the computer hacker. Somebody who learns the system in order to subvert it.

LM: Do you think of yourself as having a natural "voice" that you bring to your fiction—a voice you could identify as "you"?

HJ: It's better not to have a specific voice now. It's more appropriate to be protean. Keep one step ahead of the Mind Police.

A Rose to Look At
An Interview with Robert Kelly

Larry McCaffery

Say it all
over again.
but say it all.
Write everything.
— *The Loom*

The literary task Robert Kelly has set for himself—that is, to "write everything"—is, to be sure, an ambitious undertaking; but in a career that now spans some forty years Kelly certainly has a good running start—some fifty-odd books published, most of them poetry; several volumes of wide-ranging essays; an unduly neglected novel, *The Scorpions* (1967), which blends detective and science-fiction genre motifs with Eastern mysticism and epistemological concerns in the manner of Borges and Nabokov; and four collections of fiction that appeared in rapid succession, *A Transparent Tree* (1986), *Doctor of Silence* (1988), *Cat Scratch Fever* (1990), and *Queen of Terrors* (1994). For good measure he is also some two thousand pages into the writing of *Parsifal*, a "prose narrative" or "epic" or "novel" that may finally provide a single framework large enough for Kelly to display his extraordinary range of intellectual interests, his gifts as a wordsmith (of contemporary fiction writers, only Alexander Theroux comes close to Kelly in terms of being able to articulate his concerns within the full range of words and storytelling skills available to the writer).

Although widely recognized as a leading figure in contemporary poetry ever since his early association as a theorist and practitioner in the "deep image" movement in the early 1960s, Robert Kelly is at present probably the least well known and discussed of all major American authors as far as the recognition of his fiction is concerned. This underappreciation can partly be attributed to the reputation Kelly himself has fostered as someone who only occasionally dabbles in fiction, primarily to release his excess creative energies in a form that breaks from the rigors of poetry (always acknowledged as his true vocation). Kelly's relationship to fiction as an "outsider" and "amateur"— while simultaneously having a secure reputation and position within the poetry field—has probably benefited him in the long run. Not having invested a great deal personally or aesthetically in his fiction has surely encouraged Kelly to take greater risks, to develop methods and approaches to suit the requirements of the work (and his own interests and sensibility, of course) without worrying about how the results would be received by others.

Kelly's relative anonymity also has much to do with the fact that Americans tend to view the kind of fiction he writes—dense, exquisitely crafted narrative experiments exploring the paradoxes and ambiguities of language and perception's relationship to the world—with a certain amount of suspicion. Kelly's fiction is also usually told not in the familiar slice-of-life realism mode but as fables, parables, or allegories that unfold via an eclectic array of references and allusions in lush, sensuous prose. Such work is admired in this country, of course, but usually more so if it is written by authors from other countries. Thus, Borges and especially Calvino are the writers who most closely resemble Kelly in their thematic concerns (the mysterious confrontation between human perception, language, and the ceaseless transformations of the universe) and in their richly inventive formal methods for portraying these concerns.

But for all the formal ingenuity and erudition that Kelly brings to his fiction—the many references to obscure myths and texts, arcane words, unusual sources of knowledge—his most impressive ability is to re-create the exhilarating "hereness" of physical sensation, especially the burning intensity of sexual desire, which he describes in "The Guest" (from *A Transparent Tree*) as "that inconceivable mad fainting exalting excitement when flesh touches flesh."

Kelly's work also shares with that of Lyn Hejinian and William Vollmann what might be called a "fractal quality"—a tendency of smaller pieces to resemble larger ones in their design and concerns. This tendency has to do with their mutual interest in forms that open up language's potential and push beyond both the illusionistic assumptions and implicit limitations of realistic forms. As is also true of the work of

Lydia Davis, Kenneth Gangemi, Mark Leyner, Harold Jaffe, and other writers in this volume who have worked primarily in short forms, one of the fascinating things about reading Kelly's fiction is observing an imagination struggling successfully to transcend the limitations of the short narrative format. Almost by definition, of course, the short story is associated with clarity, focus, precision: an author must quickly establish setting and character, present a problem or create a tension that will move the story forward and then supply a solution that will relieve the tension and create a satisfying sense of closure. But closure and the sense of events occurring to discrete individuals on the basis of causal laws that can be isolated and explained runs fundamentally counter to Kelly's aesthetic and philosophical outlook, both of which have been deeply influenced by Eastern mysticism's emphasis on the interaction of human consciousness with the universe around it through language and perception, and the primacy of change and flux at the expense of order, stability, and stasis.

Equally problematic (if not more so) is the whole notion of providing "solutions" and explanations. This is not to say that Kelly doesn't present characters struggling to uncover answers, make sense of things, and understand what they have done and why they have done it. Quite the contrary, like Borges, Kelly presents a cascade of richly detailed speculations concerning the nature of just about anything worth speculating about. But such investigations are typically undercut by reflexive examinations of how such speculations are grounded in specific verbal or perceptual contexts, or to introduce competing viewpoints, beliefs, or explanations that imply that other alternatives might be equally satisfying. Indeed, the central mystery that Kelly presents in story after story is that of the interaction of human consciousness with the universe around it—a process that has no solution because it is ongoing, multiple, uncontainable. And more than anything else, Kelly's experimental formal strategies—for instance, the way he often presents his narratives in the form of mosaics composed of brief passages that include snatches of action, dialogue, and personal speculation, as well as ambiguous, highly charged image patterns, almost small prose poems, which evoke rather than directly describe the obsessions and perceptions of his protagonists—aim to achieve a sense of "open-endedness" in a form that resists expressing such a state of affairs.

The following interview began over lunch in one of Manhattan's Upper East Side restaurants on a warm spring afternoon. The topic I planned to use as a framework for the interview had to do with the recent increase in Kelly's fiction output. But by the time we concluded the interview several hours later in his apartment, it was obvious that Robert Kelly's approach to doing an interview is the same as what he described (in the "Afterword" to *A Transparent Tree*) as his approach to story writing—"trying to be everything."

*   *   *

Robert Kelly: Selected Bibliography

Novels and Collections of Fiction

The Scorpions. Novel. Garden City, NY: Doubleday, 1967; reprinted, Barrytown, NY: Station Hill Press, 1985.
Cities. Novella, also included in *A Transparent Tree.* West Newbury, MA: Frontier Press, 1971.
A Line of Sight. Los Angeles: Black Sparrow Press, 1974.
Wheres. Los Angeles: Black Sparrow Press, 1978.
The Cruise of the Pnyx. Barrytown, NY: Station Hill Press, 1979.
A Transparent Tree. New Paltz, NY: McPherson Publishing Co., 1985; reprinted as *Un Albero transparente.* Italian translation by Anna Pensante. Milan: Tranchida, 1995.
Doctor of Silence. Kingston, NY: McPherson Publishing Co., 1988; reprinted as *Il Maestro di Silenzi.* Italian translation by Anna Pensante. Milan: Tranchida, 1992.
Cat Scratch Fever. Kingston, NY: McPherson Publishing Co., 1990.
Queen of Terrors. Kingston, NY: McPherson Publishing Co., 1994.

Books of Poetry

Armed Descent. New York: Hawk's Well Press, 1961.
Finding the Measure. Collected poems, 1965–66. Los Angeles: Black Sparrow Press, 1968.
The Common Shore. Books 1–5. Los Angeles: Black Sparrow Press, 1969.
Flesh Dream Book. Los Angeles: Black Sparrow Press, 1971.
The Pastorals. Los Angeles: Black Sparrow Press, 1972.
The Mill of Particulars. Los Angeles: Black Sparrow Press, 1973.
The Loom. Los Angeles: Black Sparrow Press, 1975.
The Convections. Santa Barbara: Black Sparrow Press, 1978.
Kill the Messenger Who Brings Bad News. Santa Barbara: Black Sparrow Press, 1979.
Sentence. Barrytown, NY: Station Hill Press, 1980.
Spiritual Exercises. Santa Barbara: Black Sparrow Press, 1981.
The Alchemist to Mercury. Uncollected poems, 1960–80. Berkeley: North Atlantic Press, 1981.
Under Words. Santa Barbara: Black Sparrow Press, 1983.
Not This Island Music. Santa Rosa, CA: Black Sparrow Press, 1987.
The Flowers of Unceasing Coincidence. Barrytown, NY: Station Hill Press, 1988; reprinted, Buffalo: Leave Press, 1991.
Ariadne. N.p.: St. Lazars Press, 1991.
A Strange Market. Poems, 1985–88. Santa Rosa, CÅ: Black Sparrow Press, 1992.
Mont Blanc. Ann Arbor, MI: Otherwinds Press, 1994.
Red Actions: Selected Poems, 1960–1993. Santa Rosa, CA: Black Sparrow Press, 1995.

Nonfiction

In Time. Essays and manifestos. West Newbury, MA: Frontier Press, 1972.
Afterword. *The Scorpions,* 2d ed. 189–92. Barrytown, NY: Station Hill Press, 1985.
Afterword. *A Transparent Tree,* 195–200. New Paltz, NY: McPherson Publishing
    Co., 1985.
"A Poundian Romance: Investigating Thomas McEvilley's Novel *North of Yester-
    day." Review of Contemporary Fiction* 8, 3 (Fall 1988): 108–16.
Autobiographical essay in *Contemporary Authors: Autobiography Series,* vol. 19.
    Detroit: Gale Research Company, 1994.

Reviews, Essays, and Miscellaneous Commentary about Kelly's Work

Blevins, Richard L. "Robert Kelly." In *Dictionary of Literary Biography: American
    Short Story Writers after World War II,* ed. Patrick Meaner, vol. 13. Detroit: Gale
    Research Company, 1993.
Hubinger, April. "Robert Kelly's 'The Sound': Notes Towards a Reading." *Cre-
    dences* 3, 1 (1984): 176–88.
Meaner, Patrick. "Robert Kelly." In *One Hundred Contemporary Poets,* ed. Joseph
    Conte. Detroit: Gale Research Company, 1995.
McCaffery, Larry. "Exotic, Erotic and Crazed." Review of *A Transparent Tree. New
    York Times Book Review,* 15 September 1985, p. 18.
Rasula, Jed. "Ten Different Fruits on One Different Tree: Reading Robert Kelly."
    Credences 3, 1 (1984): 127–75. This issue also includes a comprehensive bibli-
    ography prepared by Rasula.

*   *   *

LARRY MCCAFFERY: Have I been naive in taking it for granted that
when your narrator in "Hair" (included in *A Transparent Tree*) says at one
point, "I'm never bored by anything," he's *of course* speaking for you?
ROBERT KELLY: He's speaking for me. I'm never bored; if anything,
for me the reverse is true: there always seems to be too much to say, too
much to notice, too much to write. I'm usually exhausted by my own
greed. What not being bored means is being greedy about enough different things so that there's always something to feed on. Boredom is
interesting to me. Thirty years or so ago people like Warhol began experimenting in the movies and elsewhere with the psychology of boredom. But boredom is impossible to summon by willing it—the mind
simply withdraws from the image and thinks about something else, like
the wallpaper. It appears that we literally can't be bored. We're all un-
boreable. Boredom is a magical target we fail to hit. It's not just me.
LM: Are you writing more fiction these days?
RK: I suppose I am. Writing fiction seems to be something I enjoy doing
more now. I now even occasionally have a dingy feeling—one I'm not
too happy about—that maybe I should sit down and write a story. I

never before felt such a sense of obligation before to deal with that vast imaginary planet we call Ordinary Life. Then as I was working along in *Parsifal,* which is this large novel I've been laboring at for a number of years now, I kept feeling a pressure to have my characters sit down and stay—sit still in a place, go nowhere, and do nothing strange. I found myself asking: why can't I write about people staying together in the same place day after day without change? Isn't that a song too? Because nothing really changes, we know that, we shiver along in our same old shirts to the end of the road.

Gertrude Stein in one of those wonderful essays about narration which never remain in print very long (they were given in Chicago the year I was born, so seem to have a special meaning for me) says, "American literature is about things that are moving—not moving the way that emotions move but moving the way that things that really move are moving; whereas English literature is about being in the same place every day for a hundred years." So recently I wanted to know why I couldn't write about being in the same place, or about two or three people being together, if not for a hundred years, then at least for an extended period of time. Why do I have to write about going to the moon, killing people, or running around?

LM: But of course, you solve the problems that might occur if fictional characters remain living in the one place for more than one year—and without doing anything "dramatic" during that period—quite simply: you have your characters tell themselves stories.

RK: Yes. They can't stand the absence of a narration that includes them, so they fantasize themselves, or in terms of the novel, they actually do go off on different excursions.

LM: In the afterword to *A Transparent Tree* you say that you measure your life by the growth and variety of the poetry you write. Does the fact that you've been writing a lot of fiction the past several years indicate that this sense of measuring yourself by your poetry has been supplanted now to an extent by the fiction you're writing?

RK: Not yet. My involvement with fiction has to do with my "liberty." The word I want to use in connection with my writing of fiction as opposed to my poetry is "freedom." In my own mind, and to a certain extent, societally or culturally, I've always been labeled a poet, and thus I've felt completely free to write fiction. I haven't had to write current fiction or contemporary fiction or even *good* fiction. Instead I've always been able to write, as they say, the book I wanted to read—the fiction I wished I had been able to pick up and read some night when I'm staying overnight in a friend's house, where you want to take down a book and read a story before you go to sleep. So I wrote those stories that suit different moods: sexual moods or mysterious moods, moods of the sacred in some way. The notion of freedom to me meant that what I feel most committed to in poetry—that is, keeping open all the registers of possibility—is what I'm allowed in fiction automatically.

I grew up at a time in poetry when I was caught between what I perceived (and what a lot of other people I knew growing up in New York perceived) as essentially two alternatives: the academic poetic tradition of Richard Wilbur, or something coming out of William Carlos Williams that seemed extraordinary, spacious, and vernacular—but won at the price of a loss of eloquence, richness, and mystery, all of which interested me. So from my earliest moments as a poet I was trying in a polemical way to reassociate all the possible orders of poetry—somewhat the way that Pound (not to compare myself with Pound) lays out those three "powers of poetry" (telling, singing, showing). But was there any reason to pick one over and against the others?

LM: Your involvement with poetic activity has been polemical almost from the very beginning.

RK: In the poetry world I've always been fighting someone, real or imaginary (mostly imaginary as the years pass since I've outlived all the others). But at the same time fiction was always there. When I first read Borges, it used to astonish me that what was extraordinary about him is that he was able to use Kipling, Stevenson, Chesterton, Haggard, and all those wonderful writers who were completely unallowed in serious literary circles. Even now, it's scarcely permitted to say a word about them publicly. They're great mysterious figures. I don't mean to say that they are especially important to me but the kind of conspiracy of smutty silence the nineteenth century used against Sade, we use now against these late-nineteenth- and early-twentieth-century story writers, the fabulists. And it shocks me to see García Márquez celebrated as such a powerful writer when he seems like a pleasant fabulist compared with some of the great and likewise sentimental writers at the turn of the century who have been axed from the canon.

LM: Literature, maybe especially today when the production of art has been so integrated into commodity production generally, seems to work by simulacrum and commodity replacement.

RK: Exactly. We displace Kipling and Chesterton to make room for Borges and Cortázar, displace Hudson to make room for García Márquez, displace Machen and Violet Lee to make room for Blanchot. The era of the narrow neckties and the era of wide ties. Fashions. Our only weapon against them is to keep reading forward and backwards. And yet: the new is always good, in some way we have to fashion. Jacob wrestling with the angel wins blessing, but rises lame. Are we always half-crippled by our struggle to renew?

LM: Was this sense that fictional forms offered you more freedom than

poetry based on anything inherent in the nature of the forms themselves? Or did it grow more from specific historical or social circumstances that had nothing to do with formal, aesthetic universals?

RK: The "freedom" I refer to when I'm writing fiction is a social or strate-
gic freedom in that nobody expects anything of me when I write fiction.
That sense of freedom that I didn't find simply given to us in American
poetry—no one in poetry had that freedom during the fifties, and besides, it is a social impossibility, being a poet—was available to me as a
fiction writer because no one was telling me what to write. If I wrote a
poem as off the beaten track as some of the fiction I've written, I would
be thrown out of the poet's guild. Unceremoniously. But if I write something that's merely a dreary Algernon Blackwood ghost story, no one
cares. Yeats wrote such things, and no one stopped him from doing so.

But it's also true that back in the fifties, the opportunities in fiction
seemed more wide open in that, in fact, nobody knew what to write.
By the time I was old enough to write ten pages in a row, the Jamesian
(James the Henry and James the Joyce) imperatives had finally given
way in American writing to something centered more on event. *Augie
March* had put an end to that (and maybe the Jamesian revenged itself
later on Bellow). Ultimately, event itself could be character. It had been
so at the beginning. Auerbach's reading of Abraham was important to
us in those days, how the author of Genesis gave us the deed alone, without delineating the mental process. And we remember how Faust had
guessed, briefly triumphant: In the beginning was the Deed! There was
freshly renewed with us, then, the sense of the *raconteur,* of the *récit* replacing all the old artful psychological strategies. I remember the shock
we had as we read or reread the Mabinogion and the Icelandic family
sagas and the Arabian Nights and Balzac, to see that there was a domain
of action from which narrative could arise, and that psychological was
not the only momentum or gesture. Language could *enact*—we saw it
at last. Now, of course, theories of narrativity are everywhere. But back
then, telling was no way to analyze.

LM: Looking back at the late fifties and early sixties, so much seemed to
be happening: the Kafka phenomenon, the excitement of the *nouveau
roman,* writers like Beckett and Nabokov and Burroughs finally being
examined seriously, the interesting work coming out in the theater and
the cinema. All that must have had a very liberating effect on your generation of fiction writers.

RK: But some of those writers you just mentioned somehow weren't
able to liberate us. Kafka, for example, was always given to us not as a
narrator or a text but as an attitude. "It's so Kafka," people would say
about some snafu situation. I can still remember the embarrassing con-
sequence when in innocence I offered a discussion of Kafka as a comic

novelist—talking about the rhythm of his narration which seemed then, and still seems to me now, that rhythm which we borrow most from the comic or the picaresque narration—was that people seemed shocked by what I was suggesting. To them "genre" meant "mood"; since there was nothing comic about the consequences of Kafka therefore there could be nothing comic about the strategy or structural components of his work. Such confusions of issues of genre with issues of structure and issues of mood and psychology were to me exactly what the writing of the forties was about—the pit into which we had "digged" ourselves. We got out of that in the fifties and early sixties. Even before *The Sot-Weed Factor*, Gaddis's *The Recognitions*, that masterpiece of liberation which appeared in 1954, clearly shows the passageway between the two types of writing—it just took a while for people to notice. I remember reading *The Recognitions* in 1957—a tremendous moment for me. That almost self-contained one-hundred-page novella at the start was not only a magnificent opening for a novel, but seemed to me to finish Jamesian literature—eloquently, but finally.

LM: Did you start out writing poetry exclusively?

RK: I've always written stories, even though they were always written left-handedly and with a happy, almost breathless, sense of freedom. Or do I mean a senseless breath of freedom? Even now I get uneasy with the thought of being considered a fiction writer because I'm afraid that might trap me into being a fashionable one, or seeking to think what fiction writers ought to be thinking. Fiction did not strike me with anxiety. I wrote what I wanted to read, and that was the end of it.

LM: Aside from the sense of freedom you recognized, did any of the other formal principles associated with fiction intrigue you at that stage? What made it feel inherently different?

RK: Partly it was *play*. Most of my poetry begins from a phrase I hear in my head. Sometimes the phrase is something I can't find a next line for in verse, but I can find a next sentence for in prose, so to speak. That's how my work starts. For instance, the little book *Cities* that was published separately before it appeared in *A Transparent Tree* began with the question that opens the piece: "Where should I take myself now?" and I found myself thinking, "Well, where can I go with that?" The answer spelled itself out in the story of imaginary cities and wandering around in them. I seldom have an idea of what I want to write. Maybe half of the pieces in my fiction collections began with a story I can't stop thinking about. Some image intrudes into my consciousness—a head turns so that the hair whips around over the shoulder. I'm struck with that image, so can I write a poem about it? I've done that a thousand times. It's an image that haunts me. If an image like that has me, what do I do with it? Do I have to invent a whole way for her to walk up flicking her hair from one side to another? Or is it enough to "have" an image, and speak it in a poem? What I've been after consciously for twenty years or so is the sense of writing. When I was fourteen years old I applied for a library card in the New York Public Library—a big event. I came across to Manhattan (the "real city") to apply for the card, and when I was given a form to fill out, I put down "writer" where it said occupation. This seemed like such a defiant thing to write that I felt I was making a pledge to God.

LM: Have you ever wanted to change that identity from "writer" to "poet" or "fiction author"?

RK: Not really, because I don't feel myself doing a different thing by writing fiction instead of poetry. I write with the same intention whenever I write something. It seems to me that the one great thing in literature that's happened in this century is considering the possibility of writing being a single coherent act without divisions into genre. It seems to be such a small thing to say, certainly it's an obvious statement, but it's an important one to me.

LM: Once you have that image that starts a work, what seems to prompt you to work this out in fictional form rather than as poetry? It's not a matter, I take it, of your sitting down one weekend and thinking to yourself, Okay, today I'm going to concentrate on writing a poem or story?

RK: I don't even know how that feels. Usually I literally don't know what's going to happen to the image until a few minutes later when the writing has actually begun, and some scrap of language has appeared in the mind. That's where most of my poems seem to begin, seldom with a sense of occasion or purpose, just with a sudden presence of words. Later, the occasion or purpose or meaning has to make its way to the surface through the endless palavering of trying to find out where those words go. Even more rarely I might begin something with only a title. For instance, I knew "The Doctor of Silence" would be the title of the book but there was no story to go with it, so I had to write one. I had that sentence so I needed to find out what would I do with a "doctor of silence"—what would that be? Nearly always what's involved is my trying to turn this scrap of language into more language. Language is seed.

LM: You've written about your fascination with endings—you even mention that you wrote the last chapter of *The Scorpions* first. Once you've determined that what you're writing is indeed going to be a piece of fiction, is there a moment where you need to know where you're heading before you can complete what's in between?

RK: Seldom do I know how something is going to end. I had written the last chapter of *Scorpions* either first or second, but that book was really an exception. Several years ago I finished a draft of a novel called *Parsifal*, which is about two thousand pages long in typescript; I've managed to get it down to about eighteen hundred pages in typescript so far and I hope it may yet get smaller. But I didn't know where it was going until one day, after I was already maybe fifteen hundred pages into the book, an image came to me that finally let me see where the book was headed. It was a simple image of a hand holding a photograph in which the characters in the book, who are just standing there, are for the first time described. In effect this concluding image is a literal description of the characters you've been reading about interminably. It sounds clever when I say it now, but it didn't seem that way when it first came to me because that image suddenly gave me a goal to find out what these people actually looked like. It was as if I wouldn't really know who they were until the very end. In the preface I wrote for my Russian fables in Bruce McPherson's *Likely Stories* anthology, I discovered myself making a statement that still seems the root and core of my thoughts toward fiction: "Language is the only fable and is utterly able."

Curiously, the genre I find hardest to deal with, both as a critic and a writer, is drama. The few plays I've written have not made much sense dramatically—or as *anything* for that matter. Somehow I've always felt short-circuited by drama. Its language is too naked, it needs the prop of a man or woman to say it, or a dramatic situation different from and apart from language.

LM: What moves a reader of your fiction forward in your texts if not the sequential, causal structures that drama (and in different ways, fiction) relies upon? Drama, for instance, supplies a certain kind of interaction between the voice and the action that you rarely seem interested in.

RK: Basically I want readers to be propelled forward simply by this fable of language itself unfolding and revealing itself. In the case of that long, long novel, *Parsifal*, a lot of this language happens to be dialogue, which I'd guess makes up seven hundred of those eighteen hundred pages. But unlike the dialogue you find in the theater, this dialogue isn't "about" anything—or it's about everything, but it isn't going anywhere. Nothing is "established" by the dialogue, the way it is in something like Gaddis's astonishing *Carpenter's Gothic*, where everything is established by the dialogue, everything is shown and revealed, but nothing is changed by it.

LM: In the afterword to *A Transparent Tree* you discuss the "events" that took place in the exterior world that served as starting point for several of the fictions that appeared there. But when you sat down and wrote, say, "Samuel Naked," what was involved in moving from this "real event" to the work that eventually resulted?

RK: Samuel was my great-grandfather. All my life I have lived with the archetype of this man who was actually (as the story doesn't say) a painter and a writer. Much of the outer history in "Samuel Naked" about Samuel being wounded at Gettysburg, disappearing, going to India, and so on, is part of his actual life, insofar as I know it from the family. The rest is pure fiction. All I have of his work is some poems left behind which are well written and very well spelled. This is significant for someone writing in the nineteenth century (Keats, for instance, couldn't spell at all) because it indicates that my grandfather was a man of some education. But I don't really know anything about him except that his name is Welsh, that he came from the west of England somewhere, and that he finally disappeared somewhere in India—an area which is now Pakistan. At any rate, all my life I've been dreaming Samuel's experiences. I began writing the piece long before I went to India in 1983, but didn't finish it until I came back. Once after I had traveled over Persia and Pakistan, I flew over the red desert of Rajasthan, which is really *red* red when the sun is hitting rock in the afternoon, and it suddenly struck me that here was where my ancestor disappeared and where his progeny still live. I must have cousins living there whom I would like to find someday. That experience was one reason that, when I came back, I realized I could finish that work.

LM: Why aren't you drawn to more direct autobiographical or descriptive sorts of writings—ones in which the "othering" process would be downplayed in favor of a more literal transcription.

RK: I can't do otherwise. If I stand outside and describe the event, then I'm not *in* the event anymore. When something is happening to you, it's just happening to you, and all that is available to you is how you feel about what the event is. I suppose people who are drowning are saying to themselves in a kind of voice-over, "I am drowning now" (like the replicant at the end of *Blade Runner* who says, "Time to die"), but most of us just live in a world in which we are living in the world at the time we are living there. It's like Lily Tomlin's old line, "Have I reached the party to whom I am speaking?" We're just where we are. The minute you stand outside and describe it, you've lost your involvement in what is happening. Even though I didn't get to this through theoretical observations, I feel justified or permitted to be that indifferent to describing the outer shape of the event—while providing the inner species of reality that the characters are presumably going through.

LM: So in an odd way, your fiction retains an interest in autobiography and psychology.

RK: Yes, at least in the sense that my fiction always talks about how it feels to be in a situation at just that moment—not outside it or standing back to give the whole physical arc of the event. There's only one story in *A Transparent Tree* ("The Rosary") where something is described from afar, where both parties have to be seen in their separation and difference.

LM: This seems connected to what you described as the aims of "deep image" poetry that you were associated with (and polemicized about) back in the sixties.

RK: Very much so. Several weeks ago I read that deep image essay for the first time in many years, and I found myself still able to stand by it. There's hardly anything that I disown except the rather shrill tone (today I'd probably make it shriller). My manifesto writing, which I've done a lot of over the years, always seems to return to this issue of permission: don't say I can't do this, don't take away this possibility, don't let decorum replace possibility. I don't think my writing has ever taken advantage of all the possibilities I have had, let alone those that someone has presented. As a poet, I was after something that was not exhausted by describing the outer reality or by the kind of decorum I had been facing, as we all were, of the Wilburs and all the other tired forties-ish writing that came to life briefly again in the fifties when Dylan Thomas's comet-like blaze came through us and then died down into mere imitations because Thomas was doing something you can't imitate. But after years of facing that decorum, to turn and face the decorum of the Williamsites, who were going to tell me that I couldn't use *language*, that I could only mention the names of objects (as if the names of objects were somehow more concrete than the names of feelings were, whereas in fact they are both just names—the names of "hate" and "lust" and "envy" being just as concrete as "wheelbarrow" because these are all just words, imputations, and "wheelbarrow" is just as abstract as "anger" or "embarrassment." So there was one more decorum to deal with—this one based on a naive literalism of "the real" which not even Williams himself believed. And of course as we all know, the duration of every generation is brief indeed—you get only an eighteen-month period between the language school and Raymond Carver. But the keynote is decorum, which one cannot rail against without being excluded from the poetic mainstream.

LM: One of the principal decorums you and other writers of the sixties postmodernist generation were opposing had to do with the notion of the "well-made story." When I read your fiction, I feel I'm confronting fiction that refuses to rein in the "possibilities" of an event, refuses to organize itself into structures—sequence, causality, resolution, explanations—which will hide these multiple responses. The familiar structures in fiction, you seem to imply, are illusions.

RK: And why should writers or readers accept these illusions? I might be willing to rely on these things in my work if I could believe that any story ever ends (but it doesn't), or if I could feel that X ever unilaterally caused Y. But, alas, I can't.

LM: The approach to form/content issues found in so many of the postmodern authors of roughly your generation seems to have grown out of a deep metaphysical skepticism that has its roots in everything from relativity and quantum mechanics to philosophy of language, mathematics, and so on. But I've suspected your own attitudes might have more to do with the Eastern mysticism that permeates your work . . .

RK: I hope my work reflects the fact that I am a Buddhist. One of the reasons I am has to do with one of the deepest perspectives of Buddhism that is expressed in a wonderful phrase in Sanskrit, *pratitya samutpada*, which can be approximately translated as, "the co-dependent, or interdependent origination"—so that anything that exists, exists as an intersection of other forces; there's no beginning and no end, no creator. Things have complexly always been in being, the molecules have always been locked in the box and have always been pressing and expressing each other. The world has constantly been creating itself, timelessly, forever. It's a stark theory from one point of view in that it denies the consolation of a creator—and thus of a redeemer, someone who can do it for you. On the other hand, it's a wondrously spacious notion in that everything that exists, exists without hierarchical limitation. Since everything is caused by everything else, there is no preordained hierarchy of reality. The hierarchy that comes to be meaningful to you is that which comes to be meaningful through your own interaction with it, your own faith in it, your own activity, your own urgency, your own labor. In such a system, things don't immediately present themselves to you as they would in a causal system, where this causes that; instead there is a constant realm of causation, where this ordinary bottle has to be as "real" as this rare and extremely expensive vase. Each object and each event has its own ontological verity. Even as a very naive child I felt that most stories I read of the "well-made" kind were terribly disappointing, unsatisfying, unmeaty. I instinctively responded by saying, "Well, what's been happening can't end there, there must be more to it," because the naivest perspective of life suggests that life goes on. Your friend dies but his house doesn't disappear at the moment his death is announced, everything continues on. So from even the naivest perspective, stories can't end. But from another and perhaps more sophisticated point of view, even when I finish something like the stories in *Dubliners*, which are as "well-made" as anything could be, they seem beautiful and wonderful to live in right up to the end; but at the end a kind of compulsive falseness overtakes them because Joyce wants us to believe that there could be an end.

LM: How do you avoid this false "sense of an ending" (as Kermode would have it)?

RK: Sometimes I wish I could just die and leave them to their own devices! More practically, however, it seems apparent there are endings without closures. It's the closure that produces the falsities in most fiction. I want to discern endings that are natural in the way that this moment is; a moment ends when you think of something else. It's that sense of utter freedom and openness to the next moment that I would like my works to produce in the reader. There are some writers who seem to have that now. With poetry, the difference between ending and closure is the difference between Charles Olson and Yeats. Olson seemed to have a miraculous ear/mind for knowing the exact momentum of the poem, when it ends, the exact moment when the poem reaches its end, its information transmitted, its neural arc closed. And there stop. As miraculous as Yeats's sonorous and incredible acts of closure, the whole mind of the poem twanged to a stop with a rich change of key—the chestnut tree, the burning tower, the throats of birds. Olson, as so often, is the classical mind at work. When I first read "The Librarian," its ending made me remember "our" earliest poem, the *Iliad*, with its heartbreaking, absurd final line, cut off in the middle, "And that was the funeral of Hector, tamer of horses." Homer taught us from the start that the poem, for all its narrativity or imagery or preachment, arises as much from silence, and to silence recurs. After the *Iliad*'s last line, when you're a child, you turn the page wondering what would happen to Troy and the horse and the Greeks, but there is nothing! That is ending without closure. But what we would do to the *Iliad* if we wrote the ending now—how many epilogues and postlogues and afterwords and trumpets and flags we would have to include to end that work!

LM: You've used versions of detective forms in your novel *The Scorpions* and in various stories, and even make references to detective fiction in your poetry. What intrigues you about this form, which, of course, is usually seen as providing "closure" of the most extreme kind? Mainly an interest in undercutting its formal implications?

RK: Partly that, but I confess it's also a naive devotion to Conan Doyle, who strikes me as a very great master of short stories, at least in his Sherlock Holmes stories. He allows the emblematic; the ultimate irresolution of reality is summarized and expressed through an image—some little tra-la-la he provides at the end of a story that to the naive reader ends the narrative but which actually does something quite different. I know that the stories aren't finished; I know that they are finished in that the crime (or legalistic aspect) has been finished, but something else remains. Just last night I was saying how ironic it is that *Bleak House*, Dickens's greatest work, is just such a completely unresolved situation. The day I arrived in India in 1983, the first thing I read was about a law case that had been settled in Orissa (the state underneath Bengal) which had been under litigation for 740 years! Someone in 1243 (I believe it was) had sued somebody else, and the two families had been litigating ever since. *Bleak House* ponders that sort of endless process—the idea that in the real world, litigation goes on forever—and it extracts from that an image, that wonderful juxtaposition that the surrealists knew all about. Things enter and things depart, and it's enough for an artist to give us an image of this.

LM: *Moby-Dick* does this, as well . . .

RK: Indeed. It's a great anti-Cartesian work that makes no sense whatsoever in the usual novelistic manner—you can't get a feeling for the action there, with all of its structural ornamentation and Greek dramas and scenes on the forecastle. It's an absolutely unsatisfactory novel for a child, who's bound to finish it and ask, "Where did the boat go? What happened to the whale? Why did I read this book? Why was I given five hundred pages of immense potential conflict between Starbuck and Ahab, only to see both drowned almost wordlessly? What went on in Starbuck's mind in the *act* of dying?"

LM: *Moby-Dick* is obviously a book that revels in language's potentiality—and yet ultimately it winds up demonstrating its absolute limitations, its inability to explain or define.

RK: And yet it constantly delights the reader as it goes along, so that language becomes a part of love, not the thing described but the thing describing. *Moby-Dick* cures us of the notion of using the novel as a map of some imaginary reality because it is itself a reality. I like the fact that only after some familiarity with *Moby-Dick* when we reach the point where we know all that happens before we read it, are we able to be undisappointed with the experience, and see the greatness of the book. It's like the end of the *Commedia*, which is the greatest of all anti-Cartesian works: we are left looking at a rose and are told that we are looking at infinity. He who has been able to describe everything now says, "My words now fail me." And so he leaves us with a rose to look at.

LM: You have a wonderful image somewhere about being able to get close enough to a page so that it seems infinite.

RK: If you get close enough to the page it seems you are looking right through it. And I would want to look through it indefinitely. That's the balance, the dicey thing, which a writer wants to keep between the indefinite, which is just mushy, and the undefined, which is open and spacious.

LM: Despite your interest in keeping open the register of possibilities, interesting stories do emerge in your fiction. To what extent would you say you are interested in story per se?

RK: Very much so. It is the freshness of stories that is wonderful. I speak in the afterword to *The Scorpions* of Robert Duncan's anger at my book. He said I had sinned against the spirit of story. That was a serious accusation, if we conceive of "story" as different, and necessarily different, from *writing*. But Duncan himself says somewhere that "a man has no dream except the dream he tells." A dream exists only when you tell it, either to yourself or your wife at breakfast, or whoever it might be. Yet Duncan seems to believe, as almost all of us do, that there is a thing called "story" which is different from its given embodiment as an act of telling.

If I had a theoretical interest here, it would be to push language to the point where it tells its own story—language as fable—to see where there is a difference, to see whether there is hiding in the world some story different from its own telling. I'm not talking about the *Rashomon* principle, where each person tells the story of a single event from his or her own perspective, and of course each time the event is thoroughly or subtly different, yet we are made to intuit that behind all these stories there is one *happening* common to all of them, an episode you might one day discover by legalistic triangulation. Or by theology. Because just such a self-evident event is what we mean (usually) by a god. We've had our great Rashomon writers, Faulkner comes to mind, a constant voicing of a common place, a never-ending saga of relatedness. What I mean is a story previous to any teller. I don't think there is such. I think the spirit of story is the yearning of language to console us. "Writing wants to go on," said Stein. That is our deific presence.

LM: Clearly *The Scorpions* is a novel where the writing wants to go on, whereas Duncan felt the dictates of the form indicated you should resolve things and provide closure to this adventure yarn you'd set in motion.

RK: Right, he was complaining about my failure to explain what happened. He has a great piece called "What Happened" in which he addressed some literary shenanigans that went on in San Francisco—somebody had a fight with Jack Spicer or something of the sort. But what had *happened* there was very important to him; he wanted to trace the causal nexus—this person had said this, and that led to this, and so on. I can't imagine anyone more sophisticated about this sort of thing than Duncan, and yet he did believe in a simple causal path that could be reconstructed (I don't know *how* simple, but simple enough that it could be said). Maybe it could, but I don't see things operating in those terms.

LM: Surely readers should sense by the middle of *The Scorpions* that we are in the midst of a labyrinth that *can't* be resolved—perhaps the labyrinth of reality or the human mind itself.

RK: What was happening is that everything was clearly shifting into his mind—my narrator was being shown to be more and more out of control, so that when he would up killing the redheaded boy a crisis had been reached. That murder was a complete break from everything he had ever been, and his entry into the world of evil; he had now passed into this world of evil and incoherence, and so he simply ran out. People talk about "running out" of ideas or "running out" of time, and he was like that in that he was a man who had a chance, who reified his fantasies to an extent, and then lost control. So it was a story of a man going mad (i.e., going *bad*).

LM: I was frequently reminded of Nabokov (especially *Lolita*) while reading *The Scorpions*. With Nabokov there is always the sense that every element in his texts, no matter how seemingly casual or random, is part of a larger pattern that he is absolutely in control of.

RK: I admired Nabokov a lot at the time I was writing *The Scorpions*, especially his artifice and control. *Pale Fire*, which I had not read at that point, has become very important to me, as well as *Ada*, which I didn't read until the 1970s. But I had read *Lolita* when it was still in its Travelers Library edition from France, ten years or so before I wrote *The Scorpions*. I hadn't reread it when I started my own novel, but I was conscious of the resemblance of this traveling-through-America motif. Still, I felt my character was on a different enough quest—and that the America he was visiting was at once slightly more innocent in one sense and more sinister in another—that I couldn't possibly be accused of imitation. My character is more interested in America and doesn't react as violently to America as Humbert did because my character doesn't have a Lolita whom he's following. There's a curious absence of a grail there, he's following something that is not in front of him. Absence is our Holy Grail. What I most honor in Nabokov is the absolute need of unflagging attention to the text you're writing.

LM: *The Scorpions* borrows certain trappings from science fiction, and you use elements of fantasy and the fabulous in a number of your fictions. I'm again reminded of what an important influence Borges was back in the early sixties on writers of your generation in reopening the fable as a legitimate area of literary terrain.

RK: Borges used fable without being stupid or naive about it. He encouraged us to go back and read Kipling and Chesterton, and when we did we discovered that both of them were two non-naive writers if ever there were any. Kipling had naive political views at certain points in his life, which we've never forgiven him for; he also had some honest, tough writings about India which were dark and mysterious and poetic and beautiful. But Borges certainly permitted us to reexplore that area. I wonder what Borges feels like to a South American writer. I wonder what a Cortázar felt about Borges—whether he felt that Borges had gotten off into the wrong area, because Borges does smell of the library, and he *wants* to smell of the library . . .

LM: Certainly even writers like Vargas Llosa and García Márquez, who have obviously been influenced by Borges, have combined that smell of the library with other smells—of people fucking, of the political arena . . .

RK: And yet you could say much the same thing about Joyce, who lived through all those years of Ireland's struggle for liberation and finally its achievement of something like independence. Here was a man who lived through the most exciting years in Ireland's political history and yet there's nothing of this struggle in his fiction. He writes about Parnell, who was before his time, but not about Connolly or Easter Week 1916 and the Free State—none of that.

LM: Still, I've always been bothered by the frequent charges made against Borges and Nabokov about their works' lack of political involvement. Doesn't the construction of a reality out of words have important implications for the world we all inhabit—where politicians and lawyers build realities out of words and force people to accept them?

RK: Borges has one explicitly anti-Peronist fable in *The Dream Tigers* about somebody who comes and imitates Peron, but that direct political commentary is obviously an exception. In most of Borges what I feel is a kind of interestingly self-protecting sensibility, the way his blindness is a self-protection in a sense. There's that wonderful poem by García Lorca, where he keeps repeating, "No quiero verla"—I don't want to see it. The blind man is the one who has said that most compellingly to the world. Well, if ever there was a man who chose to be blind, that man was Borges. You can see this in his relationships with women, and in the way he portrays (or chooses not to portray) powerful emotions in general.

LM: Have you noticed any difference between the stories you've written most recently and those you did back in the sixties and seventies?

RK: My immediate and affectual answer is, "No, I don't think so at all." After I heard that answer in my head, I also heard myself realizing that if I were given the task of giving prose readings of my work in Japan or Kansas City, I would probably wind up reading more pieces from, say, *Doctor of Silence* than from my earlier book *A Transparent Tree* because these newer pieces are written more for the ear than what I did previously. The fictions in *A Transparent Tree* were written over such a very long period that there are concerns among them that are purely prosaic, earnest narrative, whereas with nearly all the work in the newer book there is more a sense of the ear.

LM: Not only do many of your works deal almost obsessively and relentlessly with sexuality and eroticism both directly and indirectly, but your language and imagery in nearly everything you've ever written is frequently sensuous, charged with physicality. It's as if you wanted to exhaust all the possible things to say about desire—and the ways to say it.

RK: If there is a program to what I have been doing, it is to settle (if this ever could be settled) what the relationship is between the sexual and the sensual. Those two things, which are usually presented as alternative words for the same thing, never strike me as comfortably or finally the same. As it usually presents itself, the sexual has a mode of procreation or of mastery in it—or humiliation, triumph, or various ways of appropriation, the giving up of the assertion of the will. The sensual has none of that. How to argue the full sensual reality of oneself and another without the appropriation that turns the sensual into conquest and lawsuits and judgments, all the explicit and obvious forms of possession. Those things fascinate me. The very strong sensual instinct in me also gets me into trouble. The sexual instinct is less strong, if by that I mean the sense of appropriation. There is a contradiction in this sexual/sensual distinction in that, personally speaking, I don't have any homosexual power. I don't have any feeling for it. Even though the male body is obviously as sensual as the other, I can't relate to its sensuality. It's a contradiction at the very start of my neat distinction between the sexual and sensual. If this distinction holds, why wouldn't all bodies seem equally sensuous and evocative to me? But they're not. So insofar as I can be conscious or clear about what I am after in fishing around about these things, it seems to me that a lot of writing that is really about the sensual gets into trouble when it tries to deal with the sexual; while other writing which is appropriative and *really* sexual in that Western sense has no sensual reality whatsoever. Sade immediately comes to mind in this regard: I can't see any sensual distinction between disemboweling one girl and disemboweling thirty girls except arithmetic. That arithmetic eros of Sade or even Don Juan characterizes the sexual, whereas someone like Bataille tries to go in the other direction towards the sensual. And yet Sade and Bataille are usually spoken of as if they were doing essentially the same thing.

LM: For various reasons, authors during, say, the past two hundred years have been freer to explore sexuality (and perhaps even sensuality) in their work. Would you say that writers have made "advancements" during this period, in the sense of being able to more accurately (or "appropriately"—whatever that would mean) describe or embody the sexual or the sensual?

RK: I think so. A book that comes to mind is Robert Coover's *Gerald's Party*. Some sensitive women readers just couldn't read it. They felt this was simply unmediated male chauvinist oinkery on Coover's part. I thought not, because I felt the book was extraordinary in the way it represented the upward and outward of the sexual focus—the first is all anus and shit. Then in the central section it moves to the genital, while in the last part the hand is the central physical sexual image. Whether consciously or unconsciously, Coover seems to be using this imagery to move from the basic "spanking-the-maid" fixation at the opening to a depiction of "normal" sexual relationships, both hetero and homosexual; and then at the end everything has to do with the hand, no longer sexual, not masturbatory gestures, but a gentler, sensual movement towards achievement of the Goethean notion: "One mind suffices for a thousand hands"—as if he were finally reaching for a hand to do some work with. In that sense *Gerald's Party* is a fascinating presentation of the growth of sexual awareness, both of the child in the ontogeny way, where the primitive, anal fixations of childhood progress towards a more mature relationship to the sexual, until finally there is even transcendence of the sexual. The grotesque image of woman presented in the book strikes me as very much Coover's analyzing male fixation fantasies, rather than indulging his own.

LM: Given the current conservative climate, both aesthetically and in the larger cultural and political world, do you think the freedoms broadly offered artists the past hundred years or so will continue?

RK: While we have been in the midst of this AIDS anxiety, I've often thought that we may enter a time where this freedom will be denied us, where the same Victorian fastidiousness will return and we will no longer even be able to use naughty words, much less write naughty situations.

LM: You say in one of your afterwords that your fictions often "exert themselves to conjecture at the nature and efficacy of silence." Did you choose to entitle *Doctor of Silence* in order to point to this ongoing conjecture? I find an intriguing tension in your work between the desire to say *everything* that can possibly be said (about something, about everything) and yet the awareness of the impossibility of saying *anything* about anything.

RK: The only things that can be said about anything can be said only by means of silence. Silence as a sort of music. Silence is what makes poetry happen. The silence of the line ending is what makes the line. A line of poetry can be said to be the shortest distance between two silences. The words define the silence as much as the silence defines the words. The relationship between silence and what is being said is that golden reciprocal, everything influencing everything else. With a poem you have silence in the sense that no one is talking, then a line comes into the silent mind, or the will of an attentive artist locates some talk within the chatter of the mind and a line occurs, and this line runs from silence to silence, breath to breath. In poetry, then, there is a quite obvious and quite easily talked about relationship between silence and saying.

LM: Couldn't we say a *story* is the shortest distance between two silences?

RK: We could indeed—as in the distance between the silence out of which Homer begins the *Iliad* with that word "Wrath" and its conclusion, as if the whole twenty-four book poem were just a meditation on that one word "Wrath" down to the phrase, "that was the funeral of Hector," that ends the work. Then there is a pause, as if a new thing were going to be thought about but hadn't arisen yet. So, yes, that sense of silence as also defining a story is very interesting to me, and a lot of the pieces in *Doctor of Silence* grew out of that interest.

LM: So you really are the Doctor of Silence.

RK: Yes, I very much wanted that phrase to be a description of me. I didn't have a doctorate, so I thought, "Wouldn't it be nice to have a doctor of *silence* degree—a D.S. or S.D." "D.S." would be nice because when I was a child in New York that meant the garbage man, the Department of Sanitation. It would also indicate a doctor of knowing when to shut up, because all my life I've been reproached for talking and writing too much. But even as I thought of myself as the Doctor of Silence, I realized just having that name wouldn't help me. There needed to be a little story about the doctor of silence who becomes the old peasant who sits there and doesn't say anything because he doesn't really have anything to say and can't remember anything. I was thinking of the way as little children we are taught to respect those wordless, laconic *pomposos* who have nothing to say.

LM: Your remarkable command of such a wide range of words seems related to the relentless, obsessive quality of your work I referred to earlier. It's that sense we see in Melville's *Moby-Dick* of someone determined to seek out every possible word or linguistic context to speak into existence the mystery of life. Where does this obsession with words come from?

RK: A word is a lover—or rather, one phrase or veil or imposture of the lover: Taste it in the kiss of speaking, feel it, pursue it through its roots and reflexes and branches, to find the *one* waiting behind all statements. The one you mean. I've never systematically studied words or language, I don't browse through dictionaries to memorize words, or study word lists. There must be hundreds of very important words I don't know at all, but they do come to me, these words. That is the beauty and the love of it. Grace brings us words, no? The French say *mieux la chance que l'adresse*—luck is better than skill.

LM: You've referred to the "sacred" quality of language and of writing's "religious" function. How would you describe your views about the relationship between words and whatever it is that most of us would refer to as the "Divine"?

RK: Like what we know of dreams, what we know of religion is what people *say* about it. Typically in most religions, people say over and over again every day some sacred text—liturgy is word, the "people's work" is to say the prayers. What would religion be like if there were no language? Is there a difference between the sacred and sacred texts? Every religion seems to have a "bible" of some sort, a canon of collected instances, even if it's not a written one. What interests me as a writer, though, is once again this matter of decorum allowing you or forbidding you to write certain things. When I was growing up, one thing you didn't write about was religion. The religious instinct was regarded as strictly formatory and useless to society, either because you were a Marxist or because you were, like Joyce, fighting Catholicism or whatever was dominant. But anything that people do seems interesting to me. So if people think about God, then God must be interesting, and if people think of religion, then religion is interesting.

LM: That attitude has become closely associated with postmodernism— even soup cans, football, and soap operas can be viewed as being "interesting" in some sense.

RK: But the truth is that I can't like football, and I don't understand other sports. There are certain pleasures of other people that I want to understand and find myself unable to; rather than worrying about this, it just seems important for me to pursue the ones I have some feelings for. This sounds like an excuse but it's simply the fact of the matter. It interests me that people have religious apprehensions about reality, that they think certain words have a more hierarchical reality than other words. I don't necessarily believe that, but it seems significant to me that the name "Jesus" has a higher "energy" for some people than the word "Joshua," even though they might be the same in Hebrew. Why is there a different energy level there? Of course, it comes from culture, but it's more than culture. It's a religious culture to which we consciously contribute every day of our lives, by saying, "Jesus! I've stubbed my toe" (whereas we don't say, "Joshua! I've stubbed my toe"). Culture is not a one-way street coming to us poor little victims lying in our cradles being uncultured; we *get up* from our cradles uncultured; we *get up* from our cradles and begin to act our own realities. Religion has been well-served by language, talk, and discourse and ill-served by action most of the time because religion folds back upon the mind. As a great teacher, Kalu Rinpoche, said, "It's the mind that meditates, not the sword or the hand."

LM: Are you consciously aiming at infusing your writing with this mysterious "higher energy" of religious language?

RK: It would feel grandiose if I were to say, "Yes," but it would also feel like a betrayal if I were to say, "No, I don't want that to happen." I would, however, certainly like that to happen in my work because I respond with such excitement to some of the altitudes and ecstasies that I find in reading, for example, Henry James, someone with a "secular" mind. The opening of *The Ambassadors* might be as religious a text as we have in some ways. What could be a truer image of our days than this opening description of a mysterious woman who is the goddess of true apprehension of all false things?

LM: Many of the most striking fictions in your recent collections are structured as a series of fragments with spaces—silences—in between. Why do you choose to organize a fiction in this way, rather than in a more linear fashion?

RK: I don't think of these fictions being constructed out of fragments but out of wholes. Here I'll invoke Melville again, who strikes me as our great novelist not because of what he wrote about—the ocean, the whale—but because he had a fantastic sense of chaptering. In *Moby-Dick* he had chapters ranging in length from fifteen or eighteen pages down to ones perhaps six lines long. If you merely looked at this structure from across the room, it would perhaps seem whimsical—Laurence Sterne-like (Sterne himself being the greatest of our anti-Cartesian novelists). But Melville's sense of chaptering suggests to me that chaptering doesn't have to be variegated—the long/short, long/short structure you find in his great masterpiece *Billy Budd*—but that even very short chapters have a right to exist on their own. So I think of "The Winter's Tale" and "Samuel Naked" of consisting of their own little individual chapters. Think of what a chapter looked like in a nineteenth-century novel: when you come to the end of one, there might be an ornament, and then when you turn the page you would find a Roman numeral—"XLI" or whatever. Following that there might be a little argument or preface (with Kipling there might be three or four lines of verse), perhaps even a drawing or a vignette before you get into the chapter. All that bric-a-brac to break off one chapter from the next, to force the reader's mind through a great mine-field of silence, to absorb the differences before a new chapter could begin.

In a different sense, that's what poetry has been doing all through the centuries—slowing down the reading. Prose needs that too, and one way to accomplish it is by presenting fragments; it forces readers to string the beads themselves. I don't mean cruelly to manipulate the reader—I love the reader! But I don't want the reader to read too quickly and smoothly. I suppose you could say *The Scorpions* is a cautionary tale showing the reader what happens if you read too quickly. Still, I don't really think of the sections of these novellas as "fragments" but as revelations that, as Davenport shows us in his *Archilochos* translation, one age's fragment is another age's whole. Stan Brakhage said once that fragmentation is our classicism, and in that sense a story such as "Winter's Tale" strikes me as a very classical story. I suspect that one reason why readers have liked my "Winter's Tale" and reacted to it as a very serious story is because they find it difficult, a "difficult text." In a structural, hence classically modernist way, it confronts the reader with the necessity of a series of cooperations, of deeds called reading. A story with fewer obstacles to straightforward going-on might not win the respect of demanding readers whose pleasure lies in the effort of cocreation.

LM: Was there ever such a thing as modernism? Or postmodernism?

RK: "Modernism" was a particular moment of commodity capitalism, where it became possible to sell the shape of the experience as well as the object produced from the experience. I don't mean to speak ill of modernism—I think it was wonderful—but in its preoccupation with technique and structure (over against object) it seemed at the same moment to indulge the capitalist necessity for the sellable commodity fetish at the same moment it was trying to abrogate it. That paradox of modernism has been elaborately played with, without consciously being studied. The "postmodernist" is somebody who wants his fetish back and doesn't want to be distracted by the difficulties of it. "Postmodernism" is the funniest name anyone has ever come up with. Modernism, of course, is associated with this sense of experiment, but a long time ago it occurred to me that the biggest experiment a person ever does is simply going on every day saying a new thing—opening one's mouth and seeing what the new word of the day is. Because every day has its word, just as every pencil or typewriter has its poem, and every machine or stone its story. The sense of modernism as being able to liberate from every structure and circumstance or set of molecular interactions its own characteristic music or song or story—that's the real experiment that every day should have. I can't imagine ever getting "post" it. I can certainly imagine a way of saying, "Oh, we're not interested in difficult texts anymore." But now all that postmodernism means is "easy." Modernism at its best was an experiment in complexity—in complex interactions of the time of writing and the time of reading. Postmodernism seems to mean that the reader's investment in the text is trivial—that any old time at the beach or on the subway is enough since the text reads itself. Popcorn read.

LM: Postmodernism's emphasis on "intertextuality" leads almost inevitably to an interest in pastiche or parody—which aren't things you seem interested in.

RK: Indeed, I'm not. And I'm troubled by that idea of all postmodernism being self-parodic. In a literal sense, I can't tell the difference between a paragraph of Raymond Carver and a paragraph of Stephen King. The *aspiration* of the writing in both cases seems to be identical: bearing witness to a tongue-in-cheekly imagined reality previous to our attention, and to which the prose bears some kind of measurable relation. That would be parodic—if there exists a relationship between reality and text such that texts mirror each other, just as reality mirrors itself.

LM: One of the differences frequently cited between modernism and postmodernism has to do with the goal of creating texts whose order opposes the chaos of life versus the text which, if not indulging in this chaos, at least refuses closure.

RK: But this lack of closure was part of the original modernist impulse. The idea that modernism represents some sort of magnificent order is the academic rehash of modernism. Isn't the cry of "no more master-pieces" not just a cry of the surrealists? Isn't it Joyce's hope in *Finnegans Wake*, unreadably unendable, or Pound's ever-building Old Faithful of it, *Cantos*?

LM: Are there other contemporary fiction writers you particularly ad-mire or whom you feel some kinship with?

RK: There are so many. I can hardly pick up a book I don't enjoy—un-less it's trying to tell me a story too much. The book of fiction which has most excited me is *Light While There Is Light* by Keith Waldrop, which is as unlike anything I could ever write as I can imagine. It's about growing up in Kansas, illustrated with snapshots of these bizarre uncles doing this or his mama doing that. It's an amazing, realistic book but it's a modernist book in that its structure finally yields meaning. The writers who have actually taught me the most are Kafka, Joyce, and Dos-toyevsky—these were my influences back in the 1950s. Others I enjoy now are Georges Perec, Nabokov, early Harry Mathews, Proust, Jeanette Winterson, Amos Schmidt.

LM: At the end of "Calf of Gold," the narrator, after describing a reciter who does not understand the story that he recites, adds that "under-standing is not so important to the reciter." Is understanding your own work important to you?

RK: Yes, but not while I'm in the process of writing something. So in a certain sense that paragraph you're quoting from is about my own re-lationship to my work. It takes me a long time to understand what I've written. Often understanding will come a long time afterwards, when the storyteller is in the marketplace hearing the story again. I seldom understand a work when I first encounter it, mine or anyone else's. I guess that makes me a modernist, in that modernists didn't understand anything and couldn't trust their understanding. They wanted every-thing to be a love letter to them but knew that nothing was likely to be, so they assumed nothing was and consoled themselves with urgent love letters to the dead.

Alternative, Possibility, and Essence
An Interview with Richard Kostelanetz

Larry McCaffery
Harry Polkinhorn

There are no final limits upon the materials available to the teller of stories; the practical limits upon fictional possibility are intrinsic in the creative imagination and one's chosen medium.

— "Statements on Fiction"

The following interview with Richard Kostelanetz was conducted in Calexico, California, where Kostelanetz was screening his film *A Berlin Lost* at San Diego State University's branch campus. Calexico is a small agricultural town located directly across the chain-link and barbed-wire border fence from the growing metropolis of Mexicali, capital of Baja California, Mexico. While in the area, Kostelanetz was interviewed on Radio Universidad, appeared at the State Theater in Mexicali, where he showed his multimedia production entitled *New York City*, and tape-recorded the sounds of a pair of Mexicali baseball teams for an audio project, *Americas' Game*.

Experimental fictioneer, avant-garde theorist, anthologist, and media artist, Kostelanetz has explored the outer fringes of narrative through a variety of media and approaches. He has worked in film, book art, video books, holography, the photographic essay, and graphic arts, among other media, in his drive to explore the narrative potential of materials. As diverse as Kostelanetz's concerns are, they are united by a common concern with discovering what the essence of a genre, form, technological process, or style should be or do. Primarily a writer, Kostelanetz's preoccupations, coupled with a lack of institutional affiliation, have resulted in his "outsider" status, and a presence of increasing importance in contemporary avant-garde culture. His works make obsolete the narrow categorizations upon which official strata of culture are based.

Kostelanetz's works outside the area of fiction per se suggest something of the range of his interests (fiction publications are included in the Selected Bibliography below): —Visual poetry: *Visual Language, I Articulations, Word Prints, Portraits from Memory, Rain Rains Rain, Illuminations, Turfs/Arenas/Fields/Pitches.* —Wordworks: *Poems New and Selected.* —Audio art: *Experimental Prose, Openings and Closings, Foreshortenings, Invections, New York City, Americas' Game, The Gospels/Die Evangelien.* —Video art: *Three Prose Pieces, Openings and Closings, Declaration of Independence, Epiphanies, Kenetic Writings, Kadish.* —Book art: *Tabula Rasa, Inexistences, And So Forth, Autobiographies.* —Holography: *On Holography, Antitheses.* — Theater: *Epiphanies, Lovings.* —Nonsyntactic prose: *Recyclings* (Vol. 1), *Prunings/Accruings, Recyclings* (Complete), *Prose Pieces/Aftertexts.* —Film: *Constructivist Fictions, Openings and Closings, A Berlin Lost.* To this should be added the many anthologies Kostelanetz has edited, including *Twelve from the Sixties* (1967), *The Young American Writers* (1970), *Possibilities of Poetry* (1970), *Breakthrough Fictioneers* (1973), *Essaying Essays* (1975), *Younger Critics in North America* (1975), and *Visual Literative Criticism* (1979). Kostelanetz's criticism can be found in his *Theater of Mixed Means* (1968), *The End of Intelligent Writing* (1974), *Grants and the Future of Literature* (1978), and *Twenties in the Sixties* (1979). He has also published documentary monographs on the "polyartists" Moholy-Nagy and John Cage.

In his "creative works," as he calls them, Kostelanetz is less interested in traditional thematic approaches than in the internal dynamics of the medium in question, especially as it relates to the syntactic component of language, or what Dick Higgins calls "sequences (or sometimes counter-sequence, if the ordering of the materials defies any logical trajectory)." Although fundamentally a writer (who works mostly with words), Kostelanetz's more recent preoccupations are with the possibilities that new technologies are opening up for literature and art: overlayering and reprocessing tracks of data drawn from a wide range of sources. His continuing fascination with the works of Moholy-Nagy and Cage point up both the intermedial, unclassifiable dimensions and the combinatory processes that underlie his art.

The interview was conducted in Harry Polkinhorn's house in Calexico, where Kostelanetz had been presenting a series of lectures and performances. Kostelanetz busied himself hooking up the audio equipment, then relaxed with a view out the sliding-glass doors onto a patio and backyard lined with palms and oleanders. Tanned from sunbathing, laughing frequently, the artist seemed comfortable; bottles of beer were passed around, and the interview began.

*   *   *

Richard Kostelanetz: Selected Bibliography

Books of Fiction

In the Beginning. Somerville, MA: Abyss, 1971.
Come Here. Des Moines: Cookie, 1975.
Constructs. Reno, NV: WCPR, 1975.
Extrapolate. Des Moines: Cookie, 1975; Brooklyn, NY: Assembling, 1975.
Modulations. Brooklyn, NY: Assembling, 1975.
Openings and Closings. New York: D'Arc, 1975.
One Night Stood. New York: Future, 1977.
Three Places in New Inkland (with two others). New York: Zartscorp, 1977.
Inexistences. New York: RK Editions, 1978.
Constructs Two. Milwaukee, WI: Membrane, 1978.
Foreshortenings and Other Stories. Willets, CA: Tuumba, 1978.
And So Forth. New York: Future, 1979.
Tabula Rasa. New York: RK Editions, 1979.
More Short Fictions. Brooklyn, NY: Assembling Press, 1980.
Epiphanies. West Berlin: Literarisches Colloquium Berlin, 1983.
Constructs Three. New York: RK Editions, 1991.
Flipping. New York: RK Editions, 1991.
Constructs Four. New York: RK Editions, 1991.
Fifty Untitled Constructivist Fictions. New York: RK Editions, 1991.
Constructs Five. New York: RK Editions, 1991.
Intermix. New York: RK Editions, 1991.
Constructs Six. New York: RK Editions, 1991.

Experimental Prose

Recyclings. Vol. 1. Brooklyn, NY: Assembling Press, 1974.
Prunings/Accruings. Geneva: Ecart, 1977.
Recyclings. Complete. New York: Future, 1984.
Prose Pieces/Aftertexts. Calexico, CA: Atticus, 1987.
Minimal Fictions. Santa Monica, CA: Asylum Arts, 1994.

Performance Scripts

Seductions. For sixteen male performers, in manuscript. Performed at the Whitney Counterweight, New York, 1982.
Lovings. For three or more instrumentalists, in manuscript. Performed at the Medicine Show, New York, 1991.
Epiphanies. Performed at the University of North Dakota, 1980; Vassar College, 1981.

Fiction Texts for Composers

He Met Her in the Park/Motte Henne i Parken (for Charles Dodge). 1981.
Wasting (for Paul Lansky). 1986.

Audiotapes Including Prose/Fiction

Experimental Prose. Brooklyn, NY: Assembling Press, 1976.
Openings and Closings. New York: Archae Editions, 1976.
Foreshortenings and Other Stories. New York: Archae Editions, 1976.
Asdescent/Anacatabasis. New York: Archae Editions, 1976.
Epiphanies. In progress since 1982.
Two German Hörspiele. New York: RK Editions, 1983.
Seductions. New York: RK Editions, 1991.
Relationships. New York: RK Editions, 1993.

Videotapes Including Prose/Fiction

Three Prose Pieces. Produced at Synapse, Syracuse University, 1975.
Openings and Closings. Produced at Synapse, Syracuse University, 1975.
Declaration of Independence (1979). Produced at KENW, Portales, New Mexico, 1979.
Epiphanies. Produced at Experimental Intermedia Foundation, New York, 1980.
Seductions/Relationships. Produced at the Experimental TV Center, Oswego, New York, 1987.

Prose/Fiction Films (Coproduced and Codirected)

Constructivist Fictions (with Peter Longauer). 1977.
Openings and Closings (with Bart Weiss). 1978.
Epiphanies. 1981–92.

As Editor/Anthologist

On Contemporary Literature: An Anthology of Critical Essays. New York: Avon, 1964.
The Theatre of Mixed Means. New York: Dial Press, 1968.
Panache—Special Issue: Future's Fiction (1971). Princeton, NJ.
Breakthrough Fictioneers. Barton, VT: Something Else Press, 1973.
The Avant-Garde Tradition in Literature. Buffalo, NY: Prometheus Books, 1982.

Nonfiction

Master Minds: Portraits of Contemporary American Artists and Intellectuals. New York: Macmillan, 1969.
The End of Intelligent Writing: Literary Politics in America. New York: Sheed and Ward, 1974.
Autobiographies. Santa Barbara, CA: Mudborn; and New York: Mudborn and Future Presses, 1981.
The Old Fiction and the New. Jefferson, NC: McFarland, 1987.

The Old Fictions and the New. Carbondale: Southern Illinois University Press, 1991.
A Dictionary of the Avant-Gardes. Pennington, NJ: A Cappella, 1993.
Crimes of Culture. New York: Autonomedia, 1995.
Fillmore East, Twenty-Five Years After: Recollections of Rock Theater. New York: Schirmer, 1995.

Reviews and Articles about Kostelanetz's Work

Higgins, Dick. "Richard Kostelanetz" (with selected bibliography). In *Postmodern Fiction: A Bio-Bibliographical Guide,* ed. Larry McCaffery, 437–40. Westport, CT: Greenwood Press, 1986.
Gomez, Raymond. "Towards a Critical Understanding of Richard Kostelanetz's Single Sentence Stories." *Critique: Studies in Contemporary Fiction* 35, 4 (Summer 1994): 229–36.

* * *

RICHARD KOSTELANETZ: If only to ensure that we don't get lost on the way to a proper opening, why don't I begin our conversation with a statement: I do fiction that is more radical than what anyone else is writing today, and radical in more ways. I've therefore pushed fictional experimentation in more radical directions than any other author you know. This radicalism is based upon strategies that involve working with language in severely alternative, mostly minimalist forms, and creating fiction directly in other media.

LARRY McCAFFERY: Granted there must be some overlap between the radical experimentalism you're interested in and what one finds in works by, say, the authors usually associated with postmodern experimentalism of the sixties and seventies (Sukenick, Federman, Coover, Barth, Barthelme, and so on), how would you define these differences?

RK: First off, I'd argue there's not actually much overlap at all, other than the use of the English language for our titles, as I think *they* would agree. What I have done and continue to do as a writer, as a critic, as an anthologist, as a theorist, is simply more extreme and more avant-garde in every fundamental sense. It's more pure in ways that only fiction can be, I'd like to think, because I have thought more thoroughly and profoundly about the issues of alternative, possibility, and essence.

HARRY POLKINHORN: How do you measure the relative "purity" or extremity of your avant-garde impulses, as opposed to those of these other writers?

RK: The most immediate, backass measure of this extremism is how unacceptable my fiction appears to those guys you mention, as well as to the hordes of fiction writers behind them, almost all of them extending along an aesthetic spectrum down and to their aesthetic right. Unacceptability is a simple measure of extremism, to be sure, but it's a genuine measure which has the further epistemological advantage of being easily verified. Consider that those authors you mention are invited to teach fiction in the colleges (in one case, at my own Ivy League university), while people doing the kinds of work I do and that I admire most, are, like myself, *not* invited to teach in creative writing programs.

LM: Why do you think your work has tended to be accepted more readily in the fields of music and art than in literature? How do you account for this?

RK: The easiest place to begin, though not the place to end, is that in the literary community—how can I put this most generously?—I have made a lot of enemies, sometimes by publishing strong criticism of mediocrity and mendacity, but in other, less intentional ways.

LM: What's been the main aspect of the threat you represent to people in the literary community—the kind of criticism you've just mentioned (say, in *The End of Intelligent Writing*), or the more indirect "threat" your creative works imply?

RK: The most "threatening" thing about me, especially to *Scheisskӧpfe*, is the fact that I've survived almost wholly unaffiliated for so long, without patronage or publicity—which is the threat I can do least about. Remember that "writers" who owe their visibility to positions they've held, or to the promotions of noisy publishers, or to relentless ass-kissing have enormous difficulty accepting prominence earned without positions or publicity or ass-kissing, because it exposes their own vulnerability. They fear in their gut that once their patrons or publishers are gone, they'll be forgotten. No one, in my experience, is uglier than a disillusioned cynic.

When I was beginning, some twenty years ago, the composer Milton Babbitt told me, "As a young man I had the good fortune of making all the right enemies." This hint wasn't lost on me. When I asked him recently about this advice, he told me that the "enemy" in his mind when he said that to me was Randall Thompson, a composer now forgotten who had for many years the chair in composition at Harvard. By this point in my professional life I suppose that competitive colleagues would now envy my good fortune on this point as well.

Another problem is this: what writers want most of all is the respect of their colleagues and then the respect of artists in other fields. This respect can't be bought with position; it can't be bought by publishers' publicity departments (successful though they are at buying the interest of book reviewers). I've had some success at earning the first kind of respect and greater success at earning the second kind. All this infuriates "writers" who think their professorships, their publishers, their patrons, their wholesale acceptability should earn them this kind of respect, which will never be theirs. It makes them livid, drives them bananas.

HP: Do these differences in the reception of your work have to do with the fact that musicians and visual artists are willing to treat avant-garde approaches more seriously?

RK: That's part of it. The great modernist tradition that has more presence in music and visual art than in literature. I've also lived in a visual arts community of SoHo since 1974, when it was still illegal to reside there unless you were a visual artist, a choreographer, a filmmaker, or a composer needing more space; you even had to present your credentials to a committee which, in effect, granted you a residential variance from the city. So for quite a while there simply weren't any writers around me, even though my neighbors perceived me as essentially literary, probably because, unlike them, I spend most of my days working at a typewriter and, now, also at a computer, as well as living among thousands of books. Residing in this nonliterary environment has been very conducive to my sort of eclectic sensibility.

LM: Do you feel more comfortable working within one artistic medium rather than another?

RK: There's only one art—it's called "art"—and it happens to have many forms, none of which is fundamentally superior to any other. (How often do we hear writers speak about the superiority of literature to the other arts—and then recognize that only spokesmen for writing would need to make such claims, because the most visible "literature" nowadays scarcely interests practitioners in other arts?) What I like about my own creative situation is that I can move from one medium to another without needing to warm up to dispel anxiety. Within my own house I have now one facility for editing film and another for editing audiotape in addition to drawing tables, light boxes, and computers. Otherwise, my principal material is language and literary forms.

But music, more than any other form, told me about the essences and possibilities of art. My choice for the most profound artist who ever lived, whose every work reveals his genius, is J. S. Bach. My other hero is the composer Charles Ives, whom I take to be the most inventive artist of all time. Those are my main men—one the epitome of perfection, the other the avatar of innovation—whom I'd ultimately measure myself against. Among the living artists I've learned a lot from are Milton Babbitt, whom we've mentioned already, and John Cage, whom we'll no doubt mention again. In making both aesthetic and professional decisions, I think a lot about Moholy-Nagy and often about Ad Reinhardt.

LM: The popular acceptance of performance artists like Laurie Anderson and people like Philip Glass and Robert Wilson and David Byrne who are working in different media suggests that this is a good time for artists interested in combining forms previously seen as being separate.

RK: That's true, but most of the people you mentioned have produced books but not succeeded as writers, in part because the literary world isn't at all receptive to interlopers, or even much aware of the writing that exists outside the restricted universe of commercial novelists on one side of the stream and creative-writing MFAs along with their gods on the other.

LM: Does this literary conservatism have to do with the power words have in our culture—the way they control our thoughts and actions, as opposed to sounds and colors, whose authority seems more abstract?

RK: It has mostly to do with fashions peculiar to America. Simply, the powers-that-be in the literary world here are far more reactionary than those in music, or visual art, or architecture. Within the National Endowment for the Arts, the literature program is commonly regarded as the one most deeply mired in the support of retrograde mediocrities; that's one reason why it has never been able to increase its small share of total NEA funding, recently 4 percent, to something comparable to the 15 percent allocated to the literary support at the Canada Council. This chic conservatism also accounts for why vanguard writers still choose to go abroad, even in these putatively more enlightened times. I go abroad mostly to do work, especially in radio and film, that cannot be done here. Hell, anybody who knows me well knows that I'd very much prefer sleeping in my own bed! Chic conservatism also has to do with the way art grants are awarded in this country. In the case of the NEA, so much has to do with the personalities of the judges involved, and for various complex reasons people who might be sympathetic to experimentalism have been kept off the panel. And then there's that litany of problems I wrote about in *The End of Intelligent Writing*—the confluences of coterie interests, the awful ways literary reputations are made, the crass commercialism of the book industry.

LM: *The End of Intelligent Writing* presented a persuasive but deeply pessimistic analysis of why serious writing has so few outlets in this country. Have things changed since the late sixties, when you were researching that book?

RK: They've just gotten worse. Commercial publishing has really closed down with regard to doing things we can admire. The criteria for making commercial publishing decisions have become more and more opportunistic, the rationales are more and more vulgar, precisely because editors think nearly all books in this country are sold by the chains like Dalton's and Waldenbooks. Just ask editors in so-called "trade houses" about that, and they'll bombard you with horrifying statistics. Outside merchandisers have replaced publishers' own sales managers in becoming de facto editors—no, de facto *censors*—with remarkably little public protest. One used to believe in accidents slipping through the tight system, but by now it's hard to believe that anything of any imaginative significance will come out of this deleterious situation. The dissemination of serious writing survives in this country because of independent small presses, and some of us who published commercially in the past survived professionally because we made the transition back in the early seventies to small-press publishing when it had to be done. I have a whole bookcase full of sixties fiction, most of it by authors who are no longer visible, and then a shelf full of sixties avant-garde music records. Nearly all those composers, by contrast, are still visible. I mean, you yourself have been very involved in the contemporary writing scene, so let me just ask you: what was the last book of commercially published fiction that you admired?

LM: Barth's *Letters,* Coover's *The Public Burning* and *Gerald's Party,* William Gibson's *Neuromancer,* all of DeLillo's eighties novels, McElroy's *Women and Men,* Gaddis's *JR,* and . . .

RK: Your standards are either more generous or flaccid than mine. I'd pick only the very first of those titles. However, doesn't the fact that all those authors have reputations preceding the current situation indicate to you that it would be difficult, if not impossible, for a new author of similar stature to penetrate the current impasse with fiction of comparable quality? Certainly a book like *Letters* must have really tested the limits of commercial publishing (I recently purchased several copies of the remaindered paperback for a dollar apiece). I fear for even Barth's future with those guys. Instead, we hear of a lot of young dummies who, one hopes, do not represent the best of their literary generation; we find an abundance of junk extravagantly promoted and even favorably reviewed. Can I be the only one among us to regard the *New York Times Book Review* as not a literary arbiter but a disinformation medium that is for safety's sake best ignored?

The key thing to remember with literature is that literature has always been a wholesale business, as opposed to the visual arts which is a retail business. When you're trying to persuade an audience or buyer of one, you are likely persuading a far more intelligent or sophisticated buyer than you are when you're selling to groups of twenty or thirty thousand. And when you have a greater subsidy for quality publishing as you do in Europe, you're going to get more experimental literature than you will here. In order to succeed now serious or innovative fiction in America has to develop more of a retailing sensibility—which is to say that, alas, you've got to know most of your customers (in some cases this may even approximate the conditions of retail in painting: one of a kind for a customer). The writer's ability to accept this situation—which is, after all, the perennial condition of the avant-garde, which has always known its customers—at least allows him to have his head on straight about communication and "success" and everything else practical. Lord knows, even in the precincts in which I travel, there are a lot of writers whose heads are *not* straight.

LM: But can a publisher (or a writer) turn a profit doing these sorts of art books?

RK: Not much of one, but there are institutions surviving on what profit margin there is. The model store for this sort of book is Printed Matter, near me in New York City. It has an enthusiastic clientele, albeit of modest numbers, for "artists books," as it calls them—my term is "book-art books"—about which a critical literature is being written and for which grants are given, not by NEA-Literature, to be sure, but by the Visual Arts Program. I was involved in the book-art scene when it began, a decade ago, and I think it's important for two reasons: It provides an example for certain truly fine book artists to think in terms of editions with smaller numbers; and it allows authors to assume a more direct control of the design and production of the book.

HP: Your work has been associated with the avant-garde virtually from the very beginning of your career. What initially drew you to this sort of work?

RK: I'm puzzled that I don't have an easy answer to this. I suppose I became initially drawn to the avant-garde somewhere between graduating from college in 1962 and my going to England two years later. I had reviewed Harold Rosenberg's *The Tradition of the New* in college and was impressed by his sense of eternal revolution in art, but I didn't know much about the avant-garde tradition at the time. I was more interested in politics and literature. My B.A. thesis was on Henry Miller, whom I regarded as a Norman O. Brownian anarchist; and my M.A. thesis, in American history at Columbia in 1966, dealt with politics in the Negro novel in America.

My interests changed when I returned to New York. Even though I was living in a Harlem housing project, far from the action downtown, I educated myself in the historic avant-garde. I began to appreciate Ives (whom I'd not known about before) and was given a recording of Edgard Varèse's *Ionisation*. I wrote in *The New American Arts* (1965) chapters about theater and fiction that I soon came to consider only moderately avant-garde—Albee in drama; Barth, Heller, Nabokov, Pynchon, and Irvin Faust in fiction.

In 1965–66, when I returned from England thankfully unmarried, I witnessed one of the greatest periods in the history of the New York City art world—the beginnings of pop art and intermedia. There hasn't been another time like that, and may not ever be. Thanks to my immersion in the art scene, and then my moving downtown to the East Village in 1966, my interest in the avant-garde quickly accelerated. By 1967, I could write about intermedia in *The Theatre of Mixed Means* and then about visual arts in *Metamorphosis in the Arts*, which was written at the time but, because of ugly publishing misfortune, not published until 1980. Those two books couldn't have been written by me before moving downtown.

LM: About that time you started doing critical writing, which was highly radicalized right from the get-go. Did that radicalism result from your immersion in the art scene as a critic?

RK: Right. Since I had already been critically appreciating the more extreme developments in the art world for a number of years, it seemed natural to start from an extreme position in my own creative work. I didn't need to progress through exercises in juvenilia, in part because I took my degrees in history. So around 1967 I started a creative streak that I continued along with everything else. My first creative works were visual poems, where I was trying to enhance language through visual display, rather than through the more traditional syntactical or semantic means.

One simple explanation for my "radicalism" is that I'm more *literate* than most writers; and the fact that I have so many books surrounding me at home makes me less interested in reading or seeing something that too closely resembles what I've experienced before. Conventional, mediocre fiction is intended for people who haven't read very much or have a much higher tolerance for repetition and boredom.

LM: Was it mainly this desire to push on to previously unexplored areas that led you to reject most of the usual structures of literature (traditional notions of character, plot, and so on)? Or was it also partially a practical matter of recognizing that your imagination simply didn't work with traditional forms effectively?

RK: Personal insufficiencies were married to aesthetic principles. I tried traditional forms a few times. Back in the late fifties and early sixties I outlined and at times even drafted fiction that quickly came to resemble *The Day of the Locust*. I wish I knew now what was on my mind at the time, other than a desire to write fiction as such and perhaps to impress a college friend named David Kelly. Around this same time I took a course in creative prose in college and was told by a writer whose name is familiar to us both that I had no talent for it. That might have been true superficially, but the deeper truth which he didn't see was that I had no talent for *conventional* plotting and that incapacity in turn killed whatever style I might develop. I took another course at Brown in verse writing from S. Foster Damon, the great Blakist, who taught me not how to write but how to be a writer—which is to say how to cultivate enthusiasms peculiar to oneself, how to work up a subject, et cetera.

I later learned that Gertrude Stein was told she had no talent at writing sentences and John Cage was told by no less a god than Arnold Schoenberg that he had no talent for harmony. Yet they both managed to get around these problems okay. Had I known earlier the truths of their creative careers—that personal insufficiency was not a sufficient reason for quitting—I might have not waited until I was twenty-seven before beginning to do my own poetry and twenty-eight before beginning my own fiction.

LM: Cage's example suggests how important recognizing these "personal insufficiencies" are. It would have been a shame if Cage felt compelled to produce traditional harmonies in his work . . .

RK: You'll find that nearly all experimental artists did what they did partially because they *couldn't* do something required for conventional work; they also recognized that *excluding* some standard element from their work might make it more interesting. My own general advice to any artist, in every medium, is to ignore your weaknesses and focus instead on your strengths, especially if they are strengths rare in your art.

HP: How would you list your own strengths in this regard?

RK: Memory, comedy, formal invention, courage, and restlessness. To the extent that my artworks reflect those qualities, even if they are superficially impersonal, they can be considered expressions of me. More specifically, I'd say that what makes me interesting and distinctive as a composer now is my insistence upon working with only speech and sounds recorded in the environment. I don't work with intentional pitches or scored rhythms, and don't plan to, because I simply don't have any talent, not to mention good ideas, for working with those materials.

LM: Beginning around 1974 you began to work in other media—video, audiotapes, film, and so on. Is there a thread that unites all your work, some kind of similar aesthetic problem you find yourself involved with? Or do the different media present basically different sets of challenges?

RK: My works in all these different media are all "literary" in the sense that they involve language or literary structures of some sort. That's what distinguishes me from what I've called "polyartists," who take an aesthetic idea through various media, as Moholy-Nagy adapted his constructivist sensibility to work in painting, sculpture, photography, film, and book design, or as Cage applied his bias towards nonhierarchic, uninflected time and space to music, theater, and writing. I don't think of literature as an aesthetic idea so much as content, as material, so in terms of different conflicts or problems arising with different media, I'm always asking myself the same question: "What can I do with literary structures in this particular medium that cannot be done in other media?" In the case of my video work, for instance, I wanted to discover how my own stories could be "published" on videotape in ways different from the printed page. That led me first into abstract shapes indigenous to video, to accompany my reading of the texts, and then into image-processing unique to video, and more recently into presenting my texts directly on the screen, thanks to the character generator, which is the electronic letter-making machine likewise indigenous to video.

LM: You've mentioned Rosenberg's *The Tradition of the New* as a book which had an impact on you. What were some of the other influential works?

RK: I didn't read much as a child, so it wasn't until I was fourteen that I read someone who revealed the possibilities of adult writing, as well as the image of writing for a profession. That was Sinclair Lewis, my first literary hero. The next fiction to knock me over was Jean-Paul Sartre's *The Wall*, which I read towards the end of high school. For college courses, I read and liked *Madame Bovary* and *Moby-Dick*, but among the books I read on my own and thus came to treasure for myself were Dostoyevsky's *Notes from the Underground*, Ellison's *Invisible Man*, Joseph Heller's *Catch-22*, Barth's *The Sot-Weed Factor*. Later on Ken Gangemi's *Olt* and *Lydia* helped suggest some of the possibilities for minimalist fiction.

There were a lot of nonfiction books that also permanently altered the way I thought about things: Orwell's essays, Stanley Edgar Hyman's *The Armed Vision*, McLuhan's *Understanding Media*, Paul Goodman's *Growing Up Absurd*, Hannah Arendt's *Origins of Totalitarianism* and *Eichmann in Jerusalem*, Norman O. Brown's *Life Against Death*. In the summer of 1966, I read a book that has had, and continues to have, a great influence — Moholy-Nagy's *Vision in Motion*. Though essentially about kineticism in modern art, it has a chapter on literature, which I read again and again because it identifies accurately the principal precursors of experimental literature; I later reprinted this chapter in *The Avant-Garde Tradition in Literature*. What Moholy realized in that book was a dadaist-constructivist synthesis (neither of us, you'll notice, has much taste for surrealism), from which my own work descends. As you can see from this list of influences, in terms of my own creative works I've always been involved more with fiction than with poetry, and indeed I think of my sensibility as being distinctly more "fictive" than "poetic."

LM: Could you talk about this distinction? You've said that one of your intentions in *I Articulations/Short Fictions* was to distinguish between visual poetry and visual fiction.

RK: Yes — or to distinguish between experimental poetry and experimental fiction by distinguishing between poetry and fiction in general. That's why those two titles were bound back to back into a single book, a single object, and given nearly identical covers.

It became clear to me, especially in editing *Breakthrough Fictioneers* and after reading Northrop Frye, who has always been the greatest living literary theorist for me, that poetry is about the concentration of image and affect, while fiction is about moving from one place to another and thus about narrative. Although some works, such as long narrative poems, straddle this basic distinction, 99 percent of all writing (even at the most avant-garde extremes) clearly belongs to one category or another. My colleagues working on the avant-garde fringes think of my commitment to such categories as being rather conservative and hence needing to be discarded. But I find them useful in establishing contexts, partially because I consider myself to be working in genres, influenced by the traditions and values within each genre, even as I'm trying to expand our sense of those genres. But in my own work, I've usually known which pieces are poems and which are fictions and which are essays.

HP: You've been talking about fiction as a process involving the elapsing of time, of going from place to place or the unfolding or development of something. But this happens in poetry, too.

RK: Yes, but not often; and when it does, the narrative often works at cross-purposes to the poetry. Poetry is more often the presentation or evocation of a concrete image or metaphoric statement.

HP: Or the epiphany—which seems narratively based.

RK: The epiphany is something else, because it appears within the context of a narrative, even though as such it may have a poetic quality. You'll remember that my principal fiction project for the eighties was the writing of single-sentence stories that I call "Epiphanies," because each is meant to be the jelling moment, the illumination, in a narrative that otherwise doesn't exist.

HP: What about the distinction between poetry and prose?

RK: Prose can be divided into fiction and nonfiction. Nonfiction is usually about something outside itself, is trying to define something in the world, while fiction is based upon a story and is in that sense primarily within itself. In German radio, *Feature* and *Hörspiel* (literally, earplay) are two separate departments, with the former being about the outside world and *Hörspiel* descending from the imaginative world.

LM: That's a distinction that writers like Nabokov and Borges enjoy mocking.

RK: But it is their strategy to make fictions, complex fictions, out of essentially essayistic forms; but if you interpret them as denying the possibility of understanding the world through language, I think they're wrong. I should have mentioned that Borges is another great writer for me. Oh, to have written "Pierre Menard, Author of Don Quixote." Or Nabokov's *Pale Fire*. Or another more recent, lesser known novel in this tradition, Richard Horn's *Encyclopedia*.

LM: What would you say the main "themes" are in your work?

RK: Some are very essential themes—history, growth, decay, communication. Other recurrent concerns would be the mystery and complexity of sexuality and love, the experience of living in the big city; there is also an undertone of religious experience that, since it is not too clear to me, can probably be better defined by others. My basic premise is that if you pursue form, content will take care of itself, especially if you have a head full of content, as I tend to do. To say that I refuse to make claims for my fiction on grounds of content doesn't mean it's lacking content—not at all.

LM: Your works seem to express the sensibility of someone who is obsessively a New Yorker.

RK: I'm sure they do, in more ways than I understand, though a few qualities that occur to me are the absence of nature (indeed, the utter disinterest in nature), the geometricism, the abundance of different language forms and sounds.

LM: Do you see your works as operating as social or political critiques?

RK: Of course! And rather profoundly so, but in less obvious, more artistic ways than politics appear in most literature today! It's amazing how many otherwise observant people fail to see this, perhaps because my politics are libertarian anarchist. Take the example of John Cage, whom I consider an exemplary anarchist artist. Remember his insistence on writing scores that allow instrumentalists to make more decisive autonomous decisions than they normally would and then letting them perform without a conductor. To him, as well as me, this becomes a model for anarchist society. Similarly, I think of my own work, not only as a writer but as an editor, as exemplifying my politics. I think of my life as epitomizing my politics—I've avoided power, avoided privilege, avoided everything that might give my work an unfair advantage in the literary marketplace, no doubt to a great short-term cost, in exchange I hope for long-term benefits. Partially because I refuse to be a hypocrite, I have little trust of self-styled radicals who say one thing and do another, or who decide to exclude or exempt certain areas of their lives from their politics, especially if they use their "correct politics" about issues far away as an excuse for utterly abominable politics or ignorance about matters closer to home.

Radical politics have always been a part of my life. My student interest was in fiction as a means of understanding politics, and the very first pieces I published as an undergraduate were political satires, and the Ellison chapter of my M.A. thesis has been reprinted several times. I also wrote in an undergraduate newspaper that the only humane policy towards narcotics would be decriminalization. Only later did I discover this was a libertarian position (I thought myself an anarchist in the sixties but since the early 1970s I've been voting Libertarian most of the time). I can go on about this, but won't except to say that anyone who knows Cage's work well can identify his politics, his prescriptive vision of human society as the base of his polyartistic activity, as having influenced my own work.

Consider the political implications of *Epiphanies*, which is a nonhier-archical and noncentered collection of single sentence stories. When I submit them to literary magazines I ask editors to choose which ones they want to use and to print their selections in any order they wish. This invitation has prompted the most incredibly virulent responses: "We don't consider unedited manuscripts!" "You have to choose your own!" And so on. Politics are involved here. I'm asking editors to collaborate in the publication of my fiction, much as Cage asks instrumentalists for a greater input in the performance of his music. We do this because we wish to give away power, rather than horde it, and in the belief that the executor will possibly transcend our expectations. *Assembling*, the an-nual I cofounded in 1970, is another example of a libertarian structure. We invited people whom we knew to be doing "otherwise unpublish-able" work to submit anything of their own choosing, in a thousand copies that were collated into a thousand books, precisely because we wanted to abdicate authority over "our precious pages" that other edi-tors so often abuse.

HP: In being governed by a revolutionary principle, *Assembling* poses a direct challenge to the principle of publisher-as-mediator-of-power.

RK: Exactly. We were challenging the fundamental *authority* of publish-ing and ridiculing the customary belief that because someone else is publishing something of yours, that is necessarily better than your pub-lishing it yourself. If a writer doesn't think his work strong enough on the page to survive *outside the frame* of a commercial publisher's impri-matur, without that distribution mechanism and the fakery of publicity, then that writer need not be read.

LM: Despite your attraction to anarchism and your admiration for Cage, your own creative works don't seem to follow certain anarchist impulses of Cage's—for example, his resistance to controlling the responses of his audience. On the contrary, most of your works are obviously designed to control your readers or viewers in specific ways.

RK: I understand Cage's opposition to art which programs its response to an audience. His wittiest formulation of this objection is his com-ment about Handel's *Messiah*—he says he doesn't mind being moved, but he hates to be *pushed*. But as you point out, I haven't been consistent about this in my own work. In videotapes such as *Epiphanies* for charac-ter generators, I'm interested in manipulating the speeds at which the audience reads language; and there is only one way to read certain nu-merical works of mine, where I'm interested in empiricist aesthetics.

LM: Collaboration, plagiarism, and appropriation seem central to post-modernist aesthetics. You can certainly see aspects of this in your own work. For instance, in several of your pieces you take a familiar text—the Lord's Prayer or the instructions for using the Ovral birth control pill—and alter it orally or visually. What's involved in your selection process for choosing specific texts to (I hesitate to use this phrase, but it seems appropriate here) "deconstruct"?

RK: One general reason for choosing those texts is precisely their familiarity. The fact that the original is known to my audience allows me to do a kind of structural manipulation that shortcircuits expectation. This is the case with my "Declaration of Independence," where I wanted to rearrange the reader's or listener's mentality by challenging a consciousness that has already been structured by that text. In the case of *The Gospel/Die Evangelien*, I wanted to make listeners reexperience the first four books of the New Testament, and the story of Christ ("the greatest story ever told") by having them hear all four versions at once.

LM: This sounds related to what William Carlos Williams was doing— making the reader respond to the ordinary in ways that revitalize the language.

RK: And to Viktor Shklovsky's notion of the aesthetic defamiliarization of language as well. I came upon the Russian Formalists very early on, and was enormously impressed. A friend gave me Vladimir Markov's book, *Russian Futurism*, for my thirtieth birthday. I consider those guys to be the most extraordinary experimental *group* ever.

LM: So much of what passes for "avant-garde" in postmodernism really seems to be simply reworkings of what those artists were doing over fifty years ago.

RK: That's partially because artists and critics, even those putatively interested in experimentalism, tend to be needlessly ignorant and conservative. It's amazing what otherwise literate people don't know. I get very upset with people who *think* they're talking about the avant-garde and yet consistently choose the less extreme examples—Mayakovsky rather than Kruchonykh or even Khlebnikov. Marjorie Perloff recently had an article on Khlebnikov and the extraordinary concept of Zaum' in the *American Book Review* but if one is going to discuss the radical Russian Zaum' thoroughly and accurately, it would be better to focus on the more radical avatar, Kruchonykh, not Khlebnikov, who was a more lyrical (and hence more acceptable) poet. The more radical the artist, the more challenges he is likely to pose not only to critical intelligence but to the language of criticism. This accounts for why critics who aren't as adventurous as they should be are likely to avoid extreme figures.

I was even more annoyed by the *Mississippi Review* devoted to so-called "minimal fiction." Appropriating an honorific word from visual art criticism, the epithet is used to characterize fictions by Raymond Carver, Ann Beattie, and the like, that strike me at least as rather unminimal. These writers have no relationship at all with the tough issues posed by minimalism in visual art. The organizers of the *Mississippi Re-*

view symposium are either revealing their own ignorance and intellectual opportunism, or depending upon the ignorance and flaccidity of
their readers. Neither is laudable. If you are going to exploit the hard-
earned authority of a radical term, you should have at least sufficient
literacy and integrity to choose the most appropriate examples. And if
only because *Mississippi Review* once published some of my own single-
sentence *Epiphanies*, someone there should have known better.

LM: The work you've done with sound poetry and numbers seems to
owe something to the experiments Hugo Ball and Kurt Schwitters were
doing back in the thirties. How would you characterize the differences
between what you're doing and what they were aiming for?

RK: My work in these areas is initially not so much different from what
they were doing as an extension of it—mostly thanks to technologies
now available to artists like myself. The chief qualitative differences between us is that my pieces tend to be far more complex than theirs.
Schwitters's number works were basically simple, charming demonstrations that numbers could be used in place of words in poems, whereas
my numerical works attempt levels beyond that—especially in structuring interrelationships. It's important to realize my work with audio art is
being done in the age of audiotape, which offers tremendous advantages
and opportunities for anyone working imaginatively with speech. In recently reading Apollinaire's conversation poems, composed of snatches
overheard in a café, my first thought was, Too bad he didn't have
a portable audio recorder! Those earlier artists didn't have access to
audiotape; even worse, they didn't know what they were missing. If you
read Rudolf Arnheim's pioneering book *Radio: An Art of Sound*, written
in 1934, you'll notice in the concluding chapter on future possibilities
that not even he can envision a storage medium that can be edited
without leaving behind any telltale noises and that would have separate
tracks for handling different information.

You can see the advantages such technological developments offer in
my *New York City* piece, which Westdeutscher Rundfunk commissioned
a few years ago for its Metropolis series. My initial notion was to do a
warm audio portrait of my home town. I thought of Dylan Thomas's
Under Milk Wood as an obvious model, but once I started drafting lines,
I realized that just before his death in 1953, Dylan Thomas had created
audio experience; for the final years of wire recording, which was used
for transcription but could not be edited (even if you solder two ends
of wire together the audible result would be a noisy bump). By contrast, by using audiotape, an artist creating a sound piece today can put
two or more pieces of sound next to each other in time, and via separate tracking, modify one of those sounds without disturbing the other.
It became clear to me that to do a work at this point in the twentieth

century comparable to what Thomas had done, I would have to record sounds particular to New York and then mix them together in a multi-track studio. Which is what I did.

LM: Doesn't raising the issue of the "qualitative difference" between what you're doing in sound and number poetry and what your precursors were doing involve the kinds of hierarchical thinking you were objecting to earlier?

RK: On a critical level this issue of quality is relevant, but I find that when I do something really different, it defies my capability to make qualitative judgments. Take, for instance, those very minimal stories you published in *Fiction International*. My manuscript includes all the stories that passed my critical scrutiny as their author. What I don't know now is which stories are much better than the others. One secondary reason for allowing editors to select from this manuscript (just as they were allowed to with *Epiphanies*) is that they will be making critical discriminations that are now impossible for me. My further suspicion is that several years or so from now, it will be very clear to me which stories are best, and I'll wonder why such perceptions weren't available to me when the stories were first written. The question of whether I'm making something as qualitatively superior as, say, Dostoyevsky's *Notes from the Underground* doesn't interest me as much as discovering something that no one else has done before. Once I have that, I'll leave for others the issue of Dostoyevskian quality.

LM: Are you interested in the distinction between beauty and ugliness in art?

RK: Not in art, and probably not life either, at least not in any prescriptive sense. In life, as in art, I'm less taken by classical notions of beauty than by surprise and the discovery of originality and signature—especially signature. What's initially important is that a work of art be identifiable instantly as coming from a certain person. Without that quality of signature, an artist hasn't gotten to first base, in my opinion.

LM: We've talked a lot about the advantages technology offers artists today. What about its dangers? One hears charges that, say, a composer using a drum machine instead of a human drummer distances himself from the percussion medium or that the increased use of synthesizers reduces keyboard players to technicians. The use of computers would be the relevant example for writers—the experience of reading something like Ray Federman's *Double or Nothing*, whose text is a photocopy of the typed manuscript with all his errors and deletions, would be very different from reading a computer printout of the same manuscript.

RK: I don't agree with your point. Just as Ray could provide his publisher with a manuscript one step short of retyping, I could do the same with a word processor. Indeed, if you really have a taste for evolution of process, I could give you a stack of computer disks which would represent my book at every draft. If anything, the major problem for writers with a computer—or for any artists using new technologies—is simply finding ways to overcome their own limitations. I've had a word processor for several years now, but I've not done much with it, aside from producing neater manuscripts, sometimes with the right-hand margin as evenly justified as the left-hand margin. In that sense, I haven't done much better than the mass of personal computer users.

LM: How do you reconcile this desire to move beyond your individual experience and sensibility with your attraction for art which expresses a strong sense of "signature"?

RK: There are other ways to get signature in one's art than expressing personality. John Cage's art certainly has signature without expressing his personality. Signature has to do mostly with having a unique vision of the possibilities of art, whether that be in combining words in certain unique ways, the way Faulkner did, or in the use of lines or brush strokes, the way Jackson Pollock did.

LM: You mention in your *Autobiographies* that you got higher scores in math on your SAT and GRE than in the verbal sections, but that your artistic life suggests to you that your aptitudes are much more verbal than mathematical. Yet I feel there *is* an obvious mathematical intelligence evident in a lot of your work—an interest in exploring the relationship between abstractions, an almost algebraic interest in uncovering different relationships of words, exploring different combinatory patterns, a delight in what might be termed "abstract, formal beauty."

RK: I don't agree. I can't deal with abstractions, nor can I read most philosophy or abstract thought. My anthology *Esthetics Contemporary* expresses the limits of what I can understand in this direction. My imagination might have an "arithmetic" intelligence, but as soon as you start claiming an "algebraic" side to it, I'll have to tell you that I got a C in undergraduate calculus and retired from that sort of thing. But you're right in pointing to my interest in structuring devices, and certainly in permutations as well. I've applied Milton Babbitt's notions of combinatorality and multiple serialization to my works repeatedly, but my interest in such structures is always coupled with an empiricist bias. The numbers in my pieces are always empirical, not mythic, symbolic, or cabalistic elements. I was trained in history, and if one goes to school to have one's mind given a certain cast (and this applies to artists as well as scholars), then there's no question my mind has been cast as that of an historian. This shows up in my criticism and probably in my creative works in ways I still don't fully understand.

HP: What are your views about recent critical theory?

RK: I can't relate to the major contemporary German and French thinkers. I can't find anything of use in Adorno, Derrida, Barthes, you name them. I'm at once too much of a radical and too much an old-fashioned Anglo-American empiricist to go for that sort of baloney. I doubt if my creative instincts lie in the direction of abstraction at all.

LM: You mentioned your interest in minimalist forms as being one specific direction your experimentalism has taken. What interests you in this form?

RK: Minimalism in general (as distinct from the work of any particular artist) was one of the great ideas in the art of the 1960s. It's also an area that hasn't been exhausted, at least in literature. The central influence for me here was Ad Reinhardt, whom, incidentally, I take to be a great writer as well as a great artist. You might even trace my ambition for pure nonrepresentationalism to him.

LM: You've said that reading your number pieces is supposed to be different from someone doing "problem solving" with a mathematical puzzle. How so?

RK: In fact, some of my number fictions *are* similar to arithmetic puzzles. As soon as you mentioned what I'd said about the number fictions, I got nervous because I realized that my longest numerical piece (*Exhaustive Parallel Intervals*) operates very much like a puzzle—so much so that I had to explain it in an afterword or otherwise no one would understand what I was up to. But the pieces included in *Numbers: Poems and Stories* aren't really puzzles since they're so straightforward. Take something like "Times Perceived," where I simply present various times of a clock in vertical rows. Since the title tells you it's about someone perceiving time on a clock, readers should notice that this protagonist looks at a clock a lot about nine o'clock in the morning (it's obvious he or she is nervous about getting to work), that he looks at the clock a lot about five o'clock in the afternoon (he's anxious to get off work), and then that he doesn't look at the clock at all from two to three in the afternoon (as he's probably working). Why he starts looking at the clock at 8 P.M. is a bit mysterious (maybe someone is coming at eight and they're late, or something like that); then the same person looks at the clock at two in the morning (maybe that's because he doesn't sleep too well). All this is pretty obvious, with the numbers and only numbers creating a narrative for the reader. How Reinhardtian.

LM: Don't you feel that mathematical puzzles create a kind of "narrative" in the sense of moving a "reader" from one place to the next? I've always felt there was a real sense of "poetry" and beauty in mathematics which, after all, is a *language* with its own syntax and aesthetics . . .

RK: Yes. But again I'd like to insist upon that distinction between "mathematics" and arithmetic. My work has always dealt very simply with arithmetic and numbers, but not with mathematical *forms*. The numbers in my work are doing numerical things that any nine-year-old could figure out; they don't involve algebra or other advanced math. I'm not saying that you couldn't do something very poetic or otherwise interesting with these more complex mathematics. But, unfortunately, the fact is that I simply haven't done it.

HP: We've discussed some of the ways your work extends various traditions begun by the Dadaists. Are any of your pieces absolutely original as far as you know?

RK: I think of my numerical poems and my constructivist fiction as genuine innovations that no one else had thought of before (although they are so obvious, within the traditions of Constructivism, that I wondered why, say, van Doesburg and even Moholy didn't think at least of Constructivist fictions before me). I like this best of all in my fiction because the notion of telling a story with abstract lines is probably my most significant radical innovation.

HP: Do you tend to get your initial inspirations for pieces by considering the formal issues first—the idea of a reversible narrative, or whatever?

RK: I tend to begin with structural ideas like that and then I deal with how to "fill them in" with whatever content is in my head. But it's formal ideas or puzzles or problems that I can see will generate things I haven't thought of before which always get my imagination going. I'll get an idea like: "How can I write single-sentence stories that are the epiphanies to otherwise unfinished stories?" and that will generate all sorts of possibilities. As you pointed out, I do return to the same things in my work in terms of "content," but so much of this "content" is mainly a convenience for me. I don't have any particularly startling insights into human nature that I'm anxious to share in my fiction. I do like to think that in some of my *nonfiction* I've broached such issues. One reason I don't aim for this in my fiction is because I can deal with this sort of content more easily in my nonfiction. In fact, there's a lot of things I don't need to deal with in my fiction because of my nonfiction. (I can't write a roman à clef because I portray real people in my nonfiction, or in interviews like this!)

HP: You've stated that you're more interested in the "surfaces" of art than in art which aims at "depth." Were you thinking specifically there of psychological "depth"?

RK: Yes—or rather to art which pretends to plumb these depths. Nonetheless, I'm also very impressed by rare art that actually *does* go deeper than human experience. I think Chekhov especially is extraordinary along these lines, and to a lesser degree Alberto Moravia. They're doing something I haven't done yet and probably will never do, alas. In truth, I really don't know how one goes about writing the three hundred pages of continuous fiction that would comprise an extended novel. And precisely because it remains a mystery for me, I admire anyone who can do it, simply as a feat of imagination and perseverance.

LM: Do you see much going on around you, stylistically, in the art world that interests you?

RK: There have been several recent things which have knocked me over. James Turrell's objectless visual art, for example. The piece I remember best appears to be a monochromic field until you discover it is really a frame for an enclosed illuminated space that has a palpably different density once you get close to it. I'll admit, however, that I understand the sixties much better as a cultural and art phenomenon than any other decade. One of the criticisms that could be made of me right now is that I'm still working out what I learned in the sixties. I wouldn't dispute that.

LM: At the conclusion to *Autobiographies* you say, "Kosti is finally cautious in spite of his dare devil pose." Is that really the case?

RK: Of course! And more popular, too. There are no lies in that book. None. After all, it's "nonfiction," isn't it?

Maximum, Flat-out Drug Overkill
An Interview with Mark Leyner

Larry McCaffery

men aren't worth the paper they're printed on she said and she grabbed his penis with both her hands and swung him over her head like an olympic hammer thrower and flung him through the living room window into a slow elliptical orbit around the earth and the russians thought he was american and the americans thought he was russian but we all knew that he was just a hapless naked man tumbling through space whose orbit once every year would bring him close enough to dayton ohio for schoolchildren there to discern his wistful fleeting hello good-bye, hello good-bye, hello good-bye

—"Colonoscope Nite"

The publication of Mark Leyner's wild and radically experimental book of fictions, *My Cousin, My Gastroenterologist*, by a major commercial publisher (Harmony Books) in 1990, followed by the remarkable popular response to the book (Leyner received both reviewer acclaim and notoriety in such places as *Rolling Stone, Spin*, MTV, and a cover story in the *New York Times Magazine*), was one of the major recent surprises in American fiction. But the most surprising aspect of Leyner's success story wasn't so much that a book as truly strange as *My Cousin* would be warmly received by the public—indeed, as bizarre as Leyner's fiction might seem at first, there is also a sense in which it might well strike even ordinary readers as being absolutely "realistic" in its impulses, so that even ordinary readers might respond to its energy and formal peculiarities enthusiastically, not even realizing they were reading something allegedly "avant-garde." No, what was more unexpected was that *My*

Cousin had been published (and then heavily promoted) by a commercial publisher in the first place. Probably not since the 1960s appearance of Donald Barthelme's surreal and humorous fiction in the *New Yorker* and in books put out by major New York publishers has a writer so truly innovative received this sort of commercial support and response.

Mark Leyner's sudden rise as perhaps the most notable embodiment of the "avant-pop" sensibility of the nineties was, then, at once a complete surprise and utterly predictable. Leyner had begun writing seriously in the late seventies and early eighties while receiving his M.F.A. from the University of Colorado. Partly encouraged by support he received there from several important postmodernist authors (including Ronald Sukenick, Clarence Major, and Steve Katz), Leyner published *I Smell Esther Williams* (1983) with the Fiction Collective (a small press notable for its publication of many important, innovative writers). *Esther Williams* was a book of stories whose memorable title immediately suggested the odd blend of surrealism, synesthesia, and pop culture that would characterize all his work. Although the book didn't receive much attention, it was nonetheless a remarkable and original work containing many of the same distinctive features evident in *My Cousin*. These features included a reliance more on painterly notions of collage and juxtaposition than on the structures of story and character development found in most fiction; rapid-fire rhythms and disjointed presentations of a bewildering variety of pop cultural and technical materials, all meticulously re-created and then recombined into startling (and often hilarious) new shapes and meanings; and an unusual treatment of point of view that combined elements of autobiography, metafiction, and pure invention—an "I" that was a permeable membrane between self and the outer, public personas of media figures.

Leyner labored for nearly five years painstakingly accumulating the materials that would comprise *My Cousin*, and the results of his meticulous work habits are immediately apparent. Although his new pieces continue the basic method found in *Esther Williams*, in *My Cousin* Leyner had refined his prose, raised the intensity level and rhetorical precision of his writing, thus coming very close to his avowed writerly goal (cited in the interview that follows) of making "every line be the center of the whole piece." What might not be obvious when first encountering Leyner's manic and crazed "off-the-wall" fictions is not just the aesthetic refinement of his methods but the *appropriateness* of the manner in which he illuminates, plays with, and comments upon the flattened, flickering, infinitely reproducible, infinitely rearrangeable realms of hyperreality that wash over ordinary people every day.

In short, with *My Cousin* Leyner had invented a new form of "realism" perfectly suited to the postmodern Electronic Age. The "experimental" features of his work are in fact "natural" reflections of the frantic pace of mass media (and of MTV and rock music particularly)—the feeling of image-and-information bombardment, the sense of confusion (and exhilaration) Americans feel as they flip their remote control buttons across fifty different television stations or drive past countless advertising billboards (so pregnant with meanings and promises!) on their freeways while listening to their tape decks and carrying on simultaneous conversations with their stockbrokers (via cellular phones) and their best friends. His fictions manage to burrow deeply inside the "body" of this culture (and, as the gastrointestinal metaphor in his book's title suggests, burrow inside himself) and then emerge to report back to us what he has discovered. The reports contained in *My Cousin*, then, aren't really "surreal" or "off-the-wall" at all. They're the fictional equivalent of X-ray or telescope photos—odd-seeming at first, but finally just descriptions of what we are.

The following interview is a conflation of several taping sessions that Leyner and I did in his home in Hoboken, New Jersey. Introduced to each other in the early eighties through mutual Fiction Collective friends, Leyner and I had developed a friendship that allowed me to observe the genesis of *My Cousin* over a several year period. Thus our conversations were relaxed, wide-ranging, and conducted in what could be described as a kind of "hyperinterview" mode, with both participants acting out slightly exaggerated roles of interviewer and interviewee that we had grown familiar with watching television. In person Leyner is quieter and more thoughtful than one might expect from having encountered his various fictional incarnations. For instance, on neither of my visits did I see any of the features of the exotic life-style that Leyner claims has contributed to his success—that is, I did not personally witness any flunkies or yes-men surrounding Leyner, or observe him consuming iced raw turtle eggs and chocolate-covered strawberries in a garden ablaze with hibiscus and bougainvillea; and if there were any naked slaves, perfumed with musk, who fan him with plastic fronds as he writes, they had withdrawn to a discreet distance on both occasions while we taped the interviews. But if Leyner is not quite the literal embodiment of the glamorous, body-building avant-pop persona who appears in his most recent books (*Et Tu, Babe* [a novel, 1992] and *Tooth Imprints on a Corn Dog* [avant-journalism, 1995])—well, it's close enough for rock and roll.

*   *   *

Mark Leyner: Selected Bibliography

Novels and Collections

I Smell Esther Williams. New York: Fiction Collective, 1983.
My Cousin, My Gastroenterologist. New York: Harmony Books, 1990.
Et Tu, Babe. New York: Harmony Books, 1992.
Tooth Imprints on a Corn Dog. Journalism. New York: Harmony Books, 1995.

Uncollected Nonfiction

"Mark Leyner Interviews Keith Richards." *Spin Magazine* (January 1993): 26–27.

As Editor

American Made: New Fiction from the Fiction Collective (with Curtis White and Thomas Glynn). New York: Fiction Collective, 1986.

Reviews and Articles about Leyner's Work

Everman, Welch. "The Same Pink as Pepto-Bismol." Review of *My Cousin, My Gastroenterologist. American Book Review* 12, 5 (November/December 1990): 16, 21.
Giovanti, Toni. "The Brave New World of Cyberpunk Fiction." *Gold Coast* (March 8–15): 8–11.
Grimes, William. "The Ridiculous Vision: Mark Leyner." *New York Times Magazine*, 13 September 1992, pp. 35, 51, 64–65.
Marin, Richard. "Buffing Up Is Hard to Do." Review of *Tooth Imprints on a Corn Dog. Newsweek*, 27 March 1995, p. 68.
McCaffery, Larry. "The Centennial Moment: Everything Is Permitted." In *The Novel of the Americas*, ed. Raymond Williams, 121–32. Boulder, CO: University of Colorado Press, 1991.
———. "The Post-Pynchon, Post-Modern Contemporary American Fiction." *Positive* (Tokyo) 1 (Spring 1991): 248–67.

Interviews

Deike, Marta, and Gary Sullivan. "an infinitely hot and dense talk with Mark Leyner." *Stifled Yawn: A Magazine of Contemporary Writing* 1, 1 (Winter 1990): n.p.
McCaffery, Larry. "An Interview with Mark Leyner." *Positive* (Tokyo) 1 (Spring 1991): 210–29.
McCaffery, Larry, and Duncan Bock. "Mark Leyner's Galactic Cosmology, From Dense Dot to Big God." *Mondo 2000* 5 (1991): 48–53.

*   *   *

LARRY MCCAFFERY: Have you been surprised by the commercial success and popularity of your recent books?

MARK LEYNER: Ron Sukenick gave me some extremely valuable advice once while I was at Boulder. He told me, "Think of yourself as a poet rather than as a fiction writer in terms of the commercial success you're likely to get." That made a lot of sense to me, so I never had the same expectations about popularity that people like Ray Federman and Steve Katz (and even Ron himself) have had. Those expectations were fostered back in the 1960s, when people like Warhol made it seem like you could really make it big no matter how far out your work was. Well, that might have been true for a few people, like Vonnegut and Brautigan, but overall it was mainly just a myth that probably made a lot of writers either feel betrayed when the public didn't respond to what they were doing or wind up compromising the integrity of their work in the hopes that if they made it "just a little bit less weird" that maybe people would buy it.

But having said that, I also must say that I always wanted something more than to be just a literary eccentric writing very brilliant but unreadable books for an audience of a selected few. I think every writer always wants more and more people reading his or her work. I wasn't *expecting* a big commercial breakthrough while I was writing *My Cousin,* so there was never any question about my compromising my work, toning things down or whatever. I just wrote the way I always have—the way I have to write. I've always felt that given my strategy as a writer—to try and give more bang for the buck than any other writer, to try and pack more laughs, more excitement, more events in each sentence than anyone—that I had a potentially large audience. My popularity didn't hinge on the work so much as on how it was promoted and marketed. And Harmony/Crown succeeded marvelously in promoting and marketing *My Cuz.* So, getting back to your question, I'm not completely surprised by the commercial success and popularity of *My Cuz,* but I am amazed and overjoyed at the extent of its popularity and all the attention it's gotten. I certainly never expected the *New York Times* and *Rolling Stone* to suddenly be calling me a "cult author" as they did. But if I was destined to be a cult hero to millions of rabid fans across the earth, then I must dutifully assume that responsibility. I must bow to my success.

LM: Have your basic writing methods changed from those you were using back when writing *I Smell Esther Williams?*

ML: The methods have been pretty much the same all along. In fact the process hasn't changed much since I was about seventeen or eighteen, when I first began developing this way of writing. In fact, the only story I've ever written that I'd say evolved different was "He Had One of Those Aroooooooga Horns on His Car" (in *Esther Williams*). That's the

story where you have a conversation interspersed with a horn honking—presumably to alert someone in the house that they should come
out. I sat down to write that piece with the notion that this conversation
and the horn honking would just continue on indefinitely. I had this
Platonic ideal in mind first that I thought I could execute. But I don't
normally work from that kind of preset ideal.

LM: Discovering a methodology that seems to work at age seventeen or
eighteen is obviously rare. From whence did this aesthetic spring forth—
the forehead of Zeus, a hit of acid, Jimi Hendrix, voodoo, or what?

ML: All of the above—plus Keith Richards's nasty guitar licks. The most
powerful early experience I had aesthetically (if that word is meaningful in this context) was when I saw the Beatles on *The Ed Sullivan Show*.
I was seven or eight and was sitting in a house at the New Jersey shore,
near Asbury Park, and when the Beatles came on I was so absolutely
transfixed that the ice cream cone I was eating melted down my arm. I
was still a pre-adolescent, mind you, but after that I knew I wanted to
be an artist in some way like the Beatles were.

LM: How were the Beatles able to produce such a powerful reaction in
American kids at that particular juncture?

ML: It was this very protosexual experience. From the male perspective,
a lot of this had to do with seeing all those little girls in the audience
react to them in that way. All that squealing and jumping around does
something to you. And naturally one of my first reactions to this was,
"Wouldn't it be great to have people scream over something I did?" Even
to this day, the Beatles's sound is remarkable, it affects you neurologi-
cally or something. It's the sound of McCartney's and Lennon's voices
together, something unique, unduplicatable.

Of course, there's something demagogic about the rock star's capacity
to incite public ecstasy, and frankly, demagogues—be they dictators,
Pentecostal preachers, mass media salesmen, et cetera—have always
fascinated me. I've always been excited by and attracted to people who
can stand in front of a mob and whip it into a real foaming-at-the-mouth
frenzy. When I was young I went to Hebrew school—along with the
other Jewish kids in my neighborhood—and the teachers would peri-
odically show us films about Nazi Germany. Some were comprised of
the horrific atrocity footage we associate with the Holocaust, but others
were actually Nazi-produced propaganda films—the Joseph Goebbels–
Leni Riefenstahl type of film. It was a terrible miscalculation to show
that kind of footage to adolescent boys whose moral and cognitive
faculties are simply overwhelmed by their susceptibility to fascist propaganda pyrotechnics—to that call to mindlessness. I'm talking about a
self-annulling, male adolescent susceptibility to the sheer energy, power,
and excitement of those shiny boots and helmets and tanks and flags

and marching columns and domes of searchlights. I know that on this level, *I* got turned on, and I was a well-informed kid—mindful of the abominations that this propaganda announced and portended—but it still had its effect on me! I had the same kind of visceral reaction to baseball heroes, movie stars, rock 'n' rollers—I was absolutely mesmerized by performers who had a powerful and public emotional effect. And when the Beatles came along, I intuitively knew that they were doing something wonderful and healthy that was somehow connecting with that capacity for visceral stimulation, something that was connecting with all that excitement, bewitching the psyche of *every* kid, monopolizing the headlines, making history. They were making everything *different*, at least for that global moment. And I knew I wanted to try to do something that could have—on whatever level—an effect like that.

Obviously at that age—eight or nine—I couldn't get a band together, and I couldn't make movies, but there was always pen and paper around. I suppose if I'd had unlimited resources—terribly wealthy parents who could buy me all the equipment I needed—maybe I would have done something else. But writing was something where the tools were right there, available to me whenever I wanted.

LM: What sorts of writing were you doing when you were very young?

ML: At a certain point in high school I began to write poetry. In fact, the first thing I had published was a poem I wrote when I was sixteen about Tina Turner that *Rolling Stone* took in 1972. I also wrote a column for the high school newspaper called "This Side of Paradise." My friends and I had read a little Fitzgerald (although I actually knew more about his life than his writing), so we basically fabricated this counterfeit high society; we'd have parties and get very dressed up and I'd wind up writing about the parties. When I look at those columns, I can see the beginnings of what eventually became my literary mannerisms and strategies: the synthesis of seemingly random, unrelated chunks of public discourse, media language, private codes, and raw data into something startling and perhaps even lyrical. But it wasn't really until I was in college at Brandeis that I found a method of writing that seemed to suit what I wanted to do.

LM: Were you exposed to certain writers when you got to Brandeis who might have pushed you in certain directions, influenced your sensibility?

ML: Even though I have some sense of what sorts of things made a big impression on me, aesthetically—like the Beatles or Keith Richards—in a very basic way I don't know what started me writing fiction this way. I don't think my own writing has ever been powerfully influenced by other writers. At Brandeis I began writing fiction partly by accident: I had wanted to get into a particular poetry workshop, but for some reason I was unable to. A novelist named Alan Lalchuk was teaching a fiction workshop that I applied for, and in order to get in you had to write a piece of fiction. So I wrote a piece featuring Lee Harvey Oswald and I was off and running. It didn't take me long to develop a style or a methodology that is essentially what I'm doing now, though it took me a couple of years to feel confident with it.

LM: One of the things that I would say characterizes your writing is a kind of wild, comic boldness that is undifferentiated and unrelenting—the sense that any sentence may yield something absolutely startling. What was it that excited you about fiction so immediately? What could you do with fiction, say, as opposed to poetry?

ML: I was always squeamish about how precious poetry can seem sometimes, which was a turnoff. I was interested in fucking around with another medium. I wanted to be a troublemaker, and I felt I had an idea of how to do this in fiction. I knew just by looking around at all the writers I knew and what was being written that I could cause a lot of trouble by making every sentence astonish, grab people by the balls or whatever, irrespective of the usual bullshit fictional contexts. I always had this notion that my work could be written so that you could toss up all the pages of a piece of mine, throw a dart at them while they're in the air, and no matter where that dart lands the line is going to be audacious, captivating. No matter where you pick up in a piece of mine there's not going to be a single slack verbal moment, no empty transitional phrase or routine expository sentence anywhere. This goal has been really at the center of what I want my fiction to do for a long time. The fact that I've kept to it is more than confidence, it's the result of this exceptionally strong will I've maintained about not letting even a single line relax, to make sure there is a maximum energy level in every single line. The first compliment I got that made me feel really good about my writing was at Brandeis when someone said that one of my pieces really blew her mind. Mind blowing is still what I want. I won't settle for anything less than maximum, flat-out drug overkill, the misuse of power.

LM: Making every single sentence "intense" precludes you from doing certain things—you can't create "characters" and "plots" in any usual sense, for example. Was it difficult for you, as a fiction writer, to ignore these things, or did it just seem natural?

ML: It's not as if I went through an aesthetic crisis in deciding not to write narratives. There were other influences that probably influenced this notion—music, for example, or TV; but from the beginning my prose style and my impulse towards narrative disunity came from that desire for maximal output at the level of each sentence rather than from any sense of wanting to rebel against realism. Not being able to do those realistic things has never bothered me. I never had to go through all the shit—all the polemical tribulations—that postmodernists like Barth, Coover, Sukenick, Katz, and Federman had to back in the sixties. I never had the sense of having traditional baggage that I needed to jettison or work my way through. That's a big advantage because it saved me a lot of time and effort. I came from the fictional womb as I am, the postmodern battles had already been fought and won, so I was never interested in those battles. It simply never occurred to me to write traditional, mimetic, plotted narratives. That never interested me at all. What I was interested in was finding a way to make every line be the center of the whole piece, or where every line is as important as every other line so that readers could read anything and still find this acute audacity. And if you're trying to do that, you can't create characters and plotted narratives and that other stuff. If you have to supply backgrounds, and then have characters walking into rooms and then sitting down and then starting to talk, there's going to be lulls while you're getting the reader from one place to the next. Well, I don't want those lulls—or *any* lulls, for that matter.

LM: It's the difference between someone like Little Richard or Hüsker Dü or Sonic Youth—where everything is jacked up to this incredibly fast paced, high energy level—versus someone like Springsteen, who uses pauses and varies his tempos to create his kind of effect. Another analogy would be Stevie Ray Vaughan's approach to the blues, where every moment is maximally intense, as opposed to other blues musicians who want to slow things down and build up to a specific kind of climax.

ML: Right. And my aesthetic impulse is towards the Little Richard-meets-Hüsker Dü-meets-Megadeth approach. The fast burst that never stops. I had a band in high school and I was a Rolling Stones fanatic. Or more precisely, I was a *Keith Richards fanatic*, which is a subgenre of being a Rolling Stones fan. There's a guitar solo Richards did that I use, consciously or unconsciously (it's hard to tell at this point), as a model of what my work should be like, from moment to moment. It's the guitar solo he plays in "Sympathy for the Devil," where Richards creates this sharp, shiny, incredible, nasty violent burst of raw sounds. There's no leading up to it, it's just suddenly *there*, like a rain of razors. In a way it was easy for me to maintain this "will" about what the lines in my writing should be because I had certain models, especially rock music, which weren't literary but which I had easy access to. The literature I read and enjoyed the most was by poets who maintain this constant intensity—Shakespeare, Keats. There's not much wasted energy in their works. They just seem to start, and right away it's beautiful and complicated and lyrical and sexual and rich. And it *remains* that way—you don't have to flip around looking for the good stuff. But this seemed very rare in writing, whereas I could find it in something like the Rolling Stones' music and other rock and roll, which gave me something readily available to aim for.

LM: What kinds of stuff did your band do?

ML: Pure rock band. It was great fun. I was a guitarist. It was around the time the Allman Brothers were becoming popular but I was still a loyal Rolling Stones fan, so we had certain conflicts. I was also getting interested in Bowie, T. Rex, the New York Dolls, and some of the other glam bands. Basically I wanted us to be more glittery and wild to look at, whereas the other guitar player in the band, Tom Cacherilli, was interested in having a workman-like quality band that wouldn't dress funny and would just be a bunch of guys making good music. I didn't care so much about that—I wanted to be spectacular. A spectacle. Finally we had our big concert (actually it was our *only* concert—mostly we were just playing in our basement). We played one Saturday night to raise money for our high school to pay for a drinking fountain someone had blown up. The night before we played, *Gimme Shelter* (which I had seen a million times) was on TV. So I watched *Gimme Shelter* for the millionth time that night, and my Keith Richards idolatry knob was turned up to ten or eleven. The next day I got to the school, and I was drinking bourbon the same way Keith would have. Then some girls came up to me and the other guitarist in the band and asked if we wanted to get high. Cacherilli said we shouldn't because we'd forget what we were supposed to be doing, which was reasonable, but I said, "Fuck that!" I had just seen my great hero Richards lying on the studio floor—it's that great scene of him passed out on the floor while they're playing "No Expectations," but he's *there* with that beautiful music on his headphones and those beautiful snakeskin boots he had. So with that model expanding infinitely in my brain, I was certainly going to go into the girls' room and get high with them. I even got the other guy to go with me. And sure enough, when we got onstage we forgot what we were doing. It was a disaster from a musical standpoint. The saving grace was that I *looked great!* I had this white jacket on, with a multicolored vest under it. The girls I knew then thought the whole thing was great. They didn't know we were playing shitty and probably wouldn't have cared even if they had known. So in the way that mattered most to me, it was successful. We had made a spectacle of ourselves.

LM: Your foregrounding of language and of individual sentences seems to have more in common with poetry than fiction. *Is* there a difference between your work and poetry?

ML: Not really. The main differences are probably those of attitude rather than actual content. I try to avoid the kind of smug, precious quality that poetry can assume when poets isolate and showcase their lines in the middle of the page without making sure those lines are eventful, alive, viral . . . neon! With so many poets it seems that any anemic, banal observation will suffice simply because they're writing "poetry." And this justifies wasting all that lovely white real estate?! Yech. I never wanted to do that. I figured that if I was going to have an eight-by-eleven-inch page, I should fill up the whole page. Why use just one inch of the page? I want each page I write to be like a page of blotter acid my readers are ingesting. A huge page of blotter acid, with no white spaces but with this overload of impressions that would eventually *do* something to the readers after they're a couple of pages into it.

LM: Were there other nonliterary forms that influenced your sensibility early on?

ML: Animated cartoons. A tremendous influence. Max Fleisher's Popeye, Tex Avery and Chuck Jones with Bugs Bunny, Disney's Mickey and Donald, Tezuka's Astro Boy. Animation in the hands of these masters allowed infinite possibility from instant to instant—anything could happen and inevitably did and at dizzying speeds. A character could drive a hot rod to Mars and back, pull into a diner on the highway, sing a duet with his fried chicken leg, and then become the king of the Eskimos—in five seconds! Wonderful! The first year I was at Brandeis I took a course in American painting from a guy named Carl Bells, who had also written a book on rock and roll. That course had an impact on me, particularly seeing Pollock's work and de Kooning's, and then a little later, some of the work that Rauschenberg and Jasper Johns had done. I was especially intrigued by Pollock. He was sort of a rock and roll painter in that he was after maximum intensity, using the entire canvas, having a center everywhere. But I wouldn't say I took these things and consciously decided I wanted to do the equivalent in writing. The first piece I did in the style I have now was written because I simply got sick of trying to make a story. Story wasn't really what I wanted to be doing in my writing. I had all these parts that I thought were audacious, but I didn't care about the "whole" they were supposed to be part of. I wanted to be this incredible performer at every minute, to make it impossible for anyone to say that I'm not doing what I do full throttle, to the max.

I remember a pivotal moment in writing that piece. I was living with a girlfriend on the girls' floor of the dorm, and I had to go to the bathroom on the boys' floor upstairs. I had been fucking around with this story, getting depressed working on it, so I went up to smoke a cigarette. I was sitting on the toilet when I finally just said, "Fuck it, I'm going to start putting this story together in a way that's fun *for me*, that's going to get a big response from people even if they hate it; it's going to be something remarkable for them to hate."

LM: I know that up through *My Cousin* your work has a fairly slow gestation period. Could you describe what is going on in your work habits, on a day-by-day basis, that allows you to pull together all these disparate materials? The scenes and words and images seem to be coming from everywhere: from the tomes of trendy French theorists, to the *National Enquirer*, to obscure technical manuals.

ML: My works evolve through a constant process of accumulating information or language. This come from many sources, including stuff that is purely imagined, but there is no hierarchy in my mind that places imaginary materials above things I find. I'm always writing things down that I come across on the radio or television, so materials are accumulating every day. I became fascinated with Duchamp (another hero of mine) in college. I read everything about him I could find. I loved the idea that he allowed a piece he was working on to collect dust for several months—and then he let the formation of the dust become part of the piece. That's basically the way I proceed with my work. I don't really have to work at it that much—if I'm driving in the car and I'm not listening to the radio, I'll usually compose three-quarters of a page worth of text that I memorize and then write down when I get wherever I'm going. It's as if there's this constant static or white noise around me that I can tap into. I'm a fanatic about having external things going on around me. I love having the television on. I have it on when I fall asleep. The first thing I do when I get into a hotel room is check to make sure the television is working. When I'm working I always have the television going, even with the sound off—just so it's flickering away there on the edges of perception. And I'll have a few magazines spread out in front of me, and the newspaper, and whatever I'm reading, the *Iliad* or a Jules Verne novel or a book about poisonous insects. Aside from being a writer I love the feeling of having all that information around me. Being jacked-in to all these sources of mental stimulation makes me feel very comfortable. This seems to be my nature. I suppose I'm a model child of the media age. Some people like trees and lakes. Well, sensory overload is my environment. This is what makes me feel serene.

LM: One of the features usually ascribed to "postmodern" art has to do with what you just mentioned about your own work—the "nonhierarchical" nature of your materials and manner of presentation, your refusal to distinguish between "high" culture (or "serious" sources) and "low" culture (pop culture).

ML: That distinction is something I always hated. I despise the contemptuous attitude so many professors seem to have, for example, about television, rock and roll, and certain kinds of movies. Wonderful things like *Kojak*, Abbott and Costello, televised pro football, the Pixies, Public Enemy, musicals like *Meet Me in St. Louis*, dark, riveting films like *Cape Fear* with Robert Mitchum, Billy Wilder's remarkable films, and even multiplex fare like *Blade Runner, The Road Warrior, The Hidden, Robocop, The Terminator, Total Recall* . . . who dares underestimate the complexity of Schwarzenegger as pop icon? Personally I could never see the qualitative difference between E. C. Segar's Popeye and Thackeray's Becky Sharp. Part of this attitude is motivated by my hatred of any kind of authority figures, especially academics, professors. One of the things I liked about my work, once I realized what I was actually doing, was that it was so elegantly written that it was impossible for academics to criticize or dismiss it as being "only pop culture." That was very important to me because I wanted to confront people who made these false distinctions about my work by showing them that you could be elegantly and audaciously trashy! "Electrified," "elegant," "hard-core," "beautiful"— all these adjectives can apply to my work simultaneously. The hierarchical structure that prohibited them from coexisting seemed like something worth demolishing. And there's been this sense of perverse glee in knowing I've found a way to do this.

That's one of the reasons I've always felt so drawn to Duchamp. Duchamp personally was very elegant—he was very handsome and smoked his cigars in a beautiful manner and he played chess and wrote about it beautifully. And meanwhile he was making these radically audacious objects—and making them so well. The beauty and precision of the way the screws were set into his constructions! So even though his works were formally daring and funny and bizarre, they were also unassailable because he had made them so well. He wasn't just some sloppy weirdo throwing a bunch of shoddy stuff into a museum, and so his work was profoundly troubling, even to people who hated what he was doing because its beauty and elegance couldn't be denied. And that's the kind of response I want my work to have.

LM: Your generation of writers seems to have a different relationship to pop culture than, say, the earlier generation of writers like Coover, Sukenick, and Federman—it's simply part of your milieu.

ML: I suspect this is pretty much true of nearly everybody in my literary generation—the cyberpunks and the new "minimalist" writers and so on. I think that earlier generation felt somehow outside this pop culture arena. They feel like they're able to look at pop culture, and comment upon it, but from the outside. Whereas I am totally inside it. I'm literally made of it. It is me. The other day I was reading some T'ang poets, Li Po and Tu Fu, and I thought to myself, "I'm in the 'tang dynasty'"— you know, as in people who have grown up drinking Tang, this simulated, completely artificial orange juice product. That's as much a part of me as the color of my eyes, so it's not like I'm making a choice about whether or not to acknowledge it or comment on it. It's in my genes.

LM: What's specifically involved in your composition process? Since you don't use the usual devices of plot and character to organize your writing, how do you know when a given section is finished—or is this mostly an arbitrary decision?

ML: It's definitely not arbitrary, but it's "not arbitrary" in a certain way that's difficult to talk about. There were certain pieces that I've decided to finish simply because I had a reading coming up and wanted a finished piece to read. That doesn't mean I just arbitrarily stopped at that point but that I consciously used this arbitrary deadline as a means of forcing myself to work it through until it was finished. What I call "finishing" involves achieving a certain manipulation of the energy of the piece that I feel comfortable with. There is a sense of closure in my pieces that has nothing to do with plot denouement or plot development but which I'm quite aware of when I've arrived at it. There are formal concerns of various sorts in a given piece that you won't find in the next, and it's working through these concerns that partially produces my sense that a piece is finished. For instance, I was very aware of "Gone with the Mind" [in *My Cousin*] being a liturgical piece, so that when I read it I feel like a preacher.

LM: Hmmm—I notice you're also beginning to sound a bit like David Byrne in "Once in a Lifetime." Does what appears in the final, published version of your stories pretty much follow the chronological sequence involved in your writing it?

ML: Not at all. There is a certain point I arrive at when I have been gathering materials (and I am always gathering materials, this is just part of my life) where I decide to enter a new stage. It's almost like I'm now entering the text, this information, bodily—I dive into it and begin to metabolize the stuff. I dance in it, play around in it, like I was in a pool. And then certain things start happening, I start to see certain relationships and rhetorical possibilities.

LM: What leads you to that next stage—do you reach a saturation point in terms of accumulation, where you sense that it's time to start dancing with it?

ML: A lot of times it's a sense of despair or boredom that sets me off. Writing can become very depressing to me. It's a very difficult process. I'll be accumulating all this language and worrying about it and not seeing what is interesting about it anymore. Usually, just at the absolute nadir of those feelings, I'll decide to do something, perhaps for audacity's sake alone. It's like having a huge painted white wall in front of me and suddenly deciding to have an elegant, exotic obscenity painted on it. So I'll plunge into all this accumulated verbiage and find a line to start something with like "Gather the 10,000 americans in irreversible comas." It's as if suddenly I've found that guitar solo to open with: POW! Let's give the people their money's worth.

LM: One of the motifs that seems to appear in a lot of the stories in *My Cousin* is violence.

ML: That's because I'm personally obsessed with violence. Obviously, I'm appalled at the level of brutality and violence that we accept in our lives today—but it fascinates me. I think about it all the time—awake and in my dreams—maybe because I live in such an extremely violent area, my charming New York metropolitan area where the nine-millimeter semiautomatic has become the de rigueur accessory for today's fashionable young man. And my wife Arleen, who's a psychotherapist, deals with the victims of sexual abuse and domestic and street violence every day in her work. But in terms of my writing, I'm primarily interested in violence to the extent that it's so pervasive a part of our public discourse, because I think it would be fair to say that public discourse is my "area of speciality" as a writer. Also, I think many people find my writing style itself to be violent—they perceive the work as formally violent. They're talking about the rapidity and abruptness with which characters, settings and contexts and modes of rhetoric mutate in my fiction. I intend this to be "exhilarating"—some people find it "violent." Perhaps it's just a matter of semantics. Having said all this, I have to add that I have an abiding personal fascination with what I call micro-*Machtpolitik*—violence on the local, interpersonal, and even cellular level, where pure brutal power is the essential means by which life resolves itself. There's macrophage versus bacteria, tiger versus antelope, cannibal versus missionary, et cetera, et cetera—perhaps this is what David Cronenberg meant by "insect politics." Darwinian natural selection is merciless, as you'll experience in the section of *My Cuz* entitled "Saliva of the Fittest." Maybe this all explains my obsessive weight lifting and why I've started studying kung fu and why there's a giant portrait of Bruce Lee over my white formica escritoire. Y'know, Larry, my writing is so powerful that my American publisher put a "no-drug" clause in my new contract. My urine is tested twice a week to make sure that I'm not writing under the influence of anabolic steroids.

LM: There are references throughout your work to "Mark" and to other people in your "real life" (whatever that is supposed to refer to). So when all is said and done, can we read your work as being a kind of autobiography?

ML: Absolutely! Really, there is nothing in *My Cousin* that hasn't happened, in one way or another. Now admittedly, by the time I've gotten around to writing "Mark" or "Arleen" down on the page, those pronouns have come a long way. Still, there is something interesting about the trace of that designation. Obviously readers are going to look at a book written by a person named "Mark" and they are going to see a Mark in the book—which is going to change the resonance of that rhetoric. That resonance interests me. It also interests me to try to fashion something ludicrously mythic out of my banal life. I'm very interested in Homer, for instance. With the *Iliad* and the *Odyssey*, you have texts made of completely public characters in which you can't find a single sentence that's not about some sort of gigantic, larger-than-life event. Talk about not having transitional sentences! Today we don't have that kind of subject matter so much, which is why it interests me to project it into my work.

This relates to why I've become so interested in body-building. Body-building is finally a very adolescent thing (maybe I think my real audience is eventually teenage boys). I'm fascinated in things that display some kind of arrested development. I fantasize about becoming a gigantic god, picking people up with my fingers and talking to them. On a very personal level I'm conscious of being immersed in all this adolescent, macho heroic fantasy stuff—kung fu movies and televised pro sports. You can see this very clearly in something like "i was an infinitely hot and dense dot," which is about this person who literally is getting bigger and bigger.

LM: An "infinitely hot and dense dot" is how the beginning of the universe is described, at the instant of the big bang.

ML: Or the beginning of the first stroke on the page. This small thing that bursts into a gigantic thing. It's a pretty simple parallel. But that's what I mean about these pieces all having happened to me—I really have always empathized and fantasized a lot about growing and expanding into an all-powerful being.

LM: There's something very powerful lurking just beneath the surface of teenage boys with their arrested developments—these things find their outlets in all sorts of weird things. I say this because there is something "adolescent"—in a good sense—about your writing. It's like you're tapping into something very wild and outrageous that leaps over the bounds of "good taste" and "common sense" the same way some teenage boys do on Saturday nights.

ML: When I was a teenager I was interested in any kind of extreme or obsessive behavior. I still am. A lot of the things that captivate teenage boys fall into the category of extreme and excessive behavior, and in that sense I agree that my sensibility has this teenage tilt to it. Teenage boys are interested in stories of men who eat nothing but jellyfish for three weeks on a desert island. One of the first things I remember thinking was really great was that scene in *Mutiny on the Bounty* where some poor malfeasant sailor is getting whipped with a cat-o'-nine-tails. It's an old story: the teenage boy with a strain of S and M fascination. But this has to do less with S and M than with the way adolescents sexualize everything they come in contact with. Younger teenage boys traditionally can't be sexual yet (because you're really not supposed to have a girlfriend when you're thirteen) so all this sexual energy winds up being projected out onto all the objects and people they're involved with—sports, violence, ways of dressing or of being outrageous in the way they talk to people. There's all this powerful sexual energy you have nothing to do with that ends up fetishizing external objects and situations. I hope I can tap some of this remarkable "adolescent" energy in my work.

LM: Two related questions. One, did you conceive of *My Cousin, My Gastroenterologist* as a collection of stories or more as a novel—or as some kind of uncategorizable text? Secondly, I know you had the title of the book chosen very early on (in the author's note to *I Smell Esther Williams* it mentioned you were working on a book by this title, which means you had it in mind long before the book really began to take shape). What gave you the idea for the title and how did this idea help you focus on what you were doing during the years it took you to write the book?

ML: I consider *My Cousin* to be more a novel than a collection of stories in that there's a thematic network interrelating the individual pieces in a much more cohesive way than you'd find in a story collection. But maybe it's neither. At any rate, the engine runs, the radio works—it gets you there, quickly. As to the title, you're right that it's been part of the book for a long time, even before I had any idea of exactly what I was going to do with the book. I got the idea because I really do have a cousin who is a gastroenterologist. And just as I was finishing *Esther Williams* I went through a year or so when I was having all sorts of gastrointestinal ailments. The title for *My Cuz* doesn't operate in the same way as *I Smell Esther Williams*, which functions purely as an emblem of the way the book is going to read. All the things one could say about my work—the kinetic quality of the prose, the way it uses cultural references, and so on—are there in the title. It seemed like a perfect image to emblazon on the cover, the first thing readers would see, so it would be hovering over the rest of the book once people got into it.

The title *My Cousin, My Gastroenterologist* has something of the same quality, but it operates differently. It still implies that it's somehow about *me* but instead of using the "I" directly, it uses "my," which almost makes it seem as if it's going to be a story about someone else. As I mentioned earlier, this area interested me almost from an abstract standpoint—this playing around with how pronouns are used, with how readers were going to be decoding this "I" and this "my" that they're encountering. But in *My Cousin*, these pronouns actually unify the book in the sense that readers are supposed to feel some connections between the "I's" that appear in the different sections. That wasn't so true in *Esther*

Williams, where you're supposed to realize that these "I's" are different narrative voices.

LM: The title also implies that this is going to be a book about the "inner" you . . .

ML: Exactly. Have you ever had a colonoscopic examination? That's where they snake this fiber-optic tube up through your intestines. It doesn't hurt (they give you Demerol and Valium in an IV) and it's absolutely fascinating. They've got very advanced technology to do all of this—they can put a video camera on the end of this snake so you can watch the whole thing. It's a weird experience, lying there, high on Demerol and Valium, watching your intestines on a TV screen—probably the most introspective view of yourself you'll ever have. No kidding, you should have one done even if you don't need one.

Anyway, I wanted *My Cousin, My Gastroenterologist* to be like a colonoscopic examination of my insides (that's what I meant earlier when I said it describes what's been happening to me over the past several years) and of the insides of this body of information I've been swimming in. That's why I maintained interest in the gastrointestinal metaphor the whole time I was working on the book. I had originally planned to use one of my lower GI X-rays for the cover of the book (I doubt if *that* had ever been done before)—that seemed like a great way to get across this sense of an author exposing himself. Just before I finished the book, I had this idea in the shower of how the book could end: the narrator/protagonist, through the use of growth hormones and his weight lifting, was going to become galactically immense, so in order to get this macrocosmic look of his insides, scientists had to perform the colonoscopic operation by snaking the optic tube through one of those large observatory telescopes. I wound up not using that image to close the book, but I'm still convinced it would have been a great way to end it.

LM: One of the things you do fairly frequently in *My Cousin* is to create these wonderfully ludicrous juxtapositions by describing something utterly mundane or grotesque—but with these highly technical terms. Like that scene in the bar (in "i was an infinitely hot and dense dot") where the guy starts jerking off and "shoots a glob of dehydrogenated ethylbenzene 3,900 miles towards the Arctic archipelago." Do you actually "research" any of this—would any of these technical terms actually "fit" these situations, or are you purely playing with the sound of things?

ML: Mostly I'm playing. In the case of all those chemicals I use to describe that guy's sperm and the substances that the woman uses to rub on her clitoris, well, I had an idea about what some of those things actually *were,* because I got them out of an issue of a chemical engineering magazine, so I knew that they were at least liquids. But as to what they would do on contact with actual human skin, I have no idea. What interests me in creating a passage like that isn't so much the reality of what I'm describing but what it feels like to *read language like that*. Using that elevated, exotic jargon in an ostensibly intimate context creates an interesting opportunity to analyze the way this rhetoric functions in our lives. And of course part of the point in describing the scene that way is to see how this technological jargon confers authority, how it sounds so tough and peremptory in this masculine, macho kind of way. When I say this hunk swaggers into the bar and he's got a dick made out of "corrosion-resistant nickel-based alloy" that can ejaculate "herbicides, sulfuric acid, tar glue" and so on, I mean, just the sound of that rhetoric designates this guy as one state-of-the-art motherfucker! It's this collision of different kinds of language—phallic language and the language of technology—that together produces an exponentially bogus sense of power and authority. One kind of jargon is associated with "hunks" and another is associated with science. They're really not that different in a sense (or their effect isn't much different)—this sort of hard-boiled, tough-guy lingo and scientific prose that's all no-nonsense, confident and self-validating. And when you crossbreed these two species of language, it's also very funny.

LM: And using these very technical terms to describe such primal, mysterious human actions—touching or fucking—adds an odd dissociation in a certain way.

ML: Right, it's like the disjunction you feel between hearing the technical name for an illness or any physical dysfunction and the actual physical sensation of illness. So in that same scene I have that woman sitting at the end of the bar who's written a poem about temporomandibular joint dysfunction that won a Grammy for the best spoken word recording. These ailments seem to flash into popular awareness and then fade out—like this jaw problem seems to be a pretty hip thing to have right now—so that the specific discourse for describing specific ailments is suddenly in the air right now. Tomorrow it'll be something else. But sitting at a bar and hearing someone give this sixty-four-letter name to a physical disorder she has is farcical—it's as if people who use these words with such faith and seriousness are suffering from the discourse rather than from the ailment. They can't see how politicized that kind of naming and language really is, how our taxonomies actually determine the way we live. But if I can create a certain kind of literary context that really shows how ludicrously apparent this is—or that shows how similar the kind of sexual jargon we have for "hunks" is to this technoscientific jargon—then you can see the politics surrounding these discourses more clearly.

LM: It would seem most fiction writers rely on structures like plot and character to raise readerly expectations about what's to follow. Without those devices, how do you move your readers on from sentence to sentence?

ML: There are a million ways *not* to do it, and I find myself having to deal with these whenever I'm working on a piece. What I want to do is to be working with structures that give me as much imaginative freedom as possible—I want my readers to go on to the next sentence because they have this sense that it literally might contain *anything*. So for me to be working successfully, I have to create a context for my writing that is deliberately very weird, fluid, shifting. I want to be dancing myself into a posture where I can do whatever I want to in the next moment. That's why I don't like relying on traditional structures of plot and character. Plot and character are constantly eliminating possibilities, whereas I want these possibilities to always be available. But no matter how hard you try to create a structure that isn't narrative and that opens up these possibilities, it is very easy to find yourself getting penned in, writing yourself into a confining context. It's at those points where I find myself falling into creating a character somehow, or having written some scene that demands to be "developed," that I usually completely lose interest in working on something. Because at that point I've lost that freedom to do whatever I want in the next sentence. It's that freedom to do whatever I want that gives me the maximum ability to be truly interesting in every sentence.

LM: We've been talking about the ways you've devised structures that allow you to move freely from moment to moment. This sounds very theoretical, abstract—but there's a sense in which I'd say this approach is very much grounded in the world I live in. Wouldn't you agree that your writing, in a sense (but a crucial sense) is actually very "realistic"— that it "represents" the world around us just as "mimetically" as the nineteenth-century realist novel did for its day?

ML: I'd say my work presents the world the way people like you and I actually live in it, the way we receive and perceive it. That myth of narrative life, with all *that* implies, is something you'd think would have been jettisoned a long time ago. We live from instant to instant, with things constantly changing, kaleidoscopic. Our cultural matrix intensifies the whole natural process of information appearing in front of us and then disappearing. So you see huge headlines in the New York *Post* and *Daily News* announcing portentous things that you think everyone in the world must be reading about. But then they're gone the next day. Or you get up in the morning after having this strange dream, and then you're facing the pink and white tile in your bathroom. And then you go eat your strange breakfast cereal and you read the back of the cereal box, while the TV is blaring out another text and maybe your children are telling you some other kind of story. And all the while this white noise is filtering in from outside your window. The point is that our days are very fragmented, with a million things happening, affecting our perceptions, that have completely arbitrary relationships to one another.

LM: You'd think that these sorts of experiences would encourage people to stop thinking about their lives as if they were living in an eighteenth-century empiricist novel—relativity and quantum mechanics (just to name two obvious examples) are such revolutionary ways of looking at how things operate that they should have changed the nature of the kind of narratives we see ourselves existing in.

ML: They would have changed our narratives, if they had affected the structure of our thought and the language we use in a profound way. But they haven't had that effect yet. But things will change. For example, I'm not even sure that literature as such will remain a medium that artists will continue to use because I'm not sure how much longer book reading is going to last. People may be doing other things that are just too interesting to put down in order to read something. And that won't be because people are going to be stupider or less intellectually inclined but because the other art forms or sources of information are going to be offering people more input, more stimulation.

LM: Wouldn't you say, though, that there is something about the intimacy and nuanced, aesthetic complexity that exist in the reading of a great book that you don't feel in other art forms? Or is this just nostalgia for a mode of art whose time is running out?

ML: Of course we're all a bit nostalgic about it—after all, the written word seems somehow "homemade." I don't think we have developed other art forms yet, though, that can give you literature's speed and complexity. But I think there will be art forms to come that will do everything books do for us—and more. I'm thinking of art forms that combine words with other elements. You can use language on a screen, for instance, and have the language interacting with other images or texts or sounds even. But I don't think the novel is ever going to disappear no matter what other art forms develop. People are going to keep writing books. Whether or not it's going to be fair anymore to condemn people for not being interested in those books, though, is another story. One reason I do what I do is because I feel it has to be the writers' responsibility to make fiction a viable alternative to other art forms that are out there now. If it's not a viable alternative, then it's the writers who have let us down. It's not the readers' fault that they're turning on the television or buying tickets to see the Butthole Surfers instead of curling up with a nice book at night.

LM: I also think that there's a misapprehension that whenever you introduce technology into something—like the arts, for instance—that you automatically wind up "dehumanizing" it. That just isn't necessarily the case. If you take an art form like the blues the way it was originally, where the voice and instruments aren't amplified electrically, and compare it to the postelectric blues, it's not a matter of one being more "human" (or even more "natural") than the other. Eventually you're going to have a genius like Jimi Hendrix come along who recognizes that technology gives a blues musician a whole series of fascinating new options, and who can add those possibilities to what is still the blues and do something different. But it's still the blues—and just as human as what Robert Johnson or Blind Lemon Jefferson were doing.

ML: I've certainly never seen technology as not being human. The Japanese, apparently, are much more comfortable than we are with the idea of technology being an extension of human activity; so there's not this split between nature and technology built into their system of perceiving things and evaluating them. But as I said before, the information output of technology is the natural environment I've grown up in; it's more or less a second nature to me. I don't see technology as being something alien or unnatural that people have to keep under control and resist. Interacting with technology seems like a very natural, human activity to me.

Beneath a Precipice
An Interview with Clarence Major

Larry McCaffery
Jerzy Kutnik

From the turntable, The Jimi Hendrix Experience jumps through the room with the force of Goya dancers.

— *Reflex and Bone Structure*

Clarence Major first achieved literary recognition during the social and aesthetic turmoil of the late sixties. This recognition was initially due to Major's work as an editor, poet, and anthologist; later, the appearance in 1969 of his sexually charged, highly controversial first novel, *All-Night Visitors*, from Maurice Girodias's Olympia Press, began to establish him as one of postmodern fiction's most versatile and radical innovators. Major's first publication was a pamphlet of (mostly forgettable) poems entitled *The Fires that Burn in Heaven* (1954); following a stint in the Air Force, Major began editing *Coercion Review* (from 1958–61), which gradually brought him into contact with such leading poetry figures as William Carlos Williams, Robert Creeley, and Allen Ginsberg. Over the years, Major has continued to make editorial contributions to such journals as *Journal of Black Poetry*, *American Book Review*, and *American Poetry Review*, as well as publishing two anthologies of student work, which he edited, *Writers Workshop* (1967) and *Man Is a Child* (1969). He has also published a wide variety of reviews, manifestos, and critical essays (some collected in his 1974 critical study, *The Dark and Feeling: Black American Writers and Their Work*).

But Major first gained national attention with the publication of *The New Black Poetry* (1969), a controversial anthology of contemporary black poetry whose eclecticism drew criticism from both conservative and liberal factions of the black artistic community, who were both already heatedly discussing the implications of the "black aesthetic" being promoted by writers like Ishmael Reed, Ed Bullins, and Amiri Baraka. In terms of his own work, Major's first important poetry collection, *Swallow the Lake* (1970), explored some of the interests that would recur in his later fiction (music, alienation, and psychic dismemberment, male-female relationships, the relationship of art and reality, sex and death, and so on) in a wide variety of styles and voices; *Swallow* was rapidly followed by three more collections, *Private Line* (1971), *Symptoms and Madness* (1971), and *The Cotton Club* (1972). Major's poetry is characterized by the same rich, unsettling mixture of humor and anger, passion and abstract intellectual interests, self-consciousness and let-it-all-hang-out energy, and formal daring found in his fiction.

Because Major has mainly avoided the social realist mode favored by most black American writers in favor of expressionistic, metafictional modes, his fiction has subsequently been analyzed primarily in terms of its "experimental" or "antirealist" features. Unfortunately this focus has tended to relegate Major to the "avant-garde ghetto" where his works have never attained the popularity or critical acclaim given his more publicly visible contemporaries like Alice Walker, Toni Morrison, and Ishmael Reed.

However, as with many other figures from postmodernism's first wave of literary innovators, what once seemed antirealistic to a generation raised on the illusionistic assumptions of traditional realism can be recognized today as simply new approaches to realism, either in the sense of describing a reality that seemed increasingly "unrealistic" by earlier norms or (as is more relevant for Major's work) of finding fresh methods to depict irrational, contradictory inner lives and selves that resist traditional formulations. Many of the features of Major's fiction are in fact designed to give voice to various irrational impulses and contradictory versions of self and personal identity that traditional realism could not express. Thus, Major's best fiction often presents a fiercely passionate vision of jagged, tortured beauty that is analogous to that found in Goya, Van Gogh, Hendrix, or Eric Dolphy. While such nonliterary analogies are always suspect, they are appropriate in this case due to Major's convictions concerning the inadequacies of verbal logic to convey the truth about experience.

The themes and forms of these books seem to trace a movement away from the radical sense of personal fragmentation and insecurity, graphic sexuality, and outrage found in the early works (*All-Night Visitors* and *NO* [1973]), to a middle period where his interests in metafictional explorations of the fiction-making process, metafictional methods, and formal concerns find their most extreme expression in *Reflex and Bone Structure* (1975) and *Emergency Exit* (1979), to his recent explorations of more narrative styles and formal structures in works like *Such Was the Season* (1987). But as Major takes great pains to suggest in the following interview, such an evolution represents less a move "away from antirealism towards realism" than different stages in an ongoing effort to find a suitable means to give expression to his sense of himself.

As it happens, most of the early versions of "self" are prismatic, cubistic constructs reflecting not self but a shifting series of public, private, and imaginary selves. Most of Major's fiction unfolds as a bewildering array of discrete bits of visual images, fragments of contradictory plot elements, different voices, and reflexive ruminations about fiction. Major's novels nearly all focus on men whose lives are either coming apart or never had achieved any unity in the first place. Reading Major's important middle works like *Reflex and Bone Structure, My Amputations* (1986), and perhaps his most successful novel, *Emergency Exit*, you feel much as you did in reading Kerouac and Burroughs, Rimbaud and Artaud—figures who, like Major, felt the need to refashion an entire new language and set of narrative assumptions in order to conjure up "spaces" of the imagination and emotion never given voice to previously. Major thus developed a variety of discontinuous, collage-like structures to capture the movement of a mind which refuses to reduce his experiences to the sorts of unified narrative voices and causally related plot elements found in the realistic novel. As with other writers from this period who were exploring similar methods—for example, his fellow Fiction Collective writers Steve Katz, Ray Federman, and Ronald Sukenick—the result is akin to a jazz musician's improvisations, whose various tones, rhythms, motifs, and other sound patterns, expressed in different keys and tones, provide a means of access to the artist's inner self. The act of writing down the work we are reading thus should be seen as being not an effort to find a unified self, voice, or plot but an effort to provide a means to give expression to these multiple, contradictory aspects of himself. His novels, then, represent not the illusions of realism but the illusoriness of those illusions.

Although the influence of jazz, blues, and poetry on Major's fiction has been widely noted, his writing has probably been even more deeply influenced by the visual. Major began his artistic career as a painter (he attended the Chicago Art Institute briefly at age seventeen), and he has continued to produce paintings, which he has exhibited in galleries and exhibitions on numerous occasions. Major remarks in the following interview that he is "a visual thinker," and this quality is evident in the important role that visual descriptions and imagery have always played in his narratives. Although *Emergency Exit* is his only book in which Major has introduced reproductions of his paintings to reinforce or analogize the written materials, his use of visual images as a kind of objective correlative that reveals emotional resonances of the inner, literally unspeakable emotional lives of his narrators and characters has been a constant feature of his fiction.

The following interview took place at Clarence Major's home in Davis, California. Before the interview, the interviewers, along with McCaffery's wife, Sinda Gregory, and Major's wife, Pamela, had gone out for lunch in order to catch up on news and gossip. Back at Major's house, there was time before the interview to roam about examining the plants and small trees (whose presence indoors seemed not at all incongruous) and the many paintings by Major that hang on the walls. The conversation was friendly but serious, the atmosphere and mood combining with Major's reflective comments and soft voice to create an aura of quiet reflection.

*   *   *

Clarence Major: Selected Bibliography

Novels and Collections of Fiction

All-Night Visitors. New York: Olympia Press, 1969. Italian translation: *I Visitatori Della Notta.* Milan: Olympia Press Milano, 1969. German translation: *Damonen.* Frankfurt: Olympia Press Sonderreiche am Main, 1970.
NO. New York: Emerson Hall, 1973.
Reflex and Bone Structure. New York: Fiction Collective, 1975. Reprinted, San Francisco: Mercury House, 1996. French translation: *Reflex et ossature.* Lasagna, Switzerland: L'Age d'Homme, Vladimir Dimitijeric, 1980.
Emergency Exit. New York: Fiction Collective, 1979.
My Amputations. New York: Fiction Collective, 1986. German translation: "Meine Amputations," *Sehreibheft Zeitsehrift zur Literatur,* 31 (May 1988).
Such Was the Season. San Francisco: Mercury House, 1987.
Painted Turtle: Woman with Guitar. Los Angeles: Sun and Moon Press, 1988.
Fun and Games. Duluth, MN: Holy Cow! Press, 1990.
Dirty Bird Blues. San Francisco: Mercury House, 1996.

Uncollected Fiction

"Ulysses, Who Slept Across from Me." *Olivant* (Japan) 1 (1957): 53–56.
"Tattoo." In *American Made: New Fiction from the Fiction Collective,* ed. Mark Leyner, Curtis White, and Thomas Glynn, 155–64. New York: Fiction Collective, 1986.
"My Mother and Mitch." *Boulevard* 11, 4 no. 2 (Fall 1989): 1–11. Reprinted in *The*

Pushcart Prize, XL: Best of the Small Presses 1990–1991, ed. Bill Henderson, 110–20. New York: Wainscott, 1991.
"Chicago Heat." *African-American Review* 28, 1 (1994): 29–33.

Poetry Books

The Fires That Burn in Heaven. Chicago, 1954. Variant reprint, *Galley Sail Review* 20 (1968).
Love Poems of a Black Man. Omaha, NE: Coercion Press, 1965.
Swallow the Lake. Middletown, CT: Wesleyan University Press, 1970.
Private Line. London: Paul Breman, 1971.
Symptoms and Madness. New York: Corinth Books, 1971.
The Cotton Club. Detroit: Broadside Press, 1972.
The Syncopated Cakewalk. New York: Barlenmir House, 1974.
Inside Diameter: The France Poems. New York: Permanent Press, 1985.
Surfaces and Masks: A Poem. Minneapolis: Coffee House Press, 1988.
Some Observations of a Stranger at Zuni in the Latter Part of the Century. Los Angeles: Sun and Moon Press, 1990.
Parking Lots. Mount Horeb, WI: Perishable Press, 1992.

Nonfiction

Juba to Jive: The Dictionary of African-American Slang. New York: Viking, 1994.
Dictionary of Afro-American Slang. New York: International Publishers, 1970. Reprinted as *Black Slang: A Dictionary of Afro-American Talk.* London: Routledge and Kegan Paul, 1971.
The Dark and Feeling: Black American Writers and Their Work. New York: Third Press, 1974.
"Clarence Major Interviews Jacob Lawrence, the Expressionist." *The Black Scholar* 9, no. 3 (November 1977): 14–25.
"A Meditation on Time and Space in Bamism." In *Postmodern Fiction: Performance and Representation*, ed. Maurice Couturier, 38–47. Montpelier, France: Publication de l'Universit, 1982.
"The Crunch on Serious Fiction, Part One: The Commercial Press." *American Book Review* 2, 1 (1979): 14–15.
"The Crunch on Serious Fiction, Part Two: The Small Press." *American Book Review* 2, 2 (1979): 6–7.
Review of *Beloved*, by Toni Morrison. *American Book Review* 9, 6 (January/February 1988): 17.
Review of *Letoumeau's Used Auto Parts*, by Carolyn Chute. *New York Times Book Review*, 31 July 1988, p. 9.
"In Hollywood with the Zuni God of War." In *Dynamics of Violence*. Durham, NC: Duke University Press, 1992.
"Necessary Distance: After Thoughts on Becoming a Writer." *African American Review* 28, 1 (1994): 37–47.

As Editor

The New Black Poetry. New York: International Publishers, 1969.
Calling the Wind: Twentieth Century African-American Short Stories. New York: Harper Perennial, 1993.
The Garden Thrives: Twentieth-Century African-American Poetry. New York: Harper Collins, 1996.

Interviews and Recorded Remarks

Bolling, Doug. "Reality, Fiction and Criticism: An Interview/Essay by Clarence Major." *Par Rapport* 2, 1 (1979): 67–73.
Bunge, Nancy. "An Interview with Clarence Major." In *Finding the Words: Conversations with Writers Who Teach.* Athens, OH: Swallow Press, 1985.
Klinkowitz, Jerome. "Clarence Major: An Interview with a Post-Contemporary Author." *Black American Literature Forum* 12 (1978): 32–37.
Major, Clarence. "Licking Stamps, Taking Chances." *Contemporary Authors Autobiography Series* 6: 175–204. Detroit: Gale Research, 1988.
———. "Necessary Distance: Afterthoughts on Becoming a Writer." *Black American Literature Forum* 23, 2 (Summer 1989): 197–212.
———. "Self-Interview: On Craft." In *The Dark and Feeling: Black American Writers and Their Work*, 125–31. New York: Third Press, 1974.
O'Brien, John. "Interview with Clarence Major." In *Interviews with Black Writers*, ed. John O'Brien, 125–39. New York: Liveright, 1973.

Essays and Reviews about Major's Work

[*Note*: The Spring 1994 issue of *African-American Review* devoted a special issue to Clarence Major, guest-edited by Bernard Bell. The issue included new work by Major (poems and fiction), an excerpt from the interview included in *Some Other Frequency*, a portfolio of photographs and artwork by Major, as well as numerous critical essays which are listed individually in my bibliography.]
Bell, Bernard. "Clarence Major's Homecoming: Voice in *Such Was the Season.*" *African-American Review* 28, 1 (1994): 89–94.
Bloom, Harold. "Clarence Major." In *Twentieth Century American Literature, Vol. 4: The Chelsea House Library of Literary Criticism*, 2436–41. New York: Chelsea House, 1986.
Bolling, Doug. "A Reading of Clarence Major's Short Fiction." *Black American Literature Forum* 13/2 (Summer 1979): 51–56.
Bradfield, Larry D. "Beyond Mimetic Exhaustion: The *Reflex and Bone Structure* Experiment." *Black American Literature Forum* 17 (1983): 120–23.
Coleman, James W. "Clarence Major's Kalabanic Discourse and Black Male Expression." *African-American Review* 28, 1 (1994): 95–108.
Hayward, Steve. "Again Commodification: Xuni Culture in Clarence Major's Native American Texts." *African-American Review* 28, 1 (1994): 109–20.
Klawans, Steward. "I Was a Weird Example of Art: *My Amputation* as Cubist Confession." *African American Review* 28, 1 (1994): 77–87.
Klinkowitz, Jerome. "Clarence Major's Superfiction." In Klinkowitz's *The Life of Fiction.* Carbondale: Southern Illinois University Press, 1977.

————. "Clarence Major: An Interview with a Post-Contemporary Author." *Black American Literature Forum* 12, 1 (Spring 1978): 32–37.

————. "Clarence Major." *Dictionary of Literary Biography: Fiction Writers since World War II: Supplement,* ed. Richard Ziegfeld. Columbia, SC: Gale Research, 1982.

————. "Clarence Major." In *The Self Apparent Word: Fiction as Language/Language as Fiction,* 84, 87, 108–22, 116–17. Edwardsville: Southern Illinois University Press, 1984.

————. "Clarence Major's Innovative Fiction." *African-American Review* 28, 1 (1994): 57–63.

Mackey, Nathaniel. "To Define an Ultimate Dimness: Deconstruction in Clarence Major's Poems." *Black American Literature Forum,* 13, 2 (Summer 1979): 61–68.

Martin, Stephen-Paul. "Clarence Major: Persephone in Fragments." In *Open Form and the Feminine Imagination,* 121–32. Washington, DC: Maisonneuve Press/Institute for Advanced Cultural Studies, 1988.

McCaffery, Larry. "The Fiction Collective." *Contemporary Literature* 19 (Winter 1978): 100, 105, 107–8.

McCaffery, Larry, and Sinda Gregory. "Major's *Reflex and Bone Structure,* and the Anti Detective Novel." *Black American Literature Forum* 13, 2 (Summer 1979): 39–45.

"The New Black Poetry." *New York Times Book Review,* 3 February 1972, p. 3.

Perry, Richard, "Hunting the Thief of Identity." *New York Times Book Review,* 28 September 1986, p. 30.

Roney, Lisa C. "The Double Vision of Clarence Major, Painter and Writer." *African-American Review* 28, 1 (1994): 65–75.

Weixelman, Joe. "Notes on a Novel in Progress: Clarence Major's *Emergency Exit.*" *Black American Literature Forum* 13, 2 (Summer 1979).

————. "Toward A Primary Bibliography of Clarence Major." *Black American Literature Forum,* 13, 2 (Summer 1979): 70–72.

————. "Clarence Major." In *Dictionary of Literary Biography: Black American Authors since 1955,* ed. Thadious Davis and Trudier Harris, 153–60. Columbia, SC: Gale Research, 1984.

* * *

JERZY KUTNIK: To what extent do you see yourself as consciously working in the "black aesthetic" or black narrative tradition?

CLARENCE MAJOR: There is no single "black aesthetic." There has been a sequence or series of scenarios that can be defined as "black aesthetics" corresponding roughly to historical periods. So in the nineteenth century there were the black writers of the antebellum (1853–1865), the postbellum (1865–1902), the Old Guard (1902–1917), and Harlem Renaissance (1917–1929), and the period of social protest (1929–1959). They had their ideas about what a black writer in America should be doing, who a black writer should be addressing, and so on, that emerged out of specific literary and historical contexts. Despite all the different agendas throughout all the various periods, black writers were always working against a single dominant impulse in American culture: the use to which white America put blackness. Whiteness was about not being black. As such, black people were invested with all the negative crap against which white America defined itself. Black writers worked always to humanize black people and to overthrow the burden of this symbolism. To be human meant to be *whole*—good and bad, complex, and so on. At the same time, the Old Guard, for example, was resisting the young writers of the Harlem Renaissance, who were trying to assert a new kind of black presence and consciousness.

JK: And this presence wasn't likely to be accepted by whites?

CM: The point had less to do with white models or white acceptance and more about not feeling they had to be "proper." The accommodationists were about putting one's best foot forward for the white world, or for an equal reading public. In other words, you should never hang your dirty laundry out, never let the world know what's going on behind the scenes. If you have marital problems, family problems, drinking problems, all that should be kept quiet. Meanwhile you emphasize the positive, put your best face forward, that kind of thing. That was the black middle-class take on reality, and it should be the take presented in literature, which should be very uplifting. Then along comes Claude McKay with a book like *Home to Harlem*, which lets it all hang out, which shows the prostitutes and the pimps and the numbers runners and all the other good-time people—it was about people and situations that people like Weldon Johnson were calling the dirty laundry.

The point is that what people refer to as "black aesthetics" isn't some mysterious, inherent set of guidelines, but a set of historical motives. Aesthetics aren't a set of abstractions existing outside historical circumstances and daily reality; they're always grounded in the needs and aims of specific artists and audiences, influenced by the social setting and context. Richard Wright was concerned with the conditions of poverty, injustice, and so on that Sinclair or Wolfe and other white protest writers of the thirties were. Chester Himes wrote about those kinds of conditions too in books like *Cast the First Stone* and in some of his other forties novels. Later on in the sixties, you get this idea of the black aesthetic which comes out of Black Nationalism and operates as the cultural arm of that political movement. It's meant to be purely functional in relation to the political aim, but it seemed to me to be essentially replacing Eurocentric thinking with Afrocentric thinking.

LARRY MCCAFFERY: It's always struck me that there was a risk in this whole approach. Even if Afrocentric thinking seems somehow more "appropriate" to the experience of black people, the insistence on having black people adopt this mode of thinking winds up substituting one set of limitations, controls, norms, for another.

CM: That was essentially the problem I wound up having with this whole "black aesthetics" concept. The thrust of the movement wasn't so much an attempt to say Eurocentric thinking is limiting our attempts to function as artists and as individuals—I would have obviously supported anything concerned with opening up options, fresher or more liberating options for black people. Instead, you had this attempt to replace the Eurocentric with something that *closed down* the view of the writer and restricted it to the service of certain political ideologies that were as stifling as the ones they hoped to replace. That's why I instinctively opposed it, even before I could articulate the sources of my opposition. I knew there was something wrong. What I tried to propose even that early in the sixties (and what I still propose today) was something far more flexible, which is what I was trying to do with my anthology, *Calling the Wind: Twentieth Century African-American Short Stories*—namely, to find the terms on a more personal level, to get the best of all the different kinds of cultural influences feeding into my experience, and to come up with a personal aesthetic. It might at least be liberating for me.

LM: You can make the same argument about the great debate raging these days on college campuses about the canon.

CM: Exactly! We talk about opening up the canon so that we can bring the rest of the world into Western thinking, get outside of the restrictions we've traditionally imposed on our educational system, and somehow open up the whole process. Now of course I'm all in favor of the opening up of Western thought to other modes of thinking (who *couldn't* be?), but the minute you start talking about challenging the Western canon, the people who depend on it for their living get very terrified. It's not that anybody wants to derail Shakespeare—sure, everyone should have to study Shakespeare. But everyone should also have to study equally important writers and philosophies of other cultures. Why not?

LM: Since you started publishing fiction back in the late sixties, your work has consistently been discussed by critics like Jerry Klinkowitz and myself primarily in terms of its concern with its own processes and status as pure invention. Unfortunately, this emphasis on your works' alleged "nonreferential" or "nonrealistic" features ignored the possibility that these features might function in the service of a new kind of realism; it's also been used to relegate your work to the rarified "art for art's sake" (or the "narcissistically self-indulgent") category and hence marginalize it. How would you yourself describe the role that formal innovation has played in your fiction? Is the common distinction between "realism" versus "experimentalism" valid?

CM: Absolutely not. Those distinctions have always seemed superficial. Since *Such Was the Season* looks very much like a piece of realism on the surface, some people claimed that I had jumped ship, betrayed my experimental goals. But that book is just as "experimental" as my other work in terms of realistic norms. For example, even though Juneboy appears in what *passes for* a realistic setting, he's also being presented through this folksy, down-to-earth woman's point of view, which filters everything through colloquial speech mannerisms and idioms in an utterly subjective manner.

LM: In the interview that appeared in *Finding the Words*, you described writing as a way of finding yourself both as a writer and as a person, adding, "I think the two processes are integral and interchangeable and inseparable—the continual redefinition of self and the process of learning how to write every day. I find that it's an endless lesson; you don't really carry that much information and skill from one piece to the next unless you're doing the same thing over and over. Each act of writing becomes a whole new experience, which is why it's so difficult" (Bunge, 53). You went on to say that your writing reflects the fact that you literally feel different every day. I mention this because subjective or not, Annie Eliza's perspective in *Such Was the Season* is undeniably more *stable* or consistent than what we find in your earlier work. Is this stability a reflection of your now feeling less fragmented personally, more certain of who and what you are?

CM: In terms of my own psychology, I do feel more secure—secure enough at least so I don't feel the need to ask the same questions that drove me to create characters like the ones you find over and over again in *All-Night Visitors* and *NO*. But what we're talking about here, both in terms of my writing and my life, is an evolution, not a sharp break. Exploring different personae in my earlier novels was something that grew out of my sense of personal fragmentation. Those feelings have changed somewhat as I've gotten older and had the opportunity to resolve some of those conflicts about myself and recognize integration rather than separation. When you're young, you haven't had the experiences that allow perspective on who you are or how to know what "you" consist of. From a personal standpoint, of course, this confusion can be very troubling, but an artist needs to take advantage of these things to produce anything worthwhile. Back when I was starting out to write, it felt perfectly natural to have my work reflect this sense that I was literally a different person every time I sat down to write. It was an interesting challenge to find narrative contexts for different parts of myself that needed voices to express themselves. So in something like *Reflex and Bone Structure* I consciously played with this whole concept of author-narrator identity, though in fact there were several personae there: the narrator, the protagonist, and the implied author. In *My Amputations* I had an implied author, the protagonist, and the narrator all working together in a concerted way. To write a novel in those days with stable characters or narrators would have basically falsified my own experience. Today the opposite would be equally false. All along it's seemed that to do anything *but* reflect my own self (or selves) wouldn't make sense. Why write out of some phony sense of narrative stability if that doesn't reflect how I feel about myself? There was a sense I didn't really *want* a stable identity, at least in terms of being an artist. There was something liberating about *not* knowing who I was going to be when I sat down to write. Projecting myself into these different personas let me discover things about these concrete presences which were outside of myself but also coming out of myself. In the process, I learned a lot about myself.

JK: In this regard, your presentation of Annie Eliza in *Such Was the Season* seemed a departure for you in that she somehow *didn't* seem to be someone based on yourself.

CM: There's been a steady movement in my writing toward diminishing that dependency on self. By the time I got to the creation of Annie Eliza, I had made an enormous breakthrough: this was my first novel where I was not the model for the main character. The Zuni novel, *Painted Turtle*, was a further leap in that direction, and now I'm writing a novel whose main character is not remotely like me.

LM: Readers of *Such Was the Season* may not be encouraged to identify you with the narrator—but what about Juneboy? Weren't there autobiographical impulses that started the book?

CM: I started *Such Was the Season* after I had taken a trip to Atlanta, and to some extent Juneboy is based on some of my experiences on that trip. But—and this is pretty true in terms of all the autobiographical material in my work—those correlations start to break down very quickly once narrative and aesthetic demands and all sorts of other things start to operate on these "facts." Like Juneboy, I hadn't been to Atlanta since I was eighteen, but I didn't stay a week like he did. And I didn't make a trip with my aunt to try to find my father's grave site either—or discover that it was under ten miles of concrete in, or rather under, a housing development. There was also no political scandal in the works like there was in the novel, although like Juneboy I did meet the mayor of Atlanta and Martin Luther King's wife, Coretta, at a dinner party at my cousin's house. But overall I'd say my own presence is so diminished in Juneboy's identity that he is at best a catalyst rather than a true persona. By the time you get to *Painted Turtle* "I" am not present at all, except in the design and creation of the book. These very general connections between autobiography and fiction are always present in my books, somewhere, though you may have to dig deeper in some works than others to recognize them. But as a novelist I've always felt that my obligation is to follow whatever ideas I'm trying to work through in a particular book, not to something which actually took place.

JK: Your *Contemporary Authors* autobiography essay mentions that you began *Painted Turtle* with a woman narrator but finally decided you couldn't write it effectively that way. Were you feeling that it was some-how inappropriate to write from a woman's perspective? What finally allowed you to maintain a female narrator's voice throughout *Such Was the Season?*

CM: I don't believe gender-specific arguments about the impossibility of men writing from women's perspectives (and vice versa), just as I don't believe that blacks can't write about whites, or whites can't write about blacks. If you can make it come alive, you can write *anything.* With *Painted Turtle*, what happened was that for various reasons I was unable to make that particular Zuni woman come alive. *Painted Turtle* taught me that if I was going to write in a woman's voice, it had to be a voice I felt com-fortable with—one that would come naturally rather than something I'd have to completely invent. That was a big help when I started *Such Was the Season* a year later, but for reasons that are hard to explain, I found in *Painted Turtle* that I felt closer to the voice of the guy who falls in love with her. Strangely, a lot of people remember the book as being nar-rated by a woman. Maybe her voice is still present as a kind of subtext.

At any rate, from the outset I felt more secure with the woman's voice I was using in *Such Was the Season.* I didn't have to think about inventing that voice because I'd grown up hearing it, I knew its rhythms from the way my relatives in the South speak. It was already there, so all I had to do was just sit at the computer and correct the voice by ear, the way you would write music. If the rhythm was wrong or the pitch off, I knew it instinctively because I'd lived with that voice all my life.

JK: Do you recall what the origin of the Zuni novel was?

CM: It had to do with the fact that a black man—a huge African—appar-ently visited the Zunis in the sixteenth century with a group of Spanish explorers and then stayed on. He must have seemed extremely com-manding to the Zuni because he became some kind of god for them—he had dozens of wives, and he appears in a lot of early Zuni legends and stories, and so on.

JK: I don't remember him appearing in the novel . . .

CM: He doesn't. It turned out he was irrelevant to contemporary Zuni culture, which is finally what I wound up wanting to explore. For what-ever reason, this black man's presence is no longer found anywhere in recent Zuni culture. And since, in effect, he's been dead for them for a long time (since the nineteenth, or maybe even the eighteenth, cen-tury), I decided he wouldn't have any presence in my novel, either. Letting go of this story was disappointing—after all, he had triggered my interest in the Zunis in the first place, which had started me going down to New Mexico, visiting the reservation, and getting to know some people. But in the end his presence just didn't fit in to my story.

LM: What sorts of research did you do for *Painted Turtle?*

CM: The trips I made to New Mexico (I was teaching at the University of Colorado at Boulder then) helped me get a sense of the Native American cultures in that part of the country; I also did a lot of research while I was teaching at UC-San Diego in 1984. To make that novel come alive, I had to learn a whole different culture. This took three years of research during which I absorbed tons and tons of stuff that was arriving from every conceivable discipline and in every conceivable way. I read the myths and anthropological transcripts, plus lots of sociology about the kinds of health conditions you find at Zuni, their education, really just about everything. I started writing the book right at the kitchen table in San Diego while still fascinated by the African man, so in early drafts he was present as a kind of mythic figure.

LM: Gerald Vizenor has recently argued that there are interesting analogies between Native American narrative traditions and those being described today in terms of "postmodernism." As you got to know Zuni storytelling modes better, what kinds of conclusions did you draw about their writing practices?

CM: Zuni storytelling is completely nonlinear. The traditional stories about Coyote never build towards a resolution the way Western narratives tend to do. Coyote wanders around involving himself in a complex network of activity that defies morality (and sometimes common sense logic). He gets involved in one thing after another, but these episodes aren't put together so in terms of progression, tension-and-resolution, and the other things we associate with the novel. It's the same with the various birds of the various festivals. They have their acts, their routines, but there's always an open-endedness, a resistance to closure. Things don't have to turn out the same way at the end of the process.

LM: Did your own experiences as a black American make you feel a special sense of empathy with Zuni culture?

CM: I think so. Certainly in the sense of identifying my own experience with the Zunis as a subculture. Being a black man also probably allowed me to sense things that individual Zuni characters might feel in any given situation. I could immediately relate to what they would feel in social situations where they would feel uncomfortable, marginalized, that kind of thing. In fact, I found that Native Americans often suffer as much discrimination as black Americans, right in their own area, the minute they cross the line of the reservation. Indians can walk in to just about any motel in New Mexico and find themselves being turned down for no good reason. That's just how it is. This might not happen as often to a black American in the West.

LM: One of the things about *Such Was the Season* that rang very true to me had to do with Annie Eliza being so wrapped up with the soap operas that they seemed every bit as real as anything else. Your early novels and poems also frequently examined technology's effect on people—usually from a negative perspective, it seems.

CM: Television *is* a very "real" part of life for a lot of people. It's an extension of what their daily lives are all about, not something removed from them. I've known any number of people who are basically housebound or who simply don't go out doing things in the world for whatever reasons. People like Annie Eliza become personally or even metaphysically wrapped up in the world of television so that its boundaries literally become the boundaries of their world.

LM: It's like what Baudrillard talks about regarding Disneyland—the illusion not only *seems* more real than the real world, it *is* more real.

CM: Right. Since Annie Eliza's television is never turned off, that world is always "on" for her; she goes to sleep with it on, and it's on when she wakes up—what could be more real than that? It's the way she lives. Besides, it's what she needs. When old people who have always had their family around them suddenly find themselves in a silent house, well, you can imagine how much they miss this bombardment of voices. Television fills the void, provides familiar voices, even if the voices are artificial. At least that space that's been vacated isn't empty.

LM: Since your generation of innovators emerged in the sixties, there's been an ever-increasing expansion of the so-called "media-culture"— this rapid expansion of images, advertising, information (the "dance of biz" as Bill Gibson refers to it)—into just about every conceivable aspect of our public and personal lives. This expansion may have especially dramatic, and potentially harmful, effects on black persons because the images, the people, and the situations they're encountering in the media are so predominantly white and middle-class—and as such they have the potential to distort people's perception of reality. But you seem to be looking at the positive role that, say, television plays in Annie Eliza's life rather than implying she's being manipulated or having her sense of racial norms or values impaired.

CM: That's because Eliza is looking at *human issues*—love, death, pain— that she's known all her life (and known completely) rather than racial issues. In her own life she has always identified with universals like raising children, deception, infidelity, seduction that have nothing to do with relative things like color or caste. Another important thing about her situation is that she's middle-class. She's owned her own house for thirty years and she identifies with the financial level of these people she's watching on the soaps. So on the social level their world is accessible to her. In my view, this is not such a huge leap either. Writers too can make this entry, imaginatively, into other cultures and genders, and make it viable and real in their works.

LM: In the interview you did with Jerry Klinkowitz in the seventies, you said: "All words are lies, in any arrangement, that pretend to be other than the arrangements that they make on the page." The idea that words and fiction are essentially formal aesthetic constructions rather than representations of something existing outside the page was, of course, very much in the air in the early days of postmodernism. Do you still agree with that? Or was this something that very much needed to be emphasized at a certain moment, but not at others?

CM: Using such an emotionally charged term as *lies* in that statement may have deflected readers away from the point I was making. What I meant to say—and this seems perfectly reasonable to me today as it did then—is that a word is just a sign, a symbol, and as such it can never really represent the thing it names. Words are entirely different from things, separate from their referents. They're autonomous entities, with their own linguistic realities, their own history, their own separate presences. Like other authors working against the grain of traditional realism, it seemed important for me back in the seventies to keep reminding readers that when writers start putting words on the page, they're not "representing" anything except the way their mind works. But once you say that, what does a writer *do* with it!? Having said this fifteen years ago, and then worked through all those reflexive concepts in my books, I simply don't need to do that again.

JK: And except in very broad ways, you don't repeat yourself very often, either thematically or in your formal concerns. With each new book, it's as if you've thrown yourself into a literary void—which is a risk for any artist. But in this sense, choosing to write *Such Was the Season* in a seemingly realistic mode was perfectly in keeping with what you'd been doing all along—that is, trying out new approaches.

CM: Like I said, writing *Such Was the Season* that way didn't mean I'd abandoned an interest in innovation. I was trying out all sorts of new things when I was writing *Such Was the Season*, even if these didn't have to do with my earlier compulsion to keep readers constantly focused on the page. The voice is what is innovative in that novel. I wanted to give that voice such a commanding presence that it would, in fact, become the main subject matter of the novel. I wanted to make it impossible for readers to stop thinking about the voice once they had started reading the book, to make that voice always uppermost, so that even though it was describing the things that were going on (the way voices do in traditional novels), they'd be constantly having to confront its own presence.

JK: Were there any models you had for the kind of thing you were after here with voice?

CM: *Huck Finn.* Before starting *Such Was the Season*, I had just reread *Huck* and once again, sentence after sentence, I found myself wondering, How did Twain make that voice come alive like that—make it so real? I may not have succeeded, but what I wanted to do in *Such Was the Season* was create a voice that would have the same kind of undeniable presence as the one Twain had created for Huck. I wanted to create a text in which the voice is literally the book's main subject matter—as I believe it to be in Twain's book.

LM: What you're saying would at first seem to contrast with the work you did for the *Dictionary of Afro-American Slang*, which distinguishes Afro-American idioms and voice from their English equivalent. I'm reminded of the remarks made by certain black writers to the effect that, "English is my enemy." Obviously having someone like Twain be such a strong influence indicates that you don't personally feel the sense that, as a black American author, you have to be constantly working "against" the English language—the language of oppression, and so on?

CM: My interest in this area doesn't really conflict with my appreciation of mainstream American idioms. What black people speak is actually very much in the mainstream of American speech. Not only is it not separate, it actually informs American speech in all sorts of ways. You can even argue that it's the nucleus of American speech, one of its roots. Black speech, as a matter of fact, influences Huck Finn's voice, as well. The history of the American language can't be separated from black speech. It's just *been there* all along, so intrinsic to American speech that there's no conflict whatsoever.

JK: Has black slang changed much in the last fifteen years?

CM: Absolutely, especially with all the new slang that's been emerging out of these new subcultures—hip-hop, rap, and so on. I've compiled thousands of words and phrases that have been coined or just surfaced in the last ten years. I find them in different places and not necessarily print sources—magazines, journals, and novels, but also rock videos, songs, films, street talk.

LM: In the courses I teach in rock music I use rap as a way of talking about the role that language has played in black communities and the admiration for the person that can speak well. This whole tradition of "rapping" and "dissing"—improvised contests to see who can use language most skillfully—has always been there in black culture.

CM: The saying always was, "He's well spoken. He's got a preacher's voice. That boy's gonna grow up to be a preacher, he's so well spoken." [laughs]

LM: You were immersed in blues and jazz, growing up. You lived in Chicago in the late fifties and early sixties, when the music scene there was really happening. Muddy Waters, and so on. That scene obviously had a strong impact on your work, just as it did for so many others, white guys like Kerouac, Coover, Sukenick, and Federman, as well as black writers.

Is rap going to have a similarly liberating effect or influence on young black writers today?

CM: It's already happening. I can see the evidence of rap running through a lot of the works of the younger writers I included in *Calling the Wind: Twentieth Century African-American Short Stories.*

LM: Jazz, blues, and rap are distinctly black art forms that use black vernacular, the idioms you hear out on the streets, in the ghetto, and so on, as well as having formal roots in earlier folk arts. But at least in this century, you've also got all these white musicians just waiting to "borrow" features of these forms and turn them into something more "refined" that white audiences will relate to (and purchase). You've also got brilliant, formally innovative black artists like Charlie Parker, Ornette Coleman, Jimi Hendrix, Prince, who keep pushing things to the next level, practically reinventing the forms, maybe to stay ahead of the white guys.

CM: Yes, although I personally have trouble with the concept of artistic "refinement" whenever this winds up moving so far in certain directions that it becomes inaccessible to people. You can see this in the social history of jazz in particular—the way it's become institutionalized and removed from our lives. Jazz has its roots in the folk tradition—in blues and even going back beyond blues. When you follow its evolution, you see a progression of refinement that removes it from everyday accessibility. After a while, it becomes an acquired taste; in order to really hear what's going on, you have to be educated in classical music, and it becomes something you have to learn to appreciate. Pretty soon you find yourself putting on a tux when you want to go listen to it, rather than having it as part of your daily life, the way it should be, even if it is highfalutin music.

LM: You began your career apparently thinking you were going to be a painter—you were at the Chicago Art Institute for a while, and so on. Did this background in the visual arts have any lasting impact on your literary sensibility?

CM: No question about it. I was drawn to painting in the first place because I'm a visual thinker, which isn't something that's going to disappear later on when you're writing.

JK: Who were some of the writers and other artists who had a significant impact on your literary sensibility early on?

CM: Van Gogh and Cézanne among the painters. Gertrude Stein, Jean Toomer, Rimbaud, Henry Miller, D. H. Lawrence, Richard Wright, Radiguet, and Genet among fiction writers. Bud Powell has to be mentioned here somewhere as well.

JK: What do you mean when you say you're a "visual thinker"?

CM: I remember things better visually than verbally. I make connections between things more on the basis of visual associations than verbal or logical ones. If you tell me your name, I may not hear it as well as I can see it.

JK: How does your being a visual thinker relate to writing fiction versus poetry? Most people would say that in poetry you think more in terms of images, visual things.

CM: That's true, creating poetry is more directly involved with images. But this isn't an either/or thing. I often try to get those same kinds of images in my writing of fiction.

JK: Do you find any differences in the creative process involved in writing poetry versus fiction?

CM: There are, of course. When you're writing a poem you're concentrating on pushing language in certain directions that you don't ordinarily travel in when you're writing fiction. I try to use the language of poetry when I'm writing a novel, but only up to a certain point. You don't want to push things so far that your material becomes inaccessible as a story.

LM: What "poetic qualities" are you looking for in your fiction writing?

CM: Mostly a certain lyrical quality. Tone, pace, cadence, the music of speech. This isn't true in every case—there are things I attempt in fiction that don't lend themselves too well to a lyrical treatment. That's okay. I don't need to do the same thing over and over. But overall when my fiction is at its best, it usually has a kind of lyrical quality. I think Annie Eliza's voice, for example, has a kind of lyrical quality. Even though her voice seemed familiar to me, it wasn't something I thought of as being my private voice, which meant that the lyrical, poetic quality was something I had to consciously think of while writing.

LM: You've said that you think of some of your recent stories as being prose poems really; you've also said that sometimes some of your poems wind up being stories. When you start out writing something, how clear is it that something is going to be a story or a poem? What's the basis of this judgment?

CM: I don't always immediately know. *Usually* I do, because there's a different engagement involved in writing poems versus fiction. This gets even more complicated when you factor in other kinds of writing I do. For example, *Surfaces and Masks* started off as a journal I was keeping when we were living in Venice. Somehow these entries kept resisting being turned into prose, so after a very short time I let them come out in terms of lines. I realized that something about the material needed to be rendered in terms of measure, meter, and stanza breaks rather than in journal entry form.

LM: Is there any actual difference between the narrative voice you create in your fiction versus the one in your poetry?

CM: Formally, yes, and in the classroom I try to make those distinctions because I don't want to confuse students. But for all practical purposes, I don't separate things out like that. In fact, I'm usually trying to *bridge the two* by informing the narrative possibility with a lyrical quality.

LM: When an interviewer once said that audiences tended to have difficulty with even relatively mild disjunctures in fiction that they would readily accept in poetry, you made an interesting point about audience acceptance of truly radical narrative structures in film. Can't fiction writers take more chances today precisely because readers are now used to dealing with film and TV shows based on the principle of juxtaposition and montage?

CM: The problem is that audiences today tolerate a lot less disjuncture in fiction than they do with other art forms. People were much more willing to accept innovations in film even as early as the twenties. Audiences had no trouble with any of the stylistic innovations introduced by Chaplin or Buster Keaton. Jump cuts, leaps, animation, and all that camera technology stuff—they all made perfect sense to audiences. Whereas when you try out something analogous in a novel, you're somehow put aside as unreadable, inaccessible. Narrative or fictive conventions have had a longer time to rigidify, so readers have more difficulty when somebody is doing something different with narrative material; whereas with film or rock videos or whatever, the medium is so new that its audience just accepts the idea that its conventions are more fluid.

JK: Why didn't the radical experimentation of work written by your generation of postmodernist fiction writers help break down these readerly expectations?

CM: What happened is that the spirit of radical experimentalism and innovation gradually mellowed out during the seventies and eighties and are now finding their way into the mainstream of American writing. That's true of a lot of other things about the sixties that have filtered into our daily lives without our being aware of it. Certainly that's true of fiction. The radical fiction that writers like Barthelme, for example, were doing in the sixties was so radical in nature that it had to affect later writers. Subliminally their influences are there throughout just about the whole spectrum of American fiction today—so much so that we don't notice that they're present in a more diffuse way in the culture and in American fiction writing. This summer I read two hundred novels for the National Book Award and I can see the innovation there. It's more muted today than it was back when I was starting out as a writer, but it's there nevertheless. I remember a story about a couple of guys who are waiting down beneath a precipice to shoot a lion. A couple of lions are up above them, not knowing the men are down there, and the guys can't move, of course, because the lions might come down on them. What does the writer do with this situation? At the end of the story he says: "Well, I've given you this dramatic situation, and I hope that's enough. I mean, what more do I need to do? This is it, this is life!"

LM: I agree that the sixties brand of radical experimentalism has had a pervasive effect on recent writing, but there are also some crucial differences. Part of this just has to do with changes in the world today, especially the expansion of the media culture, the greater bombardment that everyone today is subjected to, the greater facility with which everything can be reproduced, reified, commodified. This changes the whole function of innovation: "the new" becomes merely another commodified style rather than having any social or aesthetic impact.

CM: Part of what's new is the constantly changing technical means by which literature is being made and consumed. I'm thinking of computer network fiction. Hypertexts. The speed which new technologies erode is equally staggering. The minute I upgrade my computer it's already obsolete. So, what's new? "New" in the Ezra Pound sense no longer stands still, even for a moment. And at the same time—even with all our questing for the self-directed technologies—the younger generation of writers seem to be desperately reaching back for the homespun, the tried and tested formulas of the past, despite the innovations they've absorbed. And I see all of this as exciting and very promising.

LM: In the interview that appeared in *Finding the Words*, you argued that trying to create the distinction between poetry and prose turns out to be a trap and that "a book that was written a hundred years ago becomes not only a literary experience when you read it, it's like a historical experience because the language is not our language anymore . . . literature is unlike any other art form because it has the problem of language as its material, and also the problem of our perception which is always gouged out of this thing we call reality" (Bunge, 57). You seem to be making a distinction between perception and language, and then locating literature's uniqueness as having to do with the fact that since its "materials"—language—change over time, it necessarily always has this "problem of language." But isn't this true of other art forms as well? For instance, in painting don't you find changes in perception also affecting the "materials" it's created out of? If you look at impressionist paintings (which I know you love), you can see artists registering these sorts of changes. In other words, is literature really so unique in its ongoing concern with the elements that produce meaning in it?

CM: Literature is unlike the other arts. If we're talking about oral storytelling—the essence of literature—we're talking about pure language. Naturally it's going to be limited to those who can speak and understand it. And it's also always evolving in ways that lines and colors (in painting) and stone (in sculpture) are not. Those materials evolve in their own very different ways and aren't subject to the constant practical communication uses language is subject to. A word's purity can be destroyed in a way that the color yellow, theoretically, cannot.

JK: Do you see any connection between your painting and your writing, beyond your having such a visual imagination? Are there any formal issues or problems that you found yourself being drawn to early on in your painting that you took up in your fiction as well? It would seem that painters have to be reflexively concerned with the materials they're using in a way that's analogous to the reflexive concerns you were dealing with so much in your early novels.

CM: The reflexive "problem" all writers have to face is that the materials fiction is created out of—that is, *words*, language—"mean something" in the sense of making references to the outside world. That's why I feel these materials are so different from those used for painting and sculpture. Colors and textures and shapes in these other forms don't "refer" to anything. The same is true for dance, of course, which has no "material" except the body—and the body isn't really operating in the same way as paint, texture, and color do in painting, or the way language does for literature. With dance you have space defined by the presence of the body.

LM: I was really struck with a passage in *My Amputations* where your narrator says: "He came to realize he wanted it all flat, or upright and permanent like Cubism. Like things, surfaces." Did that express what you're aiming for when you're writing? Why did he want it this way?

CM: He wants it flat like cubism because in art you control, define, and assign meaning to things otherwise swept along in the tide of time and space. In cubism, he would be able to use all sides of the experience, stop, weigh it. Think about it. Reflect on it. Cubism is just a term to refer to an attempt to gain control of the shape of his life and to give it meaning.

JK: An unusual formal feature of *My Amputations* is the way prose is presented almost as physical objects—"blocks" of materials that aren't related the way that paragraphs or other organizing principles are in linear narratives. This seems like it might be related to the visual orientation of your imagination.

CM: That's because I literally tend to "see" my books this way. In the case of *My Amputations*, I remember the very day the book came to me. Pamela and I were walking up a hill to the Jewish cemetery in Nice, and I said, "I'm going to write a book in blocks of prose. Just panels. Not paragraphs." The only thing I needed to know at that point was that this book had to be a book composed in blocks or in panels.

JK: "Such Was the Season" is from Jean Toomer. What's involved for you in selecting titles for your works?

CM: Sleeping on it seems to work best for me. I let it be the last thought before I fall off to sleep, and by the time I wake up the title will have taken care of itself. I always have a title when I'm working on something, although I don't always end up using it. I grabbed "My Amputations," for example, somewhere along the way in the middle of the book. The same was true with "Such Was the Season," which was called "Juneboy" for a while; then I realized that wasn't a good title since it's not June-boy's story at all, which made me start shopping around for another title until I was eventually led to "Such Was the Season."

LM: Your early novels, *All-Night Visitors* and *NO*, dealt obsessively and relentlessly with sex (which maybe isn't a strange preoccupation for a young writer) but also with *death*, both individually and the way it connects with sexuality. How do you explain that fascination?

CM: Thank you for bringing that up. When people talk about those two books they always mention the sex but they forget the death. [Laughter.] But is there anything particularly unusual about my preoccupation with death? In fact, this preoccupation with sex and death is probably more of a young man's thought or activity, than it is for an older person who's had a chance to adjust after the initial shock. If they're alert at all to what's up, young men are inevitably very interested in sex. That typically comes first, followed a bit later when they're around twenty-one by the shocking news that they're going to pass on. It may take five or six years for the shock to wear off. Death really is one of the biggest discoveries you ever make in your life: "My God, I'm going to die!" That news can kick your ass for quite a while until you get used to it.

LM: Were there any more abstract sources for your interest in the relationship of sex and death—had you been reading Freud early on, for example?

CM: Yes, I had read widely in psychology when I was young. There's no escaping Freudian thought for any of us in the twentieth century, certainly not for our generation. I was definitely aware of that as a young man but I was also interested in trying to define another kind of self outside those kinds of definitions. But all that sex-death material was gut-level stuff that came not from anything I had read but out of my own personal reaction to getting the news. I honestly wasn't consciously putting much of *anything* into those early books. Beyond wanting to keep the energy level up, I was just including whatever bebopped into my head and hoping for the best.

LM: I gather, though, that you find yourself incorporating intellectual interests into your works more than earlier. Does this interfere with keeping your creative energy level up?

CM: Maintaining that early energy level is just as hard to sustain as the creative recklessness we just talked about. And, yeah, I'm reluctant to try and write out of areas that don't have any experiential, gut-level basis to them. So I consciously try to keep my intellectual interests out of my writing. I've found that those things interfere with my writing rather than help.

LM: Tell us a bit about the circumstances surrounding the publication of *All-Night Visitors*. The story goes that Girodias forced you to edit (or hatchet) the book, the result being that all the sex was left in but much of the background materials were jettisoned. Being edited that way certainly made your book have a very peculiar feel to it. You must have been disappointed in the way your book was cut, but weren't there some benefits that came of this? The cuts probably made it look more radically experimental than it would have if the full version had been published.

CM: Well, it's important to note that since I did all the revisions myself, I had some control over the end result. This wasn't a matter of having somebody else go through my book and having no input on what happened. I thought about it and decided I wanted the book published enough so that I was willing to do what they were asking, and then I tried to edit the book in such a way so that it would still be something I could live with.

LM: You mentioned earlier that your early works seemed to feed off your own personal sense of fragmentation. I'm wondering about the "creative problems" that being in a more secure personal position pose. Many of the writers I've interviewed admit that they were rather displaced people when they were younger—and that this in a sense helped them gather material for their works, the incoherence of their daily lives and the kind of experiences that they were having fed into their work. But what happens when you find yourself a more stable person? Can *that* fuel your imagination as much as the earlier situation? Or can you simply "recall" this earlier point in your life and feed off of that?

CM: You're describing something that most writers don't want to admit (or talk about at all!) but that affects almost any artist who does a significant amount of early work living on the margins, somehow, of success. In my own case, becoming a university professor, having a stable relationship with Pamela and a more secure sense of myself—these things have placed me in a radically different life-style and personal situation than what I was in when I started out writing. Of course, these changes have been enormously beneficial to me from a purely personal standpoint, but almost inevitably they are also going to present creative challenges. What happens is that you sacrifice some things—certain "negative" emotional energies that you can sometimes channel into your work, maybe a kind of direct empathy and contact with situations and people you don't encounter later on, or a kind of attitude like, "Since I'm out there on the margins, I'm going to do this really wild stuff that seems right to me, and fuck the establishment!" In other words, there's frequently all sorts of frustrations, financial and personal difficulties going on in the lives of many artists that can produce a positive, exciting sense of creative recklessness and originality in their work (though it's only fair to add here that probably *most of the time* these circumstances wind up just destroying the artist). If you do manage to make worthwhile art out of this situation and gain some recognition, that youthful sense of recklessness and energy will almost inevitably be sacrificed; but hopefully those sacrifices are offset by the other things you've gained—financial security, medical care, that whole range of middle-class comforts. Sometimes I don't think people are really fair about this with artists. You wind up being put on the defensive when "The Good Life" finally appears one day, miraculously it seems after everything that's come before. It's as if the audience is pissed off because now they're not going to be given their vicarious share of pain and anger and humiliation any more.

Still, there's no question that lessening your anxieties and gaining these middle-class comforts do wind up having an impact on your work. I know I'm not as adventurous as I used to be—or let's say that being adventurous doesn't come as "naturally" as it did when I started out. I have to work harder to find innovations, I have to struggle against being content with what's familiar or the experimental approaches I've already used. Having a lot more experience in doing innovative work limits your options. I do know that I have to work harder to achieve the kind of genuine recklessness that came as second nature to me when I was younger. I remember sitting at my desk when I was twenty-five, banging the typewriter, throwing the carriage bar, radio going on this side, the window open, the neighbor beating their children. I was *in that world*, watching and listening and writing and getting the sounds of that world into my work. Not thinking about it, just letting whatever was in my soul come pouring out on the page. Well, I can't do that anymore. What I can do, though, is still try to be daring. I still find myself sitting down to write something (now at the computer terminal rather than the manual typewriter I used to peck away on) and feel myself pushing for some of that sense of recklessness I used to inhabit, come on, come on, push for it! Devil may care, get it in there!

In terms of creativity the good side to all this is that I don't think you ever completely lose touch with whatever it was that drove you to do what you did earlier on. Or at least if you want to keep it bad enough, you don't have to lose it. For instance, I think this six-hundred-page novel I've been recently working on has some of that craziness. It's just that now you've got to want it, whereas earlier it was just in the air, all around you, something you didn't have to grab because it was the air you were breathing.

Photograph courtesy of the author

Sad Jazz
An Interview with Derek Pell

Larry McCaffery

I still find Sade's cruel wisdom a comfort, his rancor a delight, and his penetrating insight into right and wrong a blessing
— "The Elements of Style"

One of the great undiscovered treasures of the "Art-Lit" scene in America, Derek Pell has also probably done more than any other artist to keep satire alive as a serious literary endeavor. Claims regarding Pell's "undiscovered" status need to be qualified, however, since in the late seventies he did enjoy a brief period of near-celebrity (and near-financial solvency) among mainstream audiences when his *Doktor Bey* collage books were being published by commercial houses and shorter works were regularly appearing in mainstream publications such as *Playboy*, *National Lampoon*, *The New York Times Magazine*, and *Screw*.

Since that period of relative prosperity, Pell has attracted little serious critical attention despite continuing to publish widely in literary journals both in the United States and abroad, and having published two highly original book-length works: *Assassination Rhapsody* (1989), a deconstructive series of hilarious and eerie textual transformations based on the Warren Commission Report; and *X-Texts* (1994), a collection of satirical pornographic pieces.

At least part of the reason for Pell's relative anonymity is that many of his best works—which include poems, fictions, collages-and-texts, book objects, mail art, and numerous unclassifiable "things"—have appeared

under the names of pseudonyms and alter egos. These disguises—
notably Doktor Bey and Norman Conquest—have been adopted by Pell
in part to mock the notion of authorial originality but also to give the
different personalities in his imagination a means of expressing themselves. The most important of these early pseudonyms was Bey, the mysterious scholar who was born simultaneously in New York and Tibet in
1877 and who is the alleged author of the wildly comic, satirical *Doktor Bey* series—*Doktor Bey's Suicide Guidebook* (1977), *Doktor Bey's Bedside
Bug Book* (1978), *Doktor Bey's Handbook of Strange Sex* (1978), *Doktor Bey's
Book of Brats* (1979), and *Doktor Bey's Book of the Dead* (1981). Using scissors and glue for his cut-and-paste techniques (Pell did not begin using
a computer to develop his illustrations until around 1991), Pell added
his own irreverent and darkly comic texts to illustrations snipped out
of nineteenth-century magazines and medical books and reconfigured
in new contexts. Full of nonsense, wordplay, absurdist humor, sick humor, and visual puns, the *Doktor Bey* books systematically exposed and
gleefully mocked the absurdities of American culture's attitudes toward
death, sex, war, and politics.

The visually oriented works created by Pell's alter ego Norman Conquest have recently been receiving wider and more favorable notice
than anything Pell himself has been doing. Like Pell, Conquest dropped
out of Chicago's Art Institute to open an activist bookshop in Massachusetts, where he first began experimenting with verbal-visual works.
In the eighties, he moved with Pell to Los Angeles and became a pro-
ponent of correspondence art, creating Fluxus-like multiples and editing the magazine *Letter Bomb*. His notorious mail-art performance "The
Buck Stamped Here" (in which Conquest applied postage to a dollar
bill, rubber-stamped it, and mailed it to a friend in New York) got him in
trouble with the FBI for "defacing U.S. currency." Conquest responded
to FBI charges that he was defacing U.S. currency by commemorating
his original act in a mixed-media work featuring a defaced dollar bill
and a huge color facsimile of the original bill affixed to a stolen post
office poster.

In 1989 Conquest founded the international anticensorship art collective *Beuyscouts of Amerika*. His early scout-inspired work, a matchbook
whose stems comprised the American flag, created considerable controversy in Soho and put the collective on the map. His conceptual works,
book objects, multiples of political satire, and collage-text manipulations have been exhibited widely (several were also recently chosen for
the permanent collection of the Museum of Modern Art). Examples
of some of Conquest's recent work include postcard art, subtly altered
Norman Rockwell illustrations, decals (Uncle Sam pointing a finger and
saying "Clean Up Your Art"; the Good Helmskeeping Seal outlined by

"No Fag Art or Blasphemy; Prison Terms for Offensive Art"), book objects such as "3-de Sade" (a bloodstained bound copy of *Justine* with a large hook extending from it, suitable for a wall display), and "art products" like *Foucault-Text*, which punningly conjoins textual materials by the renowned French theoretician with ad copy for sanitary napkins. Since 1991 Conquest has been using advanced computer technology (an area Pell has curiously remained largely uninterested in) to explore "potential images," hypertext, and "cyberart."

Of Pell's works—which at this point are fairly clearly distinguished from Conquest's by their textual (that is, nonvisual) orientation—the book that is probably best known is *Assassination Rhapsody*. Functioning almost as a minimalist version of Don DeLillo's maximal treatment of the fateful intersection of Lee Harvey Oswald and JFK, *Rhapsody* is a collection of different sorts of texts and collages based on the Warren Commission Report. A listing of a few examples suggests the remarkable range of formal methods and discourses employed by Pell and his alter egos: lipograms ("The Magic Bullet"), illustrations ("A Bullet-Theory Poem"), a biography of Lee Harvey Oswald composed of a sequence of brief snatches of autobiographical information ("Oswald appears to have taken with him a Spanish-English dictionary") linked to seemingly irrelevant or banal drawings (for example, a snowman holding a branch),[1] and an appendix of "Commission Exhibits" (visuals include a composite of ears, mysterious maps and photographs, and a page entitled "Oswald's Underworld Ties" that displays bow ties, silk ties, and so on). But the greatest triumphs of *Rhapsody* are Pell's deconstructive versions of actual textual materials drawn from the Commission Report. Here, in texts such as "The Revolver," "The Nature of the Shots," and "The Long and Bulky Package of Dreams," Pell subjects materials from the original report to various mechanical methods of transformation associated with artists like Raymond Roussel and the OuLiPo group (both greatly admired by Pell). The result is a series of wondrously crazed new texts that brilliantly and hilariously display the labyrinthine meanderings, pseudo logic, misplaced specificity, and rhetorical posturing that ultimately make the Warren Commission Report useless in terms of solving the mystery of JFK's death. What Pell's small volume demonstrates better than any other recent book, however, is that precisely the qualities that rendered the Commission Report useless in one sense are also responsible for making it the quintessential postmodern document of our era.

---

1. Most readers are able to "find" connections between the illustrations and the text, but in fact these accompanying images were originally done by Henri Zo, who is best known for illustrating the works of Raymond Roussel.

Pell's work, then, is "refined" not in the usual sense of "sophistica-
tion" and "maturity" (features that Pell, like Rimbaud, the dadaists and
surrealists, and his chief avatar, Alfred Jarry, was highly skeptical of) but
in a manner that might be termed "regressively refined." That is, his aesthetic strategies frequently seem deliberately designed to make his works
seem *less* mature, more aggressively childlike in their rejection of traditional notions of "authority" and "seriousness," more openly irrational
and playful. But it should be stressed that these aesthetic strategies have
more than mere parodic intent; rather, the silliness, lunacy, surrealism,
and parodic impulses found in Pell's best works are aspects of a fiercely
moralistic, darkly humorous, and ultimately deeply *pessimistic* personal
vision—a gaze (often an exaggerated version of the "male gaze") that
unmasks a wide range of social and literary hypocrisies and pretensions.
This blend of aesthetic anarchy, black humor, social commentary, and irreverence establishes Pell as currently the most wickedly funny writer in
America—a country that suddenly seems to have lost its sense of humor.

*   *   *

Derek Pell: Selected Bibliography

Books of Fiction, Collections, and Collage-and-Text Books

Advantages of Being a Saint. New York: H. P. Oliver Books, 1970.
Doktor Bey's Suicide Guidebook. New York: Dodd, Mead, 1977.
Doktor Bey's Bedside Bug Book. New York: Harcourt Brace Jovanovich, 1978.
Doktor Bey's Handbook of Strange Sex. New York: Avon, 1978.
Scar Mirror. Oak Park, IL: Cat's Pajamas Press, 1978.
Brother Spencer Goes to Hell. Union City, CA: The Fault, 1979.
Doktor Bey's Book of Brats. New York: Avon, 1979.
Doktor Bey's Book of the Dead. New York: Avon, 1981.
Expurgations. London: Bizarre Angel Books, 1982.
Morbid Curiosities. London: Jonathan Cape, 1983.
Assassination Rhapsody. Brooklyn, NY: Semiotext[e], 1989.
X-Texts. Brooklyn, NY: Autonomedia, 1994.
The Marquis de Sade's Elements of Style. San Francisco: Permeable Press, 1996.

Poetry Collections

Frozen Sunlight. Westport, CT: Black Journal Books, 1968.
Uncle Sam. Westport, CT: Black Journal Books, 1968.
Apple Meat. Vineyard Haven, MA: Not Guilty Press, 1969.
The Invention of Style. New York: Not Guilty Press, 1978.

Illustrations for Books

Cover art for *Living in the Boneyard*, by John Oliver Simon. Oak Park, IL: Cat's Pajamas Press, 1975.
Cover art for *Hojo Supreme*, by Bernie Bever. Oak Park, IL: Cat's Pajamas Press, 1978.
True Tiny Tales of Terror (with Ann Hodgman). New York: Perigee Books, 1982.

Uncollected Stories, Poems, Text-and-Collage, Photographs, Anthology
Appearances, Miscellaneous

Three poems. *Pulse* 1, 1 (1967).
"Fuck This War Up the Ass." concrete poem. *Kick Ass* (Suffolk, England) 1, 3 (1968): 23–24.
Two photographs. *Village Voice*, 12 July 1973, p. 1.
"Yo, Mo!" Photograph. *Rolling Stone*, 30 August 1973, 32.
"Thirteen Things You've Forgotten about Watergate." Nonfiction. *Crawdaddy*, November 1973, pp. 35–39.
"Surrender." *Village Voice*, 28 April 1975.
"The Future of Meat." Poem. *Not Guilty!* 1 (1975).
Three photographs. *Nexus* (Spring 1975): 38–39.
"Blood Bank." In *New Voices Anthology #5*, ed. Don Fried, 277–79. New Paltz, NY: N.p., 1976.
"Car Crash." *Coldspring Journal* 10 (1976): 3.
"The Riddle of the Universe." *Mid-Atlantic Review* 1, 4 (1976).
"My Secret Life with Father." Text. *The Agent* (Paris) (1976): 21–23.
"Peeping Toms." Photograph. *New York Times Magazine*, 6 March 1977.
"Cartoon Sagas #42." Poem. *Iron* (England) 27 (1979): 16.
"The Day Judge Crater Came Out of the Linen Closet." Story. *Strange Faeces* 20 (1980): 9–12.
"Fuck Death Dummy-Humping Competition." *Newrite* 1, 1 (1980).
"Judge Crater Goes to the Seashore." Short story. *Androgyne* 6 (1980): 34–39.
"Position of Parts." Text. *Not Guilty!* 5/6 (1980): 27.
"A Season Gone." Essay. *Bridgehampton Sun*, 17 September 1980, p. 9.
"Don't Wake Rimbaud." Poem. *Telephone* 17 (1981): 58–61.
"Factory to You." Collage. *Zone* 8 (1981): 18.
"The History of Sex #2." *Newrite* 2, 1 (1981).
"How to Dress When Visiting." Text. *Only Paper Today* 7, 10 (1981): 20–23.
"Physiognomical Readings." Text and drawings. *Caprice* (London) 3 (1981).
"Reading for a Beautiful Bosom." *Caprice* (London) 3 (1981).
"Thérèse and Isabelle." Text. *Fly by Night* 1, 1 (1981): 29–30.
"The Erotic Adventures of Zippy McCode." *Best of Screw* 30 (1982).
"The Socratic Hustle." Text and drawings. *Benzene* 5/6 (1982): 83.
Collage. *Times Literary Supplement* 4, 207 (1983).
"Endangered Beasties." *Lightworks* 16 (1983): 28–31.
"Judge Crater on the Moon." Story. *Bizarre Angel* (London) 4 (1983): 18–21.
"A Surname Saga." Text. *Word Ways: The Journal of Recreational Linguistics* 16, 1 (1983): 11–14.
"Literary Physiognomy of the Sixteenth Century." Text and collage. *London Review of Books* 5, 24 (1984): 11.

"Doktor Bey's Carnal Freak Show." *National Lampoon,* January 1985, pp. 70–73.
"Night of the Living ISMS." Text. *L.A. Weekly* 7, 49 (1985).
Sound-text. *The Fred* 1, 5 (1985): 64–68.
"More Joy of Celibacy." Text and photos. *National Lampoon,* October 1986.
"The Topsy-Turvy World of Edward Hopper." Text. *Fiction International* 17, 1 (1987): 60–61.
Collage. *Egad* (1988): 8, 55–57.
"Madeleine's Answer, An Erotic Lipogram." *Libido: The Journal of Sex and Sensibility* 1, 2 (Winter 1988): 28–31, 66.
"The Joy of Phone-Sex." Text and drawings. *The North* (Yorkshire, England) 6 (1989).
Three texts. *Paragraph* (Fall/Winter, 1988): 18–20.
"Stillbirth." In *The Poets' Encyclopedia,* ed. Michael Andre, 254. New York: Unmuzzled Ox Editions, 1979.
"Dr. Bofwad's Secret Manor." Text and collages. *Playboy,* November 1979, pp. 167–69.
"The Joy of Celibacy." Text and collages. *Playboy,* March 1981, pp. 115–17.
"The Evolution of the Moral Majority." Text and collages. *Playboy,* September 1981, pp. 137–39.
"The Joy of Necrophilia." Text and collages. *Screw,* 20 January 1986.
"Four Short Works by New Women Writers." *National Lampoon,* March 1986, 11.
"Funding for Godot." Text. *Playboy,* March 1986, p. 19.
"The Films of Annie Sprinkle." Text. *National Lampoon,* August 1986, 44–47.
"The Surgeon General's Guide to Safe Sex." Text and collages. *Screw,* 20 June 1988, pp. 9–11.
"Emmanuelle, A Definitive Text." *Cake* 2, 1 (1988): 10–12.
"Gestures of Arousal." Poem. *Rampike* 6, 3 (1988): 69.
"The Old Farmer's Aphabetum Graecum." *ZYZZYVA* 4, 1 (1988): 28.
"Two Drawings." *Atticus Review* (Winter, 1988).
"Eight Adult Males." Text and drawings. *Stiffled Yawn* 2 (1993).
"The Elements of Style." In *Avant-Pop: Fiction for a Daydream Nation,* ed. Larry McCaffery, 49–81. Normal, IL: Black Ice Books, 1993.
"No Coitus." *Black Ice* 10 (1993): 68.

Books as Norman Conquest

Interiors: A Book of Very Clean Rooms. Tokyo: Gallery 612, 1986.
A Beginner's Guide to Art Deconstruction. San Francisco: Permeable Press, 1995.
Extremely Weird Republicans. San Francisco: Permeable Press, 1995.
Straight Razor (with Harold Jaffe). Normal, IL: Black Ice Books, 1995.
By Any Means. San Diego: Hob Press, 1996.

Contributions to Journals, Books, and Miscellaneous Publications as Norman Conquest

"Groupie." Text. *Starscrewer* (Montgnac, France) 7 (1974).
Collage. *Brain Cell* (Moriguchi City, Japan) 30 (1986): 16.
Collage. *The Brain Factory* (Forte dei Marmi, Italy) (1986): 32.
Collage. *Smile Art* (Minden, West Germany) 4 (1986).

"Mailart Marriage to Janet-Janet." Text. *Schism* 13 (1986).
"Postal Boxes and Their Generic Names." Text and drawings. *Lightworks* 18 (1986): 53–56.
"Aviary." Sound recordings. *Birds*, ed. Kalus Groh. Edewecht, West Germany: Audio Editions Ammerland, 1987.
Cover art. *Baby Boom* 14 (1988).
"The Assassin's Alphabet." *Global Tapestry* 20 (1988): 57.
"Autobiography." *Atticus Review* 17 (Summer 1989).
Collages (video). *Arise: The Subgenius Video.* Dallas, Texas, 1989.
Collages. *Stark Fist of Removal* 7, 43 (1991): 3, 6.
Collages. *Stark Fist of Removal* 17, 41/42 (1989): 7, 32, 82, 112.
Anticensorship decals. *Umbrella* 13, 1 (1990): 32, 35.
"3-de Sade." *Art Papers* 14, 3 (1990): 37.
Three illustrations. *Bakunin* 1, 3. (1990): 10, 15, 20.
"Generic Protest." Postcard. New York: Beuyscout Editions, 1992.
"Good Helmskeeping." Decals and interview. *Interview*, July 1990, p. 36.
"Necroglyphics." Collage. *Exquisite Corpse* 8, 5 (1990): 3.
"René Magritte's Alphabet." *Fiction International* 19, 1 (1990): 11.
Two reproductions. *Central Park* 19/20 (1991): 10, 197.
Frontis illustration. *Asylum* 7, 3/4 (1992).
"Autobiography." *Atticus Review* 17 (1992).
"This is Not Magritte." Drawing. *On the Bus* 5, 2 (1993): 226.
"Eight Adult Males." Text and drawings. *Stiffled Yawn* 2 (1993).
Illustration. *Witness: Special American Humor Issue* 7, 2 (1993): 62.
"Self-Portrait." Collage/drawing. In *The Politics of Everyday Fear*, ed. Brian Massumi, 112. Minneapolis: University of Minnesota Press, 1993.
Cover art. *Fiction International* 26 (1994).
Cover art. *Nobodaddies* 1, 1 (1994).
"The Lesson." Collage. *Fiction International* 26 (1994): 131.

Reviews, Essays, and Commentary about Pell's Work

Connolly, Kevin. "New Fiction." Review of *Assassination Rhapsody. What!Contemporary Writing and Ideas* 23 (July/August 1990): 43–44.
"Derek Pell" (unsigned entry). In *Encyclopedia of Short Fiction*, ed. Walton Beacham, vol. 7. Salem, CA: Salem Press, 1981.
Franklin, Penny. "Conversation with an Absurdist." *Hamptons Magazine*, 23 June 1983, pp. 6–7, 14.
Greco, Stephen. "Interview with Conquest." *Interview*, July 1990, p. 36.
McCaffery, Larry. "The Velvet Rims of Derek Pell's *X-Textual* 'Hot Rod.'" Introduction to Pell's *X-Texts*, 2–9. Brooklyn, NY: Autonomedia, 1994.

* * *

LARRY MCCAFFERY: Your work is often either directly collaborative in nature (as with all those obscure nineteenth-century artists you jam with in your text-and-visual collage works) or otherwise filtered through other personas, pseudonyms, manipulations of public texts, public images. Of course there's a number of interesting and attractive aesthetic aspects to collaborative approaches, but one thing it seems to do in particular is (pardon my French) "deconstruct" or dismantle traditional notions of artistic originality, identity, authorial intention, and so on. Indeed, collaboration seems to me to be one of the defining features of postmodernism at this point—you find it being practiced by most of the postmodern writers I like (people as varied as Vollmann, Coover, Acker, Sukenick, Daitch, and Barth) as well as by musicians like John Zorn, Hal Willner, and the Butthole Surfers.

DEREK PELL: I can't speak for anybody but myself (and I have a hard time doing that), but I enjoy the process of lifting materials out of the proverbial shitcan where they're destined to be forgotten and reconstituting them into collaborations that give them new life. In that sense, I see what I'm doing as being "reconstructive" rather than "deconstructive." I'm also very interested in the notion of removing myself as an author, dissolving myself into anonymity. Ultimately we could evolve to the point where artists wouldn't sign their paintings, so people would go into galleries (if there are still galleries) and choose works they actually like rather than for the artist's name. Books could also be published anonymously—an attractive idea. Of course, I have already achieved perfect anonymity without even striving for it. But what does "originality" really mean today, anyway? I certainly don't know. Maybe that's the postmodern dilemma. The Italian artist Nannucci addressed this question by reproducing a type-designer's motto: "Always strive to find an interesting *variation*." What interests me as an artist is finding new variations, so that what you do becomes new by the context you've chosen. Everything is a variation of something else, so why disguise this when you're creating art? The surrealists were doing something like this. Bringing together two objects that didn't go together, so that they appear in a new context, created an interaction that produced the third reality—"sur-reality"—owing its existence to something outside both collaborators.

LM: In *The Invention of Style*, you say, "In the future, or eventually if brave, we move on to a future without walls only windows." That sounds almost like an aesthetic manifesto.

DP: There are many different ways to talk about aesthetics in my work. I'm not personally comfortable with a lot of the subjects I've dealt with—death, for example. Nobody is comfortable with death except morticians. It should be obvious from my books that I don't have an enormously optimistic outlook about a lot of things. My basic view is that the world is a terrifying place. There's a lot of *rage* in my work that comes from very basic things: this sense of being alive but not having any answers to the meaning of existence; the anger inherent in whatever religious upbringing I was supposed to have had that I didn't respond to. Being alone in the world can be a very terrifying situation. My response to this, at least in my work, has often been that of rage and satire. I'm also a very political person, and I've always viewed my writing as a means to express my outrage at society and all governments.

LM: And yet for all of your anger and pessimism, there's something optimistic about your view that forcing people to confront disturbing things can be a positive, liberating experience. This method also seems more effective (and certainly more interesting) than writing polemical "political" fiction—which often winds up simply reassuring people.

DP: I don't want my works to preach to people but to *wake them up*. Getting people to feel shock or a sense of disturbance proves to them that they're alive. Unfortunately, most of the books I read or art I see these days leaves me totally unmoved. Art and literature should grab you on some level and shake up your sense of what the world is. Meanwhile, we're living in a time when people are encouraged *not* to think or feel— to *not live*, really. People are anesthetized by television, music has no content any more. An age of passivity.

LM: Rimbaud is a figure who recurs in your work, and you've even written a poem specifically addressed to him ("Don't Wake Rimbaud"). Rimbaud's program of the "systematic derangement of the senses," his disgust with the limits and traps of "rational discourse," and his general effort to free himself (and language) from the limitations of traditional forms of writing—all these aspects of his work would seem to be appealing to someone like you, since your work often seems to be aiming at producing responses that lie outside language.

DP: As Stefan Themison wrote, "Rational systems miss the point." I've always wanted to free myself from the forms imposed from outside. Part of this results from the constrictive education I was getting when I was first thinking about being an artist. As an artist, you want to be as free as you possibly can, which is why I made a concerted effort to educate myself in nonmainstream ways. The possibilities for real education were in the books being published by small noncommercial presses, and by Grove and City Lights. Personally and artistically, I was trying to find a place to escape to where I had the freedom to create. One of the reasons I gravitated to the world of art was that I never enjoyed competing with people to get ahead. I didn't feel comfortable with that aspect of manipulating people and situations so you can arrive at your own comfortable niche to survive. Art seemed to be an avenue where that whole process was irrelevant, where people could create freely and hopefully have some kind of impact on the world.

LM: In your first letter to me you referred to "the untethered ghost of the great Alfred Jarry." Like Rimbaud, Jarry is an almost mythic avant-garde figure. What makes him such a source of inspiration for you?

DP: Jarry the writer and Duchamp the artist are the two spirits I most identify with. Jarry is certainly a mentor. I see Jarry as an angel who hovers over my head, protecting me and my work. He keeps me honest. His satirical spirit was something I tapped into as soon as I discovered him. I discovered pataphysics (his science of imaginary solutions) when I was about twenty-two, and I still consider myself a pataphysician.

LM: You've done a number of pieces that use pornography as central vehicles. What interests you, pruriently or aesthetically, about this area?

DP: I'd like to announce right here: I am not a pornographer! But I've always been interested in eroticism and pornography—which aren't necessarily the same thing. I like eroticism and take it seriously. I wonder why more erotic fiction isn't being done, and why it's been the French and not the Americans who have pioneered this form. So even though I've satirized and parodied erotic forms, I've done so lovingly. They haven't been explored enough, especially here in America, where most of what is published in this area is simply awful. The reluctance of writers to do erotic fiction seems to have mostly to do with the sense that it's dangerous territory—and because you can expose a lot of yourself when you get involved in writing it.

LM: Writing about sex would seem to be one of the biggest challenges facing a writer. Not only are you trying to write about something that is so utterly ineffable and nonverbal, but the whole area seems so contaminated by the clichés and words and modes we've already developed for it. Is that why many of your erotic pieces seem less interested in arousing readers than in examining the forms and codes that other writers have used in this area?

DP: I'm interested in both objectives. But I agree that erotic writing is definitely one of the most difficult things to do well. Not only is sex nonverbal, but it's also utterly subjective. Robbe-Grillet, for example, can spend five pages eroticizing a doorknob. That ability of language to transform an object, an encounter or a scene into something genuinely erotic interests me enormously. Perhaps my problem here is that when I find the writing truly erotic, it's very difficult to remain at the typewriter.

LM: I can relate. What's the basis of your distinction between pornography and eroticism? Could Robbe-Grillet write an "erotic" description of a doorknob that's not pornographic?

DP: You've just given me an idea: a pornographic novel called "The Doorknob." It will feature the abuses suffered by an inexperienced young welcome mat. But if you want a definition of pornography, perhaps you should ask Jesse Helms. Baudrillard says somewhere words to the effect that if the obscene is a matter of representation and not of sex, then it must explore the interior of the body—the viscera and so forth. In fact, I'm working on a piece that does just that—describes in excruciating detail the physiological processes of two bodies making love. Baudrillard's expression "an orgy of realism" implies that pornography is obsessed with the physical body, the genitals, while eroticism is centered in the mind. Most of the writers I've chosen to satirize—Marguerite Duras, Sarraute, Anaïs Nin—certainly aren't pornographers. Pornographers are more comfortable dealing with robots or stick figures that can be manipulated into various mathematical formulations or recombinations in order to arouse an audience of unimaginative readers. But reading should require an enormous involvement. An erotic novel isn't simply a manipulation of signs to achieve arousal. It deals with actual human emotions, passions, and imaginative situations, not necessarily just imaginative *sexual situations.*

LM: We hear a lot today about the "death of the avant-garde"—the idea that not only have the stakes been raised in a way (artists have gone about as far as they can go in terms of presenting shocking, extremist materials), but that capitalism now is able to instantly commodify even very radical artistic materials (from punk to Warhol and Mapplethorpe and so on). The example of Sade almost suggests that certain areas, like sexual extremity, were exhausted two hundred years ago.

DP: This is related to why no one (with the possible exception of Burroughs) has been pushing these sorts of boundaries recently. Is this because we've already reached all the extremes, so there's nothing left to be done? If so, this has profound implications for artists working outside the mainstream. I had a conversation with Ed Sanders in which we agreed that nothing is *weird* anymore. Ed said that the most radical thing to do nowadays is to write about flowers or the beauty of a sunset, since it was impossible now to shock anyone. This has to do not only with the insane violence going on all around us on the street, but also with television—the way the media culture puts us in touch with images of this violence but also anesthetizes us to the reality of those images.

LM: Ron Sukenick points to a change in the self-conceptions of the avant-garde during the sixties, using Warhol as a kind of exemplar or model. His point is essentially that whereas previously avant-garde artists self-consciously saw themselves as operating outside of (and in opposition to) "The System," the success of Warhol and other avant-garde artists prompted a change in which members of the avant-garde began to feel, "Hey, I can be 'avant-garde' and *still* make it big!" Part of this has to do with capitalism's ability to appropriate even radical, anticapitalist art and recirculate it. Even *you*, after all, have had several books published by major commercial houses (though I notice that they're all now out of print . . .).

DP: This change has definitely been happening, and it certainly raises the issue of whether or not "avant-garde" art (or whatever you want to call it) hasn't been devalued by our system—whether or not even rebellious art doesn't actually just confirm the viability of capitalism. I've thought about this a lot, especially given my early romantic feeling that writing could actually change something. My relationship to the commercial publishing industry is interesting in this respect. I look at my commercially published works—the Bey books, and so on—as essentially lucky accidents. When I originally conceived them, I planned on publishing them myself at my own expense. It was only through my friends saying to me, "Oh, come on, take these books around, get an agent," that I was finally persuaded to see if they might interest a commercial house. I bounced around Manhattan with the manuscripts under my arm for a period, and wound up at Candida Donadaio, a fine literary agency that miraculously took me on. Almost immediately the *Suicide Guidebook* was sold, and the others were sold quite rapidly afterwards. I still feel this was a giant mistake on the part of the publisher because I had never remotely considered the books to be commercial.

LM: *Assassination Rhapsody* deals with the event I usually cite as symbolically launching the postmodern era in this country—the Kennedy assassination on November 22, 1963. Where were you that day, anyway?

DP: In a junior high school class. The teacher came in the room and told us we were all being sent home because the president had been shot. Like everybody else, I sat around the television for the next three days with my family, watching the funeral procession and Oswald's murder, and so on. Obviously, it made an enormous impact on me, although I was still very young then, with no notion that there had been any conspiracy or anything like that. In fact, when I saw Oswald's murder on TV, my first reaction was a sense of unreality, of watching a *televised event*, a drama. My parents reacted with shock and anguish, and it was their reaction that made me see that this was something different from *Dragnet*. At the same time, the overall impact was the shock of history. In retrospect, this was the end of innocence for everyone of my generation.

LM: What was the original inspiration for *Assassination Rhapsody*? Did you start out by writing a single piece and then realize there were larger possibilities, or did you conceive of a longer series of interrelated pieces from the outset?

DP: I began *Assassination Rhapsody* in the spring of 1987 while I was living in Los Angeles, and I wound up finishing it in the fall of that year. I read the *New York Times* version of the Warren Commission Report, and almost immediately realized that I was going to have to do something with this material. Absorbing all the minutiae and the bizarre, discontinuous narrative trails and verbal "noise" was like confronting this gigantic, unbelievably complex edifice that had somehow been constructed to blot out the truth. The more you got into it, the further you got from the reality of what actually happened. The more detailed it became, the less you knew. It was fascinating—and *funny* from an absurdist point of view. When I finally finished reading it, I started going through the text to see what I could do with it. It started out as a series of experimental pieces, but then I suddenly saw I could collect these things into something larger. Actually I could have taken it a lot further. A *lot* further.

LM: There's a quote in your poem, "Scar Mirror" (1978), where you refer to the bond between myth and history by saying, "The mythology of actions and afterwards the history of selection . . . selecting events and selecting words—all that is left out, left behind, driven into dust is the real reality." There's a way in which that passage seems almost like a gloss on *Assassination Rhapsody*—that sense of the way the words and images we associate with the Kennedy assassination have absolutely displaced whatever "reality" surrounded the actual events.

DP: All that's left for people today is a myth—a television-created myth, a conspiracy myth, a myth of events. The irony is that we actually *saw* what happened. We saw, for example, Oswald get shot on television. But it wasn't real, none of it. From the very beginning people were questioning whether that was the "real Oswald" or just an Oswald double, a CIA plant, a simulacrum from Mars. Even though these enormously significant events were taking place right before our eyes, there was a peculiar sense of unreality about everything.

LM: At the very opening of *Assassination Rhapsody* you provide a dictionary definition for "assassination" ("to harm or ruin one's reputation") and for "rhapsody," ("any ecstatic or extravagantly enthusiastic speech or writing" and "an instrumental composition of free, irregular form suggesting improvisation"). Could you talk a bit about those definitions—or whatever it was that made you select "Assassination Rhapsody" for your title?

DP: I approached the Warren Commission Report as a kind of music. Sad jazz. At first, I was tempted to omit any mention of the president from the text. As I was getting deeper into the material, it struck me that Kennedy becomes almost a throwaway in the midst of this conglomeration of data. At one point I even considered keeping Oswald out of the book, but then I saw that Oswald was the mythical creature dominating everything while Kennedy was virtually an irrelevancy in this music of conspiracy and alleged fact.

LM: "Rhapsody" is certainly an appropriate term for the different ways you transform the language of the Warren Commission Report into your own texts.

DP: Certainly the lawyer jargon you find in the report is "extravagant." I wanted to find where this language, with all its pseudo logic and labyrinths of data, begins to *break down*, and to encourage this in my own texts. It was a very natural process of letting the language disintegrate. It was like somebody chasing after the truth while it's disintegrating, like fog. This chase creates a kind of musical effect, as you weave your way through this mass of words and information.

LM: I was struck with the different ways you present what we might call "Oswald-as-simulacra"—the various *images* of Oswald, the facsimiles of Oswald, all those many transformations of Oswald that at once point towards the real man but which in the end have wound up mainly just pointing to his absence, his mystery. I'm thinking of something like that sequence of dots that eventually creates an image of his face—an image you caption, "This is not Oswald."

DP: The reference there, of course, was to Magritte's *This Is Not a Pipe*. I was constantly struck with the issue of who had been *controlling* the imagery we've received about the assassination. We'd seen the televised version, but only in the version they'd shown us. And what we *didn't see* was probably more interesting. The same thing was true with the report—the facts not revealed, the hidden images. Whoever controlled the media was controlling our perceptions of the event, which contributed to that feeling of unreality when we *did* see something.

LM: And you often seem to be foregrounding the way our perceptions have also been shaped by the *language* of the media—that sense of Oswald and the other participants in this drama as having only "semiotic" or "textual" existence. You even refer to Mrs. Bledsoe several times in "The Wonder on the Bushbuck" as if she was merely a word ("all ten letters of her").

DP: I altered or invented names in many other cases, but Mrs. Bledsoe was an actual witness and so her name needed no alteration. But in terms of the report, Mrs. Bledsoe quite literally *is* merely the ten letters that make up her name; there's no connection made between her testimony and who she is—no photograph of her, no background provided. She's a creation of the report. As far as I know, she doesn't really exist. This is intriguing because after the report came out there were lots of disappearances of witnesses, and nobody really followed this up. As a result, all the witnesses became less real people than characters in a mystery written by Robbe-Grillet. *Last Year at Marienbad* set in Dallas.

LM: A lot of this, of course, relates to different aspects of the current debate about what constitutes postmodern culture: the media inundation of images and words producing substitutions that stand in for the real.

DP: We're all losing a sense of the original, of the origins of things. Baudrillard's "Precession of Simulacra" is absolutely real. The copy today comes before the original. The "real" is lost in that "forest of signs" we inhabit. I prefer to call it a "jungle" of signs because this environment seems much more dense, umbrageous and confining. But "forest" is what most people feel comfortable with. You can see this in people's response to the report: they were impressed with the sheer accretion of detail, with the bulk and heft, this sense that "Here it all is, now we can touch it, lift it." They were impressed with this the same way they are by big buildings or anything else whose physical presence seems undeniably "real" and which therefore makes them feel tiny, insignificant. What we're exposed to daily on television has a similar, ongoing effect on our lives. We're so continuously exposed to all this *stuff* that we're gradually beaten down, subconsciously convinced that this profusion must somehow be real.

LM: The "Commission Exhibits" at the end of *Rhapsody* are "unsituated" in the sense that readers aren't given any guidelines about how they're supposed to "read" them. Were these invented by you or based on actual visual materials from the Commission Report?

DP: Except for the maps (which have been altered), and Kennedy's eyes that I superimposed over Oswald's in that one image, none of the visuals are from the report.

LM: Could you talk about the function of some of these images? For example, the image on page 114 of what looks like a jail cell or tenement apartment has a spooky appropriateness—you know it can't really be Oswald's apartment, but the ambiance seems "right" somehow . . .

DP: That's Alfred Jarry's apartment, although it's not important for the reader to know this. What I'm hoping will happen is that the reader will see this image and ponder what it means, or how it ties in with the other materials. I chose it because it has a sense of foreboding and alienation. The same with Kennedy's eyes—the victim's eyes superimposed on the assassin's face. When the assassin looks in the mirror, does he see himself? Or perhaps his victims?

LM: What about the comic book images (pp. 112, 118)—did you draw them or were these found materials?

DP: They were found. It should be obvious with the collages I've done in *Assassination Rhapsody* that I'm not trying to fool any reader into thinking these are "real" images. Quite the contrary. In the Bey books, where I created collages from nineteenth-century line illustrations, I often tried to make pictures where you wouldn't be able to detect the transpositions. In terms of the final effect, that's always been an interest of mine: manipulation by collage. But I've also gone in the other direction by working up collages where the elements have been assembled so that the effect is intentionally jarring. Visual hyperbole. I felt that the "Commission Exhibits" in *Rhapsody* should appear forged, altered, collaged because reality was already tampered with. The "truth" itself had been folded, fondled, mutilated—in fact, *assassinated*. As far as I'm concerned, Kennedy was less a victim than the public.

LM: The image of the building with all the windows (p. 111) has an odd resonance because it's so ambiguous; you don't know what this is, and so there are so many possibilities for interpretation.

DP: That's precisely the point. Your first response is probably, "Is this the book depository?" Well, no. So what is it? And which of these windows is the significant one? Of course, there's no arrow provided to help you; in fact, I considered having arrows inserted pointing to *all* the windows. Finally, it's irrelevant, just as most of the information in the Commission Report has little bearing on whether Oswald actually killed Kennedy. It's just one of these wild tangents that have no relation to what is supposedly trying to be ascertained by gathering this data. I included images like that purely for "feel," for texture, to pose an additional mystery that is irrelevant to the *actual mystery* that is never solved. But the picture should be interesting enough for you to see that there's a potential enigma involved here as well. There's a potential mystery involved in everything . . .

LM: What factors were involved in your choice of the picture of the man screaming that appears on the back cover and then inside the book a couple of times (on the first page and then in juxtaposition with Oswald, and so on)? It reminded me somehow of Edvard Munch's painting *The Scream* . . .

DP: I originally had a series of pictures of people screaming that I wanted to put together into something called "The Alphabet of Screams." But the man in this particular illustration seemed to duplicate the famous image of Oswald's death-scream—he was another of those pseudo-Oswald's, an automaton-Oswald, one of the many missing Oswalds. The shadowy quality of the figure in the painting—the eyes shaded beneath the bowler, the identity being masked, the bandaged brow—struck me as a perfect way to symbolize the quality of what Oswald became: The Mythic, Masked, Shadowy Assassin.

LM: The text for "The Biography of Lee Harvey Oswald" appears to be snippets of materials taken from the details of Oswald's actual life (mostly ludicrously *irrelevant* details). Meanwhile, the accompanying illustrations only occasionally seem to be reinforcing or "illustrating" the text. How did that piece evolve? Who did the illustrations?

DP: Most people won't recognize these illustrations. They were done by a French hack artist named Henri Zo (if you look closely you can see his signature on most of the drawings). Raymond Roussel commissioned him to illustrate *Nouvelles impressions d'Afrique*, and I decided to steal these for the book. I wanted to carry through the biography but to constantly change the readers' reactions to what they were seeing and reading, so that at one point you'd be following things and then at the next you'd be standing on air. I chose the irrelevancies in Oswald's biography because his life was in a sense an irrelevant life. We never gained access to the main traumas in his life or were never treated to any serious investigation of his psychology. I decided to foreground the fact that what we have are mostly irrelevancies by selecting the most trivial items from his biography—say, the fact that his mother worked at Burt's Shoestore when he was in the eighth grade, that a woman named Mrs. Paine gave him a driving lesson on October 12, his having bought some postcards.

LM: There was something very moving about the sequence of materials on page 106 that leads into "Oswald's Secret": the November 21, 1963, date (which we know is the day before Oswald will murder Kennedy), the drawing of the nighttime sky (with that suggestion of immensity and grandeur), and the text describing the routine details of Oswald watching television while the women are cleaning the house . . .

DP: What I wanted there was to find a way to get right to the heart of the tragedy of Oswald's life—leading this totally lonely, desolate life, and never being given the opportunity to express himself in art. I'm glad you felt something when you saw that last page because I meant it to express the poignancy of the fact that the assassination was the only thing that ever gave Oswald any recognition as a human being. The entire rest of his life, he was always someone who never had any effect, not just on history (most of us don't have any effect on these larger processes), but even on other *people*. If you remove the tragedy of the assassination, Oswald's life is the epitome of the emptiness and loneliness you find in most people's lives (of course, some of us grow up to be artists instead of assassins). At any rate, it felt right to conclude the book on the eve of the assassination. And what did Oswald do on that portentous night? He cleaned his gun, had dinner, and went to bed. How did he sleep that night? Probably very well.

LM: The first Commission exhibit in the appendix is a series of photographs of people's ears. Are these random ears or have they been selected from among the main participants in this absurdist drama?

DP: Random. But the Commission might well have photographed everyone's ears—Kennedy's, Ruby's, Oswald's, Marina's hairdresser—and examined and measured them because this would have had no relevancy to the crime whatsoever. Besides . . . the walls have ears.

LM: Your sequence of "bullet texts" (including "A Bullet-Theory Poem") were hilarious but, once again, also capture the spirit of the report. Surely this is the most analyzed bullet in history, it's been mythicized, its physical makeup and trajectory have become part of collective memory.

DP: Like so many other things in the Warren Commission Report, the sections about the bullet are very funny from a certain perspective. All I did was turn the absurdity knobs up just one notch further. Certainly the actual report about the bullet is so utterly bizarre and full of meaningless "facts," digressions, and details that it is almost impossible to follow. All I needed to do was foreground the confusion and absurdity to make absolutely certain nobody could follow the thinking process being depicted. Really: I only turned the knob up one click!

LM: Were there things in your background that account for the direction your work has taken? I'm wondering what might have influenced you to work so extensively with visual materials or to combine visuals and texts, rather than working in either a visual or verbal medium.

DP: Well, it's obviously relevant that my dad is a commercial photographer. He tried to steer me into advertising and copywriting, which I resented enormously. I felt that whole area of commercial photography was simply a form of prostitution. I wanted to be a writer before I was doing any artwork. I was writing plays and stories when I was twelve or thirteen. I was a terrible student, always fooling around and getting into trouble. It was one day when I was held after class by a substitute teacher that I discovered *Howl*. I had started snooping around her desk after she walked out of the room and came across this little book. At that point I knew nothing about the Beats or the mythology around City Lights; all I knew was that when I picked up that poem and started reading, I was absolutely *blown away*.

LM: What was there that made this thing stand out? The exotic content, the "obscenity," the sheer extremity of everything?

DP: Mostly the language. It seemed so much more vibrant, alive somehow in a way I could relate to. That experience was a turning point for me. I immediately started writing my own personal *Howl*, and then got involved reading all the Beats; that in turn led to surrealism and dada. Meanwhile I had absolutely no interest in the stuff I was assigned to read in school. It was simply dead to me, nothing there that had any relevance to my life. So instead of going to class I used to go to the local bookstore, sit on a couch in the back, and spend the next several days educating myself reading stuff that was meaningful to me—like Jarry's "pataphysics."

LM: How much later was it before you started including visual materials in your work?

DP: I started cutting up books and working with different forms of collage around 1968. From that point on, there was almost a complete fusion of the use of words and images. At this point now, I literally can't separate my visual from my written works. When I think of "texts" I automatically think in terms of pictograms and hieroglyphs.

LM: Were you aware of the work William Burroughs was doing with collage and cut-ups?

DP: Burroughs was a major influence on me in this area—he basically showed artists of my generation the possibilities of what you could do in this area. Burroughs influenced just about every experimental writer around. He opened up so many different doors that nobody had thought to open before.

LM: At what point did the mysterious Doktor Bey enter the picture?

DP: I had the idea to do *Doktor Bey's Suicide Guidebook* (the first one) in 1968. Initially I was thinking about doing a series of textual instructions —"How to write the suicide note," et cetera—that weren't connected with Bey. But while reading *Justine*, I came across a section where Durrell mentions a toxicologist, "Doctor Faud Bey," and for some reason I really fell in love with the name. Soon I was signing my letters that way (I added the "k" for pure weirdness). The connection of Doktor Bey to the "Suicide Guidebook" idea to form *Doktor Bey's Suicide Guidebook* was inevitable. Even better, it seemed instantly right: weird and melodic. Just what I like in a title.

LM: How did the Bey series evolve?

DP: Back in the late seventies, the book market was absolutely saturated with self-help books. It always struck me as both sad and repulsive that all these people were spending all this money on self-help books that would transform them into human beings, teach them how to breathe and feel good about themselves, and so on. So the logical way to respond to this was to do a series of self-help satires. I was at a party where my editor introduced me to Edward Gorey as the fellow who had just done this how-to book for suicides. Gorey's reaction was, "It's about time!" One of the modest high points in my career.

LM: What's involved in the actual physical, mechanical process of transforming these source images into what appear in your books?

DP: Cutting and pasting. Literally. Very few people know what a collage actually is, so reviewers have frequently mislabeled the pictures "cartoons." That's frustrating, because what I do with collage is very different than a cartoon. The truth is that I feel *possessed* when I work on collages. What I do is get down on the floor, spread out thousands of pictures in front of me, and try out things with my trusty scissors and X-acto blades, glue sticks, and a Scotch Spray Mount (a wonderful high when you breathe it); after something works out well, I start laughing maniacally (I guess it's pretty weird, when you think about it). What's involved is mainly allowing myself to be in a space—literally and creatively—where marvelous accidents can occur, and being tuned in to recognize which ones of these accidents (there are many of them) are interesting or funny. Inverting a picture can suddenly suggest a face, for example, or yield up something else you wouldn't ordinarily see. There can be discoveries, everywhere, on the spot, and when that happens the process seems very magical.

LM: I first became aware of this type of work not through Burroughs but through the kind of things Donald Barthelme was doing in books like *Sadness, City Life, Guilty Pleasures.*

DP: Strangely enough, I wasn't aware of Barthelme's collages. Even more than Burroughs, the most obvious person for me to have been aware of and influenced by was Max Ernst, but instead the artist who suggested what you could do with collage long before I discovered Ernst and Schwitters and the others was Norman Rubington, who had done a series of satirical pornography for Olympia Press using the pseudonym of Akbar del Piombo. I had discovered his *Fuzz against Junk* back in high school; it was a collage book done with nineteenth-century illustrations about the narcotics brigade going after the beatniks. Really remarkable stuff. Because I was not a trained artist, it was also important that collage struck me so immediately as being an *accessible* form. Something more obviously daunting, like sculpture or even traditional landscape or portrait painting, might have scared me off.

LM: Many reviewers of Doktor Bey's *Book of the Dead* and his *Handbook of Strange Sex* saw both books as being satiric treatments specifically of Victorian rituals and cultural attitudes towards the "big topics"—sex and death. Given your anarchic sensibility, though, I wonder if your works really possess the kind of "prescriptive norms" that satire usually implies. There's rage and mockery and black humor in nearly everything you write, but it's presented in a sense that's more nihilistic and deconstructive (however you want to define that) than satiric—though destructive in the positive sense we associate with Burroughs and postmodernism generally. You're often mocking these literary structures (often cruelly and bitterly), but you're also obviously *playing* with them, wrenching things out of their familiar contexts and forcing them into new ones, and so on. That itself seems very valuable—maybe more valuable than satires, which offer specific alternatives to what's being made fun of. It also seemed to me that the absurdities of Victorian contexts wasn't the point at all—that you were using these materials as a means of presenting a commentary on *today's* absurdities.

DP: Frankly, I can't understand anybody who *doesn't* do satire. How can an artist, who is presumably struggling against the same things that enslave us as I am, *not* use such a powerful weapon—especially since it's a struggle that we are apparently *losing!* In terms of those two Bey books, of course I was mocking Victorian attitudes, but is it really news anymore that the Victorians had absurd attitudes and values? The Victorian vehicle created a kind of imaginative bridge that my readers were expected to cross over and arrive at where we are today—which is not very far from Victorian England. For all our denials, most Americans are still defined by our Victorian hang-ups.

LM: Are there any other writers or artists that you admire or feel affinities with?

DP: One would be Colonel A. W. LeMar, Sr., USAF Retired, author of the extraordinary novel, *The Romance of Hilga and George*, that deserves far more attention than it has received. A lost classic. Crank literature is America's gift to world culture. When it comes to eccentric books, we're in the lead and the Japanese can go fuck themselves. Without revealing the intricate plot of LeMar's book, let me simply read you the last paragraph (it won't spoil the experience—promise): "The love and devotion that existed between Hilga and George seemed to grow with the years, as they only thought of each other's comfort and happiness. Their romance could be considered one of the classic romantic love stories of the era." Indeed!

LM: Stunning. . . . Throughout the 1980s, your mysterious (and infrequently photographed) alter ego Norman Conquest has produced an increasing (and increasingly various) number of artworks—mostly nonliterary art pieces. Could you introduce us a bit to Norman, talk a bit about why you found it necessary to invent him, and how his works differ from those of Derek Pell?

DP: Conquest's work began around 1979, mostly in collage and assemblages. And correspondence art. You'll notice that his is very different stuff from what you find in the Bey books, mostly because they're so much less word-oriented. The name was chosen for its historical inevitability, and using it helped me separate some of my nonverbal art from the other books; it was all getting too confusing, both to me and I'm sure for my readers. Becoming Norman also helped me find homes for some verbal-visual works in mags that had previously rejected works by Pell.

LM: I hope Pell doesn't fall prey to the kind of petty jealousies you find so often when two people are both artists working out of a shared experience—those kinds of situations can get pretty . . . explosive.

DP: And in fact, a really strange sense of competitiveness *is* developing. In some ways I actually envy Norman's career. I'd kill for some of his credits.

LM: Like I said: chill out. It all comes out of the same spigot. Some of Conquest's postcard art strikes me as one way artists can bypass this whole system that coopts and incorporates artists.

DP: That's specifically the incubator Conquest emerged from. In 1979 I became involved in the international mail-art scene, and Norman's work with postcards soon followed. This scene has been going on since the fifties; it's essentially communication among artists through the mails, where artists use the mail system as part of the art process. The French artist Ben Vautier did something wonderful with this called *The Post-*

man's Choice: he had postcards printed whose sides both had places to put addresses; he would then put a stamp on each side, address them to two different parties on either side, and then let the postman decide whom to send it to. The conceptual idea was having the postal system, as well as the individual postman, involved in the act of sending. The idea of artists swapping artwork back and forth among themselves, with no commercial considerations connected to the process, appealed to me a great deal. For one thing, you didn't have to get involved in the gallery scene, and it's also just a much more exciting network than the "real" art world. I must have produced hundreds of these works while I was living in Los Angeles during the mid eighties.

LM: Has Conquest really almost taken on a life of his own? Your visually obsessed alter ego?

DP: Sometimes it really seems this way, yes. This isn't so strange when you consider how different Conquest's artworks are from Derek Pell's. How to explain this? Really, it's almost as if I switch into another personality when I'm doing Norman's stuff. The work changes.

LM: Of course, you've been playing around with pseudonyms for a long time now (all the way back to Akbar del Piombo, as I recall . . .)

DP: Yes, but I've noticed this alter-ego thing more with Conquest than with any of the other pseudonyms I've used. Probably that's because I never produced enough work for this schizophrenic process to harden. But at least on a purely artistic or aesthetic level, there's enough real difference that Conquest's works are getting accepted at places that won't touch Pell's work. Very bizarre. To be honest, the way things have been going recently, it's entirely likely that Derek Pell will have totally disappeared in a year or two, another anonymous artist sunk beneath the wave of anonymity. I could even change my name legally to Norman Conquest, get a divorce from Pell (or at least a restraining order). I can see the headlines already in the *Daily News* or the *Weekly World News*: "Schizophrenic artist obtains restraining order—*against himself! Fragmented fop's fed-up alter ego's not optimistic about trial separation.*" Maybe someday it will come to light that Derek Pell was the real fabrication all along.

On Thin Ice, You Might as Well Dance
An Interview with Gerald Vizenor

Larry McCaffery
Tom Marshall

"The trouble with humans is they believe their disguises are real, but not imagination, or their dreams," said the panther.

— *The Heirs of Columbus*

As Gerald Vizenor explains in the following interview, the act of going
away has allowed him to return home richer as an individual and as a
writer. Asia has been especially important in this regard: it was in Japan
just after the Korean War that Vizenor experienced his first major literary discovery—haiku, a form whose exterior simplicity encouraged
him to begin discovering the richness of literary forms generally. Then,
more than twenty years later, after having published numerous books of
poetry (including several books of haiku) and journalism, a year teaching in Tianjin, China, resulted in Vizenor's first novel. As he says, "mixed
bloods loosen the seams in the shrouds of identity."

Tom Marshall and I wanted to talk with Gerald Vizenor because of his
reputation as a talker as much as because of his books. We anticipated
that talking with Vizenor would be fun—and it was. He tells an anecdote
with all the verve of a true storyteller and more. The following interview
was based on a conversation held in Vizenor's office at the University of
California at Berkeley, where he is a professor in the Native American
Studies Department. This was just a few months after the publication

of *The Heirs of Columbus,* Vizenor's retelling of the American discovery myth and a work that, appearing as it did in the face of the quincentennial, announced in no uncertain terms, "I'm not a victim of Columbus." For a mixed-blood American, that was quite an assertion.

The Heirs of Columbus provides a perfect example of how Vizenor has used his "trickster" literary program to construct a means of escaping victimization. This trickster approach offers a variety of ways to use the act of writing to reshape histories. The willingness to use history for his own purposes—to use the fissures and gaps that exist in even the most meticulously recorded historical event—is one of several aspects of his work that Vizenor shares with his "postmodern" contemporaries William Vollmann, Kathy Acker, and Harold Jaffe. This connection isn't really that surprising. Vizenor, who has read widely in poststructuralist critical theory, has argued persuasively in *Narrative Chance: Postmodern Discourse on Native American Indian Literatures* (1989) that traditional Native American writing was "postmodern" before there ever was even a "modernist movement." Among the "autobiographical myths and metaphors" of *Interior Landscapes,* Vizenor claims, "the tricksters raised me in imagination."

Gerald Robert Vizenor, born in 1934, is an enrolled member of the Minnesota Chippewa tribe, White Earth Reservation. In *Interior Landscapes* (1990), Vizenor combines factual information about his life with personal anecdotes, tribal myths, flights of fantasy, and photography to produce an "autocritical autobiography" which emphasizes that the materials of the past are shaped by memory and imagination to serve the needs of present consciousness. He does this in telling his own story in "Crows Written on the Poplars." He does it in conversation in ways that challenge an interlocutor's equilibrium. And he certainly does it in his fictions. The more recent autobiographical accounts in *Interior Landscapes* are bluntly straightforward but still involve the power of retelling; and like Leslie Silko's *Storyteller, Interior Landscapes* introduces a wide range of discursive methods—including fables, "straight" autobiography, myths, public documents, and photographs—as a means of providing multiple entryways into the past and memory. *Landscapes* creates a vivid sense of Vizenor's life. He was a reporter, a soldier, an entertainer, a writer, a student, an activist, an organizer, a poet, and more, not necessarily in that order.

As we talked, we occasionally glanced over Vizenor's shoulder at the European movie poster on the wall in front of us, which sported an emphatic image of an American Indian. Image and imagination move across Vizenor's times, accumulating and melding like living waters. Like the tricksters who inhabit most of his fiction, Vizenor himself won't be any one thing for long. Vizenor continues to reshape his life in stories, poems, film, journalism, memoirs, and numerous unclassifiable forms, joined by the trickster who assists him in remembering "how to turn pain and horror into humor."

Such a transformation is no mean trick; certainly this re-remembrance isn't a mere introduction of a wish-fulfillment fantasy that allows one to forget how things "really are." In fact, all of Vizenor's public activities—talking or writing or teaching or reporting—seem positively transformative. Myth, life, story, history, and poetry mix each other up to form a stream of clarity in motion. He can tell the plain truth in a way that scares the pants off your assumptions. The reports in *Crossbloods* (1990) prove that Vizenor can reason with a tongue that goes beyond mere cheek. Thus, when he argues in "Bone Court" that tribal bones are actually narrators that have the legal right to be represented, you cannot deflect the force of his ideas, even with nervous laughter.

As Kimberly Blaeser has pointed out, Vizenor's recent novel *Dead Voices: Natural Agonies in the New World* (1992) calls for our liberation from all invented Indian stereotypes ("Trickster Signatures," 6). That's *our* liberation, mine and yours, not just his from us. He's not out to do us any easy favors, but he knows how to think through a question like this to its openings. As he explains in the interview, it's about "survivance," not just reacting to life's burdens and surviving under them but lifting one's view to play over the circumstances. Vizenor tells the Chippewa tale of Naanabozho, who finds himself in the middle of his own shit and has to invent a whole new world out of it to find some freedom. Gerald Vizenor's New World is like that.

Vizenor's work continues to hunt for something to confound each side of the traditionalist-postmodern rift which has alternately celebrated and attacked his work. Read on. The bibliography will tell you what he has written, and the books will tell you about his life, and much more.

In an early book, Vizenor reworked some songs that ethnologists had collected from his people around the headwaters of the river they call the "misisibi." We can see him carefully imaged in one of those song-poems:

two foxes
facing each other
sitting
between them

*   *   *

Gerald Vizenor: Selected Bibliography

Books of Fiction

Darkness in Saint Louis Bearheart. St. Paul, MN: Truck Press, 1978. Expanded and revised edition published as *Bearheart: The Heirship Chronicles.* Minneapolis: University of Minnesota Press, 1990.
Earthdivers: Tribal Narratives on Mixed Descent. Stories. Minneapolis: University of Minnesota Press, 1981.
Griever: An American Monkey King in China. New York: Fiction Collective, 1987.
The Trickster of Liberty: Tribal Heirs to a Wild Baronage. Minneapolis: University of Minnesota Press, 1988.
The Heirs of Columbus. Hanover, NH: Wesleyan University Press (published by the University Press of New England), 1991.
Landfill Meditation: Crossblood Stories. Hanover, NH: Wesleyan University Press (published by the University Press of New England), 1991.
Dead Voices: Natural Agonies in the New World. Norman: University of Oklahoma Press, 1992.
Shadow Distance: A Gerald Vizenor Reader. Hanover, NH: Wesleyan University Press, 1994.

Books of Poetry

Born in the Wind. Privately printed, 1960.
The Old Park Sleepers. Minneapolis, MN: Obercraft, 1961.
Two Wings the Butterfly. Haiku. Minneapolis, MN: Privately printed, 1962.
South of the Painted Stones. Minneapolis, MN: Obercraft, 1963.
Raising the Moon Vines. Original haiku in English. Minneapolis, MN: Nodin Press, 1964.
Seventeen Chirps. Haiku. Minneapolis, MN: Nodin Press, 1965.
Slight Abrasions: A Dialogue in Haiku (with Jerome Downes). Minneapolis, MN: Nodin Press, 1966.
Empty Swings. Haiku. Minneapolis, MN: Nodin Press, 1967.
Anishinaabe Adisokan: Tales of the People. Minneapolis, MN: Nodin Press, 1970. Reprinted in *Summer in the Spring: Ojibwe Lyric Poems and Tribal Stories.* Norman: University of Oklahoma Press, 1993.
Anishinaabe Nagamon: Songs of the People. Minneapolis, MN: Nodin Press, 1980. Reprinted in *Summer in the Spring: Ojibwe Lyric Poems and Tribal Stories.* Minneapolis, MN: Nodin Press, 1981.
Matsushima: Pine Islands. Haiku. Minneapolis, MN: Nodin Press, 1984.

Books of Nonfiction (Reviews, Essays, Articles, Autobiography)

Escorts to White Earth, 1868–1968: One Hundred Years on a Reservation. Minneapolis, MN: Four Winds Press, 1968.
Thomas James White Hawk. Minneapolis, MN: Four Winds Press, 1968.
Tribal Scenes and Ceremonies. Minneapolis, MN: Nodin Press, 1976.
Wordarrows: Indians and Whites in the New Fur Trade. Essays and stories. Minne-

apolis: University of Minnesota Press, 1978. Translated into Italian as *Parole frecce*, trans. Maria Vittoria D'Amico. Pisa: University of Pisa, 1992.
The People Named the Chippewa: Historical Narratives. Essays and photographs. Minneapolis: University of Minnesota Press, 1984.
Crossbloods: Bone Courts, Bingo, and Other Reports. Minneapolis: University of Minnesota Press, 1990.
Interior Landscapes: Autobiographical Myths and Metaphors. Autobiographical writings and photographs. Minneapolis: University of Minnesota Press, 1990.
Manifest Manners: Postindian Warriors of Survivance. Hanover, NH: University Press of New England, 1994.

As Editor

The Everlasting Sky: New Voices from the People Named the Chippewa. New York: Crowell-Collier, 1972.
Narrative Chance: Postmodern Discourse on Native American Literatures. Albuquerque: University of New Mexico Press, 1989. Includes Vizenor's preface (pp. ix–xiii), "A Postmodern Introduction" (pp. 3–16), and "Trickster Discourse: Comic Holotropes and Language" (pp. 187–211).
Touchwood: A Collection of Ojibway Prose. St. Paul, MN: New Rivers Press, 1987.
Native American Literature: A Brief Introduction and Anthology. New York: Harper-Collins College Publishers, 1995.

Dramas and Films

A Season for All Things. Drama. Washington, DC: Office of Economic Development, 1967.
Harold of Orange. Thirty-minute film. Minneapolis, MN: Film in the Cities, 1984.

Uncollected Short Fiction

"The Psychotaxidermist." *Minneapolis Star Saturday Magazine.* August 1978. Reprinted in *The Minnesota Experience,* ed. Jean Ervin, 220–28. Minneapolis: Adams Press, 1979.
"Rattling Hail Ceremonial: Cultural Word Wars Downtown on the Reservation." *Shantih* 4, 2 (Summer–Fall 1979): 40–41.
"Word Cinema." In *Book Forum, American Indians Today Issue,* ed. Elaine Jahner, 5 (Summer 1981): 389–95.
"Reservation Cafe: The Origin of American Indian Instant Coffee." In *Earth Power Coming,* ed. Simon Ortiz, 31–36. Tsaile, AZ: Navajo Community College Press, 1983.
"White Noise." In *White Noise, the Fellin Sisters, and The Man of Sorrows,* ed. Gerald Vizenor, Lon Otto, and Jonis Agee, 1–13. St. Paul, MN: Fodder Press, 1983.
"Luminous Thighs." In *The Lightning Within: An Anthology of Contemporary American Indian Fiction,* ed. Alan R. Velie, 66–90. Lincoln: University of Nebraska Press, 1991.

"Stone Columbus." In *Avant-Pop: Fiction for a Daydream Nation,* ed. Larry McCaffery, 199–206. Normal, IL: Black Ice Books, 1993.

Essays

"I Know What You Mean, Erdupps MacChurbb." Autobiography. In *Growing Up in Minnesota: Ten Writers Remember Their Childhood,* ed. Chester Anderson, 79–81. Minneapolis: University of Minnesota Press, 1976.
"Crows Written on the Poplars: Autocritical Autobiographies." In *I Will Tell You Now,* ed. Brian Swann and Arnold Krupat, 99–110. Lincoln: University of Nebraska Press, 1987.

Books, Reviews, Essays, and Interviews about Vizenor's Work

Ainsworth, Linda. "History and the Imagination: Gerald Vizenor's *The People Named Chippewa.*" *American Indian Quarterly* 9, 1 (Winter 1985): 49–54.
Ballinger, Franchot. "Sacred Reversals: Trickster in Gerald Vizenor *Earthdivers: Tribal Narratives on Mixed Descent.*" *American Indian Quarterly* 9, 1 (Winter 1985): 54–59.
Blaeser, Kimberly. *Gerald Vizenor—Writing in the Oral Tradition.* Norman: University of Oklahoma Press, 1993.
———. "Trickster Signatures." Review of *Crossbloods, Bone Courts, Bingo and Other Reports, Interior Landscapes: Autobiographical Myths and Metaphors, Landfill Meditations: Crossblood Stories,* and *Dead Voices: Natural Agonies in the New World. American Book Review* 15, 5 (December 1992/January 1993): 6–7.
Bowers, Neal, and Charles L. P. Silet. "An Interview with Gerald Vizenor." *Melus* 8, 1 (Spring 1981): 45–47.
"Gerald Vizenor" (unsigned entry). In *Contemporary Authors New Revision Series* 21: 460–61. Detroit: Gale Research, 1990.
Haseltine, Patricia. "The Voices of Gerald Vizenor: Survival through Transformation." *American Indian Quarterly* 9, 1 (Winter 1985): 31–47.
Jahner, Elaine. "Cultural Shrines Revisited." *American Indian Quarterly* 9, 1 (Winter 1985): 23–30.
———. "Heading 'Em Off at the Impass: Native American Writers Meet the Poststructuralists." In *Smoothing the Ground II,* ed. Arnold Krupat and Brian Swann. Columbia: University of South Carolina Press.
Keady, Maureen. "Walking Backwards into the Fourth World: Survival of the Fittest in Bearheart." *American Indian Quarterly* 9, 1 (Winter 1985): 61–72.
Krupat, Arnold. *The Voice in the Margin.* Berkeley: University of California Press, 1989.
Lincoln, Kenneth. *Native American Renaissance.* Berkeley: University of California Press, 1982.
Owens, Louis. "'Ecstatic Strategies: Gerald Vizenor's Darkness in Saint Louis Bearheart." In Vizenor's *Narrative Chance,* 141–53. Albuquerque: University of New Mexico Press, 1989.
———. "Gerald Vizenor: Selected Bibliography." *American Indian Quarterly* 9, 1 (Winter 1985): 75–78.
Ruoff, A. LaVonne Brown. "Gerald Vizenor: Compassionate Trickster." *American Indian Quarterly* 9, 1 (Winter 1985): 67–73.

Silberman, Robert. "Gerald Vizenor and *Harold of Orange*: From Word Cinemas to Real Cinema." *American Indian Quarterly* 9, 1 (Winter 1985): 4–20.
Velie, Alan. "Gerald Vizenor: Post Modern Fiction." In *Four American Indian Literary Masters*, 124–56. Norman: University of Oklahoma Press, 1982.
———. "The Trickster Novel." In Vizenor's *Narrative Chance*, 121–39. Albuquerque: University of New Mexico Press, 1989.

*   *   *

LARRY MCCAFFERY: You've recently presented a number of discussions concerning the "postmodern" features of Native American literature. Your analysis runs somewhat along the same lines as what Japanologist Maseo Miyoshi has said about the way that early Japanese literature exhibits many of the stylistic tendencies associated with postmodernism long before even "modernism" came along in the West. Obviously a lot of issues related to this topic come down mainly to a matter of definition and perspective—the problem being that in the West we always wish to see artistic "evolution" and development in terms of our own cultural paradigms and history.

TOM MARSHALL: My reaction to my friends' description of you as a "postmodernist" has been to reverse what they're implying by suggesting that your "trickster" brand of postmodernism should be seen as being "traditional" in a sense. [Laughter.]

GERALD VIZENOR: I can see the angle you're taking there, as well as what Miyoshi is driving at. It's closely connected to my argument that Native American storytellers were the first postmodernists. Making that assertion stick is tricky because of course this implies you could have a narrative tradition that's postmodern before it's ever gone through a "modern" phase. Premodern postmodernist.

LM: What's the theoretical basis of your claims for Native American literature as a postmodernist form? Or in making these claims, are you mainly just adopting the trickster position of playing with terms to reveal their limitations?

GV: First of all, I don't approach this topic theoretically because that would mean I'd have to carry back a formula for discovery. Instead I use the idea of postmodern *conditions*, which is Lyotard's notion. So I don't impose a theory—in fact, I'm very careful about not doing this because I argue against that.

TM: How would the "conditions" you're referring to here relate to Native American writing?

GV: The conditions are that, first, no story is the same. The conditions are postmodern because of their connection to oral expression which is usually a kind of free-floating signifier or a collection of signifiers, depending on who's present. The "meaning" of such stories that are orally presented depends on a number of interesting, lively, immediate, temporal, and dangerous, dangerous conditions.

LM: What do you mean here by "dangerous"? A linguistic or conventional danger—the danger of a speaker upsetting the expectations?

GV: Something like that. "Dangerous" not specifically in the sense of life-threatening but dangerous *in language*. Telling a story is as "dangerous" as hunting—dangerous because your life depends on your catching something. It's dangerous because it's an encounter with something unknown—something generally understood, but specifically unknown that may come together, alive or present in the telling or the hunting. It's also survivance. I'm serious about the use of the word "survivance" rather than survival. Survivance is a condition, not a mere response to domination. Survivance is the end of dominance in literature. Life is a chance, a story is a chance. That I am here is a chance. This interview is a chance survivance. The advantages to survivance are that it provides a way to accept this condition, reverse what's been imposed on us—and play with it.

LM: This seems related to what you're doing in *The Heirs of Columbus*, where you take the elements of the Columbus myth (and history) and reassemble them into new shapes.

GV: That's exactly the game of chance I wanted to play there. Now that doesn't mean politically that the experiences are anything but tortuous, miserable, and dangerous. It means from this moment, this chance encounter of my life experience, I have the pleasure and the privilege of playing this material back in a way so that it seems to be a different song. So, for example, the corrupted French name "Vizenor" comes from Vezina; and the Peter Vezina who adopted this name was a French-Canadian Indian living at what was to become the White Earth Reservation, including that area that wasn't a reservation yet. When the reservation was created in 1868 and he was asked his name by the Indian agents of the U.S. government (I'm guessing he couldn't write), I suspect that he said, probably in a French-Canadian accent, "Vezina," which they spelled as "Vizenor." And it has been a colonial creation ever since.

Now the pleasure of the moment is that none of this makes any difference to me. Having this colonial name "Vizenor" wasn't a personal burden for me—in fact, it's a personal advantage. I know that any Vizenor I ever meet comes from White Earth because "Vizenor" is a purely invented name. Not many families out of Ellis Island can say that. At least in my case, people know it's a new, invented American name.

TM: Is *survivance* an invented word in this sense—in addition to having it's French equivalence of "survival"?

GV: I wanted the term to have a broader meaning as a conditional experience rather than a burden of victimization. To me *survivance* is not just carrying this burden and surviving—showing that I'm a survivor of victimization, for example—but also inventing a world view. It's an attitude of play—play in a very serious sense. Survivance is also existential, a source of identity. I wouldn't say it's the French atheistic existentialist but a new kind of existentialism—tribal existentialism or spiritual existentialism. I'm hesitant using the word "spiritual" here because I have to qualify it too much, whereas saying "tribal" leaves it open. The discovery of self through action, through being present, is the part of existentialism I borrow from Jean-Paul Sartre, but when I add to this the dream, the preexistence of experience, I get more mystical than Sartre and the others ever allowed.

LM: This attitude or outlook seems to be a very "positive" or opportunistic one in the sense that it gives you the chance to *create* something out of these chance situations rather than rejecting them or feeling victimized by them—I'm thinking of your reacting to the circumstance of your name as being an opportunity rather than, say, the way so many black Americans seem to feel victimized and controlled by their given names, which they feel need to be rejected so they can go back to their original name.

GV: Well, I just don't feel the name "Vizenor" is revisionist. It bears the experience historically of the time, so it contains within it its own story. I have not revised it, and have no desire to. I have only discovered it and have the pleasure of it. A revisionist approach to this—and this is ongoing for many people—is to reach back and impose a dream on present existence. So you might have someone who adopts a sacred tribal name and takes it up, even as a mixed-blood. Many mixbloods do this—their middle name becomes something descriptive, sometimes fanciful and attractive: "Whirlwind," or "World Wing" or something of that sort.

LM: Back in the sixties, writers like Robert Coover, John Barth, and others associated with the beginnings of postmodernism in America were consciously returning to prenovelistic forms for sources of inspiration for much the same reasons you've been discussing—that is, they recognized that even familiar or clichéd cultural literary archetypes, like fairy tales and myths, had often been reduced to a single "meaning" or set of associations that prevented the richness there from being recognized. Coover, for example, felt that creating alternate versions, or toying around with the material in various other collaborative or improvisatory ways, was an "exemplary act" of the literary imagination in that it demonstrated the way narratives can display multiple meanings depending on the context of the teller.

GV: Coover is very good at that sort of thing, which is something I also associate with Calvino. There are so many different elements that came together almost at the same time in this recognition, but in a way it was all the reaction against the realistic novel form with its foolish insistence on representation. You could also say that in earlier times even the creators of realistic books were looking for experiences that were different or liberating, too. Very often these involved travel to exotic places, adventures an ordinary reader might never have—an example might be Jack London. But with television and film and other sources of experience, we don't need that. In fact, it's boring and takes too long. And it's not representational *enough*. But what troubles me more than anything is that people have lost their power to hear stories and respond to them with pleasure.

LM: What's behind this loss? The impact of the media—television and so forth?

GV: It's more complicated than just the media, although that's certainly important. What it comes down to, though, is that people don't *believe* stories anymore. What I mean by that is that a storyteller could always signal that what was about to be presented is language-play and imagination by simply saying, "Once upon a time . . ." Just saying that phrase freed us from social realism and announced, "This is play," and someone who knows how to put the story together is going to tell one that's recognizable. All that's trite now to most people, but I still think it's a terrific way to start a story—in fact, I think it's such a nice gesture that I often have to repress the urge to say, "Once upon a time." I like having this said because you're relieved of embarrassing someone with a stupid question like, "Excuse me, but is this real or not?" What a horrible thing to ask someone who is in the middle of a story! Who gives a shit?!

LM: Did *The Heirs of Columbus* have its origins in all the hubbub already surrounding the five hundredth anniversary of Columbus's arrival, or did you get started with it for other reasons?

GV: There were a number of origins of this book. For more than ten years I've outlined and worked on an idea for a novel of revolution, something describing the creation of a new nation. The first location I had in mind for this was Northwest Angle, which is a detached piece of the U.S. It's a natural, you know, it could be a new state, it has international boundaries. The scheme I had originally ten years ago had to do with a group of tribal idealists and radicals hijacking an airplane that's loaded with the best and brightest of the Indian world—teachers and lawyers on their way to a conference. The burden here is, can these best and brightest deal with the *real* problems? That's the ironic test. So my radicals hijack this plane and land it on the ice, right on the international border between Canada and the U.S., with one wheel on each side, so that it's right up to Northwest Angle. Now they've got a couple of months to negotiate, and then the plane breaks through the ice and sinks into the water. I had a nice time with the story, and I still think this is a good outline for a book, but then *Columbus* came along, and then in the past decade I became much more haunted by a couple of other things. One was trying to understand the impact that bingo is having on the tribal experience of life—both its positive and negative consequences.

LM: You've had a number of almost science fictional motifs in *Heirs* and in some of your other recent works—references to genetic engineering, mutation, biological experiments, and so on.

GV: That has to do with maybe my other main area of concern these days, which is the burden of healing. I'm totally preoccupied with the horrible legacy of genetic mutations of the chemicals on our lives. Literally and metaphorically it's a legacy of the "Chemical Civilization," which is what I call Western civilization, with its five-hundred-year history of chemical usage. We have in our bodies, all of us, the mutation of this great experiment in civilization. We eat it, we inhale it. And the consequences are horrifying. I brought together all these ideas—my deep trouble and concern about mutations, this idea about a new nation, and bingo—into *The Heirs of Columbus* five hundred years later. The idea was to somehow co-opt or colonize Columbus. Turn (or return) the whole thing around, make Columbus serve the revolution and to be responsible for healing the victims and the mutants of the first five hundred years of the Chemical Civilization. In some mythic way I wanted to make Columbus and his name responsible and accountable for these five hundred years.

TM: Turning things around like this sounds like one of those acts of *survivance* that you were referring to earlier . . .

GV: It's also a trickster approach to storytelling. A story that serves the contradictions of time and energy. It essentially says, "It's ridiculous to say I'm a victim of Columbus! I'm not a victim of Columbus, Columbus has no measure in my life." That settles that, so now what *else* do you want to talk about? And I wanted to make my revisionist story of the last five hundred years serve *tribal* interests and changes, rather than continuing to serve the white liberal interests of having Indians as victims. I wanted to heal the mutants, not perpetuate the idea of colonial victimization. Just as importantly, I wanted to tell for the first time ever (which I think it is) an Indian version of the story of who Columbus becomes. To do this, I had a group of people telling their stories every year, and the year this novel opens it happens that their best stories are about Christopher Columbus. He's just this mythic figure that they can transform in their storytelling into anything they want to. What Columbus "means" and becomes is all a matter of the context of storytelling. They even make Columbus somebody interesting! Far more interesting than he was in his own life.

TM: Based on the bits and pieces I've picked up about Columbus, along with having traveled through Spain and Europe, and then back to the Americas, I feel I know just enough about things to feel that, yeah, maybe Columbus really was like that.

GV: God forbid, it might make more sense than the historical version! As you can probably tell from having read the book, there are a lot of new moves you can make with the original stories, rich new narrative possibilities that arise because there are so many open seams in this historical account. Luckily so, for the stories I want to tell. If all the details about Columbus's life were well-documented, then you would have to find a way to confront the documentation somehow. For instance, you could tell the story ironically, or you could say something about the corruption among these historians who deliberately withheld this information. There are other strategies of subversion, as well, but they'd be different ways of telling the stories. Fortunately that wasn't the case here. Everything is so delightfully open to our imagination and pleasures of storytelling. We can tell our story in a much more imaginative way than just reciting another tale about colonialization in which we ourselves figure merely as the victims, a symbol of colonialization. Telling our own version of the story allows us to avoid this victimization, make Columbus accountable and responsible. The incredible irony is that Columbus never amounted to anything anywhere except in America. Columbus should forever be grateful that he was discovered by a constitutional democracy because nobody else gives a shit about discovering it! Only a constitutional democracy which is still struggling with the revisions of its history and the consequences of its potential evil and colonialization can make so much of somebody like Columbus who was abandoned a long time ago. I mean, he lost out for beatification, his name was in the process of being lost to history; he was hardly ever mentioned in Spanish exploration or colonial history.

LM: There's a wonderful image that appears near the beginning of *The Heirs of Columbus* where Naanabozho is standing around up to his nose in the water and is forced to take a shit by the water demons; in order to liberate his mind over his own excrement, he creates trickster stories and the New World. That scene has recurred enough in your other works that I wondered if it didn't have some special resonance or mythic quality for you . . .

GV: That's an origin story, one of the Earthdiver tales. There are many versions of it that can be summarized along these lines: you have this trickster standing on the highest point around, up to his nostrils in water, with the flood rising steadily; he's about to expire, so he has to figure out some act of survivance—which, true to life and in spite of the demands upon his survivance, turns out to be taking a great shit. Well, when this happens, the shit naturally floats around his nose, so he's got to *do* something or otherwise just stand there and accept it. And what he does is invent this whole new world. It's a wonderful metaphor: here in the middle of your own shit, you have to think about creating your own world besides. With some assistance from animals and birds and the turtle's back, he builds a new nation, a new world, on the back of a turtle.

LM: Your use of this origin story—this recycling of prior materials, some drawn from your own work, some from traditional works, and then playing with and improvising with the elements of these things until you have a more pleasing or useful version—is a strategy that seems increasingly common among so-called postmodern writers. Of course, the motivations for adopting this approach can be very different from writer to writer, but what seems to be involved for all of you is the desire to present storytelling as a truly open-ended process rather than something finished that readers can passively consume.

GV: That's an important point to emphasize because it ties together not only the idea of the tribal existential postmodern—that is, its being and presence, or the equivalent of identity, is discovered in the telling—it's the action of the telling that's important, it's the dream and vision in the telling. And that's different every time. It free floats in this way: these myths and stories are free-floating. They fit the existential moment of creation and telling, not some design that's been imposed on them. I don't want to sound too romantic about creation, but a good story arises *as a chance*. Of course there are occasions when people come together specifically for the purpose of communicating or telling or showing. Ceremonial functions would be an example. But even here, the stories are always varied; and these variations depend upon who's present, what kind of gossip exists in the air at that time, who's doing what and not what, and so all these things come into the story itself in a very subtle way, either through emphasis or omissions or parallel metaphors in very playful, subtle ways.

LM: There were similar kinds of improvisational literary forms in medieval Japan—but these largely disappeared when Western notions of literature (and philosophy) started entering Japan freely. Has this happened with this Native American tradition?

GV: These approaches certainly didn't end with Western contact, nor did they end with a university education, or with the written language. Life is still as dangerous as it always has been *in the telling*. It still is a dangerous encounter with existence and survivance and play—an existential discovery of being, of being and presence in the telling. In that postmodern sense, the trickster is always around—unplugged, ready, and willing to be drawn into a story in some way.

LM: In that creation scene in *The Heirs of Columbus,* you also describe Naanabozho as the first trickster of the stone. Wasn't the Chinese Monkey King also born from a stone?

GV: Indeed he was. In fact, you may remember that in *Griever* I specifically mentioned that the Monkey King, the first version of the Chinese trickster, was born from a stone. I was trying to show how the beginning of life comes from something substantial, like a rock. *Dead Voices* actually opens with the trickster story and goes on for some time about this. You have the trickster brother of the stone that can't move any more, so trickster has to come back all the time and tell him what he has been doing. Eventually he gets more or less pissed off and wants to do his brother in. So he says to the stone, "I'm getting sick of this! I mean, I hit you, I try to break you, but I can't do it. How can I kill you?" The stone replies, "That's easy—just heat me up and then throw cold water on me; I'll break into a thousand pieces." Well, the brother does that and, sure enough, in the early tellings, the trickster-stone bursts into millions of pieces and covers the earth—and today every stone from anywhere on this world is metaphorically from that first breakup of the trickster. So the character in *Dead Voices* collects stones, which represent the metaphors of the stories. They fit the stories, allow her to tell and imagine stories, and give her presence and existence in a story. That's everywhere, always.

LM: Had you already researched the Chinese version of the trickster—that is, the Monkey King—before you went over to China? I'm interested, for example, in what connections and differences you found in the presentations of the Chinese and Native American versions. It's certainly significant that this figure appears in both sets of mythology.

GV: I studied Chinese and Japanese literature in graduate school. I read Arthur Waley's translation of the Monkey King. I have to say, though, that the way it was presented in class as a cultural document made it difficult for me to relate this stuff to my own world. I make this very same argument today about the way tribal stories are represented by anthropologists. The Monkey King that I studied in graduate school didn't connect with me as a trickster until I arrived in China. Up until then it was just this cultural document to me, a folk story.

LM: Obviously, then, learning more about this Chinese Monkey King trickster figure wasn't specifically involved in your trip to China . . .

GV: Not at all. I went because it was a chance. I gave up my tenured position at the University of Minnesota. Then this position in China was open. I had some interests in writing a few situational journalistic pieces about my experiences there for a newspaper. I'd just have to see what would come of this. Maybe nothing would, but depending on what happened, I thought I might be able to do one of these journalistic pieces a month—not travel stuff or magazine writing, but if something interesting was happening, I knew I could make a story out of it.

Then what happened was that in the fall, a month into teaching over there, I was invited to see a production of some of the scenes from the monkey king opera. That experience changed everything for me. The theater was overflowing with Chinese, of course, and at first I was overwhelmed by the audience—not simply because the place was so jammed but because the audience was dynamic, so completely engaged in the production even though there's no applause. Everyone in the audience must have changed seats at least twice, maybe more (we, of course, were the only people in the whole place who stayed in the same seats!); people would go out to the lobby to gossip, come back in when their favorite scene was about to be performed, and then rush right up to the stage. Then they'd leave again, and nobody would applaud.

LM: I saw some theater performances in Beijing and, like so many other things I experienced over there, I found that there were some very interesting and exciting things going on if you're willing to get used to it. I felt that way at first when I'd be out at public banquets—initially you feel uncomfortable by the sheer noise and smoke and intimacy of the situation, but pretty soon you're spitting out your bones on the floor, having a go at the Peking duck's brain, and generally having a hell of a good time.

GV: Exactly! I mean, at first I was distracted by this rich and powerful dynamic between what was happening on the stage and in the audience—and also by the smell of garlic and all these other good things. Of course, what's going on is also revolutionary, but not in this case revisionist or social realism, the way most theatrical productions were in China. In other words, this Monkey King material hadn't been converted to serve the state. The revolutionary state accepted these not as bourgeois spiritual pollution, but as folk culture, original literature that represented the Chinese consciousness. They accepted it for what it was because it was in their soul—and the soul in this case was not dangerous to the Communist Party. This was on-the-street stuff, a bit like puppet theater, not an elitist-Communist Party performance. So there it is. This probably sounds naive on my part, but it's true. And these wonderful distractions with the audience, I started paying attention to the play and of course it was only then that I began to recognize all the stuff I had read about the Monkey. Then, in one of those occasional strokes of insight you get, I suddenly saw the trickster figure.

TM: I agree with your point about the way that even really powerfully resonant materials so often wind up deadened when they're presented in a classroom situation.

GV: Somehow this transferral kills it, drains it of all its emotional and aesthetic significance. This isn't intentional on the part of teachers, of course, who are often wonderful people and good educators. In the end, students become a passive witness to art that has no life. Dead voices. But when I saw this stuff performed in this other context, there it was, suddenly alive, and I was thrilled. I knew immediately that I had a book. I didn't know what it was going to be exactly, but I knew I had a book somewhere.

TM: How did the book begin to take shape?

GV: I started telling playful stories about what was happening to us. Not systematically. I didn't make notes about things and I knew I had to be careful politically, so I didn't want to have a lot of written stuff around that looked like I was keeping track of things with any regularity. I would just tell stories, knowing that something would eventually give these stories a shape that would pull things together by the time I got back to the States. When I got back, I still didn't have a book, although I did have a powerful theme—the idea that the only figure in a story who could confront the oppressive bureaucracy and contradictions existing in the People's Republic of China would have to be a mind monkey or trickster. The trickster Griever bashed at habits and rules in an established historical context.

LM: What sorts of actual experiences led to these playful story versions? The story in the novel about replacing the Chinese martial music with John Philip Sousa struck me as a likely candidate because of my own experience in Beijing of being awakened every morning at seven and hearing Ace's "How Long Has This Been Going On" blasting out of these awful loudspeakers. If I could have figured out a way to do what Griever did . . .

GV: Well, we were being driven absolutely mad by the morning martial music. In our case it was especially maddening because we were in the middle of two campuses so it came to us from two directions. And it was always just slightly off. I could imagine sneaking over there at night and putting a Sousa tape on, so I told myself that delightful story instead of just sitting there every morning having to put up with that awful martial music. Things like this would happen all the time to my wife Laura and me, and when we'd bump into something especially frustrating, I'd think of it in some sort of fantastic, playful way and we'd be free for a while. And there were plenty of stories to tell. Stories surrounding bureaucratic obstacles or some stupid contradictions in its dysfunctional machinery; and others about the wonderful delights of Chinese humor.

LM: It's difficult to talk about this quality without sounding either naive or condescending.

GV: China is the only place I've ever been where I've been able to use the word "innocence." Even people who have been there think I'm being romantic about this because they don't trust these experiences;

they think for me to use a word like "innocence" is pure rubbish—the Chinese and the Communist Chinese Revolution are *innocent*!? But it's true. There's a playfulness and sense of innocence there, a lack of the kind of cynicism and ironic detachment you find so often in the West.

LM: I certainly found that sense of playfulness everywhere I went in China—along with the determination of the Party and its massive bureaucratic machinery to squash that spirit, transform it into something as stern and petty as it was. That's why I loved the way your absurdist trickster alter ego kept popping up in the middle of this Kafkaesque maze of regulations and monotony to play around, fuck things up.

GV: If you take all that public Party posturing about conformity and following regulations seriously (as most Westerners do), it can drain all the life out of your experiences in China. It can spiritually kill you, just like it does to the Chinese who allow it to. But my own personal response to what I saw over there was telling myself stories that contradicted all that. It was my way of liberating my spirit and it wouldn't let me be brought down by this shit. In other words I *imagined* my own liberation as play. That's when I discovered that the Chinese have been doing this, both artistically and in their daily lives, forever. Play is what the Monkey King did.

TM: Isn't that also exactly what Native American tricksterism is all about—play?

GV: Play is the theoretical basis of that whole tradition. I have recently been developing a theory of trickster discourse having to do with the notion that the discourse of the trickster tale is always in fact an act of liberation—that the best storytellers in this tradition always come to this moment of surprise where imagination takes over and transforms the ordinary, limiting, and banalizing features of the world and *liberate* themselves through the process of existential play and language.

LM: Almost by definition this discourse can't be representational or "realistic"—

GV: You can't have liberation if you're confined to discourses based on the real. Once you're confined to the real you're trapped; your stories lose all their magical power, you're limited by all sorts of restrictions that trickster discourse wants to explode, deny. Trickster discourse is liberating because it's *not representational,* because it operates exactly opposite that kind of storytelling.

LM: For all the tricksterism in *The Heirs of Columbus* and *Griever* I noticed that both books are impressively grounded historically.

GV: I tried to be. The street names are right. I have Phillipe stay at all the places that Pocahontas visited in London. In other words, she essentially repeats the itinerary of Pocahontas. She walks the same streets, takes the same boat. I did the same thing in *Griever*—all the place names and descriptions of the colonial architecture, for example, are correct. That wasn't as easy as it might sound because maps are considered dangerous items in China to begin with—especially maps of the colonial period. In fact, they simply don't exist (or at least they're no longer made). Luckily I found a map of Tianjin's colonial concessions in the twenties stuck on the top of a drawer. How else would I ever have known these street names? The major boulevard that bordered the French and British concessions actually had two different names that people would use depending upon what nationality or culture they belonged to. Even when a writer like John Hersey referred in his books to Victoria Boulevard and Race Course Road, things like that, I wouldn't know where those were now (he described them but didn't locate them). So I had a map of all these streets, including all the Japanese street names, like Matsushima, which is the title of my haiku book and also a place in Japan. For a while I even thought about drawing a map up front.

LM: Since it's the metaphorical or imaginative quality you seem to be most interested in, why go to all the trouble of providing this sort of factual accuracy?

GV: It just seems to work out best for me this way. For reasons that I can't fully defend or explain, I take a great deal of pleasure being very responsible for the accuracy of all the research and background details in my books. Given the choice, I'd just rather not invent places with purely imaginary histories. Knowing that all the details in my books are as accurately rendered as I can make them somehow seems to make it easier for me to give a freer reign to my imagination when I'm using my imagination to create something that's going to interact with this basic framework.

TM: So the function of historical accuracy isn't so much a representational one as providing something "substantial" that your imagination can play off of?

GV: Representation—at least as it's usually understood in the West, that is, using language to signify something—is simply not one of my interests as a writer. I want to find a way to deal with the "real," yes, and making sure my facts are accurate is certainly one way to make it impossible for readers to deny that what they are responding to is undeniably "real." But creating that underpinning of the "real" isn't a goal in and of itself; these details just provide me with a framework solid enough for me to jump off of, let my imagination take flight. That's one reason that even after I had gathered all that information about the original street names of Tianjin, I still decided not to provide an actual map for the book. Maps signify in a limited representational way rather than metaphorically—which is more flexible, open, expansive. I'm not interested in signifying or representing something that strongly. I mean, what's the point

—to trick readers into believing that the story you want to tell actually took place? Why bother with this charade? My interest is in telling a story that leaps out of those narrative "gaps" you always find in historical narratives. Even the most fully documented accounts of history have lots of places that are full of magic, ambiguity, and narrative potential—providing the author doesn't feel some mindless, slavish obedience towards the historical material. Exploring those places and discovering the possibilities of what happens once you start bringing the implications of those places out to interact with the "solid" historically documented materials is like letting the genie out of the bottle of my creative imagination.

TM: You began primarily writing poetry, but at least since *Griever: An American Monkey King in China* you've mainly been writing in fiction or prose narrative forms rather than poetry. What are some of the reasons behind this shift in emphasis—and how do you see the role of poetry in the overall development of your own work generally, and in terms of making traditional culture visible specifically?

GV: I don't want this description to be too tidy, because what is involved here is very complicated. A couple of things are obvious. One is that although I've read about, written about, and thought about stories all my life, my first novel, *Griever*, still came together really powerfully for me as a result of my going to China. An interesting contradiction: go somewhere else to put something together. Something like that had happened to me much earlier—when I was eighteen. I joined the Army and ended up in Japan and discovered haiku. In that earlier case, what happened was the pure, innocent delight and understanding of the images. There was no distance in my imagination, no distance between me, experience, and imagination. My experiences with haiku were coming to me instantly, without any cultural, literary, or historical mediation. I didn't have to go to school or know anything to appreciate this literature. That was a first for me because I was obligated to a teacher for pretty much everything I'd ever read before. I was even still thinking of the so-called "escape readings"—genre fiction, that sort of thing—in some connection to an institution. But suddenly with the haiku there was instant gratification, immediate access. I didn't have to go through an interpreter or a scholar to respond to this. This was all wonderfully liberating and exciting to me. Now I know that's anti-intellectual, but I experienced an immediate pleasure with literature that I'd never felt before. It was the first time in my life, such pleasure with literature— and I had to have it in Japan. I don't believe I could have found it in America. I could have found a teacher, true, but I hadn't found one up to that point. In fact, at that point I had no knowledge or expectation of college. I was a high school dropout. My life was a total adventure, everything was open. I saw nothing to do. I had nothing to do.

LM: Not having any prior familial or institutional expectations can actually wind up opening up options because that means there haven't been any limits set for you. Of course, that also means you haven't received any *support* for what you might want to do, which can be a scary feeling . . .

GV: Well, if you're walking on thin ice, you might as well dance. I was living up to no one's expectations. My family life was so complicated and diverse that I lived out no one's fantasy except maybe the negative ones that I'll never amount to anything. I had no family obligations, no expectations invested in me either by institutions or individuals. I was escaping and this was wide open. What a contradiction for me to be saying this now, but the military was paradise, paradise! You can imagine the reactions of my friends years later in the peace movement when I would talk like this! They would be going on about the military-industrial complex and so on, and then I'd laugh and start saying this stuff about the military being paradise for me when I was a kid. They'd say, "Oh, God, there goes Vizenor again talking about being in love with the Army and all those other contradictory things!" They wouldn't believe me, and I'd just laugh some more. But I meant it. I really did. Listen, it's the only place in my life where nobody wanted my imagination or my mind. It's also the only time in my life (except maybe, in a very different way, in teaching) where I was allowed to do whatever I was *good at.* That had certainly never happened to me. Before I joined the Army there was class, race, lies, and counter lies, all sorts of shit going on that you had to get through before you could ever get to do something. Nobody would believe in performance. I was always feeling, "Hey, just give me a minute, and I can show you I can do this." The military, meanwhile, was grateful if somebody could do something. If you could do it, and do it well, you were somebody with some value.

TM: Other than its immediate accessibility, did the haiku have other formal features that seemed particularly interesting?

GV: The fact that it wasn't tied to representationalism was wonderfully attractive to me. And it wasn't obligated to pronouns. Almost all haiku have this wonderfully direct connection between the inner and outer: The first person was the discoverer of the image.

LM: Were there any prose writers who had a similar effect on you back then?

GV: Thomas Wolfe had the most profound effect on me. And because his prose is also imagistic and very descriptive, it also had all this powerful stuff I could get to without going through an interpreter. Wolfe published a collection of prose pieces, *A Stone, a Leaf, a Door,* that was beautifully put together. I discovered the book on a shelf in a military library and soon found myself utterly transported by his very moving, emotional imagistic prose. There was something in his language (and probably something I was learning from haiku) that came together when I opened that book. His prose literally transported me and I lost recognition of time and place until I had finished the book. When I looked up, it was as if I had been on a mystical journey. Something like this happens to you once or twice, and then you see it happening again, your self-consciousness and awareness interrupt the sensation. That's what I mean by bits and pieces—and unfortunately only in *short* bits because you can't actually go into this state consciously.

LM: Did you ever reread the Wolfe book afterwards—just to see if you could remember what took you to that place you'd never been to before?

GV: Yeah, I went back and read it. And, sure enough, I couldn't remember what the hell it was about the book that had transported me that way. I read some other books that also affected me deeply at the time. Michener's *Sayonara*, for example, was published that year. Another GI and I had very serious relationships with Japanese women, and when Michener's book came out, it was like the handbook of lovers' remorse. I couldn't believe how much this book seemed to be written for me at that time.

LM: My own experience is that living abroad allows you to recognize things about yourself and your culture that you'd never have discovered if you'd continued living in familiar circumstances. It defamiliarizes the ordinary and let's you see it in a fresh perspective.

GV: Certainly in my own case those couple years in Japan had a profound impact on my sense of literature and identity. Getting out was a way for me to get back. This was true about my trip to China, too. I had to get out to get back. Metaphorically speaking, I think every imaginative person has to get out to get back, every spiritual or inner journey is getting out to get back, every healing act and event is getting out to get back. It's the course of imagination, it's the condition of creative ecstasy. Quite simply, this getting out to get back is the condition of life.

TM: You've worked in a wide variety of forms—sketching out traditional Native American poems and stories, journalism, autobiography, essays, novels, even film. Do you see any constants running through them?

GV: The first writing was poetry and short stories. I should say these were "vignettes," since they weren't really structurally short stories. I did them when I was quite young. As I've said, haiku had a real impact on me; I studied Japanese literature, trying to work on the idea of the haiku, and then I published several books of haiku. The most recent is *Matsushima*.

LM: At least since the Opium War in the nineteenth century, the Chinese people have certainly been "victims" in various ways—victims of a succession of colonial oppressors, victims of their own governmental oppression and misrule, victims of Mao's Cultural Revolution. But the Chinese at least seem to have escaped the fate associated with the analogous "victimization" of Native Americans in that their victimization hasn't been so widely *represented* in the mass media. Your writing often seems to be consciously designed to liberate Native Americans from what we might call the "prison house of representation."

GV: I'd been preoccupied with this topic for a long time before I went to China, but my experiences over there somehow brought into focus all the business about the terrible burdens tribal people have to bear due to the way they've been represented by outsiders. Representations of Native Americans were some of the first "products" exported by Westerners back to Europe. In our own lifetime, you can see this in mass media representations—film and pulp novels are the most common—but in anthropology and literary history as well. The problem is that these representations usually depict Native Americans primarily as victims—sometimes noble or savage victims, but nearly always it's the victimization that comes through. And constantly having your life represented this way can be a terrible, terrible burden. You see yourself this way enough times and it becomes a distorting mirror that eventually makes it difficult to see the *real you*. All this had preoccupied me, but when I got to China, I couldn't get over how no one had obligated the Monkey King to representation. Somehow this wonderful innocence and play of the trickster Monkey King had escaped all that—including the obligation of being represented as a victim.

TM: I would have thought that the Communist Party would have demanded that the Monkey King somehow be brought into social realist forms.

GV: But nobody had ever used the Monkey King as some kind of cultural artifact to describe, modify, or contradict behavior. I couldn't imagine a Chinese family saying to their child, "You're acting just like the Monkey King!" All along, you see, the Monkey King was seen as language play, an act of liberation; it wasn't obliged to anything other than that. This insight is incredibly important to me because that's what I believe occurred in a tribal storytelling situation. Tribal stories were never representational. Both the tellers and listeners were smart enough to know this. They were, however, very good storytellers—often brilliant, in fact.

LM: We seem so bound up in our own literary and cultural traditions—which we take to be "natural" and sophisticated—that we haven't yet been able to recognize the brilliance in other forms, or see how they might connect with our own traditions.

GV: That failure has come about for a number of reasons. One, anthropologists have mucked it up because they've looked for the wrong things and they're obligated to prove how these wonderful stories relate to culture. Also, since they're not trained in imagination they've never appreciated the subtlety and brilliance of pure language play and game; they've never understood a language game where somebody can tell a story knowing that the figures are playful and imaginative, without obligating any realism to it.

TM: Or any single interpretation.

GV: But interpreting is always play as well, isn't it? People are drawn into it for those reasons; they aren't looking for proof or morals or ethical direction. Unfortunately, when these stories have been translated or transposed into other cultural situations, they're often used to prove some sort of moral attitude or philosophy rather than as opportunities for play. That's always a mistake.

Moth in the Flame
An Interview with William T. Vollmann

Larry McCaffery

> Would nothing ever end? When would he reach the final measurement?
> —*Fathers and Crows*

Still in the early stages of his career, William T. Vollmann is nonetheless the only American author who's appeared in the past twenty years for whom I can confidently predict "greatness." Vollmann is the recklessly daring Captain Ahab of a new generation of "post-postmodern" authors who have emerged during the past decade. These writers, who include such diverse talents as Nicholson Baker, Mark Leyner, Stephen Wright, Ricardo Cortez Cruz, Susan Daitch, David Foster Wallace, Richard Powers, and Steve Erickson, possess sensibilities shaped by very different circumstances from those responsible for the lawbreaking, psychedelicized exuberance of their sixties literary grandparents or of the defensiveness of their more staid parents during the mid-1970s to mid-1980s. They have arrived full-throated, with plenty of old-fashioned news about contemporary life and writing in America.

And certainly no one currently writing—of any generation—has more news to relate than Vollmann, whose monstrous elegance, utter fearlessness, and voracious appetite are of a kind one associates with Melville, Whitman, Thomas Wolfe, and Pynchon. Since 1987, Vollmann has published in rapid succession a staggering array of books, including several massive, unclassifiable works. *You Bright and Risen Angels* (1987) is a wild, hallucinogenic cartoon-like portrait of the artist as a young bug who continuously falls onto the thorns of love, bleeds words, and leads a failed revolution. His best-known book, *The Rainbow Stories* (1989), uses a New-Journalism-by-way-of-Burroughs approach to create windows onto the mostly invisible lives of pimps, prostitutes, street alcoholics, skinheads, serial killers, and other marginalized people living in San Francisco's Tenderloin District. And the first three of a projected seven volumes of "dream novels" that will eventually comprise what Vollmann describes as a "symbolic history" of North America include *The Ice-Shirt* (1990), which deals with the labyrinth of history, blood, and personality that fueled the early Vikings' violent intrusions into and subsequent expulsion from this continent; *Fathers and Crows* (1992), an account of the equally bloody encounter between the French Jesuits and Native Americans during the seventeenth century; and Vollmann's most emotionally engaging and fully realized book to date, *The Rifles* (1993), which describes with harrowing, poetic intensity the conflated stories of John Franklin (the celebrated nineteenth-century British Arctic explorer who perished, along with several hundred seamen, while searching for the Northwest Passage) and a different sort of Northwest passage—an affair with a Inuit woman that leads to tragic consequences—undertaken by a narrator resembling Vollmann himself.

Vollmann also has published other books only slightly less expansive, ambitious, and formally peculiar: *Whores for Gloria* (1991) is a dark and disturbing description of an ex-Vietnam veteran's last days wandering the streets of San Francisco's Tenderloin District (the wandering Vollmann's symbolic home and the most frequent setting in his fiction) in search of the wondrous (and perhaps imaginary) prostitute Gloria. *An Afghanistan Picture Show* (1992) is based upon Vollmann's 1982 experiences entering Afghanistan with Islamic rebels. *Thirteen Stories and Thirteen Epitaphs* (1991) is a mosaic comprised of thirteen paired "stories and epitaphs" that reflect and illuminate each other, texts constructed of bright, broken fragments—shards of autobiography, travel writing, and reportage, anecdotes told by a rogue's gallery of drifters and grifters, artists and con artists, Thai prostitutes, crack addicts, witch doctors, gangsters, and Generation-X slackers—which mix together with other materials to establish unexpected connections among topics widely separated by time, distance, and literal context. *Butterfly Stories* (1993) is a coming-of-age novel set mainly in the same whorehouses, bars, and backstreets of Southeast Asia that Vollmann repeatedly visited in the early nineties, often accompanied by his friend and collaborator, photographer Ken Miller.

These works are presented by Vollmann through a range of voices, literary allusions, and references to an eclectic array of other sources (scientific, anthropological, geological, geographical, historical, and so on), perspectives, and metaphors. In terms of sheer virtuosity and ambition, this achievement hasn't been matched by a writer at this stage of a career since Pynchon published *V* in the early 1960s. Indeed, this truly prodigious burst of creative energy has probably been unrivaled in American fiction since Faulkner was turning out one masterpiece after another in the early thirties.

Vollmann's books thus far tend to share certain motifs, thematic tendencies, and stylistic impulses. Most of them could be described as "prose assemblages" or "proto-hypertexts," in which Vollmann introduces his personal experiences and then allows these to interact with various other fictional and historical materials, literary and other scholarly references, meticulously researched details about exotic places and people, maps and illustrations (drawn by the author), glossaries, appendixes—you name it. These books share other concerns: with metamorphosis, the connection between sexuality and violence, and between secret, inner histories and larger, public realms. Finally, all have tended to deal with characters who are outcasts, who have been wounded in love and had that love transformed into hatred and violence.

The difficulty and peculiarity of Vollmann's talent have thus far denied him the popular and critical recognition that his works will no doubt eventually attain. What seems clear at this point is that Vollmann has established a relationship with his readers based on such old-fashioned notions as sincerity (surely the most truly radical approach an author can pursue these days) and the promise of real rewards rather than the "funny money" handed out by most other contemporary fiction writers. Certainly his work provides strong evidence that reports of the death of serious fiction have been greatly exaggerated indeed.

*   *   *

William T. Vollmann: Selected Bibliography

[*Note:* The most complete bibliographical listings for William Vollmann can be found in John Dinsmore's twelve-page desktop publication "William T. Vollmann: Bibliographical Checklists" (Lexington, KY, 1993; available from John Dinsmore, 1037 Castleton Way South, Lexington, KY 40517). These listings include a descriptive bibliography of Vollmann's first editions, a checklist of anthology appearances, periodical and newspaper articles by and about Vollmann, and a descriptive checklist of productions from his private publishing concern, CoTangent Press.]

Novels and Collections of Fiction

You Bright and Risen Angels (with illustrations by the author). London: André Deutsch, 1987; New York: Atheneum, 1987.
The Rainbow Stories. London: André Deutsch, 1989; New York: Atheneum, 1989.
The Ice-Shirt. Vol. 1 of *Seven Dreams: A Book of North American Landscapes.* London: André Deutsch, 1990; New York: Viking, 1990.
Thirteen Stories and Thirteen Epitaphs. London: André Deutsch, 1991; New York: Pantheon, 1991.
Whores for Gloria. Paperback edition, London: Pan-Picador, 1991; hardcover, New York: Pantheon, 1992.
An Afghanistan Picture Show. New York: Farrar, Straus and Giroux, 1992.
Fathers and Crows. Vol. 2 of *Seven Dreams: A Book of North American Landscapes.* London: André Deutsch, 1992; New York: Viking, 1992.
Butterfly Stories. London: André Deutsch, 1993; New York: Grove Press, 1993.
The Rifles. Vol. 6 of *Seven Dreams: A Book of North American Landscapes.* London: André Deutsch, 1993; New York: Viking Penguin, 1994.
The Atlas. New York: Viking Penguin, 1996.

Fiction, Essays, and Journalism in Periodicals

"Scintillant Orange." *Conjunctions* 11 (Spring 1988): 45–99.
"The White Knights" (with seven photographs by Ken Miller). *Conjunctions* 12 (Fall 1988): 172–222.
"The Quest for Polar Treasures." *Conjunctions* 14 (Spring 1989): 70–84.
"The Grave of Lost Stories." *Conjunctions* 14 (Fall 1989): 213–38.
"Divine Men." *Grand Street* 9, 4 (Summer 1990): 132 ff.
"The Cave of Sheets." *Grand Street* 10, 3 (1991): 34ff.
"An Incomplete Life of Amantacha the Huron." *Conjunctions* 17 (Spring 1991): 277–358.
"The Butterfly Girl." *Conjunctions* 18 (Spring 1992): 261–65.
"The Prophet of the Road." *Los Angeles Times Magazine,* 28 June 1992, pp. 18, 36–37.
"DeSade's Last Stand." *Esquire,* November 1992, pp. 161–76.
"Letter from Somalia: Killing Time with the Widowmakers." *Esquire,* May 1993, 63 ff.

Reviews, Miscellaneous Nonfiction

Review of *Biography of Conrad Aiken,* by Edward Butscher. *San Francisco Chronicle,* 18 September 1988, p. 5.
Review of *The Hot Jazz Trio,* by William Kotzwinkle. *Los Angeles Times Book Review,* 19 November 1989, p. 8.
Review of *The Drummer of the Eleventh North Devonshire Fusiliers,* by Guy Davenport. *Philadelphia Inquirer,* 2 December 1990, pp. 1, 3.
"American Writing Today: A Diagnosis of the Disease." *Conjunctions* 15 (Spring 1990): 355–58.
Review of *Pinocchio in Venice,* by Robert Coover. *Philadelphia Inquirer,* 27 January 1991.

Review of *The Choiring of the Trees,* by Donald Harington. *New York Times Book Review,* 5 May 1991, p. 23.

Review of *The Terrors of Ice and Darkness,* by Christopher Ransmayr. *Philadelphia Inquirer,* 21 July 1991, p. H-1.

Review of *The Mysterious History of Columbus,* by John Noble Wilford. *Philadelphia Inquirer,* 13 October 1991, pp. 1, 2.

Review of *Regeneration,* by Pat Barker. *Philadelphia Inquirer,* 19 April 1992, p. M-1.

Review of *Raven's Children,* by Richard Adams Carey. *Los Angeles Times Book Review,* 5 July 1992, p. 2.

Review of *Wrong: Stories,* by Dennis Cooper. *New York Times Book Review,* 26 April 1992, p. 13.

Forum reply in *Fiction International,* "Sex/Porn and Censorship Special Issue," 20 (1992): 47–48.

Review of *Cry Me a River,* by T. R. Pearson. *New York Times Book Review,* 11 April 1993, p. 11.

"Something to Die For." *Review of Contemporary Fiction—Younger Authors Issue* 13, 2 (Summer 1993): 25–28.

Review of *They Whisper,* by Robert Olin Butler. *Philadelphia Inquirer,* 13 February 1994, pp. H-1, H-4.

Review of *Arise and Walk,* by Barry Gifford. *New York Times Book Review,* 3 July 1994, p. 5.

CoTangent Series (Book Objects and Limited Editions)

The Convict Bird (with twelve black-and-white illustrations by author). Limited edition (ten copies) of original illustrated "children's poem" bound in quarter-inch steel plate by Mathew Heckert, with padlock and hand-forged hasp, hand-etched portrait engraving, barbed wire, and prostitutes' hair. Undated.

The Convict Bird. Mass edition (ninety copies), the same except without the steel case and so on. Undated.

The Happy Girls. Limited edition (fifteen copies) of "The Happy Girls" (a different version appears in *Thirteen Stories and Thirteen Epitaphs*). Bound in birch-wood and glass by James M. Lomino. With peephole, buzzer, red lamp, bra-strap harness, "whorish fabrics," photographs by Ken Miller, and watercolors by author. Four D-cell batteries and spare bulb included. Undated.

The Grave of Lost Stories. Limited edition (fifteen copies), based on the text that originally appeared in *Thirteen Stories.* Bound in sarcophagus of white marble covers by Ben Pax, with custom hinge, spring-loaded skeleton hands, custom screws, and screwdriver with cast silver skull-headed hands (for special screws). Undated.

The Grave of Lost Stories. Mass edition (twenty copies). Same as the limited edition, without the marble covers. Undated.

Whores for Gloria. Limited edition (thirteen copies). Bound in archival eight-ply matboard, with nickel-plated hinges, cover shaped like a woman's legs drawn up against buttocks, photographs by Ken Miller, illustrations by the author. Undated.

Butterfly Stories. Limited edition (fourteen copies). Bound in lingerie, with butterfly wings, illustrations, facial studies, hand-printed figures, illustrations, and watercolors. Undated.

Interviews

Coffey, Michael. "PW Interviews William T. Vollmann." *Publishers Weekly*, 13 July 1992, pp. 36–37.

Dinsmore, John, and Chase Crossingham. "An Interview with William T. Vollmann." *Firsts: Collecting Modern First Editions* 3, 9 (September 1993): 32–33.

Laurence, Alexander. "William T. Vollmann Travels to the Edge." *Cups (A Cafe Journal)* 3, 9 (October 1993): 10–11.

McCaffery, Larry. "An Interview with William T. Vollmann." *Positive* (Tokyo) 1 (1990): 230–47.

———. "An Interview with William T. Vollmann." In *Review of Contemporary Fiction—Younger Authors Issue* 13, 2 (Summer 1993): 9–24.

———. "Running on the Blade's Edge: William Vollmann." *Mondo 2000* 8 (1992): 91–95.

Reviews and Essays about Vollmann's Work

[*Note*: The Summer 1993 *Review of Contemporary Fiction—Younger Authors Issue* I edited includes an interview with Vollmann (listed above) and several essays on his work (listed below). This is currently the best single source of detailed criticism of Vollmann's works.]

Bell, Madison Smart. "Where an Author Might Be Standing." *Review of Contemporary Fiction* 13, 2 (Summer 1993): 39–45.

———. "William T. Vollmann's Risky Business." *New York Times Magazine*, 6 February 1994, pp. 18–21.

Bock, Duncan. "The Ice-Shirt Cometh." Review of *The Ice-Shirt*. *American Book Review*, October–November 1992, p. 25.

Dinsmore, John, and Chase Crossingham. "Bright and Risen Author: William T. Vollmann." *Firsts: Collecting Modern First Editions* 3, 9 (September 1993): 28–31 (includes "An Informal Checklist with Prices in First Edition").

———. "William T. Vollmann's Co-Tangent Press." *Firsts: Collecting Modern First Editions* 3, 9 (September 1993): 33.

Kelly, Robert. "Notes Towards Four Mediations on W. T. Vollmann." *Review of Contemporary Fiction* 13, 2 (Summer 1993): 62–63.

Kobak, Annette. "Send Stronger Americans." Review of *An Afghanistan Picture Show*. *New York Times Book Review*, 26 July 1992, pp. 10–11.

Laidlaw, Marc. "Suicide Notes on William T. Vollmann's *You Bright and Risen Angels*." *Review of Contemporary Fiction* 13, 2 (Summer 1993): 46–52.

Max, Daniel. "In Parkman's Footsteps." *Newsday*, 26 July 1992.

McCaffery, Larry. "The North American Novel at the Quincennial Moment: Everything Is Permitted." In *The Novel of the Americas*, ed. Raymond Leslie Williams, 56–76. Boulder: University of Colorado Press, 1992.

———. "Shock Appeal." Review of *Thirteen Stories and Thirteen Epitaphs*. *Los Angeles Times Book Review*, 1 August 1993, p. 1, 11.

———. "Vollmann Starts What May Be Extraordinary Dream." Review of *The Ice-Shirt*. *San Diego Union Book Review*, 4 November 1990, p. 1.

McIntyre, Tom. "Vollmann's Visions" (interview, with photos by Ken Miller, and "Flowers in Your Hair," from *Thirteen Stories*). *San Francisco Examiner Image*, 22 August 1993, pp. 12, 19, 21.

Moore, Stephen. Review of *The Rainbow Stories*. *Review of Contemporary Fiction* 9 (Summer 1989): 258–59.

———. "William Vollmann: An Artist in the American Grain." Review of *An Afghanistan Picture Show* and *Fathers and Crows*. *Washington Post Book World* 32, 31 (2 August 1992): 1, 10.

Skow, John. "Collision of Cultures." Review of *Fathers and Crows*. *Time*, 31 August 1992, pp. 69–70.

Smith, Carleton. "Arctic Revelations: Vollmann's *The Rifles* and the Frozen Landscape of the Self," *Review of Contemporary Fiction* 13, 2 (Summer 1993): 53–61.

Spielmann, Katherine. "The Book as Apparatus: William Vollmann's Special Editions." *Review of Contemporary Fiction* 13, 2 (Summer 1993): 64–67.

Texier, Catherine. "The Girl of His Dreams." Review of *Whores for Gloria*. *New York Times Book Review*, 16 February 1992.

* * *

LARRY MCCAFFERY: In researching your books, you've placed yourself into demanding physical situations of considerable personal danger that most people would never even consider—entering into Afghanistan with Islamic commandos for *An Afghanistan Picture Show*, hanging out with skinheads, pimps, drug dealers, prostitutes, and other street people in *The Rainbow Stories, Whores for Gloria, Thirteen Stories*, traveling to Sarajevo or to the Arctic wilderness for *The Ice-Shirt*, and then spending an extended period of time alone at the magnetic north pole for *The Rifles*, miscellaneous trips to Somalia, Madagascar, and so on. Why are you really doing this? Pure self-destructiveness on your part? Because you think these excursions are likely to yield results that are interesting from an aesthetic standpoint (because you think they'll produce good writing)? Or is it more a matter of your finding these challenges interesting from a personal standpoint?

WILLIAM VOLLMANN: I'm sure there's some self-destructiveness involved here, but every dog likes his own little corner that he can mark with his own piss. One of the ways I can mark my own corner is by going off to someplace most writers wouldn't dare to go. That way I don't have to worry about the competition writing better things than I could. I'm also attracted to the extreme because frequently the extreme case illustrates the general case—and sometimes it can do this more forcefully and memorably than the ordinary is able to.

The other thing is, sure, I'm still fascinated by exotic things. I suppose I always will be. And very often, if you want some kind of direct contact with exotic things, you find yourself in a dangerous situation, almost by definition. If there isn't some barrier between you and the exotic, it's usually not exotic. What creates this barrier has to be either danger or difficulty. When I have time and I'm feeling like a coward I take the difficult things; when I need to get things done quicker, I do

the dangerous things. On the other hand, nothing I do is *that* dangerous. Others have built a mystique around my activities.

LM: The moment in *The Ice-Shirt* when the Indian picks up the ax after
killing one of the Norsemen with it, and then looks at it and decides to
throw it back into the water, reminded me of the scene in *2001: A Space
Odyssey*, where the caveman throws the bone up in the air and the bone
is transformed into a space station. Both scenes seem to be describing
one of those absolutely pivotal moments in history where technology is
being introduced.

WV: I wasn't thinking specifically of the Kubrick movie when I wrote
my own scene, but I certainly see that moment in *The Ice-Shirt* as being
the beginning of American history. The Norse, with their characteristic
combination of courage, ruthlessness, and arrogance, had decided they
are going to take over this territory. To their mind-set, these Indians
are outlaws and can therefore be killed at will. The Indians, of course,
don't see it that way at all, so there's a battle. In that battle the Indians,
with their stone axes, lose to the Norse, with the iron axes; but in the
long run the Indians don't lose because they're so numerous and the
Norse technological superiority is not so much greater to give them any
hope of ever being safe there. Eventually the Norse leave, but in one
of the battles (and this scene, by the way, is actually described in one of
the Norse sagas) you have that scene where one of the Norse axes has
killed an Indian; when another Indian picks up the ax and kills somebody else with it, he understands how sharp and strong it is but decides
to throw it away anyway. I thought that gesture of rejection was an odd,
extraordinary moment when I first came across it. It's describing the
first confrontation between a native, established way of life and a new
force which these natives had never seen before. I imagine ice as being
at the beginning of this force. It was a new power that was going to
transform the landscape and pretty much ruin the native Indians—and
pretty much ruin us, as well. Rejecting that power was the opening act
of American history; a scene many years later where the Eskimos accept
the rifles from the Westerners closes off the whole process.

LM: You remark somewhere in *The Ice-Shirt* (you're discussing the history
of the "Blue Shirt") that, "Answers are nowhere and everywhere." That
comment reflects the same paradoxical sense I get from your books regarding the role of erudition and "book learning" in assisting people to
find answers to their lives and destinies. That is, on the one hand, your
books are often overflowing with information, specific names, dates,
accurate descriptions of exotic flora, fauna, and people, the whole way
you've been framing your works with these elaborate charts, glossaries,
footnotes, appendixes, and so on. But in the end, you refuse to supply
the kinds of "answers" we expect in novels—there's never a sense that

you're observing this from any sort of privileged position that allows you to provide final explanations or solutions for anything. If anything, your books seem to be operating the way DeLillo's recent works have—as deepening a certain sense of mystery even as they provide new perspectives on things. When you set out to write something, are you usually looking, in some sense, for answers to specific questions that you feel you can answer for the reader? Or do you go into the writing process with the sense that writing itself can be a form of discovery for you?

WV: I usually have a fairly specific issue that I'm interested in when I begin most works. If it's not particularized and mysterious enough in a way that interests me, and if there's not some sort of naive hope inside me that makes me feel I might be able to understand the issue and maybe help readers to understand it, then I'm just not going to want to put in the time and effort required to write about it. The way I think about writing is that you've got to care enough about words and ideas to justify what's involved in producing something worthwhile. And finally there's a trust between the writer and reader that needs to be maintained or the whole process becomes diminished. In the case of *The Ice-Shirt* I wanted to understand what this whole business with axes meant. But whenever I'm trying to understand a specific issue I always find that it becomes more and more complicated—which is why the books get longer and longer. With the Afghan book I wanted to understand, first of all, whether the Soviets or the Afghans were right. Secondly, if the Afghans were right, then what I could do to help them. As I said, I ended up realizing that it's a very difficult process to help other people and that issues like these become very confusing and ultimately almost unknowable. What winds up happening, then, is much less a matter of me providing answers or explanations about something I know in advance than the process of me trying to deal with all this ambiguous material. What you're left with is a movement of narrative more than anything else. Answers really *are* everywhere in the narrative. But also nowhere.

LM: That helps explain the comment you made somewhere about your view that the "diffusedness" of *Angels* was the main virtue of the book— while it was also the quality of the book most criticized by reviewers.

WV: The reactions to *You Bright and Risen Angels* were interesting. Some people seemed to be really bothered by the "diffused" quality of the book, while others have been increasingly disappointed with succeeding books precisely because they don't do that. My editor for *Angels*, Bob Harbison, was a big fan of that book, but he's pretty much hated everything I've written since. He has a right to feel that way because the other books are very different and in a sense (though not *every* sense) less ambitious.

LM: On the other hand, I see a lot of connecting threads through all of your books. And I certainly wouldn't say that *The Ice-Shirt* is less "ambitious" than anything else you've done.

WV: This has nothing to do with "ambition," but I've certainly tried to *improve* myself from book to book. For instance, I think that in each book my general ability to depict character has increased. I'm especially proud of this in the sequel to *The Ice-Shirt—Fathers and Crows.* I'm also learning more about plot as I go—recognizing what's essential and what's extraneous. I'll never write a perfect book because no one ever has, but I feel that my books are constantly getting better. Which makes me happy.

LM: Why do you refer to yourself on the title page as "William the Blind"? Is that a reference to your worries about your eyesight, or is it something more metaphorical?

WV: It's partly playing around and partly due to the fact that the sagas often have little monikers attached to the characters, "So-and-So the Lame," or "So-and-So the Priest," that sort of thing. "William the Blind" seemed like an appropriate one to give myself because I'm so nearsighted. It's maybe especially appropriate because I am always trying to understand or "see" things and I never really do.

LM: It's a little like the way psychotherapy sometimes isn't able to help you change the way you are, but it helps you accept the way you are, so you don't feel so bad about it.

WV: That's all you can ask really. And being able to change yourself isn't necessarily going to make you happy. You might be *less happy* if you could change, who knows? The people in *The Ice-Shirt* aren't necessarily happier when they have the power to change from human to animal. King Ingjald wants to be manly so they give him the wolf's heart to eat, but even though that experience changes him, he ends up being this terrible, horrible person. He probably would have been better off if he'd just said, "Well, nothing I can do will ever make me be manly— but that's all right."

LM: Many readers are going to see what you've been doing in Marxist terms—so in *Angels*, the Blue Globes and the Electricity people are on the side of the capitalist system, with Bug and the other guys representing the communists.

WV: Sure!

LM: Given the way this revolutionary approach becomes corrupted and goes bottom up, are you implying that the whole Marxist notion of revolution is basically just a nineteenth-century utopian pipe dream?

WV: Do you remember the guy who said, "If you're not a Marxist when you're under thirty you have no heart, and if you're still a Marxist when you're over thirty you have no brains"? There's some truth to that. Socialism, or something equivalent, seems to me to be a good system, something to strive for. All these puny little dogs who've been yapping about how the turn away from communism in Eastern Europe and elsewhere proved that socialism is bankrupt forever don't know what they are saying.

LM: There's a lot of specific historical contexts involved in those turns that don't have much to do with "socialism" at all.

WV: It's like people saying the Inquisition proved that Christianity is no good—whereas it didn't prove anything. I'm personally hopeful that some day there can exist something like what the communists are talking about. The basic idea of "from each according to his ability, to each according to his need" is very beautiful. And at some point it may be necessary to try for it.

LM: Isn't it possible to imagine a situation in which political systems do not resort to violence? And assuming that repressive political systems do invoke violence, is it possible to have a revolutionary response that's not going to be infected with violence and bloodlust in the way it happens in *Angels*?

WV: Probably not. Not even if your motivations are genuinely noble and pure. Violence is a part of the human character and always will be. It can't be avoided. For instance, I don't consider myself a conservative (I subscribe to a lot of notions that most conservatives would be horrified by, I'm sure), but I'm in favor of the death penalty. There are always going to be vicious, brutal, horrible people who have to be put to death for putting others to death. In that sense I think that revolutions will always have to be violent. To defend themselves against violence, they'll have to be violent too. Possibly the ugliness we've seen in Marxist governments (or so-called Marxist governments) in this century has not been the fault of the governments. I don't know. I'm no admirer of people like Stalin, but it might be that the violence used against them by the rest of the world, compelled them, at least in the beginning, to react violently. I don't know whether Lenin was actually compelled to murder the Romanov family and the little kids. I find that pretty vile. But I can imagine that maybe he did. When Hitler attacked the Soviet Union, obviously the Soviet Union had to respond. And we can understand the reasons, say, for the way that Albania and North Korea have become these horrible static fossils. Maybe it's not even their fault at all—although that still doesn't justify them to exist in the way that they exist.

LM: There's a way that the sorts of permutations of accidents and destructions that we find in J. G. Ballard's work seem similar to what one encounters in the shows of Mark Pauline and his Survival Research Lab, to whom you devote a chapter in *The Rainbow Stories*. In both cases, the "message" seems to be mainly just that there's nothing to say or feel anymore. On the other hand, my own sense is that these shows by the SRL actually evoke fairly complicated responses from the audience.

WV: No question about it. Part of what SRL does is very good and very much in keeping with what they say they're doing—which is to educate people about the extremely violent world we live in, and to help them get in touch with these vicious, empty, mechanical feelings and understand them. But another part of what they do is also very self-serving because people like to watch that stuff for the same reason they like to watch horror movies. Not because they're going to learn how to avoid it, but because they like to rub their own noses in it. It may well be that seeing those things make people *more violent.*

LM: There's something about this spectacle of machines crashing into one another that's very powerful to me, emotionally. It's like the response people have to car crashes, airplane crashes, or any machine malfunction. You get a kind of empathy or thrill watching machines being destroyed—the empathy of horror of watching this machine's "body" malfunction. And part of it may have to do with feeling that since we're imprisoned in this mechanical world, there's a private glee of liberation when we can watch the machines losing it.

WV: Absolutely. For most of us the world we live in now is an immense trap. Or torture chamber. Everything outside this torture chamber has been destroyed by the torturers, so now there's just this vacuum. In this situation, we naturally take joy when we see that the torturers are malfunctioning. But at the same time we know that if we were to exert ourselves and actually destroy this thing we live in, then all the air would come rushing out and we'd suffocate. That would be the end. That's why violence is a very tricky issue, both for artists and ordinary people. We all share these violent impulses, but we have ambivalent feelings about these feelings.

LM: Beginning with *You Bright and Risen Angels* and many of the pieces in *The Rainbow Stories* and then continuing on through all your recent books, violence seems to be a twisted response to love, or lack of love, or love with the wrong kind of thing.

WV: I think this kind of thing has happened in most violent people. They had feelings of yearning, or longing, or love, or whatever you want to call it, which couldn't be realized for some reason. So that love either becomes frustrated and they become violent in certain ways, or maybe the love is just completely burned out of them, so they don't care what they do to people. The other possibility (which is probably the most dangerous of all) is when these feelings of love become manipulated by someone who's suffered one of those other two things—someone who can then use that love for his own end. Someone who is a damaged soul, like Eichmann, would be an example. If Eichmann hadn't happened to have lived in Germany at a certain time, he would have died unknown. He was such a puppet of his setting that what he wound up doing wasn't completely his fault. He wanted somebody to love and then Hitler came along to fill that need; so Eichmann had to do what his puppet master made him do.

LM: That strange combination of brutality and insensitivity mixed together with passion and longing is something you really captured in *The Rainbow Stories.* For all the fascism and cruelty you depict in the skinheads, for example, there were also ways that they seem infinitely superior to people like middle-class businessmen or politicians.

WV: Absolutely. That's one of the things I wrote about in *Thirteen Stories.* There's this one guy in San Francisco who always calls Asians "gooks." Once he went into this Vietnamese restaurant and started screaming and yelling about "gook food" and how the gooks were an inferior race. Well, the door to this place didn't close properly, and later on, when he was finished screaming, he goes up to the woman and says, "Do you want me to fix your door for you?" She just looks at him and lets him. So he spends about three hours fixing the door, and then just kind of shrugs, goes outside and says, "You goddamn gook!" Then he goes off and leaves them. Now of course, you just know that it would never occur to most of these people sitting in the restaurant who thought this guy was such a horrible person for saying "gook" to fix her door. Life is strange.

LM: It's like what you just said about Eichmann. What people want to think about the skinheads or the Nazis or the people behind the Cultural Revolution in China is just that they were basically evil assholes.

WV: That's the easy way because it allows you to feel this distance and sense of superiority. Whereas the truth is a lot more difficult to accept or deal with. Like that guy in the restaurant—what should you feel about that guy? I'm sure that's how most of the Nazis were, too. Perfectly fine people in their way.

LM: One of your biographical statements said that you lived inside of books as a kid. Were you one of those kids who read all of the time and inhabited these realms in your imagination?

WV: Pretty much so. I sat inside reading while the other kids were out playing. I really felt like I was *inside* those books, like I was trapped in them somehow. I was writing when I was six or seven, and I wrote a science-fiction novel when I was in sixth grade. It was about these astronauts discovering another solar system, and various awful things happening to them at each planet until finally they were all killed off. I guess my work really hasn't changed too much. [Laughs.]

LM: Were you writing pretty much steadily from the time of that science-fiction novel onward?

WV: I've always been writing. I wrote stories and other stuff all through college, much of which I've since destroyed. I also wrote a novel just before I started the Afghanistan book.

LM: Were there any writers then who were influencing your sensibility, either through college or from your own reading? I was wondering in particular if you had discovered William Burroughs early on, simply because he's about the only writer whose works I could think of which vaguely reminded me of *Angels*.

WV: When I was working on *Angels* probably the writer I was most interested in was Lautréamont, not Burroughs. I've been impressed and influenced by different writers at different times. Right now, for instance, it seems like I've learned a lot from Mishima, Kawabata, and Tolstoy. Pynchon is the other writer people kept mentioning as a likely influence, but I never really saw the connection.

LM: I don't either. Maybe there's some similarities in your use of scientific language and metaphors. But Lautréamont's *Maldoror* seems like a more interesting possible source because of his emphasis on the grotesque and the dreamlike, transformative qualities.

WV: Yeah, that's a wonderful book. Lautréamont's language is almost perfect. Poe was another writer who was influencing me; "The Grave of Lost Stories," which is one of the stories I included in *Thirteen Stories and Thirteen Epitaphs*, is even about Poe. In rereading Poe recently I was surprised at how limited the poor guy was. Basically his best few stories are almost duplications of each other.

LM: What were the backgrounds of "The Happy Girls" and "The Convict Bird"?

WV: "The Convict Bird" is about a friend of mine who is serving a life sentence in prison. I did it partly to raise a little bit of money for her, which I guess goes against this fallacy that somehow you can help people with books. I knew no one else would publish this poem in the way I wanted it to be published, so I decided I should do it myself. And since I was going to do it myself, I decided I might as well go whole hog and make it exactly the way I wanted it. Matt Heckert of Survival Research Lab wound up doing the steel plate that binds the manuscript.

The text of "The Happy Girls" is in my collection *Thirteen Stories and Thirteen Epitaphs*. In my CoTangent version it appears without the epitaph. As soon as I'd written the text I knew that Ken Miller's photographs would be appropriate because he and I knew some of the people in this massage parlor, and he'd taken pictures of them. I also knew about his experience taking photographs of these prostitutes in Thailand, so a collaboration seemed like a nice idea. Our third collaborator is my friend James Lombino, who is a mechanical engineer who works for Steinway. I knew he could build an interesting box to house all this other material. But I was the person who mainly designed all these Co-Tangent book projects. So with "The Happy Girls," I wrote the story, made the metal plates, printed and painted it by hand. Ken Miller took the pictures and printed them and cut the mats, and James built the box.

LM: Were there moments during the process of gathering materials for *The Rainbow Stories* when you were frightened, or started thinking, "Uh oh, maybe I shouldn't have done this."

WV: Sure, and I've mentioned a few of those moments in *The Rainbow Stories.* When I started out doing the prostitute stories, I was pretty nervous about the pimps and drug dealers. One time a whore ran off with my money; when she saw me writing up my notes she must have thought I was a cop, so she had her pimp ambush me; I would have felt disgusted with myself if I had run away, but when I tried to just walk he took a shot at me (only one, though, luckily). For a while I was scared enough that I'd bring someone else with me, but that wound up being self-defeating. But these personal anecdotes aren't something really worth dwelling on. If I were to go on and on about them at great length, the whole point of what I was trying to do would be lost. It would sound as if the book is just about me. Obviously, I didn't like it when those things happened to me. They were unpleasant and scary, and I did what I could when they happened. But that wasn't the meaning of the experience.

LM: A lot of readers would probably find it surprising that these people would talk to you at all. But my own experiences with, say, skinheads is that if you sort of talk with them on their own level and don't treat them condescendingly, they're happy to talk with you. I mean, a lot of them were raised in the suburbs by parents who were lawyers and architects.

WV: I never had any problem with the skinheads. A lot of them were warm, generous people. They all seemed to respect me when I'd show them what I'd written. I actually enjoyed the time I hung out with them. The street people were a lot harder to live with simply because their life is so awful—you had the fleas, this horrible booze you had to drink, the smells, shaking hands with people whose hands are covered with shit because they don't have any toilet paper. But the street people whose brains hadn't rotted were really interesting in a lot of ways, and they were willing to tell me their stories. Really, I think anybody will open up if you seem like you have a little bit of respect and show a little bit of your own vulnerability. A lot of times, they're afraid they're more vulnerable than you are, so if they have some way they can get back at you and hurt you too, then they feel more comfortable.

LM: *An Afghanistan Picture Show* is based on your experience entering

Afghanistan with Islamic commandos in the early 1980s. What were the circumstances that led to that?

WV: While I was in Pakistan in 1982 on a tourist visa, I made some contacts in the refugee camps with some of the resistance forces; eventually I crossed into Afghanistan illegally with Islamic commandos. I'd hoped to be there for about a month, but we had to wait on the border for about ten days for our ammunition. At the time the commandos would slip in at the beginning of the season and pretty much stay there until the end of the fighting season in the fall; they couldn't leave any of their ammunition behind, so they'd bring as much of it with them as they could. Anyway, since we had to wait so long at the border I only wound up being actually inside Afghanistan for a couple of weeks.

LM: You said earlier that *You Bright and Risen Angels* was written in a sense as a response to what you'd done in the Afghanistan book—that notion of creating a fictional situation where the good guys (Bug and his group) could triumph over the bad guys.

WV: It's hard to remember. With a long, involved book like *Angels* that wound up having so many twists and turns in it, it gets confusing as to what the initial idea really was after you're finished. The *main* impulse was probably just wanting to start a new book, since I'd just finished the previous one. But my conception of *Angels* also involved having seen all these bad things in Afghanistan and wanting to right the balance somehow. Writing the novel was the only way I could do this, since I couldn't do it anywhere else. Like I said, though, it wound up that in the process of writing the novel, I saw that actually there was no way of righting the balance. And that there never could be.

LM: Since your conception of the book changed so dramatically while you were writing it, you obviously weren't writing from an outline. Is that the case with all your books?

WV: I never outline in detail. The very general scheme I've come up with for the *Seven Dreams* project is as far as I've ever gone with trying to formulate in advance what I'm going to be doing.

LM: Since you weren't working from an outline, or even from any kind of preset notion of what is going to be happening in the novel, how did you know the book was over? What was there about that very last scene with Frank and Brandy that made you realize the book should end there?

WV: At that time, I didn't really analyze it. It just felt like this was right for the book to end. Later on, I realized that was the right place because in a way what the whole book is all about is disappearances. This happens with the characters, so that everyone dwindles away and vanishes. And even the richness of the language at the beginning becomes much more austere toward the end. Finally, the only thing that's left is just this debased war. It's not only that the Reactionaries have won. Their monolithic order is cracking and rotting and sprouting ivy; there are shorts and brownouts and everything is generally falling to hell. All we're left with is people like Frank—these overly adaptable, empty beings scuttling around in their shells, trying in their mediocre way to still love and manipulate people. Frank has basically been taken advantage of by everyone throughout the whole book. In fact, one of the passages I cut from the book was about how the title of the book should have really been "Frank Fairless"—how the book was really *his* book in a way, but he was so pathetic and ill-used that even in his own book he doesn't appear very much. Everyone has been using him: Dr. Dodger is pumping him and getting all this stuff out of him; Bug is trying to turn him into a revolutionary; Milly hates him. Everyone kicks him around. Eventually, the only chance he thinks he has for love is this prostitute, Brandy. But of course all she's doing is manipulating and getting money out of him, not really giving him love or anything else. At the very end of the novel, Frank realizes that all he needs to do to get her under his thumb is to start treating her the way that all these other people have been treating everyone else in the book—which means he should just start promising her all these things that he doesn't have and is never ever going to give her. So the book ends with old Frank sort of coming into his own. Now he's just as crummy and "mature" in his own way as the Blue Globes are.

LM: What was the origin of that image of the Blue Globes?

WV: The first commercial transmission of alternating current took place in Telluride, Colorado, around the turn of the century. They originally used wooden power poles, which weren't creosote or anything, the way they are now. As a result, often times the power poles would short and even catch on fire, and there would be these huge blue globes of ball lightning on top of the globes.

LM: There are several mysterious figures who are mentioned and kind of appear offstage—like that guy Phil Blaker, who is described as "owning Mars." I kept expecting you to clarify what the situation was with him, and the Martians (and the "Vegans") and so on, but you never did. Were you originally intending to do more with Blaker and the Mars business?

WV: No. Blaker was never more in the book. I just enjoyed having him there. His presence in the book was absolutely pointless and inscrutable—just another one of the many sides of the Reactionaries squabbling among themselves. All the reader can know about him is that he was as vicious and awful as the other Reactionaries, and that's all you really need to know about him. Actually in terms of the Mars business, I'd thought at one point of having Wayne go to Mars. Wayne was doing these twelve Herculean labors for Parker and Mr. White—attacking the Beetle Guards, recovering the lenses of the miraculous Macropodia (which contains the entire universe in it), and in the end killing the Great Beetle and destroying the insect breeding grounds. I could have very easily whisked him off to Mars to do something for one of his other labors, but finally I felt like it wasn't needed.

LM: What was it that gave you the initial idea to use the bugs in all these different ways?

WV: Originally, I didn't know where the bugs were going to be in the lineup—whether they'd be with the Reactionaries or against them. But once I started working with them I realized that bugs are a good metaphor for what most of these characters are deep down. Because bugs are amoral. You can't blame them for being that way. Bugs aren't courageous. They're always scuttling in and out of crevices, always trying to better themselves; they're always prepared to hide and always ready to attack. With the possible exception of social insects, they don't have concepts of friendship or kindness or mercy. In other words, bugs have developed the same kind of practical survival mechanisms that all the people in *Angels* have. Survival by this amoral expediency of hiding, scuttling, grabbing what's available, attacking when you have to. I also thought it would be interesting to imagine how bugs feel . . .

LM: At the beginning of the interview you said that sometimes the extreme case helps dramatize the general one. I'm reminded of your epigraph to *Angels*, "Only the expert will realize that your exaggerations are really true." I think there's an interesting aesthetic at work there that you find people like Kafka and the magic realists applying: by pushing something to the exaggerated or fantastic, the "reality" of the thing can come through more clearly.

WV: There's a lot of truth to the idea that if there's any meaning or backbone to something, a lot of times the way to get at it is to keep forcing it into a more exaggerated caricature of itself. Eventually you'll reach some kind of limit where nothing is left but the exaggerated essence of the thing. Then you can see what the thing really is because everything is in sharper relief. That surface "realism" of ordinary life (and of most fiction) covers up a lot of important things that artists need to recover for people. You can also go at this from the opposite direction, where you take something real but extraordinary and make it sound ordinary, like what you find in Richard Hughes's *A High Wind in Jamaica*. It's about these kids who get kidnapped by pirates, who are very cruel; then later on when the kids get a chance they turn the tables and get the pirates horribly punished. The book works because it's so understated.

LM: Clearly thus far you've not been much into understatement . . .

WV: Well, certainly the reason that *Angels* works (if it works) is because it's an overstated book. There's no pretense of hiding the cruelty and anguish and everything else that the book is about. At the same time I wanted people to be entertained by the book and enjoy it, which they can also do when it's a cartoon.

LM: This method seemed very close to magical realism you find in García Márquez and some of the other Latin American writers. Were they people you were interested in?

WV: Sure. I loved *One Hundred Years of Solitude.* The problem right now, of course, is that this whole magic realism thing has become a gimmick; it seems very easy to do, so everyone is doing it. But at its finest it's really beautiful. I'd say that what I do with my own use of exaggeration isn't quite like this, though.

LM: Early on in *Angels,* referring to Ambrose Bierce being saved by Dr. Dodger's Special Elixir, and his inability to remember things, you say, "Such mental haziness is in order, given the delightful vagueness of the terrain—springy moss padding the continent, golden idols and lost gimcrack empires a dime a dozen, sentient insects and clean mountains without sharp peaks to puncture balloons and dreams; and a foggy sort of peace generally" [3]. That passage seemed to have to do with that idea of the "diffusedness" that you mentioned before—and why it's appropriate in this book. It's almost like a gloss on the narrative strategy you're going to use here.

WV: Yeah, I agree. It's the same kind of thing as when I refer to Wayne's "cartoon heart." You find phrases like that throughout the book, just by way of reminding people that, of course, the thing they're reading is far off and distorted from the literal truth—things never really happen this way, and there's no reason to pretend that they do. That's fine, because these distortions help us look at things more closely. If, for instance, instead of bugs and electricity, I was talking about capitalists and communists, or white people and black people, most capitalists, communists, white people, and black people wouldn't be able to read it and get the point because they'd already be emotionally or intellectually involved in their own particular side of things.

LM: So by taking it out of the realm of so-called reality, you make it more available to everybody.

WV: Right, because ultimately who cares whether the Blue Globes or the Bugs win? Turning everything into this cartoon helps us see the struggle for what it is. It's a bit like what happened with that Deutscher biography of Stalin. He wrote somewhere that certain people would sometimes say that his biography was too hard on Stalin (the Stalinists would all say so, for example), so they would then have the book banned in their countries. Then some other people would say that the book was too *soft* on Stalin and have it banned in their countries. He ended up feeling that these contradictory reactions indicated he had probably done a pretty good job. Which I think he did. But it's nice that *Angels* can avoid that problem because in terms of your response to the book, it won't matter whether you're pro- or anti-Stalin.

LM: I'm not so sure—I mean, in the end, you're pretty pessimistic about the prospects for any revolutionary program.

WV: Okay, maybe what I should have said was that if you were pro-Stalin and you were *smart*, you probably wouldn't like this book. You'd be irritated.

LM: The point of view in *Angels* is very unusual—there's nothing I can really compare it to. You have Big George, who implies he is able to shift in and out of various characters who were dead; and you also have "The Author," who is able to press the resurrection button and bring to life Bug, Catherine, and Parker. It almost seems there's a conflict going on there between Big George and "The Author." What gave you the idea to use this very peculiar point of view?

WV: It had to do with what I mentioned earlier about the book's initial purpose and failure to fulfill that purpose. You might say that "The Author" is the one who wants Bug to save the world (and the Afghans, and everybody else) while Big George is the one who actually controls events and makes sure that this can't happen. Another way to put it would be to say that "The Author" was the one who wanted his characters to be able to realize themselves and Big George was the force of life and fate, or God, or whatever you want to call it—or the computer. What George represents is that even if people realize themselves, eventually they're going to age and die. To start with, people are most likely not going to get what they want; and even if they *do* get what they want, they won't be able to make use of it. That's simply what life is. So "The Author" is optimistic and Big George is pessimistic—or realistic, depending on your point of view.

LM: So these perspectives are really aspects of your own divided self.

WV: Yeah. Except I like to think I'm a nicer person than Big George is.

LM: On the other hand, *Angels* struck me as a very brave novel on your part precisely because even there you reveal a lot of your own vulnerability and foolishness in the book. You did this in various ways, not only as embodied through characters, but also through your presentation of "The Author" and his relationship with women, his blindness about love and the pain this causes him. You see this very strongly near the very end of the book, when you're talking to Catherine, the Queen Bee. All this by way of saying: Didn't you feel that you were revealing a lot of yourself in that first book, too?

WV: Sure I did. But in *Angels* these revelations are partly covered up simply because it's sometimes more difficult to know exactly where the fiction or the imagination stops and the reality begins. In *The Rainbow*

Stories it's usually a lot clearer which things actually happened. When I did things that a lot of people would disapprove of, I didn't try and hide or disguise them by presenting them through those layers of ambiguity that the narrative perspective creates in *Angels*. I don't want to knock down the way I was dealing with these things in *Angels*. It simply wasn't as direct.

LM: One of the commonplaces about writers is that it's usually their first novel that's the most autobiographical in some kind of direct sense. And even though it's obvious that *The Rainbow Stories* is the most "nakedly" autobiographical one of your books (and you interject yourself into *The Ice-Shirt* in a lot of ways, too), I still had a sense that a lot of the materials in *Angels* had powerful autobiographical sources. Those scenes with Bug and the swimming team, and a lot of the other adolescent scenes, seemed very authentic in the way it *felt*, even though they often seemed very fantastic from a literal standpoint.

WV: You might say that *Angels* reveals more of my emotions, *The Rainbow Stories* reveals more of my actions, and *The Ice-Shirt* reveals more of my thoughts.

LM: The color symbolism in *The Rainbow Stories* is one of the things that seems to unify the book in various ways. How did the use of color begin to work in with the evolution of the book?

WV: The color symbolism occurred to me very early on, although it wasn't something I started out with. When I work, I tend to write several different things at once. In this case, the first things I started on were "The White Knights" skinhead story (which originally had a different name), "Yellow Rose," "Blue Yonder," and "Ladies and Red Lights." The first pieces I finished were the skinhead story and "Yellow Rose," followed by "The Wild Blue Yonder." About that time I suddenly realized that this color symbolism was starting to emerge. I didn't have much of the book completed at that point so it was easy to go back and adjust those pages to make them fit into the rainbow symbolism. "Violet Hair" was finished last and was the one easiest to write. It's also the one I think that is actually the best. The Poe epigraph I put in when I had about three-quarters of the stories finished.

LM: Once you recognized that this color symbolism was emerging, did you begin to consciously seek out certain types of experiences that would in some ways fit into this framework? Or was the framework always something you imposed later on?

WV: I won't pretend that once I had the color scheme pretty well fixed in my mind that then I started cold-bloodedly trying to go out and make every experience I had try to fit this scheme. I knew more or less what I wanted this collection to be about, and the color scheme simply seemed to supply a kind of overlay or connection between the things I wanted to talk about. I thought of the book almost like a novel because it has a structure that allows specific patterns of themes and symbols to develop and clarify themselves. That's why I resisted when some of my editors wanted to cut and rearrange some of the stories. For instance, they thought that "Scintillant Orange" was anti-Semitic and so it shouldn't appear in the book at all. I wouldn't let them do that for various reasons. I feel very strongly that there is a real movement in the arrangement of the stories. So, for instance, the stories are arranged so that "darkness" gradually emerges more and more from the stories, until at the end, you wind up with the X-rays, which aren't even in the visible spectrum. And this whole business about trying to know the other, see into these other worlds should gradually become more and more obvious. I also more or less alternated the documentary stories with the imaginative stories to make the point that it doesn't matter in these worlds whether these things literally happened or not. They're both true in different ways.

LM: So these imaginative pieces were conceived concurrently with the more journalistic ones—they weren't works you had written earlier and then integrated later on?

WV: They were all written at the same period I was writing the San Francisco pieces and more or less finished up at the same time too. That's why I feel the book falls somewhere in between a novel and a collection of short stories. There's definitely a certain movement and progression that's important in the book, that unifies what's being presented and justifies its arrangement. On the other hand, certain stories could have been replaced by other stories about different characters, so in that sense it's not quite a novel either. I'm not sure you can call something a novel if you can cut out one episode and replace it with a different episode involving different people without it really mattering.

LM: You've mentioned your desire for *The Rainbow Stories* to allow readers to share different roles and worlds. Does your ability to move into these other worlds, literally and empathetically, imply that the act of writing is for you a deliberate leap into a kind of insanity or schizophrenia? Or is it the case that maybe you weren't ever able to really get into that other world?

WV: My primary world is just this one basic "dream world" that I've been in from the time I was a kid. All these worlds that I see and write about are equally real and can coexist, so it's not like I have to leave my own world in order to inhabit them. That's my ability I guess. But this also means that these different worlds are also equally *unreal,* so I can't take anything too seriously. None of them take precedence over any others.

LM: Your works often have a powerful edge of extremity and violence to them. Were you involved or drawn somehow to the punk scene back in the seventies, while you were growing up?

WV: No, I never was. I was aware that it existed, and of course being in San Francisco I saw it. But, no, I was never involved with it. I wouldn't say that I have ever been part of any movement.

LM: Were there any other figures you feel might have influenced your sensibility while you were growing up? Painters or artists working in other art forms? What about other authors (I was wondering, for example, about Burroughs).

WV: My influences are pretty spread out. I wouldn't say that there's anyone that has influenced me more than anyone else. I haven't read all of Burroughs's books, but some of them I like a lot. I think *The Ticket That Exploded* is terrific, and I liked *Junkie* a lot, too. In terms of visual artists, like I said earlier, I've never had any formal training in painting or drawing. I've been learning to express myself more with things like watercolors, prints, drawings, and even photographs. Certainly, there are a lot of visual artists I admire, like Paul Klee, who's given me a lot of intuitions in his work. I've gotten a lot of the obsessive love stuff from Klimt (and it's helped sometimes to look at his faces).

LM: One of the things that's usually associated with postmodernism is something you seem to do very naturally or intuitively—that is, the way you problematize all sorts of distinctions that people used to make between fiction and autobiography, or between "realism" and fantasy or science fiction. You seem very comfortable with the notion that all these different worlds or perspectives coexist and provide "windows" into each other. And in fact, it seems to me that your generation takes a lot of this for granted in ways that, say, the sixties generation of experimental writers couldn't.

WV: At this point, what you're describing is probably true throughout the culture, not just in the arts. You see it in advertising, in television, in shop windows, anything. The gain from that is obvious: greater freedom in every way, more available options. The loss from it is a sense of disorientation, plus when it's done sloppily (the way it often is) there's no thought given to context. I honestly believe that most people nowadays, including writers, know less of the body of facts, and aesthetics—the basic core of information about the work and culture and so forth, that makes up our heritage—than people did earlier. That's very unfortunate because it makes it impossible to place these new options or combinations within any context that means anything.

LM: Certainly one thing that strikes anybody reading your books is simply this wide, encyclopedic range of reading. Where does that come from?

WV: About 95 percent of what I read is done for my work. But since my work is pleasure, I'm also reading for pleasure. The other readings I do are from random things I pick because they look interesting. For instance, the day before yesterday I went out to the bookstore and bought a catalog on torture instruments of the Inquisition, Mishima's novel *The Sound of Waves*, this Eliade book on shamanism that I really want to read, a book on artistic methods (it's about various ways of painting and drawing and sculpture). That's pretty typical of what I might be looking at, excluding the stuff I read for my work, which I keep in this white box over here. It's mainly anthropological works about Indians, but also some religious materials.

LM: In *Angels* you created a lot of long paragraphs that seem to have a kind of musical structure to them (improvisation); it's almost like the reader can physically see your imagination grappling with an idea or image and just going with it, pushing it on down the page in the paragraph. That seems less obvious in *The Ice-Shirt*.

WV: I'd say that all the books in *Seven Dreams* are probably going to be more terse in that regard. In many ways when I'm working with these symbolic histories my own proclivities have to become more muted. I like what I'm doing here as much as anything else I've written, but the stylistic effects are more reined in by the overall structure I'm working with. Unfortunately, you can't do everything in a book anchored by fact that you can with something where your imagination is completely unbounded, like *Angels*. It can't be as spontaneous because it gets its legitimacy from something else. Hopefully, what it gains from that is greater than what it loses the other way.

The same thing is true with this stack of papers here called *Whores for Gloria*. It's a novel that was my first attempt to create a symbolic history. It's really a series of true stories which were taped. The basic devices are about this alcoholic who imagines this perfect woman, Gloria, whom he loves (we don't know if she actually existed or not). He pays all these prostitutes not just to have sex with him but to tell him happy stories he can use as memories of himself and Gloria. When I was interviewing prostitutes I found that these whores would start telling a happy story that would end up being just terribly sad. They could never tell a happy story. So this guy always keeps twisting these stories around in his mind to make them happy again, which they aren't. He's not either. He's a terribly pathetic, unhappy person.

LM: Do you ever wonder or worry about suffering the fate of the moth who, as you say in "Scintillant Orange," "must die happily in the flame"?

WV: Fire is neither a big attraction nor a phobia for me. But when my time comes to die, I hope I can die like the moth in the flame. That seems like the best way to go.